CLIMATE CHANGE
Nature is in Control

Third Edition 2024

©2020 John Maunder

All rights reserved.

No part of this book may be reproduced or used in
any manner without written permission
of the copyright owner, except for the
use of quotations in a book review.
For more information contact:
john.maunder@gmail.com

First Edition 2020:
Fifteen Shades of Climate
ISBN-13: 979-8565519549

Second Edition 2023:
Climate Change : A Realistic Perspective
ISBN: 979-8-394709-92-0

Third Edition 2024:
Climate Change: Nature is in Control
ISBN: 979-8-343377217

Edited by: Elizabeth Harré
Third Edition updated 2024: Margaret Marsh
Second Edition updated 2023: Margaret Marsh
Original design and layout: Lesley Pritchard

CONTENTS

Author's Introduction	iv
Acknowledgements	v
Author's Foreword	vii
Foreword by John W Zillman AO FAA FTSE	ix
Preface	xiii
The fall of the weather dice and the butterfly effect	xv

❶ What controls the weather dice? — 1

Misrepresentation Of Climate Science	3
Climate Alarmism	6
The World of Climatism	7
Climate Change is Not a major problem	10
May the odds be ever in your favour	12
Climate Change: both sides of the story... a Rotary Conference discussion	15
Climate Change and the Villach Conference of 1985	19
Ten big climate questions answered	21
Key points about climate change	26
Net Zero	27
Air New Zealand and Green Credentials	32
Small modular reactors	34
The New Zealand Climate Commission	36
Climate overview: The last 400,000 years	39
The Maunder of the "Maunder Minimum"	41

❷ Methods of inferring/detecting changes in the climate — 43

Recording the weather	45
Homogenization of climate observation and quality control	60
The "hockey stick" graph of global warming	65
Glaciers	68
Tree rings	74

❸ Forecasting the climate — 81

Weather and Climate Forecasting	83
Blocking Highs	102
Climate forecasts - how good are they?	105

❹ The Sun — 113

Solar activity and spotless days	115
The Maunder Minimum	117
The Maunder Butterfly	118
Sunspot numbers 1700 - present	119
Sunspot numbers 1950 - present	120

i

5 Astronomical causes of climate change — 123
Milanković cycles — 125
Solar magnetic variations and the Earth's climate — 136

6 The role of the oceans — 139
Global ocean currents as climate controllers — 141
Indian Ocean Dipole (IOD) — 148
Southern Annular Mode (SAM) — 152
What are El Niño and La Niña? — 156

7 The climate record over the centuries — 159
Central England temperatures 1700-2018 — 161
Southern Oscillation Index (SOI) — 164
Tropospheric temperatures 1979 to May 2020 — 167
Global temperatures 1996 - May 2020 — 169
Global annual temperatures 1880 - 2019 — 171
Arctic and Antarctic temperatures January 1979 to January 2020 — 174

8 Lessons from history — 177
Vikings and their explorations in a warmer world — 179
Building the cathedrals of Europe... the climate factor — 185
The Dust Bowl era in the United States in the 1930's — 190
Sea level changes — 196

9 Extreme events — 199
The year without a summer — 201
Volcanic eruptions — 204
Tropical Cyclones — 208

10 Anthropogenic influences on the climate — 219
The Greenhouse effect — 221
Urban heat island effect — 225
Australian forest fires and climate — 231
Methane — 241

11 Adaptation to climate — 247
Emission Trading Schemes (ETS) — 249
Building sea walls to combat rising sea levels — 254
Declaring Climate Emergencies — 263
Climate refugees — 269

12 Energy — 275
Fossil fuels — 277
Geothermal energy — 281
Nuclear Energy — 285
Solar energy — 290
Wind power — 296
Hydroelectricity — 310
Tidal Power — 314

13 Official viewpoints — 321
Intergovernmental Panel on Climate Change (IPCC) — 323
World Climate Programme — 341
The Paris Climate Agreement — 347
World Meteorological Organization — 356
UN Climate Conference 2014 — 367

14 Political aspects — 369
Politics and science — 371
Climate change: three sides of the story — 372
The Kyoto Protocol — 374
Ozone and the 1987 Montreal Protocol — 377
Right and left of climate policies — 381
Green movements around the world and their climate agenda — 386

15 Annex — 393
The *climate4you.com* website — 395
Bibliography — 399

Author's Introduction

Since the beginning of time, the Earth's climate has been shaped by natural systems that govern the planet. To me, it is essential for all of us to have a better understanding of the complex factors such as solar variations, ocean currents and atmospheric gases that influence our climate.

To me, it is clear that "Nature" is in control, but we must work in harmony with "Nature's" rhythms to restore balance and not work against "Nature".

I have compiled this book to increase our knowledge about the natural and social science aspects of climate.

Dr John Maunder

ACKNOWLEDGEMENTS

There are many people I would like to thank for making this book possible. The idea for the book came about when I was visiting my family in Adelaide in January 2020 during a heat wave. One day when the forecast was for 45 °C my daughter Denise suggested I should stay inside, shelter from the heat and write another book. I asked what did she have in mind and she simply said "Climate the Truth". My son Philip who has lived in Adelaide for about 30 years thought it was a good idea but after a few days thought I settled on a more appropriate title "Fifteen shades of climate... the fall of the weather dice and the butterfly effect". Subsequently, in 2023 I changed the name of the book to "Climate Change: A Realistic Perspective", and this latest book is simply "Climate Change: Nature is in Control". This book includes about 60 % of the second book; but also includes ten new sections dealing with climate facets such as climate alarmism, the world of climatism, misrepresentation of climate science, net zero, small modular reactors, may the odds be ever be in your favour, and the Maunder of the "Maunder Minimum".

Many of the facets of my eighty years in the "weather business" are covered in this book. These years include my schooling in New Zealand's Golden Bay school, and Nelson College, the University of Otago, the New Zealand Meteorological Service, the University of Victoria in Canada, the University of Missouri, the World Meteorological Organization, the University of Delaware, the 1985 WMO/ICSU/UNEP Villach Conference, 1979 WMO First World Climate Conference, the 1990 Second World Climate Conference, the Stockholm Environment Institute, the University College Dublin, the weather business in New Zealand, writing several books, many scientific papers and a host of media releases. My thanks go to all my friends and colleagues all over the climate world who have kept me on the right path, even if the path has been a little different than some may have thought I should have followed.

In Tauranga I would like to give special thanks to three people, first to Lesley Pritchard who was my mentor and computer expert who prepared and formatted all 480 pages of the book. In addition, in a quiet moment Elizabeth Harré kindly offered to critically edit and proof read the whole book several times. The writing of this book went through several phases. I wrote various drafts, Lesley had formatted much of the original text, Elizabeth fine-tuned all the new text; and Margaret Marsh formatted all the additions and the final book layout.

I would also like to acknowledge the use of various extracts and analyses obtained from Wikipedia.

This is my seventh book, and it would be remiss for me not to acknowledge the wonderful support I received over the years from my late wife Melva who passed away in 2016.

I hope that this book truly reflects the wise wisdom of all those whose life had, and in many areas still has, on my writings.

John Maunder

Tauranga
New Zealand

AUTHOR'S FOREWORD

Now that I am in my 93rd year it seems appropriate that I should re-quote the words of Walter Cronkite of CBS fame, whose absolute commitment and reputation for objectivity always signed off his 6pm news bulletin with ... "And that's the way it is".

With so much information and misinformation about the climate story, perhaps the words of Cronkite should be a reminder to us all, including our educators, our decision makers, and the media, that the sun, the volcanoes, and the oceans dominate the climate system, and not us.

Of course, now that we are through the 20th and into the 21st century, one must acknowledge the important human (including domestic animals) influence on the climate system. However one must also acknowledge that prior to about 1800, the climate variations which occurred (and there were many of them), were not - with very few exceptions - influenced by the activities of humans.

There is a great amount of evidence about detecting changes in the climate, and many reasons/causes of why the climate changes.

Among the evidence for detecting climate change are instrumental records which include satellite observations, extreme weather events, historical records (eg crop records, church attendance), sea level changes, lake varves, glacial advances and retreats, ice cores, rocks, and tree rings.

Among the causes of why the climate changes is methane, carbon dioxide, solar activity - including sunspots, the Earth's orbit and rotation, the Earth's reflectivity, volcanic activity, ocean circulation, generating power, using transportation, producing food, heating and cooling of buildings, planetary cycles (e.g. Milanković cycles), and the ever increasing world's population.

In considering both the evidence for climate change and the causes of climate change, there are many questions as to the credibility of the "evidence". Some of this "credibility" relates to the reliability of the records, and this includes the "authority" making the observations. There have been many cases where the evidence for and the causes of climate change have been challenged.

I have spent the last 70 years studying and writing, as objectively as I can, about the evidence, causes and impacts of climate and climate change. I have written this book to summarise what I have learned. And, like Walter Cronkite, I would like to sign off with the assurance that, to the best of my knowledge, "And that's the way it is".

****

"... *if man examines the universe and understands it, he knows how small a part he is.*"

From *Guide to the Perplexed* by Moses Maimonides, one of the greatest of all Jewish geniuses who died in 1204. (The quote is from Robert Winston's book *The Story of God*, Bantam Books, 2005)

FOREWORD BY JOHN W. ZILLMAN

There are probably few people in the world who have originated and accumulated as much detailed knowledge of as many different shades of climate as John Maunder. He is a font of wisdom on climate matters and I believe he has served the world extremely well over the past 50 years through the way he has shared that knowledge and wisdom with the global community.

I first met Dr Maunder, when he was Chief of the Agricultural Branch of the World Meteorological Organization (WMO), at the May 1975 WMO Congress in Geneva, and again through his contribution to the proceedings of the December 1975 Monash (Melbourne) Conference on climate change and variability. The WMO Congress commissioned one of the first high-level international expert assessments of climate change and Dr Maunder's Monash Conference contribution was among the first on the international scene to preview the emerging political and economic dimensions of climate variability and change.

For the next 40 years, Dr Maunder was at the centre of the rapidly advancing international scene on climate data, research, applications and impact studies. This included academic appointments in New Zealand, Canada, the United States and Ireland. When the 1979 WMO Congress established the World Climate Programme (WCP) as an international interdisciplinary framework for understanding and managing climate variability and change, it assigned much of the responsibility for WCP implementation to the WMO Commission for Climatology of which John Maunder was a respected member and future leader.

Through the sixteen years of his Vice Presidency (1981-89) and Presidency (1989-96) of the WMO Commission for Climatology, Dr Maunder guided the international implementation of the 'data' and 'applications' components of the WCP. As a member of the WMO Executive Committee (now Council) through that period and President of WMO for Dr Maunder's final two years as President of the Commission, I saw the benefit of his wise and balanced advice to all WMO Member countries across the full range of climate matters. And, as Director of the Australian Bureau of Meteorology at the time, I was particularly pleased when he crossed the Tasman and joined the Bureau as a resident climate expert in 1990-92.

Dr Maunder has always been ahead of the game on climate matters. Before the costs and benefits of the impacts of weather became an issue of global concern, he had written a book on '*The Value of the Weather*'.

Before the rest of the world had worked out how to use weather and climate information to manage the risks and opportunities of weather and climate variability and extremes, he had captured the essence of the problem with a book on *'The Uncertainty Business'.* And before the First Report of the Intergovernmental Panel on Climate Change (IPCC) and the 1990 Second World Climate Conference had set in train the negotiation of the United Nations Framework Convention on Climate Change (UNFCCC), he had produced a climate lexicon that became, for many years, the definitive international *'Dictionary of Global Climate Change.'*

While Dr Maunder comes from a meteorological generation for whom the study of climate embraced much more than concern with greenhouse warming and before the venerable scientific field of climatology had been repackaged and narrowed to 'climate science', he also became deeply involved in the early study of human-induced climate change. His extensive background in traditional climatology and his participation in the 1985 Villach Conference on the climatic effects of increasing carbon dioxide made him a respected source of wise advice to WMO Member countries when concern with 'greenhouse warming' burst upon the world in the 1980s. No-one can keep up with it all but I know of few traditional climatologists who have kept such a careful watch on all aspects of the growing global concern with climate change over the 35 years since Villach. This book is the result and the repository of the accumulated Maunder wisdom of those years.

Dr Maunder sees himself as a 'realist' on human-induced climate change. He is troubled by the over-simplification of the climate story and sets out to foster a better public appreciation of the complexity of the climate system. But, while he goes to great lengths to present a wide range of perspectives, including many he disagrees with, he does not refrain from making clear his own views on greenhouse warming or on the many other contentious issues captured in the fifteen shades of climate covered in the fifteen chapters of this book. The issues covered, some quite succinctly but others in great detail, represent almost a complete climate lexicon in their own right and I would be surprised if any reader failed to find at least a few new and illuminating slants on some of the many fascinating different aspects of climate.

This is not a book for those looking for unambiguous scientific support for greenhouse action. But it is, in my view, among the best you could hope to find by way of highly readable and authoritative answers to many of the everyday puzzles of climate. And, for those who have come to the frontiers of climate science without a background in traditional climatology, it contains much distilled wisdom from a generation of progress in a field of study that was once described by the great mathematician John von Neumann, as the most difficult unsolved problem still to confront the scientific intellect of man[sic]. This book also provides a few sobering reminders that, despite the enormous progress of the past fifty years, the von Neumann characterisation may still be close to the mark.

I have not always agreed with everything I have found in Dr Maunder's writing but I have always regarded his books as the epitome of scientific honesty and practical wisdom on climate issues. This book brings it all together. Read any or all of its chapters and you will be wiser on the many fascinating twists of the climate story.

John W. Zillman AO FAA FTSE
Former Director (1978-2003) of the Australian Bureau of Meteorology
Former President (1995-2003) of the World Meteorological Organization

PREFACE

The explosive nature of the "climate" has brought about a significant challenge for those of us who are climate scientists to provide details of what is currently happening, why is it happening, and what is going to happen to the climate in the next month, year, and decade. An equal challenge is for media, including the social media, to present this information in a coherent manner, so that society, and political leaders at all levels - from the UN down to the local level, make appropriate decisions, whether this involves solar energy, the burning of coal, forest management, hydro electricity, electric cars, veganism, nuclear power, the building of sea walls, moving to a better climate, learning to live with whatever climate Nature provides, and even who to vote for in the next election.

There are many aspects of climate that could be written about, and my previous book Climate Change: A Realistic Perspective: The fall of the weatherdice and the butterfly effect (Amazon 2023), and this book includes most subjects that are commonly discussed in the media, which should be of interest to the public at large. As always there are continual developments in the climate scene and readers may wish to follow the current research by a simple Google search of any topic such as methane, sea level changes, global temperatures, or an answer to such a question as "Are hurricanes increasing or decreasing in frequency, or "Are polar bears increasing or decreasing". The information in this book and my previous book aims to provide a "need to know" background on weather and climate matters, climate change, and "global warming" with the aim to promote a better understanding of these matters.

In my 92 years I have been involved in a wide range of activities in the "climate business"; from watching a river overflow into the small town of Takaka, Golden Bay, New Zealand when I was eight years old and asking why it happened, and was it good or bad; to the realms of several national meteorological services and universities, to the weather business, and the World Meteorological Organization. Essentially, my book is a collection of specific activities and writings on the questions of climate, climate change, climate's variability (natural or otherwise) and climate politics over the years.

In this regard I am reminded of the physicist Leo Szilard (1898-1964) who once announced to his friend Hans Bethe that he was thinking of keeping a diary: 'I don't intend to publish, I am merely going to record the facts for the information of God.' 'Don't you think God knows the facts?' Bethe asked. 'Yes' said Szilard. 'He knows the facts, but he does not know this version of the facts'*

DR. JOHN MAUNDER

*From Hans Christian von Baeyer, author of "*Taming the Atom*", (from the preface paragraph in "*A Short History of Nearly Everything*", by Bill Bryson, A Black Swan Book, 2004).

The fall of the weather dice and the butterfly effect.

Weather dice were shown on the cover of my book *The Uncertainty Business - Risks and Opportunities in Weather and Climate*, published in 1986. The cover, which has two dice on a "monopoly board", with various weather symbols on each side of the dice, was to represent the reality that most if not all of the weather (and ultimately most of the climate) with the exception of human induced weather and climate effects, is ultimately related to how the weather dice fall.

Professor Edward Lorenz (1917-2008) was a meteorologist who worked at the Massachusetts Institute of Technology (MIT) in the United States who in 1972, during the 139th meeting of the "American Association for the Advancement of Science", posed the question: *Predictability: Does the flap of a butterfly's wings in Brazil set off a tornado in Texas?* This paper resulted in the development of "chaos theory" or simply "the butterfly effect" which among other things endeavours to explain why it it is so hard to make good weather forecasts beyond about 10 days, and has implications for making good climate forecasts, particularly when considering the natural causes of climate change.

Who or what controls the fall of the weather dice is the ultimate question for all meteorologists and climate scientists... and if the butterfly effect is correct, we may really just have to learn to live and adapt to whatever the weather and the climate provides.

1

What controls the weather dice?

> "...if man examines the universe and understands it, he knows how small a part of it he is."
>
> From *Guide to the Perplexed* by Moses Maimonides, one of the greatest of all Jewish geniuses who died in 1204. The quote is from page 335 of Robert Winston's book *The Story of God* published by Bantam Books in 2005.

Misrepresentation Of Climate Science

Science is described by William Kininmonth (in a study published in News Weekly August 19, 2024) as the systematic study of the structure and behaviour of the physical and natural world and is based on observation and experiment. That is, any hypothesis must be derived from sound representation of climate science.

The UN's Intergovernmental Panel on Climate Change (IPCC) uses global and annual average temperature as an index for describing climate change. However, this index is misleading because it hides and does not account for the regional and seasonal differences in the rates of warming that have been observed. The human-caused global warming hypothesis, to be valid, must also explain these regional and seasonal variations.

Since 1979, based on conventional and satellite observations, observations have been systematically analysed as the basis for global weather forecasting. The analyses are stored in a database (NCEP/NCAR R1) maintained by the US National Center for Environmental Prediction (NCEP). A satellite derived database of atmospheric temperature is held by the University of Alabama, Huntsville (UAH).

The observations show that the index of global and annual rate of Earth's warming of 1.7°C per century does not capture the differing regional and seasonal characteristics. Any explanation for the recent warming must be able to explain why these regional and seasonal differences occur.

Kininmonth notes that CO_2 is described as a well-mixed greenhouse gas in the atmosphere and its concentration is measured in parts per million (ppm). CO_2 is constantly flowing between the atmosphere, the biosphere and the oceans. The annual average concentration has little regional variation but there is a marked seasonal cycle with the range of the cycle being a maximum over the Arctic. CO_2 is taken from the atmosphere, primarily by way of two processes: by photosynthesis with growing terrestrial plants, and by absorption into the colder oceans. CO_2 enters the atmosphere by way of decaying terrestrial plant material, from outgassing from warmer oceans, and through emissions associated with the industrial and lifestyle activities of humans. Because of the large natural flows, the average residence time in the atmosphere of a CO_2 molecule is only about four years.

The emissions generated by human activities have grown to about 10% of the natural flows. Despite the seasonal atmospheric CO_2 concentration peaking over the Arctic, far from human settlement, it is claimed that the rising atmospheric concentration is caused by human activity. Regardless of the origins, CO_2 concentration is increasing in the atmosphere. As summarised by IPCC, the increasing concentration of CO_2 reduces longwave radiation emissions to space, thus upsetting Earth's long-term radiation balance. The slight reduction in flow of radiation energy to space, called 'radiation forcing', is claimed to be a source of heat that warms the Earth's atmosphere.

The IPCC recognises climate forcing as 'a modelling concept' that constitutes a simple but important means of estimating the relative surface temperature impacts due to different natural and anthropogenic radiative causes. A fundamental flaw in this modelling concept is an assumption that, prior to industrialisation, Earth was in radiation balance.

First, nowhere on Earth is there radiation balance: over the tropics absorption of solar radiation exceeds emission of longwave radiation to space; over middle and high latitudes emission of longwave radiation to space exceeds absorption of solar radiation. Earth is only in near radiation balance because heat is transported by winds and ocean currents from the tropics to middle and high latitudes, and second, the latitude focus for absorption of solar radiation varies with seasons. There is a need for the ocean and atmosphere transport to vary with the seasonal shift. Consequently, the seasonally changing solar radiation causes Earth's global average near surface (2 metre) air temperature to oscillate with an annual range of about 3°C.

Rather than being in balance, as claimed by the IPCC, the net radiation exchange with space oscillates about a balance point. The reason for the oscillation is the differing fractions of landmass in each of the hemispheres. The Northern Hemisphere has a higher proportion of land while the Southern Hemisphere has much more ocean surface than land surface. Because the radiation exchange with space is not in balance then the essential requirement of radiation forcing, as used in climate modelling, is invalid. Moreover, given the strong natural flows of heat within the climate system (oceans, atmosphere, and ice sheets) there is no reason to expect that, as CO_2 concentration increases, the small reduction in longwave energy to space will heat the atmosphere.

Kininmonth in his conclusion says that the hypothesis and computer modelling that suggest human activities and the increase in atmospheric CO_2 are the cause of recent warming cannot be sustained.

He says that there never was a balance between absorbed solar radiation and longwave radiation emitted to space. Earth's radiation to space changes with the seasonally varying temperatures of the surface and atmosphere; this is according to well understood physics. The radiation forcing scheme that is the basis for including CO_2 in computer modelling leads to false outcomes.

The index of global and annual average temperature used by the IPCC is crude and hides the important regional and seasonal differences in the rate of warming as experienced over the recent 44 years. It is these regional and seasonal differences, together with well understood meteorological science, that point to slow variations of the ocean circulations being the cause of recent warming.

Kininmonth concludes that the recent warming is consistent with natural cyclical variations of the climate system. Attempts to halt the current warming by reducing atmospheric CO_2 concentrations will certainly fail. Government policies that are based on the alarming but erroneous IPCC temperature projections are fraught.

Climate Alarmism

Damaging weather events inevitably lead to climate evangelists making apocalyptic claims of imminent disaster. UN Secretary General António Guterres led the most recent chorus in 2024, in talking about "global boiling" and raising alarmism to a fever pitch. Yet, more than 1,600 scientists, including two Nobel physics laureates, have signed a declaration stating that, "There is no climate emergency." That poses a serious political problem for any government that has been arguing the contrary.

An expert opinion, submitted pro bono in November 2023 to the Hague Court of Appeals by three eminent American scientists, presented a devastating refutation of climate catastrophism. Their conclusions contradict alarmists' sacred beliefs, including that anthropogenic CO_2 will cause dangerous climate change, thus obliterating the desirability, let alone the need, for net-zero policies that by 2050 would inflict US$275 trillion in useless expenditures on wealthy countries and harm the poorest people in the world's poorest economies.

Predictably, the study has been ignored by mainstream media.

The foundation for the three scientists' opinion is, not surprisingly, the scientific method, which Richard Feynman (1918-88), theoretical physicist and 1965 Nobelist, defined with trademark clarity: "It doesn't matter how beautiful your theory is, it doesn't matter how smart you are. If it doesn't agree with experiment, it's wrong." Joe Oliver writing in the *Canadian Financial Post* says on 2 July 2024 "To be reliable, science must be based on observations consistent with predictions, rather than consensus, peer reviews, opinions of government controlled bodies like the IPCC and definitely not cherry-picked, exaggerated or falsified data. The paper makes the point colloquially: "Peer review of the climate literature is a joke. It is pal review."

The World of Climatism

The *Mad, Mad, Mad World of Climatism* is the first book on climate change that is fun to read. Using figures, cartoons, and whimsical sidebars, author Steve Goreham describes our crazy world, which is far down the primrose path of global warming fantasy. Contrary to popular consensus, global warming is natural and cars are innocent. But this book is not short on science. Goreham uses charts, graphs, and references to dozens of scientific papers to support his arguments. He shows that icecap melting, stronger storms, polar bear extinction, and many other climate fears are unfounded. Learn the real story about climate change.

Goreham (Steve Goreham is an American futurist in the fields of energy and environmental policy, as well as a former engineer and business executive with 30 years of experience at Fortune 100 and private companies.) says that l bet I know your thoughts about the climate.

For many years you've heard about how Earth is warming up. How people are the cause of global warming. How the polar bears are threatened with extinction. How we each must change our lifestyle for the good of the planet. Television specials show calving glaciers and raging torrents from an ice melt in Greenland and voice concern over greenhouse gas emissions. Scientists report from Antarctica about pending disasters. A news story says that the flood in Pakistan is due to global warming. And wasn't Hurricane Katrina caused by climate change? If you listen to the news, your national leaders promote new policies to fight climate change. Your nation must embrace renewable energy and reduce greenhouse gas emissions. There is talk about new taxes and regulations that will require sacrifices, but these are necessary to solve the climate crisis.

Of course, as a good citizen, you try to follow the lead. Purchases of expensive green energy and estimating the carbon dioxide output from processes are new policies. It's politically incorrect to question these policies, so you remain silent. Your high school student comes home with concerns about climate change. It seems she has just seen Al Gore's movie in class. She asks if your family is doing enough to help save the planet. A group of wind turbines was recently constructed in the next county. They look so majestic, towering above fields and grazing livestock, but when you drive past them, many seem to be standing idle.

Yes, the world is certainly a greener place in response to all these changes. Yet, something deep down in your gut says that all this alarm about global warming just doesn't ring true. Maybe you've heard the demands for change, but they don't make sense in your daily life. Maybe you remember the 1970s, when scientists were concerned about global cooling and a pending ice age. But friends tell you now that your memory is faulty—there was no fear of an ice age back then. You've been told that our air is being filled with "dangerous carbon pollution." But, you don't see any evidence of this. You recall the smog in our cities and foul-smelling polluted air when you were a child. Somehow it seems like the quality of air has improved during the last 30 years, despite the alarms from the news media. Maybe you've just been through a tough winter, with mountainous drifts of snow and cold temperatures. Didn't the seasonal forecast call for a warm, dry winter? And what about Climategate—something about a scandal over temperature data at a university in Britain? Well, your intuition about global warming is right. There is no direct scientific evidence that man-made greenhouse gases are causing catastrophic global warming. Instead, the world has been captured by the ideology of Climatism— the belief that man-made greenhouse gases are destroying Earth's climate. Most of the leaders in government, at universities, in scientific organizations, and in business say they believe in Climatism. The astonishing thing is that CO_2 is green! Rather than being a pollutant, CO_2 makes plants grow.

Published in 2012, *The Mad, Mad, Mad World of Climatism* has had many very supportive reviews, including this sample:

"An amusing and colorful, yet science-based, look at mankind's obsession with global warming." *Publishers Weekly.*

"Goreham, the antidote for Gore!"

"This is the first book written to make you laugh at the absurdity of man-made global warming—that is, until it makes you cry. If 250 pages of facts are too much, you can simply read the amusing cartoons and quotes on every page to fully understand how the world has been misled."
— Jay Lehr, The Heartland Institute.

"I am extremely impressed with this work, easily the best of its kind I have ever read... an authoritative, well-referenced, but easy-to-understand summary of the climate scare and its dire implications for society and the environment."
— Tom Harris, International Climate Science Coalition.

"Interesting, accurate, compellingly readable, and directly relevant to one of today's most important political debates. What more needs to be said beyond, "Buy this fascinating book!"
— Robert Carter, Australian Marine Geologist and Environmental Scientist.

"Steve Goreham's insightful and readable analysis of the ideology of Climatism and its socialistic goals is an important addition to public understanding of both the facts and the critical importance of making the right decisions for America."
— Harrison H. Schmitt, PhD, Geologist, former Senator and Apollo 17 Astronaut.

"Goreham's book is an excellent, readable, comprehensive, and indispensable education for everyone. It should be required reading in all schools, universities, statehouses and Congress."
— Edwin Berry, PhD, Physicist and Meteorologist.

"This is a serious book that carefully examines the issues that have been used to create the current climate change/global warming crisis…I endorse Climatism! for its easy-to-read, well-illustrated presentation of complex science."
— John Coleman, Meteorologist and Founder of the Weather Channel.

"…one of the most comprehensive yet accessible studies I have seen… if you have any interest in the subject, you'll find it difficult to put down."
— Roger Helmer, Member of the European Parliament.

"Goreham covers the science, the politics, the history, and the consequences if we get things wrong…I'm agog at how much research he must have done to pull together so many strands. I'll be keeping this book close by. It's one heck of a resource."
— Joanne Nova, Australian Speaker, TV Host, and Author.

Climate Change is Not a major problem

Bryan Leyland (in a recent review in the New Zealand Centre for Political Research) notes that underlying almost everything we hear from the mainstream media is based on an assumption that if New Zealand reduces its emissions of greenhouse gases, our climate will 'improve'. This he says "... is nonsense because any reduction we make in greenhouse gases will swiftly be blown off into the Pacific. It is also worth noting that, according to Bjorn Lomborg, if every country that signed the Paris Agreement abided by their promises until 2100, the world would be cooler by a trivial 0.17 °C. As many countries are not abiding by their promises, we cannot expect any measurable reduction in temperature. New Zealand's only sensible option is to adapt to our ever-changing climate, and stop squandering money on a futile attempt to control it."

Leyland also notes that "We hear a lot about 1.5°C "tipping points" that, it is claimed, could melt Greenland ice, destroy Amazon rainforest, trigger rapidly rising sea levels, and so on. The evidence from ice cores is that previous warm periods were warmer than pre industrial temperatures by more than 1.5°C. The Bronze Age, the Roman and the Medieval warm periods all brought prosperity to many countries. Without a prosperous economy they could not have afforded to build so many cathedrals!"

"Regarding recent weather disasters (in New Zealand), many commentators seem to be unaware that past weather events were at least as severe and that much of the flooding was due to inadequate drainage in urban areas. For instance, Esk Valley floods were as bad in 1938 and worse in 1897. 'He who ignores history is doomed to repeat it' ".

Leyland also says that "We hear lots of claims that inaction in emissions comes with a massive financial bill from the Paris Agreement. Nonsense: the Agreement does not have penalties. Given its futility, New Zealand should either opt out of the Agreement or, like the majority of countries that have signed the Agreement, ignore it. Given that Article 2(b) says that we should not do anything that threatens food production, why are so many people complaining about removing agricultural emissions from the Emissions Trading Scheme?"

"The New Zealand Government's latest Climate Strategy says that climate change is already costing New Zealand and the costs are likely to grow. It is notably silent on whether or not anything that we do will change our climate; but the whole thrust of the strategy implies that this is the case. Deliberate deception? People don't expect governments to spend vast amounts of money for no return; but this is happening."

"The first pillar of the Strategy is to build up our resistance to inevitable climate change: this can only be a good move. The second pillar of the NZ Government's Strategy says that they will rely on the market to reduce emissions at the lowest cost. Which is certainly an improvement on the current situation where nobody considers 'the bang for the buck' of various options and chooses the best. The third pillar is to have clean energy abundant and affordable. It might be abundant but it is certainly not affordable because of the very high cost of providing backup for the times when the wind is not blowing and the sun is not shining. The fourth pillar is to have world leading innovation boosting the economy and the fifth pillar is to have nature based solutions addressing climate change. I'm not sure what they're getting at. If this includes growing 'carbon forests' and building solar farms on productive farmland then they are flying in the face of Article 2 of the Paris Agreement."

May the odds be ever in your favour

Climate tech companies can tell you the odds that a flood or wildfire will ravage your home. But what if their odds are all different? *Bloomberg.com* in a report dated August 2024 suggests that "May the odds be ever in your favour."

Bloomberg further comments that humans have tried to predict the weather for as long as there have been floods and droughts; but in recent years, climate science, advanced computing and satellite imagery have supercharged their ability to do so. Computer models can now gauge the likelihood of fire, flooding or other perils at the scale of a single building lot and looking decades into the future. Startups that develop these models have proliferated.

The models are already guiding the decisions of companies across the global economy. Hoping to climate-proof their assets, government-sponsored mortgage behemoth Fannie Mae, insurance broker Aon, major insurers such as Allstate and Zurich Insurance Group, large banks, consulting firms, real estate companies and public agencies have flocked to modellers for help. Two ratings giants, Moody's and S&P, brought risk modelling expertise in-house through acquisitions.

They further suggest that : "There's no doubt that this future-facing information is badly needed. The Federal Emergency Management Agency — often criticized for the inadequacy of its own flood maps — will now require local governments to assess future flood risk if they want money to build back after a disaster."

But, according to *Bloomberg* there's a big catch. Most private risk modellers closely guard their intellectual property, which means their models are essentially black boxes. A White House scientific advisers' report warned that climate risk predictions were sometimes "of questionable quality." Research non profit CarbonPlan puts it more starkly: Decisions informed by models that can't be inspected "are likely to affect billions of lives and cost trillions of dollars."

Everyone on the planet is exposed to climate risk, and modelling is an indispensable tool for understanding the biggest consequences of rising temperatures in the decades ahead. However zooming in closer with forecasting models, as the policy makers and insurers adopting these tools are doing, could leave local communities vulnerable to unreliable, opaque data. As black-box models become the norm across, for example, housing and insurance, there's real danger that decisions made with these tools can harm people with fewer resources or less ability to afford higher costs.

One telltale sign of this uncertainty can be seen in the startlingly different outcomes from a pair of models designed to measure the same climate risk. *Bloomberg Green* (2024) compared two different models showing areas in California's Los Angeles County that are vulnerable to flooding in a once-in-a-century flood event. The analysis considers only current flood risk. Still, the models match just 21% of the time.

Model inputs — the metrics fed into a black box and how they're weighted — obviously affect the outputs. One of the above models was released in 2020 by First Street Technology, and accounts for coastal flooding caused by waves and storm surge. (If the American public has any familiarity with climate risk modelling, it's thanks to First Street, whose risk scores have been integrated into millions of online real-estate listings.)

The other, newer model was created by a team led by researchers at the University of California at Irvine. It focuses on rain-induced and riverine flooding, and incorporates high-resolution ground-elevation data alongside granular information on local drainage infrastructure.

To fill out the picture, *Bloomberg Green* reviewed a third model, created by the property information firm CoreLogic. Its data is used by many banks and insurers, and by the federal National Flood Insurance Program to help set rates for some 5 million US home owners. When it comes to Los Angeles County properties at high or extreme risk, CoreLogic's model agrees with First Street's or Irvine's less than 50% of the time.

Much of this variation may come down to modellers' different sets of expertise — climate science, building codes, insurance, engineering, hydrology — and how they're applied. But these data disagreements can have real-world consequences. Depending on which models a government office or insurer considers, it could mean building protective drainage in a relatively safe area, or raising premiums in the wrong neighbourhood.

And while experts are well versed in modelling methods, that's not the case for all users of such tools, including homebuyers. First Street's forecasts — the company says it can predict the risks of flooding, fire, extreme heat and high winds on an individual-property level — are translated into risk scores for US addresses that anyone can check at *riskfactor.com*. Redfin and *realtor.com* include these scores in home listings.

Communicating risk responsibly requires more nuance, says Mark Pestrella, director of Los Angeles County Public Works. While the public needs to know the risks they face, there's also the potential for properties and neighbourhoods to be stigmatized.

"You have to be careful how you convey the information," Pestrella says, so as not to create hysteria and unwittingly harm "those who can least afford to buy flood insurance, who can least afford their mortgage."

—From report *Bloomberg.com* by Eric Roston, Krishna Karra, Leslie Kaufman, and Sinduja Rangarajan

Climate Change: both sides of the story... a Rotary Conference discussion

A panel discussion on "Climate Change: Both Sides of the Story" was held at a Rotary Conference in Cambridge, New Zealand on June 28 2008. I was President of the Rotary Club of Otumoetai for 2007-08 at this time, and the Rotary District Governor John Tarbutt asked me in December 2007 to Chair a discussion on the above subject and to arrange the speakers. I was fortunate to be able to obtain the services of Dr Jim Renwick from NIWA (currently Professor of Climate Science at Victoria University of Wellington in New Zealand), who in the main, took the side of "man" and Dr Willem de Lange from the University of Waikato in New Zealand who in the main, took the side of "nature".

The organisers were very generous in giving us 1 hour 20 minutes, and this discussion was held before 600 delegates. I opened the proceedings with a brief overview of the subject with reference to the fact that when I started in the "weather and climate business" over 50 years ago, nobody would have forecast that in 2007, 15,000 people would attend a climate change conference in Bali (now over 25,000 people attend such conferences). I pointed out that I was the only person invited from New Zealand to attend the key WMO (World Meteorological Organization), UNEP (United Nations Environment Programme), ICSU (International Council for Science) Climate Conference in Villach, Austria, in 1985. This was in the mind of many people "the start of the whole complex subject of what role 'man' and in particular greenhouse gases have in 'controlling' our climate".

The following is what I said in my opening remarks:

Forty-seven years ago, after already being a weather forecaster in New Zealand and Canada for a few years, I was appointed to the staff of the University of Otago as a Lecturer in geography. Among my duties as a Lecturer I presented an Honours course in climatology. At Otago the course on climatology included two main topics, first the causes of climate change, and second the evidence for climate change. At that time, little did I know, nor I suspect any of my students could foresee the explosive nature of the subject of "Climate Science" as it is now called, during the last decade, and particularly over the past few years. My involvement in climate science has subsequently involved National Meteorological Services in New Zealand, Australia, Canada, Universities in New Zealand, Canada, USA and Ireland, as well as many years involved in the World Meteorological Organization including being President of the WMO Commission for Climatology for eight years.

Among the many climate science meetings I have attended, the most significant, at least as far as this afternoon is concerned, is my involvement in the WMO, UNEP, ICSU Conference held in Villach, Austria in October 1985. One hundred experts from 30 countries attended the meeting (in contrast to thousands who now attend such meetings), and I was privileged to be the only New Zealander invited. We were all there as experts in various fields of science endeavouring to do the best we could in looking at the complexities of climate science.

Among the principal findings of this conference was...

"while other factors, such as aerosol concentration, changes in solar energy input, and changes in vegetation, may also influence climate, the greenhouse gases are likely to be the most important cause of climate change over the next century."

At that time, even though I was partly responsible for the writing of the paragraph I have just read, I, along with a few of my colleagues, had some misgivings about it, and were somewhat surprised that within a year "human-induced climate change" caught the imagination of much of the world.

Two main views held by climate scientists

Irrespective of my personal views on the matter, it is clear that there are two main views held by climate scientists and others:

The first: those who are mainly involved in the Intergovernmental Panel on Climate Change (IPCC) and many or most Government scientists, plus others, such as Al Gore, and many politicians and most journalists who consider that man, including domestic animals, is the prime cause of recent changes in the climate.

The second: those - in the main some University scientists, many retired climatologists, and a minority of politicians and journalists, who consider that nature is the main cause of changes in the climate.

One of the most fascinating things about the climate change scene is the tremendous growth in the political and economic aspects of it. In 1970, I wrote a book called *The Value of the Weather*, and later on in 1986 I published a book called *The Uncertainty Business - Risks and Opportunities in Weather and Climate*. In both books, I made only a few references to "global warming" or "climate change" but many references to variations in the weather and climate on a day to day, season to season, and year to year basis.

It is my view that these variations are still paramount but the current emphasis seems to be on what is going to happen to the climate 20, 50 and 100 years ahead, and hence the debate we are now to have here this afternoon.

Jim and Willem were each given about 20 minutes to state their case, and this was followed by about 20 minutes of questions, some of which I obtained from attendees at the conference, but most were questions which came from me. Prior to the conference, both Jim and Willem agreed that I should ask the questions. The following were some of the questions which I asked.

Questions:

1. Irrespective of the cause of Climate Change, could you explain why the media and many politicians seem to consider that, in general warming, is a bad thing, and by inference does this mean that, in general cooling, is a good thing?
2. If the IPCC was forecasting a cooling rather than a warming, what difference do you think that would make to Government, UN and *Greenpeace* attitudes?
3. The Maunder Minimum, from 1650-1715, which was a period of very low sunspot activities, and associated with very cold conditions in Europe, was a significant feature of the history of the last millennium. Are we likely to get another Maunder-like minimum in the near future?
4. During the period of Viking exploration from about 800 to 1300AD the Northern Hemisphere was associated with relatively warm conditions, and in many cases it was warmer then than during the last 30 or 40 years. During the 1200's Greenland had about 3000 settlements and yet by 1550 the last of them had disappeared. There was no human-induced greenhouse warming during that period, so is there any reason why we could not have such a period again - perhaps like what we had from about 1970 to about 2000 - unrelated to what people and domestic animals are doing?
5. I understand that the IPCC seems to be giving relatively small importance to the role of the sun. Why is this the case? Do we really know all there is to know about solar activity?
6. A key debate in the climate change arena appears to be whether increases in CO_2 (from whatever cause) causes warming, or whether warming causes increases in CO_2. When do you think we will be

able to establish the truth about these statements, or have I got it all wrong?
7. Why is an increase in CO_2 not considered to be a good thing? I understand that some scientists suggest that the biosphere is currently suffering from "CO_2 starvation", and that a doubling of CO_2 would increase plant production by 20%.
8. Many or most climate scientists who have publicly stated that they do not agree with the findings of the IPCC are labelled as "sceptics", yet economists who disagree with the Reserve Bank on monetary matters are not considered to be "economic sceptics", but simply experts who have a different view of things. Why is this so?
9. To Willem: If in the future it can be established without question that the current viewpoint of the IPCC is correct, how would people like yourself and organizations who take the contrary view of the IPCC, deal with this situation?
10. To Jim: If in the future it can be established without question that the current viewpoint of the IPCC is wrong, and that nature is the main driver of climate changes, how would the IPCC, and organizations like NIWA deal with this situation?
11. My understanding is that most climate scientists who support the view that man rather than nature is in control of the climate are Government employees, whereas most climate scientists who support the view that nature, rather than man, is in control of the climate are in the main, retired. On the other hand University Climate Scientists take a variety of positions on this subject. Is there any reason for this? Is it linked to who finances the research, political agendas, or something else?

Jim and Willem were then given five minutes to sum up. From what I heard from the attendees, the discussion seemed to be an excellent way of presenting this challenging subject, and my sense was that the majority of the audience there were yet to be convinced that man is really in control (as most media, politicians including the G8 leaders, and the IPCC believe), rather than nature.

Jim and Willem agreed on many points, but it was the interpretation of the data, much presented in graphical manner, which was the key difference in their presentation. Jim obviously took in the main the "IPCC line", but agreed with Willem that we did not know everything, and Willem took in the main the more "academic line", but also agreed that we do not know everything.

Climate Change and the Villach Conference of 1985

Among the many climate science meetings I have attended, the most significant, at least in terms of climate change is concerned, was my involvement in the UN sponsored International Conference held in the beautiful town of Villach, Austria, in October 1985. One hundred experts from 30 countries attended the meeting (in contrast to ten to twenty thousand who now attend such meetings), and I was privileged to be the only New Zealander invited.

We were all there as experts - and not representing our respective organisations - in various fields of science, endeavouring to do the best we could in looking at the complexities of climate science. This conference predated by three years the establishment of the Intergovernmental Panel on Climate Change (IPCC) established by the World Meteorological Organization (WMO) and the United Nations Environment Programme (UNEP). The first session of the IPCC was held in Geneva in November 1988.

Among the principal findings of the Villach Conference was that "while other factors, such as aerosol concentration, changes in solar energy input, and changes in vegetation, may also influence climate, the greenhouse gases are likely to be the most important cause of climate change over the next century".

At that time, even though I was partly responsible for the writing of the above paragraph, I along with a few of my colleagues, had some misgivings about this phrase, and were somewhat surprised that within a year 'human-induced global warming' caught the imagination of much of the world. Indeed today, not a day goes by without some mention of 'global warming', climate change, emission trading schemes etc., all terms which up until 1980's were the preserve of academic text books.

Despite this concern, a colleague of mine from Australia, Bill Kininmonth, who in 2004 wrote a book called *Climate Change - A Natural Hazard* has mentioned to me on several occasions that I have changed from being a 'gamekeeper' and become a 'poacher'. Whether that is true is a matter of opinion. However, irrespective of my personal views on the matter, it is clear that there are two main views held by climate scientists and others on the subject of global warming and climate change.

First, those who are mainly involved in the Intergovernmental Panel on Climate Change (IPCC) and many or most government scientists, plus others, such as Al Gore, and many politicians and most journalists who consider that humans activities, including domestic animals, are the prime cause of recent changes in the climate.

Second, those - in the main some university scientists, many retired climatologists, and a minority of politicians and journalists, who consider that "nature" is the main cause of changes in the climate.

Thirty years ago, it was unconceivable that the New Zealand or any Government would have a Minister of Climate Change; indeed back then, as weather forecasters and climatologists we just got on with our job of making the best possible weather forecast and providing the best climate advice to all those who requested information, without guidance or interference from the government of the day. How things have changed!

Ten big climate questions answered

The following was published on a website of the *New Zealand Herald* in January 2010. Weather Watch weather analyst Philip Duncan's blogs on climate change attracted a lot of reader interest when this interview took place in 2010. Duncan looked at the readers' ten most commonly asked questions and put them to Dr James Renwick, Principal Scientist, Climate Variability & Change at New Zealand's National Water and Atmospheric Research Institute (NIWA). Professor Renwick is now Head of the School of Geography, Environment and Earth Sciences, at the Victoria Univerity of Wellington in New Zealand.

1) It feels like summers in New Zealand aren't as hot as they used to be - it doesn't feel like NZ is getting hotter at all?
Dr Renwick: I hear that comment quite a lot, and I think a lot of it is psychological. My perception is that when you're young you spend a lot of time outdoors in the summer... the older we get the more time we spend indoors, in the office, less holidays etc. So our perception is that summers used to be hotter, but I can assure you that the data show it is definitely warming up and has done so over the last century.

2) If the world is heating up, why are places like USA and UK seeing record cold and snow?
That's the difference between global change and regional change. The USA and UK have had a very cold winter, but other parts of the Northern Hemisphere, such as Greenland, Alaska and the Arctic Ocean have been much warmer than average over the past few weeks, but this didn't make the headlines. We need to be careful with comparing a local region to what's happening across the whole globe.

3) Why was Global Warming replaced with the term "Climate Change"?
That's a really interesting question and I don't believe it ever was changed. My perception is that "Climate Change" has always been used in the scientific community, however the term "Global Warming" was something perhaps used more by the media and then the term stuck. There's a lot more to climate change than just warming - that's why all the scientists I know use and have always used the term "Climate Change". I don't think there has ever been an "official" replacement.

4) Last decade was NZ's warmest decade on record - but wasn't the increase within the margin of error or at the very least, a tiny change?
There are two ways of looking at that. One of the records we used was based on seven climate stations which have data for well over 100 years. The difference in the averages (between the 2000s and the 1980s) from those stations was indeed very small and within the margin of error. However it's important to note that four decades in a row have been significantly warmer than those before it. There are other records that can be used, such as the 11 reliable climate sites we described on our website last year, and in that data set the 2000s and the 1980s (next warmest decade) were more than 0.1°C different, which is significant. So the last 10 years were a bit warmer, and the last few decades have been a lot warmer than all the previous decades in the record, which shows an overall warming trend. If it was natural variability then you would expect a recent decade to have been cooler, like it was in the 1920s, say - but we aren't seeing any decades dropping back to those sorts of levels - and it's very unlikely going into the future that any will be that much cooler.

5) If the world is getting hotter, how come 2009 was cooler than average in NZ?
This is partly the same as question 2. It's important to remember that New Zealand covers a small fraction of the globe. Climate change doesn't mean every year will be warmer in every country. It also doesn't mean every year will be warmer globally. There are always ups and downs but the trend is upwards. For instance, last century the eastern US actually cooled for several decades while the globe overall warmed up significantly. In the last 25 years however, that local cooling has reversed, as the globe has continued to warm. So, the overall trend is upwards, but even then we do see some cooling regions and some cooler periods. There are patches of the globe, sometimes quite large patches, which can go against the overall trend for a while - but that misses the point...if you're thinking about global change you have to look at the whole globe.

6) Weather forecasters can't even predict the weather 2 weeks out, how can climate scientists predict 10 or 50 years out?
Well that's confusing the weather with the climate. Its true you can't predict the exact daily sequence of the weather more than a week or two out. But we (climate scientists) can say, with quite a lot of certainty, that July is going to be cooler than January in Auckland because seasonal

change in the climate is predictable... and changes in the average climate over decades are also quite predictable. We're not in the business of saying what the weather will be like in January 2050, but we can predict average conditions several decades out on the basis of greenhouse gas increase. Here are a couple of analogies that might help explain my point:
Analogy 1: Imagine you're out in the harbour on your boat. Predicting the weather is a bit like predicting the ripples of the waves on the sea caused by the wind. Predicting the climate is more like predicting the tides.
Analogy 2: Nobody can predict exactly when you and I will die, but insurance companies make a lot of money from knowing what the average death rate is - this average can't be applied to any individual. Predicting the climate is like using those life expectancy tables... we can predict the averages and the overall statistics with a fair degree of accuracy. Predicting the weather is more like tracking an individual person... certainly more variable.

7) Is 30 years of weather data long enough to use as a "guide" for predicting the future?
The four warmest decades were the last four decades... and some have interpreted that to mean we didn't have data from before that. Actually, we have good records from a lot of stations in NZ from the last 70 or 80 years and some back well over 100 years. Globally, scientists use ice cores, tree rings, and other records to estimate climate over several hundred or thousand years. Thirty years is certainly not long enough but no one is actually using just 30 years of data.

You just mentioned ice cores - but haven't they showed big warming's in the past?
Yes you're right, and that tells us the climate is sensitive... it just happens that it has been pretty stable while human society has been around. There are certainly natural things that cause fluctuations, such as changes in the Earth's orbit that drive the ice ages, but it's also clear that human activity – CO_2 greenhouse gas release – affects the climate as well... in fact, basic physics shows that today's greenhouse gas release is a much faster way to heat the planet than the slow natural warming process that ends an ice age. I often hear this argument: Because there are natural causes of variation then the concept of human-caused variations is impossible - i.e. there's been natural causes in the past so then that rules out a human

cause now. That argument just doesn't make sense. Natural influences have caused the climate to change quite a lot in the past and that should give us concern... it shows that the climate is variable, and vulnerable.

8) Are scientists scared to speak out about what they really believe for fear of being alarmist or not "going with the consensus"?
Well no (laughing)... no not at all. Scientists are in the business they're in because they want to find out what's actually happening with the natural world. I don't know one scientist who is scared to speak out about what they believe... and believe is an interesting word. Science is about observing the natural world and building understanding on those observations, it's not about belief. Scientists publish their results openly, there's no fear of speaking out at all. Going with the "consensus" is an illusion too. For instance, the IPCC is a review process - it summarises what thousands of scientists all over the world have observed, or modelled, or deduced - it doesn't dictate to them, just summarises. It turns out 99.9% of work reported does indeed form a consensus... that's a reflection of how things are, of what the real world looks like - it's a very clear picture.

9) Why does it seem that climate change is so doom and gloom? I'm burnt by warnings of things like SARS, Y2K, Bird Flu, Swine Flu etc how can I trust the experts on this one?
There isn't an easy answer to that... there have been a lot of things in the media that haven't turned out to be as important or dangerous as we are led to believe... and if you're not an expert in those fields then what do you believe? What I can say is that with climate change there is an incredible weight of evidence that shows that climate change is happening... it is definitely a problem. Almost every scientific paper out there supports this view. The IPCC process is designed to help non-experts understand the problem. There are a lot of dire possibilities with future climate change... all the scientists I know are very concerned, and have a sense of urgency about taking action. To help convey that sense or urgency to the public, we sometimes do focus on the biggest issues or risks. It's important to note though that it's not all doom and gloom... there will be some winners, at least in the short term.... perhaps more grass or grape growth in colder parts of New Zealand... but unfortunately there will be more losers than winners for the globe, and more at risk as times goes on.

10) The 2009 UN Climate Change Conference seemed like a complete waste of money...are politics helping or confusing your cause?
Science is about evidence and understanding the natural world, so scientists are not in the business of politics. But there has to be a political process to deal with this problem, one that's informed by the science. There is no alternative to dealing with this, and individual countries need to work together. Getting that cooperation going can seem slow and confusing, and a bit of a time wasting process. From my point of view it would be great if the political process was more efficient and faster. Copenhagen was a bit disappointing... but given human nature, I guess the world community has to go through these stages before we really get somewhere. I was just reading a report on Copenhagen (from the New Zealand Business Council for Sustainable Development)... and the author said it reminded him of going to a dance as a teenager... it takes a long time to get couples up on the dance floor... but eventually someone gets up and dances, and then everyone wants to dance. That was Copenhagen - things didn't really get going there, but we hope the big players will be ready to dance soon.

In the scientific community there is a great deal of concern and a sense of urgency - that we have to do something now. This hasn't quite got through to the international political world. We aren't taking it seriously enough yet... and there isn't a lot of time left to get on top of things.

Key points about climate change

1. Communities and businesses and individuals should always live within their climatic income - both now and in the future.

2. There are always surprises in science, and the science of climate change will probably never be fully understood.

3. It is not always true that the climate we have now (wherever we live) is the best one... some people (and animals and crops) may prefer it to be wetter, drier, colder, or warmer. However, some species which have adapted well to their current climate may not be able to adapt to a future climate if the rate of change to that climate is too fast.

4. Climatic variations and climatic changes from WHATEVER cause (i.e. human induced or natural) clearly create risks, but also provide real opportunities.

5. It is important that we should "clean-up" the environment by decreasing greenhouse gas emissions, but we should do so because in most cases it makes good economic and social sense to do so. If, by so doing we ALSO produce a "better" climate, then we will all be winners, but we should NOT expect to be able to "control" the climate.

6. One should always be aware that if it is really "Nature" and not "Man" in "control" of our climate, then our only choice (as has always been the case) will be to adapt to whatever "Nature" provides, and our ability to control such changes will be minimal if not zero.

7. The need to forecast the changes that will occur in the climate of the future and in particular how the current climate will vary over the next 10 to 20 years remains paramount, and the best climate-scientific brains are required to prepare all countries for whatever the future climate will be.

Net Zero

Viewpoint One

Net zero policies will have a trivial effect on temperature, but disastrous effects on people worldwide.

Richard Lindzen, Professor of Earth, Atmospheric, and Planetary Sciences, Emeritus Massachusetts Institute of Technology, and William Happer Professor of Physics, Emeritus, Princeton University in a review dated July 14, 2024, wrote that the United States and countries worldwide are vigorously pursuing regulations and subsidies to reduce CO_2 emissions to net zero by 2050 on the assumption, as stated by the Intergovernmental Panel on Climate Change (IPCC), that the "evidence is clear that carbon dioxide (CO_2) is the main driver of climate change" and is "responsible for more than 50% of the change."

They comment that they are career physicists with a special expertise in radiation physics, which describes how CO_2 affects heat flow in Earth's atmosphere. The physics of carbon dioxide is that CO_2's ability to warm the planet is determined by its ability to absorb heat, which decreases rapidly as CO_2's concentration in the atmosphere increases. This scientific fact about CO_2 changes everything about the popular view of CO_2 and climate change. At today's CO_2 concentration in the atmosphere of approximately 420 parts per million, additional amounts of CO_2 have little ability to absorb heat and therefore it is now a weak greenhouse gas. At higher concentrations in the future, the ability of future increases to warm the planet will be even smaller. This also means that the common assumption that CO_2 is "the main driver of climate change" is scientifically false. In short, more CO_2 cannot cause catastrophic global warming or more extreme weather. Neither can greenhouse gases of methane (CH_4) or nitrous oxide (N_2O) the levels of which are so small that they are irrelevant to climate. They further comment that referring to additional atmospheric CO_2 as "carbon pollution" is "complete nonsense". More CO_2 does no harm.

Quite the contrary, Lindzen and Happer say that more CO_2 does two good things for humanity: (1) It provides a beneficial increase in temperature, although slight and much less than natural fluctuations, and (2) It creates more food for people worldwide. They say that net zero efforts will have a trivial effect on temperature. More of the atmospheric greenhouse gas, CO_2, will increase temperature, but only slightly. How changes in atmospheric greenhouse gases affect radiation transfer are described by precise physical equations that have never failed to describe

What controls the weather dice?

observations of the real world. They applied these formulas to the massive efforts in the U. S. and worldwide to reduce CO_2 emissions to net zero by 2050 in a paper by R. Lindzen, W. Happer and W. van Wijngaarden, Net Zero Avoided Temperature Increase, (Net Zero Averted Temperature Increase - CO_2 Coalition; http://arxiv.org/abs/2406.07392.

They show that all the efforts to achieve net zero emissions of CO_2, if fully implemented, will have a trivial effect on temperature: • United States Net Zero by 2050 -- only avoids a temperature increase of 0. 015 °F with no positive feedback, and only 0.06 °F with a positive feedback of 4 that is typically built into the models of the IPCC. • Worldwide Net Zero by 2050 -- only avoids a temperature increase of 0.13 °F or 0.50 °F with a factor of 4 positive feedback. These numbers are trivial, but the cost of achieving them would be disastrous to people worldwide.

In the United States and worldwide, Net zero regulations and subsidies will have disastrous effects, including elimination of coal-fired and gas-fired power plants that provide the majority of the world's electricity; elimination of gas-fuelled heaters and cooking stoves; elimination of internal combustion engines for transportation and other uses; elimination of energy sources and feedstocks for producing nitrogen fertilizer that feeds nearly half the world as well as for the manufacture of nearly everything used in daily life. Investments into inefficient "green" energy technologies diverts resources from more useful purposes. These and other effects would destroy entire economies.

More CO_2 means more food. Contrary to the demonization of CO_2 as a pollutant, increasing concentrations of atmospheric CO_2 boosts the amount of food available to people worldwide, including in drought-stricken areas. Doubling CO_2 to 800 ppm, for example, will increase global food supplies by a significant amount. Thus, CO_2 emissions should not be reduced, but increased to provide more food worldwide. There would be no risk of catastrophic global warming or extreme weather because CO_2 is now a weak greenhouse gas. Reducing CO_2 emissions will reduce the amount of food available to people worldwide and produce no benefit to the climate.

Fossil fuels must not be eliminated. Net zero requires that fossil fuels be eliminated because they account for about 90% of human-induced CO_2 emissions. However, the elimination of fossil fuels will have no effect on the climate since CO_2 is now a weak greenhouse gas. The use of fossil fuels should be expanded because they provide more CO_2 which makes more food, are used to make nitrogen fertilizer that enables the feeding of about half of the world's population, and provide reliable and inexpensive energy for people everywhere, especially for the two-thirds of the world's population without adequate access to electricity.

Conclusion: All net zero actions worldwide should be stopped immediately. All net zero CO_2 regulations and subsidies in the United States and worldwide must be stopped as soon as possible to avoid the disastrous effects on people worldwide, especially in developing countries.

Viewpoint Two

An expert working group of natural scientists (especially geologists) has been established in the Czech Republic and has prepared the following Declaration for politicians and the general public in the Czech Republic (but also elsewhere in the world).

They are mostly geologists, but they work with experts in all relevant fields (including the international organisation CLINTEL). Basic geological research and mapping has provided the most evidence of ongoing climate change on Earth, long before so-called anthropogenic global warming came into vogue.

It is not true that natural climate change is very slow,(except perhaps in the case of major disasters, which recur after a very long time). There is already evidence from the relatively recent past (the Quaternary) of repeated very rapid temperature changes, and this at a time when there was no significant human influence, let alone human-induced emissions of greenhouse gases, including CO_2. On the contrary, it has been clearly demonstrated that the increase in greenhouse gas concentrations was a consequence of rising temperatures. The release or uptake of GHGs then affected temperatures only secondarily (as a positive feedback). The sensitivity of GHG concentrations to temperature changes has been demonstrated in many examples, even on short time scales at the time of instrumental measurements.

Current climatology, at least the results presented to the public as the 'consensus of scientists', unilaterally emphasizes only GHG emissions. Greenhouse gases, which prevent incident energy from being radiated back into space, are last in the chain of factors (solar radiation, reflectivity) affecting temperatures.

The significance of changes in solar activity (whose fluctuations over the period of instrumental measurements alone are energetically comparable to the reported greenhouse gas forcing) is usually ignored, on the grounds that it shows no temporal correlation with temperatures on short time scales. The period of significantly above-average solar activity, which began in the late 19th and early 20th centuries and has not yet completely ended, must have had some effect on temperatures. It has been documented that there are physical mechanisms that explain why average temperatures may not respond immediately to changes in solar activity (e.g. energy accumulation in the oceans and in the Earth's crust and its delayed release). However, some climatologists have apparently taken the attitude of 'if we can't calculate it, we'll ignore it' – which is totally unacceptable in serious science with the opportunities offered in the 21st century.

The atmosphere is steadily moving towards rebalancing with the ocean, which contains orders of magnitude more CO_2 (including other forms of carbon that can easily transfer to it). It is therefore not within human power to significantly deviate the atmospheric CO_2 content from equilibrium values in the long term view. The calculations used by the IPCC, which nonsensically separate 'natural' CO_2 from 'emitted' CO_2, lead to unrealistically high year-to-year variability in the uptake of 'emitted' CO_2 and are therefore not a credible basis for answering the question of how much CO_2 and other human-emitted greenhouse gases actually remain in the atmosphere (more precisely: how much lower concentrations would be if anthropogenic emissions were not present).

'Carbon neutrality', as the main objective of the current measures extremely affecting the economy, is therefore only of ideological significance, because maintaining certain concentrations of CO_2 and other greenhouse gases would only be realistic if temperatures did not change significantly in the long time (even from natural causes).

Concentrating a great deal of effort on preventing global warming must therefore have a very uncertain outcome even under very favourable circumstances. Much more effective is adaptation to climate change itself (which humanity has been doing for the entirety of its existence). Also important are the efforts devoted to regional or local climate, where the impact of human activity is already very real (heat islands, disruption of small water cycles, etc.). We reject the propaganda that warming is a priori bad and increases the frequency of extremes of all kinds, because such claims are completely contradicted by the geological record and current observations (there is no denying, for example, the positive effect of higher precipitation and higher CO_2 concentrations on vegetation growth, including agricultural crops, in the vast majority of the world).

Mgr. Miloš Faltus, Ph.D.,RNDr. Tomáš Fürst, Ph.D.,RNDr. Pavel Kalenda, CSc.,Mgr. Jiří Kobza.,RNDr. Dobroslav Matějka, CSc.,Mgr. Václav Procházka, Ph.D.

Viewpoint 3
From the UN Climate Action for August 2024. "For a liveable climate: Net zero commitments must be backed by credible action. Put simply, net zero means cutting carbon emissions to a small amount of residual emissions that can be absorbed and durably stored by nature and other CO_2 removal measures, leaving zero in the atmosphere."

Why is net zero in current national plans fall short of what is required?

In May 2021, the International Energy Association published its landmark report Net Zero Emissions by 2050: A Roadmap for the Global Energy Sector. The report set out a narrow but feasible pathway for the global energy sector to contribute to the Paris Agreement's goal of limiting the rise in global temperatures to 1.5°C above pre-industrial levels. The Net Zero Roadmap quickly became an important benchmark for policy makers, industry, the financial sector and civil society.

Since the report was released, many changes have taken place, notably amid the global energy crisis triggered by Russia's invasion of Ukraine in February 2022. Energy sector CO_2 emissions have continued to rise, reaching a new record in 2022. Yet there are also increasing grounds for optimism: the last two years have also seen remarkable progress in developing and deploying some key clean energy technologies.

The 2023 update to Net Zero Roadmap surveys this complex and dynamic landscape and sets out an updated pathway to net zero by 2050, taking account of the key developments that have occurred since 2021.

Air New Zealand and Green Credentials

Search for Air New Zealand's big bold climate action plan and you get a black screen with the words: This site is under review Dubbed Flight NZO (zero), the airline called it its "most important journey yet"; its commitment to finding a more sustainable way to connect with the world by buying greener planes and using greener fuel. That journey has been disrupted after the airline dropped its 2030 goal to reduce carbon intensity by nearly a third from its 2019 baseline. It has also pulled out of the Science-Based Targets initiative, a scheme involving corporates around the world.

The airline says it is sticking with the goal of net zero carbon emissions by the year 2050 and it is working on a new "near-term carbon emissions reduction target that could better reflect the challenges relating to aircraft and alternative jet fuel availability within the industry".

The move comes as airlines around the world face court action over their sustainability claims, so called greenwashing. Newsroom's David Williams says the sceptics of Air New Zealand's climate ambitions, including Tourism Professor James Higham, had warned early on that they would face greater scrutiny.

"I guess he's saying that it's very hard for an airline to claim environmental exceptionalism. It's not exceptional in terms of its ability to reduce its carbon footprint. So he would say there needs to be a bit more reality about what they're saying about their sustainability."

Despite the move, Williams says the airline is seen as a sustainability leader by the industry, particularly for it's offsets programme where customers can opt to pay for tree planting to offset their emissions. "And there's all sorts of things you can do at the airport as well to save energy and to not emit carbon; but actually the big one is the big source of your emissions and that is flying planes. It's really hard to say you're an environmental leader when you're burning fossil fuels all the time."

The airline's announcement came on the same day that the Climate Change Commission warned that New Zealand risks missing key emissions targets under current government policies. Newsroom's Marc Daalder says people often find the stories confusing and discouraging but there was some optimistic news in the same report.

"We either want to hear that we're doing well or we're not doing well but the message often takes a little bit more nuance than that. That report said on the one hand New Zealand's emissions have fallen every year in a row since 2019. That same report says we may be on track to meet our near term emissions targets but we're not on track to meet our medium and long-term emissions targets."

He explains to The Detail why government policies have played only a small part in the reductions to date; and why we're now not on target for net zero 2050 emissions. For example, he says, "the goals are ambitious and require deep cuts to the climate pollution produced from transport, energy, industry, waste and households. Compared with most other developed countries New Zealand's emissions are higher per capita, mainly due to our agriculture. New Zealand's net zero 2050 targets are also less ambitious because they do not include agriculture. We've got less stringent targets, we're just getting started on our journey and at the same time we now have a government that is cancelling a lot of climate policies, reworking the emissions plan and producing new plans that don't have us on track to meet our targets ".

"There are other countries that are facing backslides on climate or are at risk of doing so, like the United States, but New Zealand is part of a smaller core of countries that are actually taking backsteps on climate."

Small modular reactors

Small modular reactors (SMRs) are a class of small nuclear fission reactors, designed to be built in a factory, shipped to operational sites for installation and then used to power buildings or other commercial operations. Wikipedia says (August 2023) that the first commercial SMR was invented by a team of nuclear scientists at Oregon State University (OSU) in 2007.

Working with OSU's prototype, NuScale Power developed the first working model, available to the US market, in 2022. The term SMR refers to the size, capacity and modular construction. Reactor type and the nuclear processes may vary. Of the many SMR designs, the pressurized water reactor (PWR) is the most common. However, recently proposed SMR designs include: generation IV, thermal-neutron reactors, fast-neutron reactors, molten salt, and gas-cooled reactor models.

Military specified small reactors were first designed in the 1950s to power ballistic missile submarines and ships (aircraft carriers and ice breakers) with nuclear propulsion. The electrical output for modern naval reactors are generally limited to less than 165 MWe and dedicated to powering turboshaft props rather than delivering commercial electricity. In addition, there are many more safety controls absent from naval reactors due to the space limitations these reactors were designed for.

Commercial SMRs can be designed to deliver an electrical power output as low as 5 MWe (electric) or a maximum of 300 MWe per module. SMRs may also be designed purely for desalinization or facility heating rather than electricity. These SMRs are measured in megawatts thermal MWt. Many SMR designs rely on a modular system, allowing customers to simply add modules to achieve a desired megawatt output (MWe). Some SMR designs, typically those using Generation IV reactors technologies, aim to secure additional economic advantage through improvements in electrical generating efficiency from much higher temperature steam generation. Ideally, modular reactors are expected to reduce on-site construction, increase containment efficiency, and claim to enhance safety. However, other SMR manufacturers claim greater safety should come through the application of passive safety features that operate without human intervention. Passive safety is a concept already implemented in some conventional nuclear reactor types. SMRs should also help reduce power plant staffing costs, as their operation is fairly simple. and are claimed to have the ability to bypass financial and safety barriers that inhibit the construction of conventional reactors.

As of late 2023, only China and Russia have successfully built operational SMRs. The US Department of Energy had estimated the first SMR in the

United States would be completed by NuScale Power around 2030, but this deal has since fallen through after the customers backed out due to rising costs. There are more than 80 modular reactor designs under development in 19 countries. Russia has been operating a floating nuclear power plant Akademik Lomonosov, in Russia's Far East (Pevek), since October 2022. The floating plant is the first of its kind in the world. China's pebble-bed modular high-temperature gas-cooled reactor HTR-PM was connected to the grid in 2021.

The United States has plans for several modular reactors. Dominion Energy Virginia is now accepting proposals. The U.S. has nearly 4 gigawatts in announced SMR projects in addition to almost 3 GW in early development or pre-development stages, according to Utility Dive.

SMRs differ in terms of staffing, safety and deployment time. US government studies to evaluate SMR-associated risks are claimed to have slowed the licensing process. One main concern with SMRs and their large number, needed to reach an economic profitability, is preventing nuclear proliferation.

Economic factors of scale mean that nuclear reactors tend to be large, to such an extent that size itself becomes a limiting factor. The 1986 Chernobyl disaster and the 2011 Fukushima nuclear disaster caused a major set-back for the nuclear industry, with worldwide suspension of development, cutting down of funding, and closure of reactor plants.

In response, researchers at Oregon State University introduced a new strategy to build smaller reactors, which were expected to be faster to fabricate, safer to operate, and operate at a reduced cost per reactor. Despite the loss of scale advantages and considerably less power output, funding was expected to be easier thanks to the introduction of modular construction and projects with anticipated shorter time scales. The generic SMR proposal is to swap the economies of unit scale for the economies of unit mass production. Partnering with OSU, NuScale Power was the first to apply this manufacturing strategy starting in 2006.

In February 2024 the European Commission recognized SMR technology as an important contributor to decarbonization as part of EU Green Deal. In its pathway to reach global net zero emissions by 2050, Wikipedia says that the International Energy Agency (IEA) considers that worldwide nuclear power should be multiplied by two between 2020 and 2050. Antonio Vaya Soler, an expert from the Nuclear Energy Agency (NEA), agrees that although renewable energy is essential to fight global warming, it will not be sufficient to achieve net zero CO_2 emissions and nuclear energy capacity should be at least doubled.

The New Zealand Climate Commission

The New Zealand Climate Commission is the successor to the Interim Climate Change Committee (ICCC) of November 2019 of the Climate Change Response (Zero Carbon) Amendment Act. The Commission was tasked with developing an evidence-based plan for New Zealand to fulfill its climate change goals within the framework of the Zero Carbon Act. On 24 April 2020, the then Climate Change Minister James Shaw asked the Climate Change Commission to review New Zealand's emission reduction target under the Paris Agreement, focusing on New Zealand's methane and carbon commitments.

On 31 January 2021, the Climate Change Commission released its draft advice for the first three emission budgets and the first emissions reduction plan. The report proposed phasing out petrol-powered cars, accelerating renewable energy generation, reducing the number of cows, and growing more native forests to meet New Zealand's carbon neutral goals by 2050. Chairman Carr defended the advice as ambitious but claimed it was realistic and advocated "immediate and decisive" action. New Zealand Prime Minister Jacinda Ardern, claimed that the impact of the proposed reforms would not be an economic burden.

On July 30, 2024 the Minister of Climate Change released the Climate Change Commission's first emissions reduction monitoring report. The reports will in future be delivered to the Minister of Climate Change annually. This first report issued in July 2024 from the Climate Change Commission shows that New Zealand is making progress but could still fall short of future emissions budgets, says Commission Chair Dr Rod Carr.

This report will track year-on-year how the country is progressing towards meeting its emissions budgets and targets. Dr Carr says "the report provides an evidence-based, impartial view of whether the country is on course to reach its goals for reducing and removing greenhouse gas emissions. The report released today shows New Zealand is making some good progress towards meeting emissions budgets, with emissions declining in recent years," Dr Carr says. "This was partly because New Zealanders increasingly adopted low emissions technology and took actions that made a difference. Examples include building new renewable generation facilities, converting boilers to biomass and electric power, choosing to drive more electric and hybrid vehicles, and planting more forests ".

"However, the report also shows there is a significant risk that the country won't meet future emissions budgets. There is an urgent need to ensure New Zealand's climate policies will put the country on track. Our assessment highlights particular risk to sufficient emissions cuts from the agriculture and transport sectors. The annual monitoring reports are a critical part of the wider system that was created to help shape Aotearoa New Zealand's efforts to tackle and adapt to climate change. The report covers what progress has been made, what challenges the country is experiencing, and what opportunities and risks need to be considered in policy decisions. This report shows current emissions data and projections indicate the country is on track to meet the first emissions budget".

"However, there are several uncertainties and risks that could change this, such as if deforestation is higher than projected, if a dry year increases electricity sector emissions, or if transport emissions continue to grow as they did in 2023," Dr Carr says. "There are also significant risks the second and third budgets may not be met." While emissions fell steeply in 2022, around 94% of that reduction was strongly influenced by factors outside of government control, such as good hydro conditions, high fossil fuel prices, and general economic conditions."The areas that could have the biggest impact for driving down emissions are in decarbonising electricity supply, decarbonising industry, reducing on-farm emissions, adopting low and zero-emissions vehicles, and land use change to forestry. Together, these could deliver around three quarters of what's needed for the second and third emissions budget," Dr Carr says.

The Commission has been tasked by Parliament to deliver monitoring reports annually to build the bigger picture for decision-makers. The Commission draws on official data and projections including the New Zealand Greenhouse Gas Inventory, an official Tier 1 statistic, to inform the monitoring report. "While there are many different data sources available, a key part of our monitoring role is providing an accurate and regular benchmark," Dr Carr says. "Over time, we will provide a series of snapshots that build a picture for New Zealand to track progress against. This monitoring report is not just a report card with data and assessments. It also identifies opportunities to reduce emissions further, pick up the pace, and improve the lives of New Zealanders – particularly people most affected by climate change, or by lack of action to tackle them. The Commission has been clear in all its work that the Government has choices on how to act – and our monitoring report helps decision-makers understand different choices, and how they add up ".

The monitoring report includes: official data on greenhouse gas emissions up to 2022 from New Zealand's Greenhouse Gas Inventory. The Commission is required by the Climate Change Response Act to use the Inventory as base data as it is New Zealand's Tier 1 official source of greenhouse gas data, provisional estimates of gross emissions in 2023, latest projections of future greenhouse gas emissions and removals, an assessment of current government emissions reduction policies and plans (as at April 2024).

This looks at how well they set up the country to meet its climate change goals information about a range of opportunities to make further progress towards those goals, including within specific sectors.

The emissions reduction monitoring report is expected to answer four key questions:

1. What progress have we seen in emission reductions to date?
2. How is the country tracking towards meeting the first emissions budget for 2022–2025?
3. How is the country tracking towards meeting future emissions budgets and the 2050 target?
4. What is needed for New Zealand to be on track for future emissions budgets and the 2050 target?

The Commission drew on well-regarded monitoring systems here and overseas, including those used by independent climate bodies, to develop its approach for the report. The methodology was reviewed by independent experts, and the research, evidence and analysis drew on the Commission's existing independent advisory work.

Climate overview: The last 400,000 years

The website *climate4you.com* is a comprehensive website which gives links to many official climate data websites produced by NASA, NOAA, The University of East Anglia etc. The graph below shows an overview of what has happened to the earth's temperature over the last 400,000 years.

Reconstructed global temperature over the past 420,000 years based on the Vostok ice coré from the Antarctica (Petit et al. 2001). The record spans over four glacial periods and five interglacials, including the present. The horizontal line indicates the modern temperature. The red square to the right indicates the time interval shown in greater detail in the next graph.

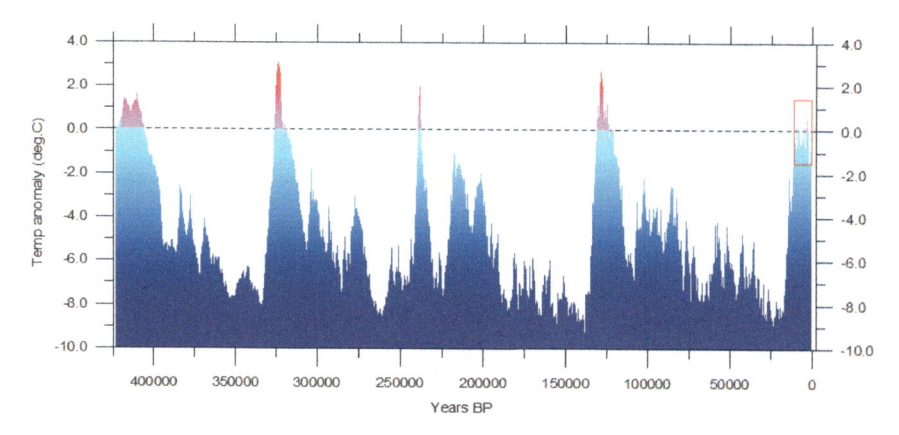

The last 11,000 years (the square on RHS in diagram above) of this climatic development is shown in greater detail in the following chart.

The upper panel shows the air temperature at the summit of the Greenland Ice Sheet, reconstructed by Alley (2000) from GISP2 ice core data. The time scale shows years before modern time. The rapid temperature rise to the left indicates the final part of the even more pronounced temperature increase following the last ice age. The temperature scale at the right hand side of the upper panel suggests a very approximate comparison with the global average temperature (see comment below). The GISP2 record ends around 1854, and the two graphs therefore end here. There has since been a temperature increase to about the same level as during the Medieval Warm Period and to about 395 ppm for CO_2. The small reddish bar in the lower right indicates the extension of the longest global temperature record (since 1850), based on meteorological observations (HadCRUT3). The lower panel shows the past atmospheric CO_2 content, as found from the EPICA Dome C Ice Core in the Antarctic (Monnin et al. 2004). The Dome C atmospheric CO_2 record ends in the year 1777.

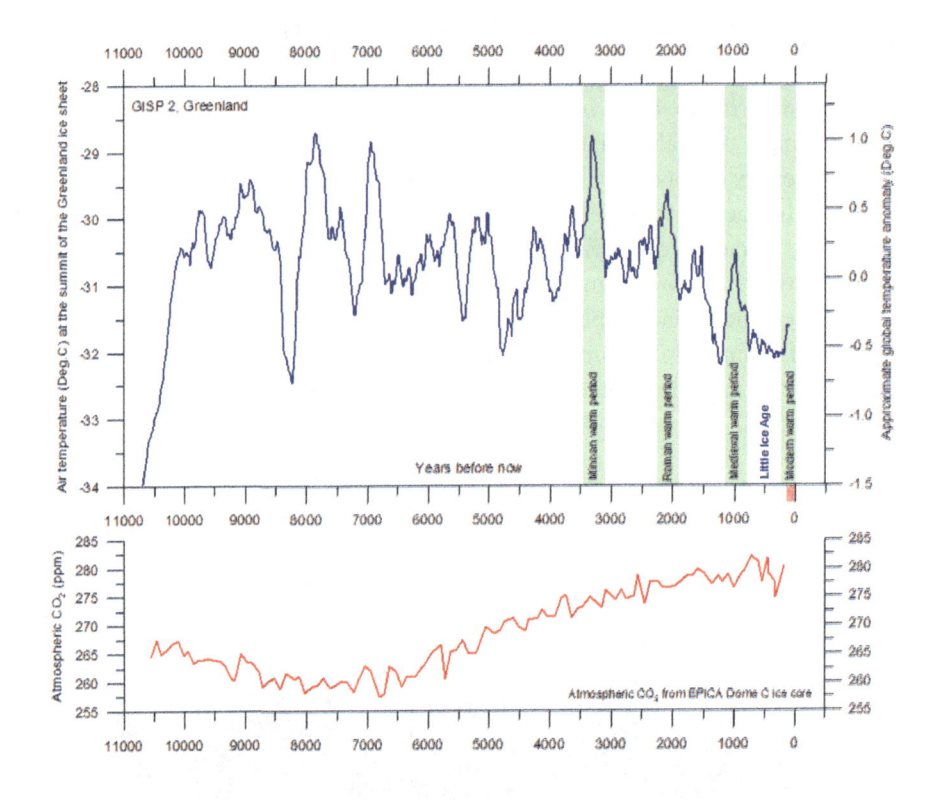

40 *Climate Change : Nature is in Control*

The Maunder of the "Maunder Minimum"

The Maunder of the"Maunder Minimum" Edward Walter Maunder (12 April 1851 – 21 March 1928) was an English astronomer best remembered for his study of sunspots and the solar magnetic cycle that led to his identification of the period from 1645 to 1715 that is now known as the Maunder Minimum.

Maunder was born in London, the youngest child of a minister of the Wesleyan Society. He attended King's College London but never graduated. He took a job in a London bank to finance his studies.

In 1873 Maunder returned to the Royal Observatory, taking a position as a spectroscopic assistant. Shortly after, in 1875, he married Edith Hannah Bustin, who gave birth to six children, 3 sons, 2 daughters and a son who died in infancy. Following the death of Edith in 1888, he met Annie Scott Dill Russell (1868–1947) in 1890, a mathematician and astronomer educated at Girton College in Cambridge, with whom he collaborated for the remainder of his life. In 1895 Maunder and Russell married. In 1916 Annie Maunder became one of the first women accepted by the Royal Astronomical Society in England.

Part of Maunder's job at the Observatory involved photographing and measuring sunspots, and in doing so he observed that the solar latitudes at which sunspots occur varies in a regular way over the course of the 11 year cycle. After studying the work of Gustav Spörer, who examined old records from the different observatories archives looking for changes of the heliographic latitude of sunspots, Maunder announced Spörer's conclusions in his own paper edited in 1894. The period, recognized earlier by Spörer, now bears Maunder's name. Annie worked as a "lady computer" at the Observatory from 1890 to 1895. In 1904, they published their results in the form of the famous "butterfly" diagram that shows this regular variation.

The Maunders travelled extensively for observations going to places such as the West Indies, Lapland, India, Algiers, Mauritius. Their last eclipse expedition was to Labrador for the Solar eclipse of August 30, 1905 at the invitation of the Canadian government. The expedition was unsuccessful due to overcast conditions.

In 1890, Maunder was a driving force in the foundation of the British Astronomical Association. Although he had been Fellow of the Royal Astronomical Society since 1875, Maunder wanted an association of astronomers open to every person interested in astronomy, from every class of society, and especially open for women. Maunder was the first editor of the Journal of the BAA, an office later taken by his wife Annie. His older brother, Thomas Frid Maunder (1841–1935), was a co-founder and secretary of the Association for 38 years. The author William John Maunder is a distant relative of the famous Maunder.

2

Methods of inferring/ detecting changes in the climate

"Everything is appropriate in its own time. ...
even so, man cannot see the whole scope of God's work
from beginning to end".

Ecclesiastes 3:11

Recording the weather

The Commission for Instruments and Methods of Observation (CIMO) of WMO ensures the accuracy of weather observation by facilitating the creation of international standards and, thus, the compatibility of measurements. The Commission, one of eight Technical Commissions of WMO, is responsible for developing the guidelines and recommendations implemented through the Instruments and Methods of Observation Programme (IMOP), one of the key components of the World Weather Watch (WWW) Programme. For over a century it has coordinated collective actions by Members in respect to their observing systems, so that the end results of their efforts far exceed what each could individually accomplish to meet its critical needs. The Commission then disseminates the results worldwide.

Today, CIMO is facing new challenges, particularly in the areas of integration and new technologies. The transition from manual observations to automatic and, now, remote-sensing wind profiler and satellite observations, requires the development of guidelines on the use and performance of these and, possibly, conducting intercomparisons to assess their relative performance. The ever growing demand for higher resolution meteorological observations in both time and space, such as for nowcasting and severe weather forecasting, and for the optimization of financial resources have obliged meteorological services to use observational data from various different sources – different systems as well as different providers – including external and private data providers. In addition, national security issues make these observations extremely sensitive. In this context, CIMO is challenged to support Members in developing guidelines to assess the quality of the observational data provided by various systems and shared through metadata.

The Commission uses the same strategies and tools that have yielded successful results in the past to face these challenges:
- The promotion of standards,
- Development and publication of guides on instruments and methods of observation,
- Instrument intercomparisons, and
- The organization of capacity building activities such as training workshops and technical conferences.

The Commission actively collaborates with instrument manufacturers – primarily through the Association of Hydro-meteorological Equipment

Industry (HMEI) – the scientific community and other international organisations. Over the years, where synergies exist, CIMO has partnered with other international organizations to achieve common goals. These include the *Bureau International des Poids et Mesures* (BIPM), the International Organization for Standardization (ISO) and the direct involvement of CIMO experts into metrology research such as with the European Metrology Research Programme (EMRP).

The terms of reference of the Commission:
- Respond to the requirements for standardized and compatible observations, including data content, quality, metadata and observational product generation;
- Provide advice, and recommendations, and promote studies concerning effective and sustainable use of instruments and methods of observation, including quality management procedures such as methods for testing, preventive maintenance, calibration and quality assurance;
- Conduct and/or coordinate global and regional instrument inter-comparisons and performance testing of instruments and methods of observation;
- In collaboration with the other international organizations, such as BIPM and ISO, promote the development of measurement traceability to recognized international standards (SI), including reference instruments within a hierarchy of world, regional, national and lead centres for instrument calibration, development and testing;
- Promote compatibility, intercomparison, integration and inter-operability within and between, space-based and surface-based (in situ and remote-sensing) observations, including conducting testbed observing experiments;
- Encourage research and development of new approaches in the field of instruments and methods of observation of meteorological, climatological, hydrological, marine, and related geophysical and environmental variables;
- Promote the appropriate and economical production of instruments and methods of observation with particular attention to the needs of developing countries;
- Support training and capacity-building activities in the area of instruments and methods of observation;

- Liaise with the scientific research community and instrument manufacturers to evaluate and to introduce new observing systems into operations.

The Commission first published the *WMO Guide to Meteorological Instruments and Methods of Observation* (CIMO Guide, WMO-No. 8), in 1954. The Guide deals with the standardization of observational procedures and techniques, and provides comprehensive and up-to-date guidelines on the most effective practices for carrying out meteorological observations and measurements. It contains guidelines on the measurement of variables related to weather and climate applications as well as to environmental (ozone, atmospheric composition), marine/ocean observations and water (precipitation, evaporation, soil moisture) applications.

Since its establishment, the scope of the Commission has widened considerably, providing worldwide services in the area of instrumentation and measurements standards. It is an important pillar in the work of the Organization. As the global community continues to increase its scientific collaboration, work in this field will continue to progress, to keep pace with the ever-increasing demand for new and high-quality observational measurements of the atmosphere and the environment around the world, such as required for the Global Framework for Climate Services and the Global Cryosphere Watch.

The success of the Commission has always relied and will continue to rely on the time and effort dedicated by experts from WMO Members.

Historical developments

Meteorological instruments are the equipment used to sample the state of the atmosphere at a given time. Each science has its own unique sets of laboratory equipment. Meteorology, relies mostly on on-site observation and remote sensing equipment. In science, an observation, or observable, is an abstract idea that can be measured and for which data can be taken. Rain was one of the first quantities to be measured historically. Two other accurately measured weather-related variables are wind and humidity. Many attempts had been made prior to the 15th century to construct adequate equipment to measure atmospheric variables.

Measuring Devices
Devices used to measure weather phenomena in the mid-15th century were the rain gauge, the anemometer, and the hygrometer. *Wikipedia* notes that the 17th century saw the development of the barometer and the Galileo thermometer while the 18th century saw the development of the thermometer with the Fahrenheit and Celsius scales. The 20th century developed new remote sensing tools, such as weather radars, weather satellites and wind profilers, which provide better sampling both regionally and globally. Remote sensing instruments collect data from weather events some distance from the instrument and typically stores the data where the instrument is located and often transmits the data at defined intervals to central data centres.

In 1441, King Sejong's son, Prince Munjong, invented the first standardized rain gauge. These were sent throughout the Joseon Dynasty of Korea as an official tool to assess land taxes based upon a farmer's potential harvest. In 1450, Leone Battista Alberti developed a swinging-plate anemometer, and it is known as the first anemometer. In 1607, Galileo Galilei constructed a thermoscope. In 1643, Evangelista Torricelli invented the mercury barometer. In 1662, Sir Christopher Wren invented the mechanical, self-emptying, tipping bucket rain gauge. In 1714, Gabriel Fahrenheit created a reliable scale for measuring temperature with a mercury-type thermometer. (Interestingly, for a country like New Zealand, the Fahrenheit scale is almost perfect in that 99% of the time daily temperatures range from 0 to 100 degrees and most of the time from about 20 to 90. In addition, the Fahrenheit scale is much more descriptive as one can refer to the temperatures in the 40's or 60's or low 90's). In 1742, Anders Celsius, a Swedish astronomer, proposed the 'centigrade' temperature scale, the predecessor of the current Celsius scale. In 1783, the first hair hygrometer was demonstrated by Horace-Bénédict de Saussure. In 1806, Francis Beaufort introduced his system for classifying wind speeds. The April 1960 launch of the first successful weather satellite, TIROS-1, marked the beginning of the age where weather information became available globally.

A thermometer measures air temperature, or the kinetic energy of the molecules within air. A barometer measures atmospheric pressure, or the pressure exerted by the weight of the Earth's atmosphere above a particular location. An anemometer measures the wind speed and the direction the wind is blowing from at the site where it is mounted. A hygrometer measures the relative humidity at a location, which can then be used to compute the dew point. Radiosondes directly measure most of these quantities, except for wind, which is determined by tracking the radiosonde signal with an antenna or theodolite. Supplementing the radiosondes a network of aircraft collection is organized by the World Meteorological Organization (WMO), which also use these instruments to report weather conditions at their respective locations. A sounding rocket or rocketsonde, sometimes called a research rocket, is an instrument-carrying rocket designed to take measurements and perform scientific experiments during its suborbital flight.

A pyranometer is a type of actinometer used to measure broadband solar irradiance on a planar surface and is a sensor that is designed to measure the solar radiation flux density (in watts per metre square) from a field of view of 180 degrees. A ceilometer is a device that uses a laser or other light source to determine the height of a cloud base. Ceilometers can also be used to measure the aerosol concentration within the atmosphere. A ceiling balloon is used by meteorologists to determine the height of the base of clouds above ground level during daylight hours. The principle behind the ceiling balloon is a balloon with a known ascent rate (how fast it climbs) and determining how long the balloon rises until it disappears into the cloud. Ascent rate times the ascent time yields the ceiling height. A disdrometer is an instrument used to measure the drop size distribution and velocity of falling hydrometeors. Rain gauges are used to measure the precipitation which falls at any point on the Earth's landmass.

Remote sensing
Remote sensing, as used in meteorology, is the concept of collecting data from remote weather events and subsequently producing weather information. Each remote sensing instrument collects data about the atmosphere from a remote location and, usually, stores the data where the instrument is located. The most common types of remote sensing are radar, lidar, and satellites (also photogrammetry). The main uses of radar are to collect information concerning the coverage and characteristics of precipitation and wind. Satellites are chiefly used to determine cloud cover, as well as wind. SODAR (SOnic Detection And Ranging) is a meteorological instrument as one form of wind profiler, which measures the scattering of sound waves by atmospheric turbulence. Sodar systems are used to measure wind speed at various heights above the ground, and the thermodynamic structure of the lower layer of the atmosphere. Radar and lidar are not passive because both use electromagnetic radiation to

illuminate a specific portion of the atmosphere. Weather satellites along with more general-purpose Earth-observing satellites circling the earth at various altitudes have become an indispensable tool for studying a wide range of phenomena from forest fires to El Niño.

Surface weather observations are the fundamental data used for safety as well as climatological reasons to forecast weather and issue warnings worldwide. They can be taken manually, by a weather observer, by computer through the use of automated weather stations, or in a hybrid scheme using weather observers to augment the otherwise automated weather station.

A weather station is a facility, either on land or sea, with instruments and equipment for measuring atmospheric conditions to provide information for weather forecasts and to study the weather and climate. The measurements taken include temperature, atmospheric pressure, humidity, wind speed, wind direction and precipitation amounts. Wind measurements are taken with as few other obstructions as possible, while temperature and humidity measurements are kept free from direct solar radiation, or insolation. Manual observations are taken at least once daily, while automated measurements are taken at least once an hour. Weather conditions out at sea are taken by ships and buoys, which measure slightly different meteorological quantities such as sea surface temperature (SST), wave height, and wave period. Drifting weather buoys outnumber their moored versions by a significant amount.

Typical weather stations have the following instruments:

- Thermometer for measuring air and sea surface temperature
- Barometer for measuring atmospheric pressure
- Hygrometer for measuring humidity
- Anemometer for measuring wind speed
- Pyranometer for measuring solar radiation
- Rain gauge for measuring liquid precipitation over a set period of time.
- Wind sock for measuring general wind speed and wind direction
- Wind vane, also called a weather vane or a weathercock: it shows whence the wind is blowing.

In addition, at certain automated weather stations, additional instruments may be employed, including:
- Present Weather/Precipitation Identification Sensor for identifying falling precipitation
- Disdrometer for measuring drop size distribution
- Transmissometer for measuring visibility
- Ceilometer for measuring cloud ceiling

More sophisticated stations may also measure the ultraviolet index, leaf wetness, soil moisture, soil temperature, water temperature in ponds, lakes, creeks, or rivers, and occasionally other data.

Except for those instruments requiring direct exposure to the elements (anemometer, rain gauge), the instruments should be sheltered in a vented box, usually a Stevenson screen, to keep direct sunlight off the thermometer and wind off the hygrometer. The instrumentation may be specialized to allow for periodic recording otherwise significant manual labour is required for record keeping. Automatic transmission of data, in a format such as METAR, is also desirable as many weather stations' data is required for weather forecasting.

Weather ships
A weather ship was a ship stationed in the ocean as a platform for surface and upper air meteorological measurements for use in weather forecasting. It was also meant to aid in search and rescue operations and to support transatlantic flights. The establishment of weather ships proved to be so useful during World War II that the International Civil Aviation Organization (ICAO) established a global network of 13 weather ships in 1948. Of the 12 left in operation in 1996, nine were located in the northern Atlantic Ocean while three were located in the northern Pacific Ocean. The agreement of the weather ships ended in 1990. Weather ship observations proved to be helpful in wind and wave studies, as they did not avoid weather systems like merchant ships tended to and were considered a valuable resource. The last weather ship was MS *Polarfront*, known as weather station M ("jilindras") at 66°N, 02°E, run by the Norwegian Meteorological Institute. MS *Polarfront* was removed from service January 1, 2010. Since the 1960s this role has been largely superseded by satellites, long range aircraft and weather buoys. Weather observations from ships continue from thousands of voluntary merchant vessels in routine commercial operation; the Old Weather crowdsourcing project transcribes naval logs from before the era of dedicated ships.

Weather buoys are instruments which collect weather and oceanography data within the world's oceans and lakes. Moored buoys have been in use since 1951, while drifting buoys have been used since the late 1970s. Moored buoys are connected with the seabed using either chains, nylon, or buoyant polypropylene. With the decline of the weather ship, they have taken a more primary role in measuring conditions over the open seas since the 1970s. During the 1980s and 1990s, a network of buoys in the central and eastern tropical Pacific ocean helped study the El Niño-Southern Oscillation. Moored weather buoys range from 1.5–12m in diameter, while drifting buoys are smaller, with diameters of 30–40 cm. Drifting buoys are the dominant form of weather buoy, with 1250 located worldwide. Wind data from buoys has smaller error than that from ships. There are differences in the values of sea surface temperature measurements between the two platforms as well, relating to the depth of the measurement and whether or not the water is heated by the ship which measures the quantity.

Synoptic weather stations are instruments which collect meteorological information at synoptic time 00h00, 06h00, 12h00, 18h00 (UTC) and at intermediate synoptic hours 03h00, 09h00, 15h00, 21h00 (UTC). The common instruments of measurement are the anemometer, wind vane, pressure sensor, thermometer, hygrometer, and rain gauge. The weather measurements are formatted in special format agreed to by WMO. A variety of these land-based weather station networks have been set up globally.

Engineering aspects of weather recording instruments
Weather forecast instruments are a vital component in our application of science and technology in an attempt to predict future conditions of the atmosphere for a given time and location. Whilst not 100% accurate, it definitely has come a long way over the millennia. Christopher Mc Fadden writing in the *interestingengineering.com* website on March 23, 2020 has some interesting insights on the engineering aspects of weather recording instruments.

These weather forecast instruments and inventions have helped define and improve how we predict the weather today.

The barometer is one of the most important instruments in weather forecasting. It is used, as the name suggests, to measure localized atmospheric air pressure. Evangelista Torricelli is widely credited with the invention of the barometer in the mid 17th Century. But historical documentation also indicates that Gasparo Berti, another Italian scientist, built a working barometer by accident between 1640 and 1643.

Berti was a friend of Galileo who in turn was the mentor of Torricelli. Berti could not explain how his 'barometer' worked, invoking a theory that the vacuum in some way held the water level in the tube and asked Galileo for advice. If this is true, Torricelli later made the connection between atmospheric pressure and the phenomenon described by Gasparo Berti in his apparatus.

He would later write: "We live submerged at the bottom of an ocean of elementary air, which is known by incontestable experiments to have weight".

Torricelli also later discovered he could replicate the phenomenon in 'miniature' using denser fluids like mercury. Traditionally, barometers came in forms such as Water (Goethe), Mercury and Aneroid (later invented in 1844 by Lucien Vidi).

Analog forms are rarely used for official weather prediction today, having largely been replaced with digital ones. Digital barometers use electrical transponders, instead of liquids in a vacuum, to detect atmospheric pressure and are the most widely used form in official weather stations today.

Air pressure, when combined with wind observations has been used to predict, fairly accurately, short-term weather forecasts since the latter 19th Century.

Wind speeds can be accurately measured using devices called anemometers. They were first developed by Italian artist Leon Battista Alberti in 1450 but were perfected much later in the 20th Century. They are a common instrument often found on weather stations. Their design has changed very little since the 15th Century.

The most easily recognizable forms used in weather forecasting include Cup anemometers and Vane anemometers. The first determines wind speed based on how fast the cup wheel spins. Improvements made to the design in 1991 by Derek Weston, also allows them to determine wind directions from the cyclical changes in the cup wheel speed. Although simple in theory, other factors need to be considered before determining true wind speeds. For instance, turbulence from the device itself and friction from the mount point needs to be accounted for.

Radar

Today, radar forms an integral part of any weather instrumentation and is used, primarily, to locate precipitation, track it and estimate its type (snow, rain, etc) and intensity. Radar can also be used to forecast precipitation associated with thunderstorms, hurricanes, and winter storms. Radar was initially developed during the Second World War as a means of detecting and tracking enemy aircraft. Personnel soon noticed "noise" or "echoes" on their displays from precipitation which revealed a potential peacetime application for the technology.

Shortly after the conclusion of the war, surplus radar equipment was repurposed on weather stations. Modern stations use pulse-Doppler Radar that is actually capable of detecting the motion of rain droplets as well as the intensity of the precipitation. They typically use dual-polarization radar that sends and receives vertical and horizontal pulses. This gives meteorologists a much clearer appreciation of the multi-dimensional situation at any one time.

Rain gauges are pretty simple instruments used to directly measure the amount of liquid precipitation in one location over a period of time. They are vital instruments for meteorologists and hydrologists alike.

Rain gauges are one of the world's oldest and most basic weather instruments around. Some of the first recorded apparatus dates back to Ancient Greece around 500 BC. Other records indicate that people living in India also started measuring rainfall in around 400 BC.

The first standardized rain gauge appears to have been developed in 1441 AD in the Joseon Dynasty of Korea. The first "tipping bucket" form of rain gauge was developed by Sir Christopher Wren in 1662.

Richard Towneley is the first person to systematically measure and record rainfall over a period of 15 years from 1677 to 1694. He later inspired other scientists of the age to follow suit, eventually leading the pioneering work of George James Symons (one of the first official Meteorologists who founded the British Rainfall Organisation).

Most modern rain gauges generally measure the precipitation in millimeters in height collected on each square metre during a certain period, equivalent to litres per square metre.

These can be simple collection systems that are later visited by meteorologists to assess rainfall or automated to gather data in situ.

Weather balloons
Weather or sounding balloons are effectively mobile weather stations that carry scientific instruments into the upper atmosphere. They tend to be equipped with suites of sensors to measure weather variables like atmospheric pressure, temperature, and humidity. This information is relayed to ground-based receiver stations to be stored and analyzed. Other information, like wind data, can be obtained by tracking the balloon's

position using radar, radio direction finding or installing GPS systems on each balloon. Other instruments are encased in small, parachute-equipped though often expendable, payloads called radiosondes. Each balloon tends to comprise a large, often up to 1.8 metres wide, helium or hydrogen-filled latex balloon. The balloons then carry an instrument payload package that encases and protects the more sensitive instruments during its flight.

Leon Teisserence de Bort, a French meteorologist, was one of the first people to use weather balloons. He launched hundreds of them during 1896 which led to his discovery of the troposphere and stratosphere.

Some balloons, called transosondes, are designed to stay aloft for long periods of time. They were initially devised to help monitor radioactive debris from atomic fallout during the 1950s.

Another basic yet fundamental instrument used for weather forecasting is the thermometer. They are generally used for measuring the ambient temperature of the air.

The device is pretty simple in design and consists of the following important component: a temperature sensor. This includes a bulb of mercury in traditional analog thermometers or a digital sensor in modern infrared thermometers. A means of converting changes in temperature to a numerical value. These are visible scales on older analog thermometers to digital readouts on modern ones.

The basic concept of the thermometer was known to the ancient Greeks but the thermometer as we know it gradually evolved from Galileo's 16th Century thermoscope in the 17th Century. Standardization began sometime between the 17th and 18th Centuries.

Hygrometers are tools used to measure the humidity or air moisture content in the atmosphere, soil or indoors. The very first, though crude, hygrometer was invented by the Italian genius Leonardo da Vinci in around 1480. More modern versions were created by Swiss polymath Johann Heinrich Lambert in 1755. Older analog hygrometers come in various forms including hair tension hygrometers and sling psychrometers to name but a few. The former, as the name suggests, uses animal hair (which is hygroscopic - water-absorbing) to 'detect' changes in relative air humidity as the hair's length changes. The latter uses a set of two thermometers, one moistened and one dry, that are spun in the air. As temperatures fluctuate above or below the freezing point of water, the 'wet' thermometer will either show a cooler temperature (if water evaporates above freezing point) or lower (if ice forms) when compared to the dry thermometer.

Modern hygrometers tend to be digital versions as they are more reliable and accurate. They use electronic sensors to detect changes in relative humidity and convert it to an easily readable numerical value.

Weather satellites
Weather satellites are the highest tech options available to weather forecasters. They are able to view and gather large amounts of data about the Earth's weather and climate with unparalleled views. They tend to hold either asynchronous orbits (therefore covering the entire Earth's surface) or geostationary (thereby focussing on a single spot for extended periods). As early as 1946, ambitions to put cameras into space were already being developed. The first weather satellite, Vanguard 2, reached Earth's orbit in February 1959. This sparked the beginning of a proliferation of weather satellite launches over the next five decades.

From orbit, they are privy to unobstructed views of the Earth's cloud systems and are able to gather information on anything from ocean temperatures to spotting wildfires or sandstorms. Weather satellites are unique in that they are able to offer meteorologists views of weather systems over large-scale areas offering the ability to observe weather patterns hours or days before more conventional systems like weather radar. They are often employed to track and monitor large-scale weather patterns like hurricanes and El Niño.

Pyranometers are a special type of weather forecast equipment used to measure solar irradiance on a given planar surface. They are also designed to detect and record solar radiation flux density (W/m^2) within a wavelength range of 0.3 to 2.8 micrometers. They have become the WMO's standard instrument and are covered under the International ISO 9060 standard. Such devices tend to be calibrated using the World Radiometric Reference which is maintained by the *World Radiation Center* in Switzerland.

Pyranometers tend to comprise of the following main components: - A thermopile, which is a sensor made of thermocouples in series and coated with a solar absorbing material. - A glass dome to restrict the wavelengths of light able to enter the device. It also shields the thermopile from wind, rain, and convection. - An occulting disc which measures the diffuse radiation and blocks beam radiation from the surface.

These devices are normally passive and do not require any power supply at all. Modern electronic pyranometers, on the other hand, do require a small amount of electrical input.

Transmissometers are weather forecast instruments used to measure the extinction coefficient of the atmosphere and seawater and by proxy estimate the visibility. These instruments send narrow beams of energy, usually a laser, through the air towards a corresponding receiver a set distance away. Any photons that are absorbed or scattered by the air between the detector and sources will not reach the detector.

By determining the path transmission and extinction coefficient the local visibility can be determined. These devices are also known as telephotometers, transmittance meters, or haze meters.

Ceilometers are devices that use lasers or other light sources to determine the height of clouds or cloud bases; they can also be used to determine cloud thickness. They also have applications for determining aerosol concentrations and volcanic ash in the atmosphere.

They come in two general forms: - Optical drum ceilometers use triangulation to determine cloud height from a spot of light projected onto the base of clouds. These tend to consist of a rotating projector, detector, and recorder. - Laser ceilometers consist of a vertically aligned laser and lidar receiver within the same location. The time taken for the reflected light to return to the lidar receiver enables the device to determine cloud cover height. This technology can also be prone to false positives because it can be affected by any form of particulate matter in the air (dust, rain, smoke, etc).

Ceilometers have also been shown to be fatal to birds as they get disoriented by the light beams emitted from them. In the worst recorded ceilometer, non-laser light beam incident, approximately 50,000 birds from 53 different species died at Warner Robins Air Force Base in the United States during one night in 1954.

The Stevenson Screen
Although not technically a weather forecasting instrument, per se, the Stevenson Screen is vital nonetheless. Also known as an instrument screen, the Stevenson screen forms the basic enclosure around meteorological instruments the world over. The main purpose of this innovation is to protect instruments from precipitation and direct heat radiation from the sun whilst allowing ambient air to circulate through to the instrumentation inside. This is important as its absence would otherwise skew the results of any instrumentation at the weather station dependent on exposure rather than actual local weather patterns.

Stevenson screens will tend to protect instruments like thermometers, hygrometers, dewcells, barometers, and thermographs. They were the brainchild of Thomas Stevenson who was a Scottish civil engineer who also designed lighthouses. His father was the famed Robert Louis Stevenson. Its current form is the result of some minor changes over the years with its standardization coming into effect in 1884. Automated weather stations are progressively replacing Stevenson Screen type monitoring stations the world over.

Ocean Station Vessels
Weather ships aka Ocean Station Vessels were ships that were stationed strategically around the world's oceans as platforms for surface and upper atmosphere weather observations. They used to be a vital means of data collection for weather forecasting before the advent of weather satellites. Weather ships were deployed around the Atlantic and North Pacific Oceans and reported their observations by radio. Such vessels also doubled as search and rescue ships, supported transatlantic flights and helped with oceanographic research.

The concept was first proposed in 1921 by Meteo-France to support their shipping and transatlantic flight operations. These ships proved very useful during the Second World War but also suffered heavily from U-Boat attacks as they were completely defenseless. So much so that the International Civil Aviation Organization (ICAO) established a global network of weather ships in 1948. This organization remained in place until 1985 with weather ships gradually replaced by buoys.

The last weather ship was *Polarfront*, known as weather station M ("Mike"), which was removed from operation on January 1, 2010. Weather observations from ships continue from a fleet of voluntary merchant vessels in routine commercial operation.

"Official" ways of recording the weather
The above description of the ways that have been, and are currently used, to "record weather" are almost exclusively related to "official" ways of recording the weather. The use of official ways of doing this is of course related to the need for "correct" observations to be made. Clearly a lot of "unoffical " observations are made, and with instruments electronic and otherwise now available and used by many people and organisations, many "near official" observations are made. While these observations are generally very valid, they lack the compatibility with the official

observations. This is the reason why all national meteorological services use and archive "official" observations. That is of course not to state the rainfall or the temperature recorded on a wheat farm in Kansas, or in a park in London is not valid and useful.

Homogenization of climate observation and quality control

Whenever data is observed the question needs to be asked: how good is the data, and how do the observations compare with what was observed in the past. These questions relate to almost all data, but it is especially pertinent when climate observations are considered. Most weather observations such as rainfall, maximum temperature, the hours of sunshine, and wind speed etc., are observed over long periods of time. In order to assess whether the climate is warming or cooling or becoming wetter or drier, it is necessary to homogenize the data so that what is observed today can be compared with what was observed in the past taking into account changes in the local environment such as urbanisation, and the growth of trees, changes in the location of where the observations are made, changes in observational authorities, and changes in the type of recording instruments used.

All of these factors are part of climatological "know-how" of climatologists, but it is sometimes suggested that the observations are "adjusted" or in the words of some people "cooked". While this may happen, and human judgements are made for some aspects of quality control, I believe that any adjustments of the data to fit a particular belief, is not done by any reputable climatologists.

Internationally, the World Meteorological Organization (WMO) is the arbiter of the homogenization of weather observations, and this is achieved by two of its Technical Commissions, the Commission for Instruments and Observations (CIMO), and the Commission for Climatology (CCl). CIMO is responsible for the design and quality control of most meteorological instruments, from mercury in glass thermometers to modern weather sensors. CCl is responsible for what happens to the weather/climate observations after they have been made.

Commission for Climatology
The WMO Commission for Climatology (CCl) notes that climate data are the records of observed climate conditions taken at specific sites and times with particular instruments under a set of standard procedures. A climate dataset therefore contains climate information at the observation sites, as well as other non-climate-related factors such as the environment of the observation station, and information about the instruments and observation procedures (called Metadata).

These factors can be associated with the changes that can affect the site, instruments or methods and procedures in the observations and data processing. Such changes can affect:
- Sheltering and exposure;
- Mean calculations, observation hours and daylight saving times;
- Units of observed elements and data accuracy;
- Urbanization and land-use changes;
- Introduction of Automatic Weather Stations or new types of instruments;
- Quality control and data recovery procedures.

The aim of climate data homogenization is to adjust climate records, if necessary, to remove non-climatic factors so that the temporal variations in the adjusted data reflect only the variations due to climate processes.

WMO in collaboration with CCl developed a set of Guidelines on Climate Metadata and Homogenization on how to deal with homogeneity problems. Main steps in data homogenization include:
1. Metadata analysis and quality control: Changes in the measurement as well as in quality control procedures can be detected.
2. Building of a reference time series: Mostly a weighted average is calculated by using neighbouring stations.
3. Breakpoint identification: It is searched for inhomogeneities in the difference between the weighted average and the candidate or in the candidate time-series itself.
4. Data adjustment: It is decided which breakpoints are accepted as inhomogeneities. At the end the assessed discontinuities are adjusted and the data is corrected.
5. For future projects and climate change studies it is important to document every step of the homogenization and data preservation.

Homogenization is necessary because much has happened in the world between the French and industrial revolutions, two world wars, the rise and fall of communism, and the start of the internet age. Inevitably many changes have occurred in climate monitoring practices. As a consequence, the instruments used to measure temperature have changed, the screens to protect the sensors from the weather have changed and the surrounding of the stations has often been changed and stations have been moved in response. These non-climatic changes in temperature have to be removed as well as possible to make more accurate assessments of how much the world has warmed.

For the land surface temperature measured at meteorological stations, homogenization is normally performed using relative statistical homogenizing methods. Here a station is compared to its neighbours. If the neighbour is sufficiently nearby, both stations should show about the same climatic changes. Strong jumps or gradual increases happening at only one of the stations indicate a non-climatic change. If there is a bias in the trend, statistical homogenization can reduce it. How well trend biases can be removed depends on the density of the network. In industrialised countries a large part of the bias can be removed for the last century. In developing countries and in earlier times removing biases is more difficult and a large part may remain. Because many governments unfortunately limit the exchange of climate data, the global temperature collections can also remove only part of the trend biases.

Inhomogeneities in data
The WMO Task Team on Homogenization (TT-HOM) is involved in providing guidance for scientists and weather services who want to homogenize their data. Historically, problems due to inhomogeneities in data have long been recognised and homogenization has a long history. In September 1873, at the "International Meteorologen-Congress" in Vienna, Carl Jelinek requested information on national multi-annual data series (Hof- und Staatsdruckerei, 1873), but decades later, in 1905 G. Hellmann (k.k. Zentralanstalt für Meteorologie und Geodynamik, 1906) still regretted the absence of homogeneous climatological time series due to changes in the surrounding of stations and new instruments and pleaded for stations with a long record, "*Säkularstationen*", to be kept as homogeneous as possible. Although this "Conference of directors" of the national weather services recommended maintaining a sufficient number of stations under unchanged conditions today basic inhomogeneity problems still exist. For example, in early times documented change points have been removed with the help of parallel measurements. Differing observing times at the astronomical observatory of the Annalen der K.K. Universitäts-Sternwarte, Wien, have been adjusted by using multi-annual 24 hour measurements of the astronomical observatory of the K.K. University in Prague. Measurements of Milano (Italy) between 1763 and 1834 have been adjusted to 24 hour means by using measurements of Padova (Kreil, 1854a, 1854b).

However, for the majority of change points we do not know the break magnitude; furthermore it is most likely that series contain undocumented inhomogeneities as well. Thus there was a need for statistical break detection methods. In the early 20th century Conrad (1925) applied and evaluated the Heidke criterion (Heidke, 1923) using ratios of two precipitation series. As a consequence he recommended the use of additional criteria to test the homogeneity of series, dealing with the succession and alternation of algebraic signs, the Helmert criterion (Helmert, 1907) and the "painstaking" Abbe criterion (Conrad and Schreier, 1927). The use of Helmert's criterion for pairs of stations and Abbe's criterion was described as an appropriate tool in the 1940s (Conrad 1944). Some years later the double-mass principle was popularised for break detection (Kohler, 1949).

Methods in Climatology
Julius Hann in 1880 studied the variability of absolute precipitation amounts and ratios between stations. He used these ratios for the quality control. This inspired Brückner (1890) to check precipitation data for inhomogeneities by comparison with neighbouring stations; he did not use any statistics. In their book "*Methods in Climatology*" Conrad and Pollak (1950) formalised this relative homogenization approach, which is now the dominant method to detect and remove the effects of artificial changes. The building of reference series, by averaging the data from many stations in a relatively small geographical area, has been recommended by the WMO Working Group on Climatic Fluctuations (WMO, 1966). The papers by Alexandersson (1986) and Alexandersson and Moberg (1997) made the Standard Normal Homogeneity Test (SNHT) popular. The broad adoption of SNHT was also for the clear guidance on how to use this test together with references to homogenize station data.

Modern developments include SNHT as a single-breakpoint method, but climate series typically contain more than one break. Thus a major step forward was the design of methods specifically designed to detect and correct multiple change-points and work with inhomogeneous references (Szentimrey, 1999; Mestre, 1999; Caussinus and Mestre, 2004). These kind of methods were shown to be more accurate by the benchmarking study of the EU COST Action HOME (Venema et al., 2012).

The paper by Caussinus and Mestre (2004) also provided the first description of a method that jointly corrects all series of a network simultaneously. This joint correction method was able to improve the accuracy of all but one contribution to the HOME benchmark that was not yet using this approach (Domonkos et al., 2013).

The ongoing work to create appropriate datasets for climate variability and change studies promoted the continual development of better methods for change point detection and correction. To follow this process the Hungarian Meteorological Service started a series of "Seminars for Homogenization" in 1996.

The "hockey stick" graph of global warming

Both the Medieval Warm Period (MWP) and Little Ice Age (LIA) have long been well established and documented with strong geologic evidence. *GeoRef* lists 485 papers on the Medieval Warm Period and 1,413 on the Little Ice Age or a total of almost 1,900 published papers on these two periods. Despite all of this physical evidence of the global MWP, the IPCC 3rd report published in 2001 reassessed the MWP on the basis of statistical manipulation of tree ring studies by Mann et al. (1998) and concluded that neither the MWP nor the Little Ice Age were global climatic events.

Mann's graph became known as "the hockey stick" of climate change and was used in the 2001 IPCC report to assert that climate had not changed over the past 1000 years until anthropogenic CO_2 began to rise. Geologists didn't take the 'hockey stick' seriously and thought that either (1) the trees they used for their climate reconstruction were not climate sensitive, or (2) the data had been inappropriately used. However, the 'hockey stick' was featured prominently in Gore's 2006 book and film, which were widely circulated along with the statement that throughout the entire history of human civilization there has never been an environmental shift remotely similar to this until the rise of CO_2.

Battle of the graphs: Mann versus Ball

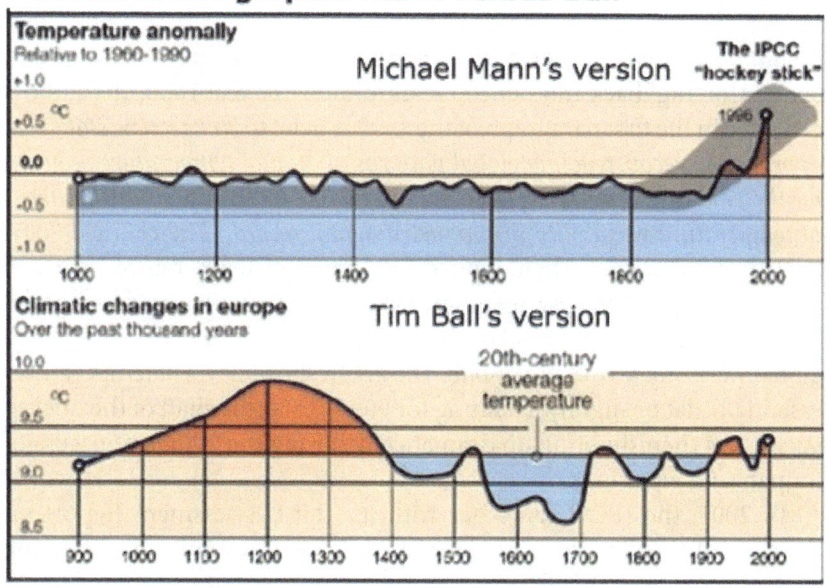

Methods of inferring/detecting changes in the climate 65

The Climategate scandal
McIntrye and McKitrick (2003) evaluated the data in the Mann paper and concluded that the Mann curve was invalid "due to collation errors, unjustifiable truncation or extrapolation of source data, obsolete data, geographical location errors, incorrect calculation of principal components and other quality control defects." Since then, emails and data disclosed in the *Climategate* "scandal" have revealed how the data was manipulated.

Comparison of the Mann 'hockey stick' graph with surface temperatures of the Sargasso Sea reconstructed from isotope ratios in marine organisms (Keigwin, 1996), reconstructed paleo-temperatures without tree ring data (Loehle, 2007). Summer sea surface temperatures near Iceland (Sicre et al., 2008) shows that the Medieval Warm Period and the Little Ice Age most certainly happened, and the consensus of the most, but not all, of relevant temperature graphs covering the the last 1000 years shows that the Mann 'hockey stick' is not supported by any credible evidence.

In the *ManhattanContraraian* website, lawyer Francis Manton reviewed the 'hockey stick' graph that took the world of climate science by storm back in 1998. Mann and co-authors Raymond Bradley and Malcolm Hughes published in *Nature* their seminal paper *Global-scale temperature patterns and climate forcing over the past six centuries.* A subsequent 1999 update by the same authors, also in *Nature,* (*Northern Hemisphere temperatures during the past millennium: Inferences, uncertainties, and limitations*) extended their reconstructions of "temperature patterns and climate forcing" back another 400 years to about the year 1000. The authors claimed (in the first paragraph of the 1998 article) to *"take a new statistical approach to reconstructing global patterns of annual temperature..., based on the calibration of multiproxy data networks by the dominant patterns of temperature variability in the instrumental record."* The claimed "new statistical approach," when applied to a group of temperature "proxies" that included tree ring samples and lake bed sediments, yielded a graph – quickly labelled the "Hockey Stick" – that was the perfect icon to sell global warming fear to the public. The graph showed world temperatures essentially flat or slightly declining for 900+ years (the shaft of the hockey stick), and then shooting up dramatically during the 20th century era of human CO_2 emissions.

In 2001, the IPCC came out with its Third Assessment Report on the state of the climate. The Hockey Stick graph dominated, appearing multiple times, including being the lead graph in the "Summary for Policy Makers" which is the only part of an IPCC report that most policy personnel read.

Of significance in this chart is that *The Medieval Warm Period* – an era between the years of about 1000 and 1300 once generally accepted to have had temperatures warmer than the present – had disappeared. The clear implication was that the earth had had a benign and unchanging climate for about a thousand years, and now humans had entered the picture with their fossil fuels and were rapidly destabilizing the situation.

A prominent sceptical climate scientist in Canada named Tim Ball accused Mann of fraud in generating the Hockey Stick graph. The famous quote, from a February 2011 interview of Ball, was *"Michael Mann should be in the State Pen, not Penn State."* In March 2011, Mann sued Ball for libel, focusing on that quote, in the Supreme Court of British Columbia in Vancouver BC. (In Canada, the Supreme Court is not the highest appellate court, but rather the trial-level court for larger cases.) The case then essentially disappeared into limbo for eight years. However, on August 22, 2019 the British Columbia court dismissed Mann's claim with prejudice, and also awarded court costs to Ball.

Glaciers

The *Brittanica.com* website has a good summary of glaciers written by Mark F Meier. Glaciers are classifiable in three main groups: (1) glaciers that extend in continuous sheets, moving outward in all directions, are called ice sheets if they are the size of Antarctica or Greenland and ice caps if they are smaller; (2) glaciers confined within a path that directs the ice movement are called mountain glaciers; and (3) glaciers that spread out on level ground or on the ocean at the foot of glaciated regions are called piedmont glaciers or ice shelves, respectively. Glaciers in the third group are not independent and are treated here in terms of their sources: ice shelves with ice sheets, piedmont glaciers with mountain glaciers. A complex of mountain glaciers burying much of a mountain range is called an ice field.

New Zealand has many glaciers. The Franz Josef and Fox glaciers, as well as being major tourist attractions have a unique position as glaciers in a temperate region with their terminal faces very close to sea level. New Zealand's GNS website information about glaciers follows:

A glacier is a large mass of ice that has been created by the compression of snow that has piled up over many years. Usually the ice is slowly moving downhill from the area of snow accumulation. As it descends to a lower altitude temperatures get warmer and warmer and tend to melt it away.

Mountain glaciers in temperate regions are subdivided into the small *cirque glaciers*, the larger, more dynamic *alpine glaciers* and the biggest *valley glaciers*.

Another type is the *ice sheet* (or *ice cap* – some people use this term only for smaller scale ice sheets). These occur where ice has built up to such an extent that the landscape features are buried and all that is visible is a flat white expanse. There is a great range in scale, from ice caps that cover an individual mountain peak to the huge East and West Antarctic Ice Sheets, the Greenland Ice Sheet and the Patagonian Ice Cap. Within an ice sheet there can be *ice streams*, where glacier ice is flowing faster, in between more stable areas. Large ice sheets can combine a lot of individual ice streams and other glaciers.

If a glacier reaches the sea without melting, it can float intact as a *glacier tongue*. A single body of floating ice that is fed by several glaciers is known as an *ice shelf*. At the edge of glacier tongues and ice shelves, the ice breaks off and floats away as *icebergs*.

At present, glaciers and ice sheets cover about 10% of the land surface of the earth. They are created in cold climates where the average temperatures are low enough to prevent at least some of the annual snowfall from melting away. Year by year more snow piles up. This means that glaciers occur high up in mountain ranges around the world as well as in the cold polar regions. They even occur in tropical regions such as East Africa and Central America where the mountains are high enough.

Ice velocities also depend on the slope angle and the amount of annual accumulation. In areas of very high precipitation such as the western slopes of the Southern Alps of New Zealand, velocities of more than 7 m/day have been recorded during high rainfall conditions. More commonly a temperate glacier might move 100 or 200m/yr (about 0.5m/day) and a polar glacier much less due to the more rigid nature of the colder ice.

When the climate conditions remain constant a glacier will be in a state of balance or equilibrium, with the accumulation of new snow and ice being exactly compensated by the downward flow and ablation over a period of a year. In these conditions a glacier will stay the same size and shape, with the terminus remaining stationary and a large terminal moraine can form.

However, when the general climate fluctuates, causing variations in local climate (such as average temperature, cloud cover, wind direction, precipitation etc.), the mass balance is pushed out of equilibrium. The mass of snow and ice being added to the upper glacier is no longer the same as the mass being lost by ablation lower down. Mass balance is said to be positive when there is a net gain of ice mass and negative when there is a net loss.

Shaping the landscape
Glaciers are powerful shapers of the landscape, acting like giant bulldozers that carve away at the mountainside and carry away the eroded rocks like a conveyor belt. Since the presence and size of glaciers is completely related to the climatic conditions, the landscape features can tell the story of past climates.

The time it takes for a glacier to adjust to a climate shift is known as the response time. This typically varies from a few years to many decades, depending on the glacier size, steepness, flow rates, and other factors.

A glacier generally responds to the local climate conditions, which vary from place to place. However there are other factors that can make glaciers behave differently. For example, some glaciers are more responsive to short term variations in the climate and may advance and retreat whilst nearby less responsive glaciers don't appear to change much at all. This can be caused by a combination of the size, shape, speed and steepness of the glacier, the rate of accumulation and the amount of rock debris covering the surface. In New Zealand, some small glaciers have vanished completely in the last 50 years, whilst large valley glaciers such as the Tasman have remained the same length due to the protective cover of rock debris; but have become much less deep due to overall lowering of the surface. The Franz Josef and Fox glaciers are highly sensitive due to very rapid accumulation combined with steep, narrow trunks that allow the ice to quickly reach very low altitudes where fast melting occurs. They periodically advance at times although on average they are in retreat.

There is a positive feedback relationship between a glacier's ice thickness and the local climate. The thicker the ice, the higher and therefore the colder the surface is. This means that some small low angle glaciers are self sustaining and survive because of their own cooling effect. This works because their surface is above the equilibrium line altitude and in the accumulation zone, even though their base is below it. Once they disappear, these glaciers won't reform again unless the climate gets substantially colder.

Other examples of positive feedbacks that help sustain an established glacier are the 'orographic effect' (increase in precipitation due to the enhanced uplift and cooling of air flowing over the glacier) and the cooling that is caused by the 'albedo effect' (reflection of solar radiation by snow).

On the *Brittanica.com* website Meier says that a significant aspect of recent geological time (some 30 million years ago to the present) has been the recurrent expansion and contraction of the world's ice cover. These glacial fluctuations influenced geological, climatological, and biological environments and affected the evolution and development of early humans. Almost all of Canada, the northern third of the United States, much of Europe, all of Scandinavia, and large parts of northern Siberia were engulfed by ice during the major glacial stages. At times during the Pleistocene Epoch (from 2.6 million to 11,700 years ago), glacial ice covered 30% of the world's land area; at other times the ice cover may have shrunk to less than its present extent. It may not be improper, then, to state that the world is still in an ice age. Because the term glacial generally implies ice-age events or Pleistocene time, in this discussion "glacier" is used as an adjective whenever reference is to ice of the present day.

Glacier ice today stores about three-fourths of all the fresh water in the world. Glacier ice covers about 11% of the world's land area and would cause a world sea level rise of about 90 metres (300 feet) if all existing ice melted. Glaciers occur in all parts of the world and at almost all latitudes. In Ecuador, Kenya, Uganda, and Irian Jaya (New Guinea), glaciers even occur at or near the Equator, albeit at high altitudes.

Newly published research shows regional climate variability caused an "unusual" period in which some of New Zealand's glaciers grew bigger, while glaciers worldwide were shrinking.

Not all glaciers are retreating

Research cited in the *phys.org* website and carried out by scientists from New Zealand's Victoria University of Wellington and the NZ National Institute of Water and Atmospheric Research (NIWA), has been published in *Nature Communications*.

At least 58 New Zealand glaciers advanced between 1983 and 2008, with Franz Josef Glacier advancing nearly continuously during this time. "Glaciers advancing is very unusual–especially in this period when the vast majority of glaciers worldwide shrank in size as a result of our warming world," says lead-author Associate Professor Andrew Mackintosh from Victoria's Antarctic Research Centre. "This anomaly hadn't been satisfactorily explained, so this physics-based study used computer models for the first time to look into it in detail."

"We found that lower temperature caused the glaciers to advance, rather than increased precipitation as previously thought. These periods of reduced temperature affected the entire New Zealand region, and they were significant enough for the glaciers to re-advance in spite of human-induced climate change." Associate Professor Mackintosh says the climate variability, which includes the cooler years, still reflects a climate that's been modified by humans. "It may seem unusual–this regional cooling during a period of overall global warming–but it's still consistent with human-induced climate change. The temperature changes were a result of variability in the climate system that's specific to New Zealand."

"New Zealand sits in a region where there's significant variability in the oceans and the atmosphere–much more than many parts of the world. The climate variability that we identified was also responsible for changes in the Antarctic ice sheet and sea ice during this period."

Associate Professor Mackintosh says they found New Zealand glaciers that advanced had certain characteristics, including specific elevation and geometry. "Franz Josef Glacier actually regained almost half of the total length it had lost in the twentieth century. However, Haupapa/Tasman Glacier, New Zealand's largest glacier – which has about a third of all of New Zealand's ice volume – continued to retreat. Because of that, New Zealand glaciers lost mass overall in this period."

The study, funded by a core NIWA project 'Climate Present and Past', used computer modelling to understand the drivers of glaciers. The model was tested using more than a decade of field observations of glaciers in the Southern Alps, and a 30-year record of glacier photographs from the NIWA 'End of Summer Snowline' programme.

Victoria University's Dr Brian Anderson and NIWA's Dr Andrew Lorrey were also lead authors on the study. Dr Lorrey says the long-term observations that NIWA maintain–which document New Zealand glacier snow line changes and high elevation climate variability–were critical to achieving the aims of the study. Associate Professor Mackintosh says, "Although glaciers advancing sounds promising, the future 'doesn't look good' for New Zealand's glaciers. Franz Josef Glacier has already retreated more than 1.5 kilometres since the end of the advance in 2008."

Forecasts of glacier advance and retreat
Not all forecasts of glacier advance or retreat are what they seem. For example, the UN's climate science body has admitted that a claim made in its 2007 report - that Himalayan glaciers could melt away by 2035 - was unfounded. The admission followed a New Scientist article that revealed the source of the claim made in the 2007 report by the *Intergovernmental Panel on Climate Change* (IPCC) was not peer-reviewed scientific literature – but a media interview with a scientist conducted in 1999. Several senior scientists have now said the claim was unrealistic and that the large Himalayan glaciers could not melt in a few decades. In a statement, the IPCC said the paragraph "refers to poorly substantiated estimates of rate of recession and date for the disappearance of Himalayan glaciers. In drafting the paragraph in question, the clear and well-established standards of evidence, required by the IPCC procedures, were not applied properly."

It added: "The IPCC regrets the poor application of well-established IPCC procedures in this instance." But the statement calls for no action beyond stating a need for absolute adherence to IPCC quality control processes. "We reaffirm our strong commitment to ensuring this level of performance," the statement said. The IPCC says the broader conclusion of the report is unaffected: that glaciers have melted significantly, that this will accelerate and affect the supply of water from major mountain ranges "where more than one-sixth of the world population currently lives". Jean-Pascal van Ypersele, vice-chair of the IPCC, added that the mistake did nothing to undermine the large body of evidence that showed the climate was warming and that human activity was largely to blame. He told BBC News: "I don't see how one mistake in a 3,000-page report can damage the credibility of the overall report."

The row centres on the IPCC's "fourth assessment" report in 2007, which said "glaciers in the Himalayas are receding faster than in any other part of the world." The claim appears in the full report, but not in the more widely read "Summary for Policymakers". The claim was attributed to a report by the campaign group WWF, but in a *New Scientist* article, *Guardian* writer Fred Pearce noted that WWF had cited a 1999 interview in the magazine with Indian glaciologist Syed Hasnain as the source of the claim. Hasnain told the magazine that "it is not proper for IPCC to include references from popular magazines or newspapers". One could of course add that much of the information about "climate change" which politicians and the public read or view originate from the emphasis of the media and "popular" magazines.

Tree rings

Dendrochronology (or tree-ring dating) as reviewed by *Wikipedia* is the scientific method of dating tree rings (also called growth rings) to the exact year they were formed. As well as dating them, this can give data for dendroclimatology, the study of climate and atmospheric conditions during different periods in history from wood. Dendrochronology is useful for determining the precise age of samples, especially those that are too recent for radiocarbon dating, which always produces a range rather than an exact date. However, for a precise date of the death of the tree a full sample to the edge is needed, which most trimmed timber will not provide. It also gives data on the timing of events and rates of change in the environment (most prominently climate) and also in wood found in archaeology or works of art and architecture, such as old panel paintings. It is also used as a check in radiocarbon dating to calibrate radiocarbon ages.

New growth in trees occurs in a layer of cells near the bark. A tree's growth rate changes in a predictable pattern throughout the year in response to seasonal climate changes, resulting in visible growth rings. Each ring marks a complete cycle of seasons, or one year, in the tree's life. As of 2013, the oldest tree-ring measurements in the Northern Hemisphere are a floating sequence extending from about 12,580 to 13,900 years.

History

Knowledge of tree rings has a very long history. The Greek botanist Theophrastus (c. 371 – c. 287 BC), as noted by *Wikipedia*, first mentioned that the wood of trees has rings. In his *Trattato della Pittura* (Treatise on Painting), Leonardo da Vinci (1452–1519) was the first person to mention that trees form rings annually and that their thickness is determined by the conditions under which they grew. In 1737, French investigators Henri-Louis Duhamel du Monceau and Georges-Louis Leclerc de Buffon examined the effect of growing conditions on the shape of tree rings. They found that in 1709, a severe winter produced a distinctly dark tree ring, which served as a reference for subsequent European naturalists. In the U.S., Alexander Catlin Twining (1801–1884) suggested in 1833 that patterns among tree rings could be used to synchronize the dendrochronologies of various trees and thereby to reconstruct past climates across entire regions. The English polymath Charles Babbage proposed using dendrochronology to date the remains of trees in peat bogs or even in geological strata (1835, 1838).

During the latter half of the nineteenth century, the scientific study of tree rings and the application of dendrochronology began. In 1859, the German-American Jacob Kuechler (1823-1893) used crossdating to examine oak trees in order to study the record of climate in western Texas. In 1866, the German botanist, entomologist, and forester Julius Ratzeburg (1801-1871) observed the effects on tree rings of defoliation caused by insect infestations. By 1882, this observation was already appearing in forestry textbooks. In the 1870s, the Dutch astronomer Jacobus C. Kapteyn (1851-1922) was using crossdating to reconstruct the climates of the Netherlands and Germany. In 1881, the Swiss-Austrian forester Arthur von Seckendorff-Gudent (1845-1886) was using crossdating. From 1869 to 1901, Robert Hartig (1839-1901), a German professor of forest pathology, wrote a series of papers on the anatomy and ecology of tree rings. In 1892, the Russian physicist Fedor Nikiforovich Shvedov (1841-1905) wrote that he had used patterns found in tree rings to predict droughts in 1882 and 1891.

During the first half of the twentieth century, the astronomer A. E. Douglass founded the Laboratory of Tree-Ring Research at the University of Arizona. Douglass sought to better understand cycles of sunspot activity and reasoned that changes in solar activity would affect climate patterns on earth, which would subsequently be recorded by tree-ring growth patterns (i.e., sunspots → climate → tree rings). The University of Arizona website notes that in 1937, the scientific study of tree-rings was formalized by the creation of the Laboratory of Tree-Ring Research (LTRR) at the University of Arizona in Tucson, US. By that time, founder Andrew Ellicott Douglass had been working with wood for over 30 years, and so the tradition of dendrochronology in Tucson is older than the Laboratory itself. The LTRR has long since had the distinction of being the only dendrochronology laboratory in the US, but helped found many dendrochronology laboratories around the world.

Growth rings

Horizontal cross sections cut through the trunk of a tree can reveal growth rings, also referred to as *tree rings or annual rings*. Growth rings result from new growth in the vascular cambium, a layer of cells near the bark that botanists classify as a lateral meristem; this growth in diameter is known as secondary growth. Visible rings result from the change in growth speed through the seasons of the year; thus, critical for the title method, one ring generally marks the passage of one year in the life of the tree. Removal of the bark of the tree in a particular area may cause deformation of the rings as the plant overgrows the scar.

The rings are more visible in trees which have grown in temperate zones, where the seasons differ more markedly. The inner portion of a growth ring forms early in the growing season, when growth is comparatively rapid (hence the wood is less dense) and is known as "early wood" (or "spring wood", or "late-spring wood"); the outer portion is the "late wood" (sometimes termed "summer wood", often being produced in the summer, though sometimes in the autumn) and is denser.

Many trees in temperate zones produce one growth-ring each year, with the newest adjacent to the bark. Hence, for the entire period of a tree's life, a year-by-year record or ring pattern builds up that reflects the age of the tree and the climatic conditions in which the tree grew. Adequate moisture and a long growing season result in a wide ring, while a drought year may result in a very narrow one.

Tree ring chronologies
Direct reading of tree ring chronologies is a complex science, for several reasons. First, contrary to the single-ring-per-year paradigm, alternating poor and favourable conditions, such as mid-summer droughts, can result in several rings forming in a given year. In addition, particular tree-species may present "missing rings", and this influences the selection of trees for study of long time-spans. For instance, missing rings are rare in oak and elm trees. Critical to the science, trees from the same region tend to develop the same patterns of ring widths for a given period of chronological study. Researchers can compare and match these patterns ring-for-ring with patterns from trees which have grown at the same time in the same geographical zone (and therefore under similar climatic conditions). When one can match these tree-ring patterns across successive trees in the same locale, in overlapping fashion, chronologies can be built up–both for entire geographical regions and for sub-regions. Moreover, wood from ancient structures with known chronologies can be matched to the tree-ring data (a technique called *cross-dating*), and the age of the wood can thereby be determined precisely.

Dendrochronologists originally carried out cross-dating by visual inspection; more recently, they have harnessed computers to do the task, applying statistical techniques to assess the matching. To eliminate individual variations in tree-ring growth, dendrochronologists take the smoothed average of the tree-ring widths of multiple tree-samples to build up a ring history, a process termed replication. A tree-ring history whose beginning - and end-dates are not known is called a *floating chronology*. It can be anchored by cross-matching a section against another chronology (tree-ring history) whose dates are known. A fully anchored and cross-matched chronology for oak and pine in central Europe extends back 12,460 years, and an oak chronology goes back 7,429 years in Ireland and 6,939 years in England. Comparison of radiocarbon and dendrochronological ages supports the consistency of these two independent dendrochronological sequences. Another fully anchored chronology that extends back 8500 years exists for the bristlecone pine in the White Mountains of California.

Dendrochronology makes available specimens of once-living material accurately dated to a specific year. Dates are often represented as estimated calendar years B.P., for before present, where "present" refers to 1 January 1950. Timber core samples are used to measure the width of annual growth rings; by taking samples from different sites within a particular region, researchers can build a comprehensive historical sequence. The techniques of dendrochronology are more consistent in areas where trees grow in marginal conditions such as aridity or semi-aridity where the ring growth is more sensitive to the environment, rather than in humid areas where tree-ring growth is more uniform (complacent). In addition, some genera of trees are more suitable than others for this type of analysis. For instance, the bristlecone pine is exceptionally long-lived and slow growing, and has been used extensively for chronologies; still-living and dead specimens of this species provide tree-ring patterns going back thousands of years, in some regions more than 10,000 years. Currently, the maximum span for fully anchored chronology is a little over 11,000 years B.P.

In 2004 a new radiocarbon calibration curve, INTCAL04, was internationally ratified to provide calibrated dates back to 26,000 B.P. For the period back to 12,400 B.P., the radiocarbon dates are calibrated against dendrochronological dates. Dendrochronology faces many obstacles, including the existence of species of ants that inhabit trees and extend their galleries into the wood, thus destroying ring structure.

Reference sequences
European chronologies derived from wooden structures initially found

it difficult to bridge the gap in the fourteenth century when there was a building hiatus, which coincided with the Black Death, however there do exist unbroken chronologies dating back to prehistoric times, for example the Danish chronology dating back to 352 BC. Given a sample of wood, the variation of the tree-ring growths not only provides a match by year, but can also match location because climate varies from place to place. This makes it possible to determine the source of ships as well as smaller artifacts made from wood, but which were transported long distances, such as panels for paintings and ship timbers.

The width of tree rings varies with, among other things, temperature. They can be used to estimate temperature for times before thermometers were in widespread use. When cross sections are taken of trees there is a pattern of annular rings. The width of these rings is, in part, a function of temperature. The website *climatedata.info/proxies/tree-rings/* shows that many things can affect ring width including:

- The age of the tree. The rate of growth varies through the life of the tree.

- Weather. In addition to temperature, ring growth is also affected by precipitation and to a lesser extent by wind speed and sunshine.

- Previous years. If a tree has grown vigorously in one year it is likely to grow vigorously in following years and vice versa.

- Atmosphere. CO_2 is necessary to growth and increased levels of CO_2 can lead to enhanced growth.

- Competition. Other trees nearby or other plants can rob a particular tree of nutrients or light.

- Parasites. Infestation by insects or fungi can slow the growth of the tree.

To overcome the above, for temperature reconstruction, the sites to be analysed are chosen so that these other factors have limited importance. For example trees might be chosen in areas where rainfall was plentiful so that water stress does not affect growth. Even in well chosen sites it has to be recognised that ring width is not a uniform function of temperature but is biased toward the temperatures during the growing period. This is sometimes dealt with by analysing early and late growth separately. It is not necessary to fell the tree first – normally samples are taken by boring into the tree with a hollow bit. Dozens of samples are normally taken from a group of trees.

The chart below shows the effect of global temperatures on tree rings widths. There is reasonable agreement between the rate of growth and the temperature record. There is one interesting feature, which may be an artefact of the method of processing; the rate of growth of tree rings appears to precede the increase in temperature.

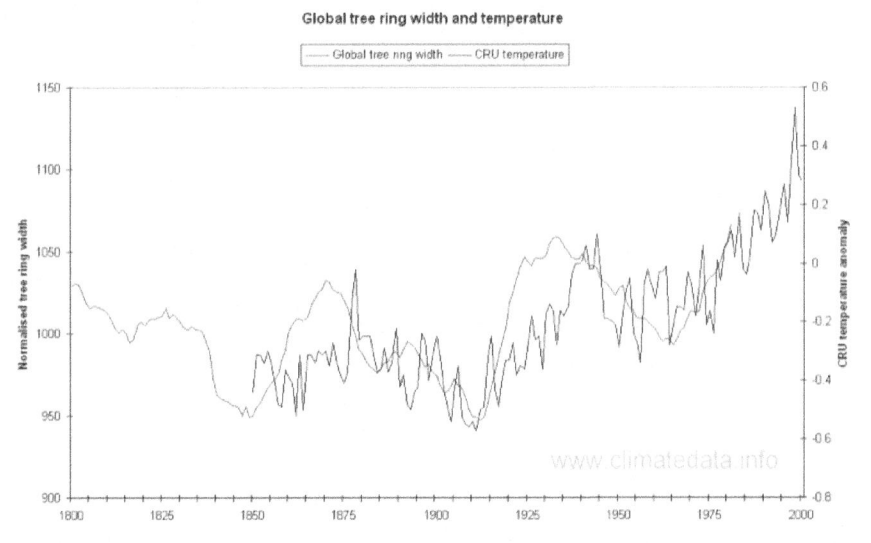

Global tree ring width and temperature

Data for the Northern and Southern Hemispheres, which show a general agreement on the pattern of rising and falling temperatures. Again the agreement is generally good except for the fact the observed temperature record shows an increase around 1940 not noticeable in the tree ring record.

The following chart is for Bristlecone Pines from the USA. This record is very long – 2000 years – and therefore potentially very valuable for temperature reconstruction. However it shows a particular characteristic, that is there is a very marked increase in growth of tree rings from the late 19th century onward. This singular increase was originally ascribed to CO_2 enrichment of the atmosphere. Another theory is that as the trees get old they become very twisted and this may lead to relaxation of the fibres and an apparent growth in ring size.

Bristlecone Pine - Tree ring widths

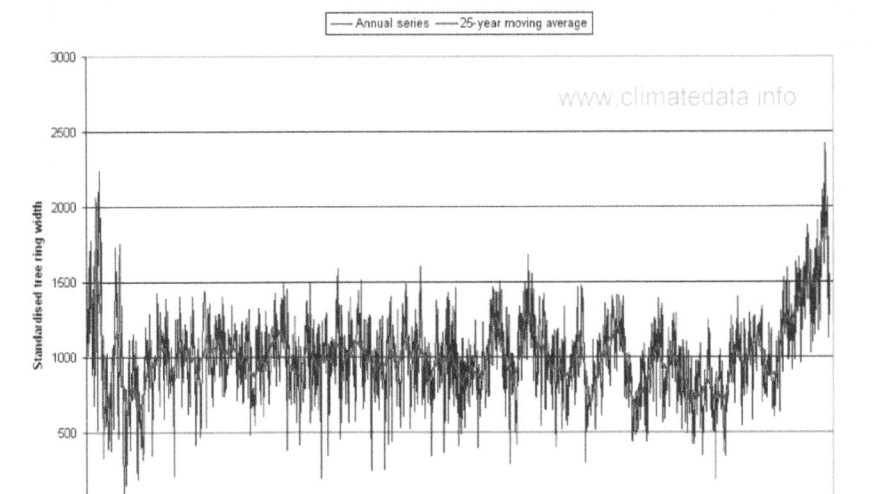

The fact that from the middle of the 20th century tree ring growth was less than might have been expected from the temperature record, as seen in the records for the US but general in the Northern Hemisphere, brings into question the reliability of tree rings as a proxy for temperature. If they do not accurately represent late 20th century temperatures how can we be sure they accurately represent temperatures in earlier times for which we have no instrumental corroboration? Whilst this phenomenon is well known among tree ring experts and has been described in the scientific literature, the fact that the discrepancy between narrower tree rings and higher temperatures has not always been made clear has led to lively debate.

3
Forecasting the climate

If you wait until the wind and the weather are just right, you will never sow anything and never harvest anything

Ecclesiastes 11:4

Do not disparage any of this: it's a good idea to look at one sign after another, and if two agree, it is more hopeful, while a third can make you more confident.

Aratus Phenomena (275 BC)

"Recent climatic extremes from snow to drought remind us of our dynamic climate. Despite what politicians believe, humans cannot control nature, nature controls us."

Don Nicholson, 2010-11 President of the the New Zealand Federated Farmers, writing in the *Sunday Star Times Dec*ember 26, 2010.

Weather and Climate Forecasting

Today people know sooner whether to carry an umbrella for a rainy day, thanks to a revolution in weather and climate forecasting. Peter Lynch writing in the *WMO Bulletin* in 2010 reviewed "Weather and Climate Forecasting: Chronicle of a Revolution".

Remarkable advances in weather forecasts during the past half-century have brought great benefits to humanity. Accurate forecasts save many lives, and early warnings mitigate the worst effects of extreme weather events, when they are available. Detailed, accurate forecasts are of huge economic value, with numerous studies showing that the benefits of forecasts outweigh the costs many times over. Advances in climate modelling over the past fifty years have also been outstanding. General circulation models have been developed and applied to examine the factors causing changes in our climate, and their likely timing and severity. When the European Centre for Medium-Range Weather Forecasts was established in 1976, forecast skill ten days ahead was little more than a dream. The centre's stated goal was to produce weather forecasts in the range of four to ten days. In February 2010, the "ten-day barrier" became reality.

The birth of scientific forecasting using thermodynamics – which took a great leap in the nineteenth century – completed the set of fundamental principles governing the flow of the atmosphere. By about 1890, the American meteorologist Cleveland Abbe recognized that meteorology is simply the application of hydrodynamics and thermodynamics to the atmosphere.

Shortly afterwards, the Norwegian scientist Vilhelm Bjerknes analysed weather more explicitly with a two-step plan. In the diagnostic step, the initial state of the atmosphere is determined using observations; in the prognostic step, the laws of motion are used to calculate how this state changes over time. But, Bjerknes at that time saw no possibility to put his ideas to practical use. The English scientist Lewis Fry Richardson was bolder. Richardson's forecasting amounted to implementation of Bjerknes' prognostic step. As Richardson observed, his scheme is complicated because the atmosphere is complicated. It involved a phenomenal volume of numerical computation, quite impractical in the pre-computer era. But Richardson was undaunted. "Perhaps some day in the dim future it will be possible to advance the computations faster than the weather advances… But that is a dream," he said in 1922.

Today, forecasts are prepared routinely on powerful computers running algorithms remarkably similar to Richardson's scheme. His dream has indeed come true.

Richardson's dream

While Richardson's dream appeared unrealizable at the time his book was published, key developments in the ensuing decades set the scene for progress. Profound developments in the theory of meteorology provided crucial understanding of atmospheric dynamics. Advances in numerical analysis enabled the design of stable algorithms. The invention of the radiosonde, and its introduction in a global network, meant that timely observations of the atmosphere in three dimensions were becoming available. Finally, the computer provided a means of attacking the enormous computational task involved in weather forecasting.

In the mid-1930s, John von Neumann became interested in turbulent fluid flows. Von Neumann knew of Richardson's pioneering work, and saw that progress in hydrodynamics would accelerate if a means were available of solving complex equations. It was clear that very fast automatic computing machinery was required. Von Neumann recognized weather forecasting – a problem of great practical significance and intrinsic scientific interest – as an ideal problem for a computer. Von Neumann discussed the prospects for numerical weather forecasting with Carl Gustaf Rossby, who arranged for Jule Charney to participate in a weather prediction project. Charney directed the Princeton Project (USA) for eight years, and led the team who performed the first computer weather forecasts.

Arrangements were made to run the integration on the only computer then available, the Electronic Numerical Integrator and Computer (ENIAC) in the late 1940s. The ENIAC integrations were truly groundbreaking; indeed, weather forecasting had been regarded as a Grand Challenge problem throughout the history of computing. Four 24-hour forecasts were made. Each 24-hour integration took about 24 hours of computation – that is, the team was just able to keep pace with the weather. The ENIAC forecasts were made using a highly simplified model. In the ensuing years, several more sophisticated and realistic models were developed.

The impact of climate change is of enormous importance for our future, and global climate models are the best means we have of anticipating likely changes. Norman Phillips (Princeton University, USA) carried out, for about a month, the first long-range simulation of the general circulation of the atmosphere in 1956. Following Phillips' seminal work, several models were developed. Solar heating, terrestrial radiation, convection and small-scale turbulence and other processes are now included in these models. Modern models include the oceans, ice and land processes. The EC-Earth model, being developed by a community of European scientists, has the Integrated Forecast System as its base. It is used to provide state-of-the-art computer simulations of the Earth's past, present, and future climate states.

Earth System Models
Comprehensive atmospheric models were among the finest achievements of meteorology in the twentieth century. These models are constantly refined and extended, and are ever more sophisticated and comprehensive. They simulate the atmosphere and oceans as well as geophysical, chemical and biological processes and feedbacks. The models, now called Earth System Models, are applied to weather prediction and also to the study of climate variability and humankind's impact on it. It is no exaggeration to describe the advances made over the past half century as revolutionary. Thanks to this work, meteorology is now firmly established as a quantitative science, and its value and validity are demonstrated daily by the acid test of any science, its ability to predict the future.

Operational forecasting today uses guidance from a wide range of models. In most centres, a combination of global and local models is used. By way of illustration, consider the global model of the European Centre for Medium-Range Weather Forecasts. The centre aims to deliver weather forecasts of increasingly high quality and scope from a few days to a few seasons ahead. Operational since 1979, the centre continues to develop forecasts and other products of steadily increasing accuracy and value, maintaining its position as a world leader.

The chaotic nature of the atmospheric flow is now well understood. It imposes a limit on predictability – unavoidable errors in the initial state grow rapidly, and render the forecast useless after some days. The most successful means to overcome this obstacle is to run a series, or ensemble, of forecasts, each starting from a slightly different initial state. To allow for uncertainty, the physics parameters of the forecast model are also perturbed at random. The combined result is used to deduce future changes in the atmosphere.

Since the early 1990s, ensemble forecasting has been operational at both the European Centre for Medium-Range Weather Forecasts and at the National Centers for Environmental Prediction in Washington. At ECMWF they perform an ensemble of 51 forecasts, each having a resolution half that of the deterministic forecast.

Probability forecasts have emerged as the key guide for medium-range prediction. They are generated and disseminated for use in operational centres. The European Centre, for example, prepares seasonal forecasts, with a range of six months. They are made using a coupled atmosphere-ocean model, and a large number of forecasts are combined in an ensemble each month.

These ensemble forecasts have demonstrable skill for tropical regions. Recent predictions of the onset of El Niño and La Niña events have been impressive. However, in temperate latitudes, and in particular for the European region, no significant skill has yet been achieved. Indeed, seasonal forecasting for middle latitudes is one of the great problems facing us today.

Forecast skill

Forecasts have improved by around one day per decade in the last thirty years, and by 2010 forecasts have been made with 10-day accuracy. Forecast skill is judged by the anomaly correlation coefficient (ACC) of the 500 hPa height forecast field. The useful range is estimated as the forecast day on which the ACC drops to 60%. On average, the 60% level is now reached at around day 8. In February 2010, the average monthly ACC remained above 60% throughout the 10-day range of the deterministic forecast for the Northern Hemisphere. Computers have enabled a revolutionary leap in forecasting. The eminent Norwegian meteorologist Sverre Petterssen noted that, prior to the computer, advances occurred in homeopathic doses.

Yet formidable challenges remain. Sudden weather changes and extremes cause much human hardship and damage to property. These rapid developments have fast and slow time scales, with intricate interactions between dynamic processes and physical parameters. Computing these complex interactions is a significant challenge.

Nowcasting is the process of predicting changes over periods of a few hours. Guidance from current numerical models can fall short of what is needed to take effective action to avert disasters. For now, the best results systematically combine numerical weather prediction products with conventional observations, radar imagery, satellite imagery and other data. But much remains to be done to develop optimal nowcasting systems, and we can be optimistic that future developments will lead to great improvements in this area.

At the opposite end of the time scale, the atmosphere's chaotic nature puts a limit on what standard forecasts can achieve. While the ensemble prediction technique provides probabilistic guidance, so far it has proved difficult to use in many cases. Interaction between the atmosphere and the ocean becomes a dominant factor at longer forecast ranges. Although there is good progress in seasonal forecasting for the tropics, useful long-range forecasts for temperate regions remain to be tackled by future modellers. Another great challenge is the modelling and prediction of climate change, a matter of increasing importance and concern.

Developments in atmospheric dynamics, instrumentation and observing practice and digital computing have made the dreams of Bjerknes and Richardson an everyday reality. Numerical weather prediction models are now at the centre of operational forecasting. Forecast accuracy has grown apace, and progress continues on several fronts.

There is a vast variety of end uses to weather and climate forecasts. Weather warnings are important forecasts because they are used to protect life and property. Weather and climate forecasts based on temperature and precipitation are important to agriculture, and therefore to traders within commodity markets. Temperature forecasts are used by utility companies to estimate demand over coming days. On an everyday basis, many use weather forecasts to determine what to wear on a given day. Since outdoor activities are severely curtailed by heavy rain, snow and wind chill, forecasts can be used to plan activities around these events, and to plan ahead and survive them. In 2009, the US spent approximately $5.1 billion on weather forecasting.

Historical weather forecasting
For millennia people have tried to forecast the weather. *Wikipedia* says that in 650 BCE, the Babylonians predicted the weather from cloud patterns as well as astrology. In about 350 BCE, Aristotle described weather patterns in *Meteorologica*. Later, Theophrastus compiled a book on weather forecasting, called the Book of Signs. Chinese weather prediction lore extends at least as far back as 300 BCE, which was also around the same time ancient Indian astronomers developed weather-

prediction methods. In *Matthew* 16:2-3 Jesus referred to deciphering and understanding local weather patterns, by saying, "When evening comes, you say, 'It will be fair weather, for the sky is red', and in the morning, 'Today it will be stormy, for the sky is red and overcast.' You know how to interpret the appearance of the sky, but you cannot interpret the signs of the times."

In 904 CE, Ibn Wahshiyya's Nabatean Agriculture, translated into Arabic from an earlier Aramaic work, discussed the weather forecasting of atmospheric changes and signs from the planetary astral alterations; signs of rain based on observation of the lunar phases; and weather forecasts based on the movement of winds. Ancient weather forecasting methods usually relied on observed patterns of events, also termed pattern recognition. For example, it might be observed that if the sunset was particularly red, the following day often brought fair weather. This experience accumulated over the generations to produce weather lore. However, not all of these predictions prove reliable, and many of them have since been found not to stand up to rigorous statistical testing.

It was not until the invention of the electric telegraph in 1835 that the modern age of weather forecasting began. By the late 1840s, the telegraph allowed reports of weather conditions from a wide area to be received almost instantaneously, allowing forecasts to be made from knowledge of weather conditions further upwind.

Beaufort and FitzRoy

The two men credited with the birth of forecasting as a science were an officer of the Royal Navy Francis Beaufort and his protégé Robert FitzRoy. Both were influential men in British naval and governmental circles, and though ridiculed in the press at the time, their work gained scientific credence, was accepted by the Royal Navy, and formed the basis for all of today's weather forecasting knowledge.

Beaufort developed the Wind Force Scale and Weather Notation coding, which he was to use in his journals for the remainder of his life. Robert FitzRoy was appointed in 1854 as chief of a new department within the Board of Trade to deal with the collection of weather data at sea as a service to mariners. This was the forerunner of the modern Meteorological Office. All ship captains were tasked with collating data on the weather and computing it, with the use of tested instruments that were loaned for this purpose.

A storm in 1859 that caused the loss of the *Royal Charter* inspired FitzRoy to develop charts to allow predictions to be made, which he called "forecasting the weather", thus coining the term "weather forecast". Fifteen land stations were established to use the telegraph to transmit to him daily reports of weather at set times leading to the first gale warning service. His warning service for shipping was initiated in February 1861, with the use of telegraph communications. The first daily weather forecasts were published in *The Times* in 1861. In the following year a system was introduced of hoisting storm warning cones at the principal ports when a gale was expected. *The Weather Book* which FitzRoy published in 1863 was far in advance of the scientific opinion of the time.

To convey accurate information, it soon became necessary to have a standard vocabulary describing clouds; this was achieved by means of a series of classifications first achieved by Luke Howard in 1802, and standardized in the *International Cloud Atlas* of 1896.

It was not until the 20th century that advances in the understanding of atmospheric physics led to the foundation of modern numerical weather prediction. In 1922, English scientist Lewis Fry Richardson published *Weather Prediction By Numerical Process*, after finding notes and derivations he worked on as an ambulance driver in World War I. He described therein how small terms in the prognostic fluid dynamics equations governing atmospheric flow could be neglected, and a finite differencing scheme in time and space could be devised, to allow numerical prediction solutions to be found.

Richardson envisioned a large auditorium of thousands of people performing the calculations and passing them to others. However, the sheer number of calculations required was too large to be completed without the use of computers, and the size of the grid and time steps led to unrealistic results in deepening systems. It was later found, through numerical analysis, that this was due to numerical instability. The first computerised weather forecast was performed by a team composed of American meteorologists Jule Charney, Philip Thompson, Larry Gates, and Norwegian meteorologist Ragnar Fjørtoft, applied mathematician John von Neumann, and ENIAC programmer Klara Dan von Neumann. Practical use of numerical weather prediction began in 1955, spurred by the development of programmable electronic computers.

As previously noted the first ever daily weather forecasts were published in *The Times* on August 1, 1861, and the first weather maps were produced later in the same year. In 1911, the UK Met Office began issuing the first marine weather forecasts via radio transmission. These included gale and storm warnings for areas around Great Britain. In the United States, the first public radio forecasts were made in 1925 by Edward B. "E.B." Rideout, on WEEI, the Edison Electric Illuminating station in Boston. Rideout came from the U.S. Weather Bureau, as did WBZ weather forecaster G. Harold Noyes in 1931.

The world's first televised weather forecasts, including the use of weather maps, were experimentally broadcast by the BBC in 1936. This was brought into practice in 1949 after World War II. George Cowling gave the first weather forecast (on BBC) while being televised in front of the map in 1954. (Many years later in 1981, I with two colleagues from the New Zealand Meteorological Service presented the weather on the *EyeWitness* programme of South Pacific Television). In the United States, experimental television forecasts were made by James C. Fidler in Cincinnati in the 1940s on the DuMont Television Network. In the late 1970s and early 1980s, John Coleman, the first weatherman on ABC-TV's *Good Morning America*, pioneered the use of on-screen weather satellite information and computer graphics for television forecasts. Coleman was a co-founder of The Weather Channel (TWC) in 1982. TWC is now a 24-hour cable network.

Numerical weather prediction
The basic idea of numerical weather prediction is to sample the state of the fluid at a given time and use the equations of fluid dynamics and thermodynamics to estimate the state of the fluid at some time in the future. The main inputs from country-based weather services are surface observations from automated weather stations at ground level over land and from weather buoys at sea. The World Meteorological Organization (WMO) acts to standardize the instrumentation, observing practices and timing of these observations worldwide.

Models are initialized using this observed data. The irregularly spaced observations are processed by data assimilation and objective analysis methods, which perform quality control and obtain values at locations usable by the model's mathematical algorithms (usually an evenly spaced grid). The data are then used in the model as the starting point for a forecast. Commonly, the set of equations used to predict the physics and dynamics of the atmosphere are called primitive equations. These equations are initialized from the analysis data and rates of change are determined. The rates of change predict the state of the atmosphere a short time into the future. The equations are then applied to this new atmospheric state to find new rates of change, and these new rates of change predict the atmosphere at a yet further time into the future. This time stepping procedure is continually repeated until the solution reaches the desired forecast time.

The length of the time step chosen within the model is related to the distance between the points on the computational grid, and is chosen to maintain numerical stability. Time steps for global models are on the order of tens of minutes, while time steps for regional models are between one and four minutes. The global models are run at varying times into the future. The UK Met Office's Unified Model is run six days into the future, the European Centre for Medium-Range Weather Forecasts model is run out to 10 days into the future, while the Global Forecast System model run by the US Environmental Modeling Center is run 16 days into the future. The visual output produced by a model solution is known as a prognostic chart, or prog. The raw output is often modified before being presented as the forecast. This can be in the form of statistical techniques to remove known biases in the model, or of adjustment to take into account consensus among other numerical weather forecasts. MOS or model output statistics is a technique used to interpret numerical model output and produce site-specific guidance. This guidance is presented in coded numerical form.

Fluid dynamics equations
As indicated by Edward Lorenz in 1963, long range forecasts, those made at a range of two weeks or more, are impossible to definitively predict the state of the atmosphere, owing to the chaotic nature of the fluid dynamics equations involved. In numerical models, extremely small errors in initial values double roughly every five days for variables such as temperature and wind velocity.

Essentially, a model is a computer programme that produces meteorological information for future times at given locations and altitudes. Within any modern model is a set of equations, known as the primitive equations, used to predict the future state of the atmosphere. These equations – along with the ideal gas law – are used to evolve the density, pressure, and potential temperature scalar fields and the velocity vector field of the atmosphere through time. Additional transport equations for pollutants and other aerosols are included in some primitive-equation mesoscale models as well. The equations used are nonlinear partial differential equations, which are impossible to solve exactly through analytical methods, with the exception of a few idealized cases. Therefore, numerical methods obtain approximate solutions. Different models use different solution methods: some global models use spectral methods for the horizontal dimensions and finite difference methods for the vertical dimension, while regional models and other global models usually use finite-difference methods in all three dimensions.

The simplest method of forecasting the weather, persistence, relies upon today's conditions to forecast the conditions tomorrow. This can be a valid way of forecasting the weather when it is in a steady state, such as during the summer season in the tropics. This method of forecasting strongly depends upon the presence of a stagnant weather pattern. Therefore, when in a fluctuating weather pattern, this method of forecasting becomes inaccurate. It can be useful in both short range forecasts and long range forecasts.

The role of human forecasters
The forecasting of the weather within the next six hours is often referred to as nowcasting. In this time range it is possible to forecast smaller features such as individual showers and thunderstorms with reasonable accuracy, as well as other features too small to be resolved by a computer model. A human given the latest radar, satellite and observational data will be able to make a better analysis of the small scale features present and so will be able to make a more accurate forecast for the following few hours. However, there are now expert systems using those data and mesoscale numerical models to make better extrapolation, including evolution of those features in time. *Accuweather* is known for a Minute-Cast, which is a minute-by-minute precipitation forecast for the next two hours.

In the past, the human forecaster was responsible for generating the entire weather forecast based upon available observations. Today, human input is generally confined to choosing a model based on various parameters, such as model biases and performance. However, the human forecaster has a place. I well remember that in 1982 when preparing my forecast to present on the Thursday before Good Friday on New Zealand Television, by chance the then Director of the NZ Meteorological Service (John Hickman) and I were jointly looking at the weather maps and we both said "we don't like the look of the situation as shown on the weather map". As a result I persuaded the TV station to allow me to expand the weather forecast that evening, and being the evening before the Easter holiday I hope that I may have saved a few lives by warning people that it would not be a good idea to go out in their boats.

Using a consensus of forecast models, as well as ensemble members of the various models, can help reduce forecast error. However, regardless how small the average error becomes with any individual system, large errors within any particular piece of guidance are still possible on any given model run. Humans are required to interpret the model data into weather forecasts that are understandable to the end user. Humans can use knowledge of local effects that may be too small in size to be resolved by the model to add information to the forecast. While increasing accuracy of forecast models implies that humans may no longer be needed in the forecast process at some point in the future, there is currently still a need for human intervention.

The analog technique is a complex way of making a forecast, requiring the forecaster to remember a previous weather event that is expected to be mimicked by an upcoming event. What makes it a difficult technique to use is that there is rarely a perfect analog for an event in the future. Some call this type of forecasting pattern recognition. It remains a useful method of observing rainfall over data voids such as oceans, as well as the forecasting of precipitation amounts and distribution in the future. A similar technique is used in medium range forecasting, which is known as teleconnections, when systems in other locations are used to help pin down the location of another system within the surrounding regime. An example of teleconnections is by using El Niño-Southern Oscillation (ENSO) related phenomena.

Forecasts from government agencies
Several countries employ government agencies to provide forecasts and watches/warnings/advisories to the public in order to protect life and property and maintain commercial interests. Knowledge of what the end user needs from a weather forecast must be taken into account to present the information in a useful and understandable way. Examples include the National Oceanic and Atmospheric Administration's National Weather Service (NWS) and Environment Canada's Meteorological Service (MSC). Traditionally, newspaper, television, and radio have been the primary outlets for presenting weather forecast information to the public. In addition, some cities have weather beacons. Increasingly, the internet is being used due to the vast amount of specific information that can be found. In all cases, these outlets update their forecasts on a regular basis.

A major part of modern weather forecasting is the severe weather alerts and advisories that the national weather services issue in the case that severe or hazardous weather is expected. This is done to protect life and property. Some of the most commonly known severe weather advisories are the severe thunderstorm and tornado warnings, as well as the severe thunderstorm and tornado watch. Other forms of these advisories include winter weather, high wind, flood, tropical cyclone, and fog. Severe weather advisories and alerts are broadcast through the media, including radio, using emergency systems as the Emergency Alert System, which break into regular programming.

Australia has one of the most variable climates in the world. The Australian CSIRO in a report on multiyear climate forecasts says that Australia's climate's natural variability is further exacerbated by extreme climate events such as drought, flooding and bushfires. Research and observations also show that the climate is changing due to anthropogenic (human) impacts, including greenhouse gas emissions and aerosol concentrations in the atmosphere. The frequency, persistence and intensity of extreme events are also shifting. It's therefore more important than ever to understand not only what long-term future climate trends may look like, but critically, how these changes will influence climate variability (and much of Australia's economy) in the near-future.

Many of Australia's industries, such as agriculture, aquaculture and energy, are climate-sensitive and are vulnerable to extreme climate events. Adding to this, decision makers, regulators and stakeholders working across these industries often plan resource management and business decisions on the one to ten year timescale – and therefore require climate predictions that can help identify periods of increased profitability and/or risk.

While current weather and seasonal forecasts can help predict conditions between several days and a few months ahead, we are currently missing a key piece of the puzzle: what will the climate look like anywhere between one year and a decade into the future? That research gap is now being filled by work in decadal forecasting, providing invaluable insights to industry and beyond.

The CSIRO has undertaken the challenge of delivering useful climate forecasts, with a Decadal Climate Forecasting Project to enable climate predictions on the annual to decadal scale. Researchers have built a system called the Climate Analysis Forecast Ensemble (CAFE). The CAFE system, which includes 100 climate models, assimilates a vast array of in-situ and remotely sensed ocean and sea-ice observations – including satellite observations, robotic instruments such as ARGO and new marine observation networks such as the IMOS (the Integrated Marine Ocean Observing System). These models provide forecasts and statistics as far out as 10 years. While the development of CAFE is still in its preliminary stages, its forecast skill is comparable to current state of the art seasonal forecasting systems.

Climate prediction on an annual to decadal timescale has the potential to deliver huge benefit to the Australian economy, as well as communities and government by informing decision-making in areas such as risk management and natural asset management.

Near-term climate prediction
Near-term climate prediction remains a huge challenge. Fortunately, even in early stages, advanced climate forecasts are of significant economic value and can equip decision-makers in agriculture, energy and other sectors with the knowledge to better manage risks and opportunities - in addition to informing where to best direct resources. The CSIRO is working with clients to explore the utility of climate forecasts for managing hydroelectric, agriculture and fisheries.

Advancing climate forecasting
"Advancing climate forecasting" in a report in *eos.or/science* in 2017 says that WMO's *World Climate Research Programme* coordinates research aimed at improving and extending global climate forecasting capabilities. The authors William J. Merryfield et al. say that as the science underlying climate forecasts continues to develop, their accuracy can be expected to increase.

Climate forecasts predict weather averages and other climatic properties from a few weeks to a few years in advance. Increasingly, forecasters are using comprehensive models of Earth's climate system to make such predictions. Researchers also use climate models to project forced changes many decades into the future under assumed scenarios for human influence. Those simulations typically start in preindustrial times, so far in the past that details of their initial states have little influence in the present era. By contrast, climate forecasts begin from more recent observed climate system states, much like weather forecasts. For this reason, they are sometimes referred to as "initialized climate predictions."

Climate forecasts are produced at numerous operational and research centres worldwide. Models and approaches vary, and by coordinating research efforts, the modelling community can make even greater progress. The Working Group on Subseasonal to Interdecadal Prediction (WGSIP) of the World Climate Research Programme (WCRP) facilitates such coordination through a programme of numerical experimentation– evaluating model responses to different inputs–aimed at assessing and improving climate forecasts.

WGSIP currently supports a project that archives hindcasts; this is a major community resource for climate forecasting research. It also supports three additional targeted research projects aimed at advancing specific aspects of climate forecasting. These projects examine how well climate forecast models represent global influences of tropical rainfall, assess how snow predictably influences climate, and study how model drifts and biases develop and affect climate forecasts.

Climate varies naturally over a wide range of timescales, driven by processes within and interactions between the atmosphere, ocean, and other components of the climate system such as land, sea ice, and the biosphere. These factors combine with long-term changes forced largely by human influences on the concentrations of greenhouse gases and other atmospheric constituents. Together, these natural variations and forced long-term trends affect society in countless ways.

All models require hindcasts to make useful climate forecasts because they enable correction of model biases and estimation of historical skill. Because of the innate complexity of these interacting natural systems, analysis of multiple models from different forecasting systems is a key to better understanding climate variability and its prediction. To support such studies, WGSIP initiated the Climate-system Historical Forecast Project (CHFP), under which historical forecasts, or hindcasts, from many prediction models are permanently archived

Hindcasts test models by seeing how well they can replicate events or trends that have already happened. All models require these hindcasts to make useful climate forecasts because they enable correction of model biases and estimation of historical skill. In addition, they provide an invaluable resource for analyzing and comparing the properties of climate forecast models, assessing the quality of the forecasts themselves, and exploring multimodel forecasting methodologies.

The heaviest rainfall on Earth occurs over tropical oceans. As water vapour condenses to form droplets in the moist tropical air, the water releases substantial amounts of latent heat. This heat produces deep convection currents that propel the resulting clouds to great heights. The accompanying uplift turns into divergent horizontal winds near the tops of these clouds, high in the troposphere.

Upper level divergent winds
Variations in climate alter the patterns of tropical rainfall from year to year. Shifts in upper level divergent winds drive disturbances in atmospheric circulation. These disturbances, known as Rossby or planetary waves, propagate eastward and poleward away from the equator in the winter hemisphere and affect atmospheric circulation in the extratropical regions, outside of the tropics. Such tropical influences on extratropical climate are known as teleconnections.

Because the predictable tropical climate influences the less predictable extratropical climate through teleconnections, tropical predictability could enable skillful predictions of the extratropical climate. These interconnections raise several important and related questions:
- How much do tropical teleconnections contribute to extratropical climate variability?
- How well are extratropical circulation responses to tropical climate variability represented in current climate models?
- To what extent can improvements in the modelling of teleconnections improve the skill of extratropical climate forecasts?

To address these questions, the WGSIP teleconnection initiative is examining how well climate forecast models represent the chain of causation connecting variations in tropical rainfall to planetary wave forcing and propagation and hence to modulation of extratropical climate. A pilot analysis of one model is being extended to many models, drawing on the CHFP archive and other hindcast data sources.

Climate forecast models
Climate forecast models show encouraging levels of skill at predicting seasonal rainfall in all tropical ocean basins during the Northern Hemisphere's winter months. Recent results indicate that teleconnections are more directly connected to tropical rainfall than sea surface temperature, which has often been used to infer teleconnection driving. In addition, climate forecast models show encouraging levels of skill at predicting seasonal rainfall in all tropical ocean basins during the Northern Hemisphere's winter months, especially in the eastern and western Pacific.

Ongoing efforts will determine how well different models represent the sources and propagation of planetary waves driven by tropical rainfall. This will then relate those model attributes to skill in forecasting winter climate variations in the northern extratropics, including the Arctic and North Atlantic oscillations.

Seasonal snow cover strongly influences surface reflectivity and exchanges of heat and moisture between the land and atmosphere across vast Northern Hemisphere regions. These land-atmosphere couplings can influence large-scale atmospheric circulation following horizontal and upward propagation of planetary waves into the stratosphere. Hence, year-to-year variations in snow could potentially serve as a source of predictability for cold-season climate. In addition, the springtime snow cover over the Himalaya-Tibet Plateau region could influence the onset of the Indian summer monsoon.

Whether such predictability can substantially benefit climate forecasts depends on the robustness of snow-climate influences and whether current models can adequately capture them. Many investigations have examined these issues but have come to differing conclusions depending on the methodology and specific observations or model employed.

The WGSIP SNOWGLACE initiative is addressing these issues through coordinated multimodel experiments comparing forecasts that use either realistic or average snow states. Through this initiative, it is hoped to learn more about the effects of snow on surface air temperature and circulation over subseasonal timescales and to assess and improve capabilities for predicting subseasonal to seasonal snow cover.

Although climate models are increasingly realistic, finite spatial resolution, approximations and uncertainties in representing small-scale processes, and other factors limit their accuracy. Each model thus simulates a climate that differs to some extent from that of the real world. When models are initialized from observed climate states, they inevitably drift toward their own biased climate.

Computational "shocks"
When models incorporate physically inconsistent initial atmospheric and ocean states, the resulting computational "shocks" can accelerate the development of errors. These influences can be difficult to separate from the drift signal. These drifts, shocks, and biases can be estimated and removed from climate forecasts through various postprocessing methods informed by the hindcasts for that model.

Model drifts and biases are important in their own right because they contain information about the nature and causes of model imperfections. Even though drifts can be approximately removed, the correction procedures themselves may introduce errors, and drifts and biases still may degrade forecasts by distorting the model representation of the observed climate system.

To provide a multimodel framework for the study of model drifts and biases and their impacts on climate forecasts, WGSIP initiated the Long-Range Forecast Transient Intercomparison Project (LRFTIP). The project has developed a data archive describing drifts in many climate forecast models and seeks to establish a standard set of model diagnostics for characterizing drift behaviour on timescales from days to months to years.

As the science underlying climate forecasts continues to develop, their accuracy can be expected to draw closer to natural limits of predictability. Realizing the potential utility of climate forecasts will require tailoring products for decision-making by different sectors and effectively characterizing and communicating forecast uncertainty. By advancing the science of climate forecasting, WGSIP projects are contributing to this process.

Climate Change: A Natural Hazard

In 2004, the book *Climate Change: A Natural Hazard* was published. The author Australian William Kininmonth demonstrated that the model of the climate system represented by the IPCC is inadequate as a foundation for future planning. In a recent paper Kininmonth has updated the views he expressed in his earlier book and the following are his current views on why the Earth's climate changes.

There are two competing views on how Earth's climate changes. The first, as espoused by the Intergovernmental Panel on Climate Change (IPCC), holds that Earth's temperature is primarily a function of the properties and atmospheric concentrations of greenhouse gases, and how these gases interact with atmospheric radiation. The second, as outlined here, is that Earth's temperature is regulated by atmospheric transport of energy from the tropics to polar regions, and how the rate of transport varies with ocean circulations, particularly the millennial period thermohaline circulation.

The radiation-centric anthropogenic global warming hypothesis has basic conceptual failings. Nowhere is there radiation balance at the top of the atmosphere, an essential requirement of the hypothesis. Moreover, greenhouse gases in the atmosphere emit more radiation than they absorb, thus tending to cool the atmosphere. Adding more CO_2 concentration to the atmosphere will not further warm the atmosphere.

An increase in the concentration of atmospheric CO_2 does enhance the emission of longwave radiation back to the surface to affect the surface energy budget. There is a reduction in the net radiation loss from the surface causing the surface temperature to rise. As a consequence, more energy is exchanged with the atmosphere by way of conduction and evaporation of latent heat. Estimates of the changes in surface energy budget components, drawn from observations and radiation transfer models, point to CO_2 forcing as being an inadequate explanation for the magnitude of the observed recent temperature rise.

Poleward transport of energy by the atmosphere circulation is required to sustain high latitude temperatures against net radiation loss, especially during winter months. The data presented here demonstrate that, as equatorial ocean surface temperatures rise and more energy is exchanged with the atmosphere, wintertime temperatures over high latitudes have risen and the melt period for polar ice has extended. The observed temperature rise over the equatorial region has been amplified over high latitudes of winter because the increased latent energy exchange over the warming tropical oceans is realised over higher latitudes as heat.

Solar energy absorbed in the tropical ocean surface layer follows three primary pathways: warming of ascending cold interior water of the thermohaline circulation; poleward transport in the ocean surface gyres; and return to the atmosphere as heat and latent energy. The inertial and thermal capacities of the ocean greatly exceed those of the atmosphere. Energy available for exchange with the atmosphere is the residual of the absorbed solar radiation after the needs of the overturning circulation and the surface gyres are met.

There is little variation over time in the rate of absorption of solar energy into the tropical ocean layer. Consequently, it is variations in the ocean gyres and the thermohaline circulation that regulate the availability of heat and latent energy for transport to polar regions.

It is estimated that the energy available from the tropical ocean for poleward transport varies by about 8.5 W/m^2 with every 1°C of surface temperature change. This points to a limit to further global warming and debunks the alarmists' scenario of 'runaway global warming'. If the overturning thermohaline circulation were to be stilled, then only about

25 W/m² of energy would be made available to the atmosphere, thus limiting the tropical ocean surface temperature rise to about 3°C.

The changing rate of temperature transport by the atmosphere has a two-fold impact on high latitude climate. Firstly, surface air temperature varies but mainly over winter months. At high summer solar insolation exceeds local emission of longwave radiation to space. Secondly, the duration when ice melt is possible varies. As energy transport is reduced then wintertime temperatures are reduced and local ice melt duration shortens, allowing accumulation of land ice. Conversely, as atmospheric energy transport increases then the ice melt duration lengthens and land ice mass reduces.

In the absence of long observation records the inertial periods of the various ocean gyres and the thermohaline circulations can only be speculative. The multidecadal oscillations in middle latitude temperatures of the North Atlantic and North Pacific oceans point to inertial periods for these gyres of the same multidecadal period. Such oscillations have been found to be important for regional climate variability.

Thermohaline circulation
The overturning period of the thermohaline circulation has been variously estimated as of the order of 1,000 years, a period that is consistent with variations in northern polar temperatures as discerned from Greenland ice cores. The period is also consistent with historical accounts of waxing and waning of civilisations over the recent few thousand years, with civilisations seeming to flourish in the warmer phases.

The annual cycle of heating and cooling over middle and higher latitudes is a powerful stimulus to the inertial modes in the ocean circulation. Oscillations associated with the inertial modes are reflected, through equatorial ocean surface temperature, in climate variability on multi-decadal and multi-centennial timescales.

The contemporary warming trend, as Earth emerges from the Little Ice Age, is consistent with a slowing of the thermohaline circulation. The warming is an order of magnitude greater than what might have been expected from the post-industrial increase in atmospheric CO_2.

Blocking Highs

Blocking patterns occur when centres of high pressure and/or low pressure set up over a region in such a way that they prevent other weather systems from moving through. When the blocking pattern is in place other systems are forced to go around it. "Blocks" are important features well recognised by weather forecasters and early in a weather forecaster's education it is learnt that blocking systems steer the fronts and the lows in the usual chaotic atmospheric circulation.

When an upper-level high-or low-pressure system becomes stuck in place due to a lack of steering currents, it is known as being "cut off". The usual pattern which leads to this is the jet stream retreating poleward, leaving the then cut-off system behind. Whether or not the system is of high- or low-pressure variety dictates the weather that the block causes. Precisely this situation occurred over the southern United States during late spring and early summer of 2007. A cut-off-low system hovering over the region brought unusually cool temperatures and an extraordinary amount of rain to Texas and Oklahoma, and a cut-off-high near the coast of Georgia caused a drought in the Southeast that same year.

If the block is a high, it will usually lead to dry, warm weather as the air beneath it is compressed and warmed, as happened in southeastern Australia in 2006 and 1967 with resultant extreme droughts. Rainy, cooler weather results if the block is a low.

The seasonal cycle of blocking
A review paper in the *Monthly Weather Review* December 2013 by Pool, Risby and McIntosh said that the seasonal cycle of blocking in the Australian region was shown to be associated with major seasonal temperature changes over continental Antarctica and Australia and with minor changes over the surrounding oceans. These changes are superimposed on a favourable background state for blocking in the region resulting from a conjunction of physical influences. These include the geographical configuration and topography of the Australian and Antarctic continents and the positive west to east gradient of sea surface temperature in the Indo-Australian sector of the Southern Ocean. Blocking is represented by a blocking index (BI) developed by the Australian Bureau of Meteorology.

The BI has a marked seasonal cycle that reflects seasonal changes in the strength of the westerly winds in the mid-troposphere at selected latitudes. Significant correlations between the BI at Australian longitudes and rainfall have been demonstrated in southern and central Australia for the austral autumn, winter, and spring. Patchy positive correlations are evident in the south during summer but significant negative correlations are apparent in the central tropical north. By decomposing the rainfall into its contributions from identifiable synoptic types during the April–October growing season, it was shown that the high correlation between blocking and rainfall in southern Australia is explained by the component of rainfall associated with cut-off lows. These systems form the cyclonic components of blocking dipoles. In contrast, there is no significant correlation between the BI and rainfall from Southern Ocean fronts.

Blocking as a "driver"

Blocking serves as an important "driver" of Australian weather and climate by influencing the suppression of rainfall in the regions dominated by the anticyclonic component while contributing to enhanced rainfall in the regions where the cyclonic components are located. An association of blocking with rainfall poses a paradox because periods of blocking often accompany extended dry spells in southern Australia, including Tasmania. By way of contrast, significant rainfall events are also known to occur over southern, eastern and inland Australia when high pressure systems dominate to the south or southeast of the continent. The explanation lies in the interactive relationship between the extensive high-latitude anticyclonic component of blocking on the one hand and the cutting off or isolation of a relatively small cyclonic component equatorward of the high.

The resulting cut-off lows are known to be major contributors to rainfall events in agricultural areas of southern Australia and to runoff in Australia's major river catchments. In blocking episodes, the Southern Ocean cyclones on the poleward side of the highs tend to be steered to higher latitudes and in exceptional cases, have been observed to cross the circumpolar trough and produce precipitation over the high plateau of Antarctica .

Blocking of atmospheric systems near the surface of the Earth occurs when a well-established poleward high pressure system lies near or within the path of the advancing storm system. The thicker the cold air mass is, the more effectively it can block an invading milder air mass. The depth of the cold air mass is normally shallower than the mountain barrier which created the cold air damming.

In the middle latitudes of the Northern Hemisphere, areas on the eastern side of blocking anticyclones or under the influence of flows from colder continental interiors related to blocks, experience severe winters, a phenomenon which has been known since the discovery of the North Atlantic Oscillation in the 1840s. These blocking patterns also have a tendency to produce mild conditions at very high latitudes, at least in those regions exposed to anomalous flow from the ocean as in Greenland and Beringia, or from chinook winds as in Interior Alaska.

Such cold winters over the contiguous United States and southern Canada as 1911/12, 1935/36, 1977/78 and 1978/79 resulted from blocks in the Gulf of Alaska or to the east of the Mackenzie Mountains directing very cold Arctic air with a long trajectory as far as the American South, as did the Western cold waves of 1889/90 and January 1950. In Northern and Western Europe, cold winters such as 1683/84, 1739/40, 1794/95, 1829/30, 1894/95, 1916/17, 1941/42, February 1947 and 1962/63 were almost always associated with high-latitude Atlantic blocking and an equatorward shift of the polar jet stream to Portugal and even Morocco.

Over Central Asia, unusually cold winters like 1899/1900, 1929/30 and 1930/31, 1944/45, 1954/55 and 1968/69 were associated with blocking near the Ural Mountains extending the Siberian High westwards to push the very cold air from the Siberian "cold pole" outward towards the Aral and Caspian Seas. Unlike other mid-latitude regions of the Northern Hemisphere, however, cold winters in Europe (e.g. 1916/17, 1962/63) are often very mild over Central Asia, which can gain warm air advection from subtropical cyclones pushed to the south under negative NAO conditions.

Climate forecasts - how good are they?

Scientists have been making projections of future global warming using climate models of increasing complexity for the past four decades. These models, driven by atmospheric physics and biogeochemistry, play an important role in our understanding of the Earth's climate and how it will likely change in the future. The *CarbonBrief* website has collected prominent climate model projections since 1973 to see how well they project both past and future global temperatures.

The following summary of the finding of *CarbonBrief* shows that while some models projected less warming than we've experienced and some projected more, all showed surface temperature increases between 1970 and 2016 that were not too far off from what actually occurred, particularly when differences in assumed future emissions are taken into account.

While climate model projections of the past benefit from knowledge of atmospheric greenhouse gas concentrations, volcanic eruptions and other radiative forcings affecting the Earth's climate, casting forward into the future is understandably more uncertain. Climate models can be evaluated both on their ability to hindcast past temperatures and forecast future ones. Hindcasts are testing models against past temperatures, and they are useful because they can control for radiative forcings. Forecasts are useful because models cannot be implicitly tuned to be similar to observations. Climate models are not fit to historical temperatures, but modellers do have some knowledge of observations that can inform their choice of model parameterisations, such as cloud physics and aerosol effects.

In the examples below, climate model projections published between 1973 and 2013 are compared with observed temperatures from five different organizations. The models used in the projections vary in complexity, from simple energy balance models to fully-coupled Earth System Models. These model/observation comparisons use a baseline period of 1970-1990 to align observations and models during the early years of the analysis, which shows how temperatures have evolved over time more clearly.

Sawyer, 1973
One of the first projections of future warming came from John Sawyer at the UK's Met Office in 1973. In a paper published in *Nature* in 1973,

he hypothesised that the world would warm 0.6°C between 1969 and 2000, and that atmospheric CO_2 would increase by 25%. Sawyer argued for a climate sensitivity – how much long-term warming will occur per doubling of atmospheric CO_2 levels – of 2.4°C, which is not too far off the best estimate of 3°C used by the IPCC today. Unlike the other projections examined in this article, Sawyer did not provide an estimated warming for each year, just an expected 2000 value. His warming estimate of 0.6°C was very close to the observed warming over that period that was between 0.51°C and 0.56°C. However he slightly overestimated the year 2000's atmospheric CO_2 concentrations, assuming that they would be 375-400ppm, compared to the actual value of 370ppm.

Broecker, 1975

The first available projection of future temperatures due to global warming appeared in an article in *Science* in 1975 published by Columbia University scientist Prof. Wally Broecker. Broecker used a simple energy balance model to estimate (Scenario A) what would happen to the Earth's temperature if atmospheric CO_2 continued to increase rapidly after 1975. Broecker's projected warming was reasonably close to observations for a few decades, but recently has been considerably higher. This is mostly due to Broecker overestimating how CO_2 emissions and atmospheric concentrations would increase after his article was published. He was fairly accurate up to 2000, predicting 373ppm of CO_2, compared to actual Mauna Loa observations of 370ppm. In 2016, however, he estimated that CO_2 would be 424ppm, whereas only 404 pm has been observed.

Broecker also did not take other greenhouse gases into account in his model. However, as the warming impact from methane, nitrous oxide and halocarbons has been largely cancelled out by the overall cooling influence of aerosols since 1970, this does not make that large a difference (though estimates of aerosol forcings have large uncertainties). As with Sawyer, Broecker used an equilibrium climate sensitivity of 2.4°C per doubling of CO_2. Broecker assumed that the Earth instantly warms up to match atmospheric CO_2, while modern models account for the lag between how quickly the atmosphere and oceans warm up. The slower heat uptake by the oceans is often referred to as the "thermal inertia" of the climate system.

Scenario B assumed a gradual slowdown in CO_2 emissions, but had concentrations of 401ppm in 2016 that were pretty close to the 404ppm observed. However, scenario B assumed the continued growth of emissions of various halocarbons that are powerful greenhouse gases, but were subsequently restricted under the Montreal Protocol of 1987. Scenario C had emissions going to near-zero after the year 2000.

Of the three, scenario B was closest to actual radiative forcing, though still about 10% too high. Hansen et al. also used a model with a climate sensitivity of 4.2°C per doubling CO_2 – on the high end of most modern climate models. Due to the combination of these factors, scenario B projected a rate of warming between 1970 and 2016 that was approximately 30% higher than what has been observed.

Broecker made his projections at a time when many scientists widely thought that the observations showed a modest cooling of the Earth. He began his article by presciently stating that "a strong case can be made that the present cooling trend will, within a decade or so, give way to a pronounced warming induced by CO_2".

Hansen et al., 1981

NASA's Dr James Hansen and colleagues published a paper in 1981 that also used a simple energy balance model to project future warming, but accounted for thermal inertia due to ocean heat uptake. They assumed a climate sensitivity of 2.8°C per doubling CO_2, but also looked at a range of 1.4-5.6°C per doubling. Hansen and his colleagues presented a number of different scenarios, varying future emissions and climate sensitivity. The "fast-growth" scenario, is where CO_2 emissions increase by 4% annually after 1981, and a slow-growth scenario where emissions increase by 2% annually. The fast-growth scenario somewhat overestimates current emissions, but when combined with a slightly lower climate sensitivity it provides an estimate of early-2000s warming close to observed values. The overall rate of warming between 1970 and 2016 projected by Hansen et al. in 1981 in the fast-growth scenario has been about 20% lower than observations.

Hansen et al., 1988

The paper published by Hansen and colleagues in 1988 represented one of the first modern climate models. It divided the world into discrete grid cells of eight degrees latitude by 10 degrees longitude, with nine vertical layers of the atmosphere. It included aerosols, various greenhouse gases in addition to CO_2, and basic cloud dynamics. Hansen et al. presented three different scenarios associated with different future greenhouse gas emissions.

IPCC First Assessment Report, 1990
The IPCC's First Assessment Report (FAR) in 1990 featured relatively simple energy balance/upwelling diffusion ocean models to estimate changes in global air temperatures. Their featured business-as-usual (BAU) scenario assumed rapid growth of atmospheric CO_2, reaching 418ppm CO_2 in 2016, compared to 404ppm in observations. The FAR also assumed continued growth of atmospheric halocarbon concentrations much faster than has actually occurred. The FAR gave a best estimate of climate sensitivity as 2.5°C warming for doubled CO_2, with a range of 1.5-4.5°C.

Despite a best estimate of climate sensitivity a little lower than the 3°C used today, the FAR overestimated the rate of warming between 1970 and 2016 by around 17% in their BAU scenario, showing 1°C warming over that period vs 0.85°C observed. This is mostly due to the projection of much higher atmospheric CO_2 concentrations than has actually occurred.

IPCC Second Assessment Report, 1995
The IPCC's Second Assessment Report (SAR) only published readily-available projections from 1990 onward. They used a climate sensitivity of 2.5°C, with a range of 1.5-4.5°C. Their mid-range emissions scenario, "IS92a", projected CO_2 levels of 405ppm in 2016, nearly identical to observed concentrations. SAR also included much better treatment of anthropogenic aerosols, which have a cooling effect on the climate.

SAR's projections ended up being notably lower than observations, warming about 28% more slowly over the period from 1990 to 2016. This was likely due to a combination of two factors: a lower climate sensitivity than found in modern estimates (2.5°C vs. 3°C) and an overestimate of the radiative forcing of CO_2 (4.37 W/m^2 versus 3.7 used in the subsequent IPCC report and still used today).

IPCC Third Assessment Report, 2001
The IPCC Third Assessment Report (TAR) relied on atmosphere-ocean general circulation models (GCMs) from seven different modelling groups. They also introduced a new set of socioeconomic emission scenarios, called SRES, which included four different future emission trajectories.

CarbonBrief examined an A2 scenario, though all have fairly similar emissions and warming trajectories up to 2020. The A2 scenario projected a 2016 atmospheric CO_2 concentration of 406 ppm, nearly the same as what was observed. The SRES scenarios were from 2000 onward, with models prior to the year 2000 using estimated historical forcings.

TAR's headline projection used a simple climate model that was configured to match the average outputs of seven more sophisticated GCMs, as no specific multimodel average was published in TAR and data for individual model runs are not readily available. It has a climate sensitivity of 2.8°C per doubling CO_2, with a range of 1.5-4.5°C. The rate of warming between 1970 and 2016 in the TAR was about 14% lower than what has actually been observed.

IPCC Fourth Assessment Report, 2007

The IPCC's Fourth Assessment Report (AR4) featured models with significantly improved atmospheric dynamics and model resolution. It made greater use of Earth System Models – which incorporate the biogeochemistry of carbon cycles – as well as improved simulations of land surface and ice processes. AR4 used the same SRES scenarios as the TAR, with historical emissions and atmospheric concentrations up to the year 2000 and projections thereafter. Models used in AR4 had a mean climate sensitivity of 3.26°C, with a range of 2.1°C to 4.4°C.

The model runs for the A1B scenario (which is the only scenario with model runs readily available), though its 2016 CO_2 concentrations are nearly identical to those of the A2 scenario. AR4 projections between 1970 and 2016 show warming quite close to observations, only 8% higher.

IPCC Fifth Assessment Report, 2013

The most recent IPCC report – the Fifth Assessment (AR5) – featured additional refinements on climate models, as well as a modest reduction in future model uncertainty compared to AR4. The climate models in the latest IPCC report were part of the Coupled Model Intercomparison Project 5 (CMIP5), where dozens of different modelling groups all around the world ran climate models using the same set of inputs and scenarios.

AR5 introduced a new set of future greenhouse gas concentration scenarios, known as the Representative Concentration Pathways (RCPs). These have future projections from 2006 onwards, with historical data prior to 2006.

Comparing these models with observations can be a somewhat tricky exercise. The most often used fields from climate models are global surface air temperatures. However, observed temperatures come from surface air temperatures over land and sea surface temperatures over the ocean. To account for this, more recently, researchers have created blended model fields, which include sea surface temperatures over the oceans and surface air temperatures over land, in order to match what is actually measured in the observations. These blended fields show slightly less warming than global surface air temperatures, as models have the air over the ocean warming faster than sea surface temperatures in recent years.

Global surface air temperatures in CMIP5 models have warmed about 16% faster than observations since 1970. About 40% of this difference is due to air temperatures over the ocean warming faster than sea surface temperatures in the models; blended model fields only show warming 9% faster than observations.

A paper in *Nature* in 2017 by Iselin Medhaug and colleagues suggests that the remainder of the divergence can be accounted for by a combination of short-term natural variability (mainly in the Pacific Ocean), small volcanoes and lower-than-expected solar output that was not included in models in their post-2005 projections.

Below is a summary of all the models *CarbonBrief* looked at. The table below shows the difference in the rate of warming between each model or set of models and NASA's temperature observations. All the observational temperature records are fairly similar, but NASA's is among the group that includes more complete global coverage in recent years and is thus more directly comparable to climate model data.

Projecting future warming

Model	Difference in 1970-2016 mean warming rate vs. Obs
Broecker 1975	+30%
Hansen et al 1981	-20%
Hansen et al 1988	+30%
IPCC 1st Report, 1990	+17%
IPCC 2nd Report, 1995	-28%*
IPCC 3rd Report, 2001	-14%
IPCC 4th Report, 2007	+8%
IPCC 5th Report, 2013	+16% (+9%)#

* SAR trend differences are calculated over the period from 1990-2016, as estimates prior to 1990 are not readily available.
\# Differences in parenthesis based on blended model land/ocean fields.

Climate models published since 1973, as reviewed by *CarbonBrief*, have generally been quite skillful in projecting future warming. While some were too low and some too high, they all show outcomes reasonably close to what has actually occurred, especially when discrepancies between predicted and actual CO_2 concentrations and other climate forcings are taken into account. However, models are far from perfect and will continue to be improved over time. They also show a fairly large range of future warming that cannot easily be narrowed using just the changes in climate that we have observed. Nevertheless, the close match between projected and observed warming since 1970 suggests that estimates of future warming may prove similarly accurate.

However, it is important to note than in almost all of the above forecasts/models the major input to forecasting future temperatures is the role of greenhouse gas and only minimal importance is given to aspects of the climate that are not human induced. These include changes in the solar output, astronomical affects, volcanic activity, and change in the oceans. In addition, there are other aspects of climate scene such as sea level variations, tidal variations, and earthquakes which are not human-induced. While most of these factors are small for most time scales, some like the absence of sunspots which occurred during the "Maunder Minimum" (1650-1715) can, if history has anything to tell us, be significant.

4

The Sun

"The sun pays no heed to human committees no matter how powerful they think they are."

This phrase with a small addition is given in a NASA release on "New solar cycle prediction", 29 May 2009

Solar activity and spotless days

The NASA solar physics website, and other websites such as the Royal Observatory of Belgium, include information on sunspot numbers, spotless days, the 'Maunder Minimum' and sunspot cycle predictions.

A sunspot is a relatively dark, sharply defined region on the solar disc – marked by an umbra, dark area, which is 2000 degrees cooler than the effective photospheric temperature. The average diameter of a sunspot is 4000 km, but they can exceed 200,000km.

The sunspot index is updated monthly and is available from 1749. The last time the value was much above 200 was in August 1990.

Solar observers have noticed that since mid-2016, the Sun has occasionally been devoid of sunspots. These spotless disks will gradually become a familiar feature as the solar cycle is heading for its next minimum, currently expected by 2020 and probably has already started. The number of spotless days can vary significantly from one solar cycle transit to another. For example, during the previous minimum solar cycle 24 (around 2008), 817 spotless days were recorded, whereas the minimum period leading into solar cycle 23 (around 1996) counted only 309 such blemishless days.

Top 25 years with most number of spotless days since 1849

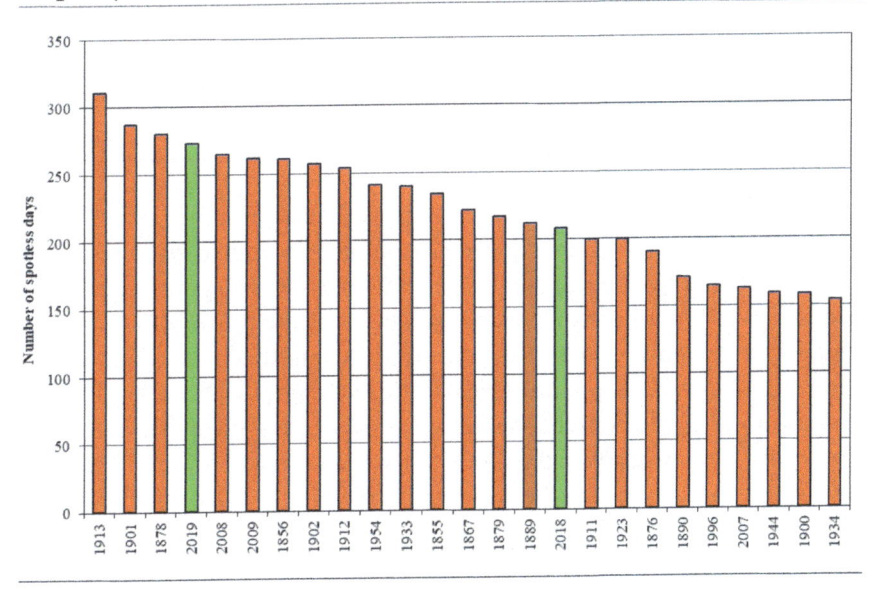

The current solar cycle 24 will gradually give way to the new solar cycle 25, and several consecutive days and even periods of 30 or more consecutive days without sunspots will become the norm. The Belgium SILSO website has created a "Spotless Days page". This page contains graphs and tables on the accumulated number of spotless days, stretches of spotless days, and comparisons to other solar cycles.

The previous minimum (solar cycle 24) surprised many solar scientists and solar observers by being the deepest in nearly 90 years. Will the upcoming solar cycle minimum show as many spotless days, or will solar cycle 25 take off much faster than expected? The "Spotless Days page" provides a front-row seat on the current status of the solar cycle minimum and the number of spotless days. Enjoy!

Since 1849, there have been 114 years (including 2019) with at least one spotless day. The chart below shows the 25 years with the highest number of spotless days. 1913 had 311 spotless days, 1901 had 287 spotless days, 1878 had 280 spotless days, while last year 2019 which ranks fourth since 1849 had 273 spotless days.

Periods with spotless days (≥ 30 days) since 1849

Rank	SC	Begin	End	Days	Rank	SC	Begin	End	Days	Rank	SC	Begin	End	Days
1	15	08 Apr 1913	08 Jul 1913	92	10	25	14 Nov 2019	23 Dec 2019	40	15	11	20 Apr 1867	24 May 1867	35
2	14	11 Mar 1901	18 May 1901	69	10	14	26 Nov 1901	04 Jan 1902	40	16	24	31 Jul 2009	31 Aug 2009	32
3	12	16 Feb 1879	10 Apr 1879	54	11	16	06 Jan 1924	13 Feb 1924	39	17	24	21 Jul 2008	20 Aug 2008	31
4	14	17 Mar 1902	04 May 1902	49	11	15	15 Jul 1913	22 Aug 1913	39	17	17	12 Dec 1933	11 Jan 1934	31
4	10	14 Aug 1855	01 Oct 1855	49	11	12	29 Dec 1866	04 Feb 1867	38	17	15	12 Jul 1912	11 Aug 1912	31
5	12	04 Apr 1878	20 May 1878	47	12	10	17 Dec 1855	18 Jan 1856	38	17	14	25 Nov 1900	25 Dec 1900	31
6	14	16 Jan 1902	01 Mar 1902	45	13	12	17 May 1876	22 Jun 1876	37	18	19	03 Jun 1954	02 Jul 1954	30
6	12	14 Sep 1878	28 Oct 1878	45	13	12	27 Jul 1878	01 Sep 1878	37	18	17	13 Jul 1933	11 Aug 1933	30
7	15	21 Jan 1912	03 Mar 1912	43	14	18	18 Apr 1944	23 May 1944	36	18	14	08 Jul 1902	06 Aug 1902	30
8	23	13 Sep 1996	24 Oct 1996	42	14	17	05 Nov 1933	10 Dec 1933	36					
9	10	22 Apr 1856	01 Jun 1856	41	15	25	02 Feb 2020	07 Mar 2020	35					

The table above shows all periods with 30 or more consecutive spotless days. The 40 days period from 14 November 2019 until 23 December 2019 is one of the longer ones since the beginning of daily solar observations in 1849, making it all the way into the top 10. A slightly longer period in recent history occurred during the solar cycles 22-23 transition, from 13 September 1996 until 24 October 1996, when the Sun was spotless for 42 consecutive days. One of the longest spotless periods (since 1818) is probably from 24 October 1822 until 12 March 1823 (140 days), but unfortunately, the series are broken on 29 December 1822 as no observation was available for that day.

The Maunder Minimum

The 'Maunder Minimum' is the name given to the period from 1645 to 1715 when the number of sunspots – 'storms' on the sun – became almost zero. The period is named after the solar astronomer Edward Walter Maunder (1851-1928), who was working at The Royal Observatory at Greenwich when he discovered the dearth of sunspots during this period.

During one 30-year period within the Maunder Minimum there were only about 50 sunspots compared with a more typical 40,000. Maunder was a driving force in the foundation of the British Astronomical Association and a Fellow of the Royal Astronomical Society. The sun was well observed during the period of the Maunder Minimum and this lack of sunspots is well documented. This period of solar inactivity corresponded to a climatic period called the 'Little Ice Age' when in Europe rivers that were normally ice-free, froze and snow fields remained at low altitudes throughout the year. There is evidence the sun had similar periods of inactivity during the years 1100-1250 and 1460-1550. Sunspots generally follow a cycle of about 11 years, but cycles have varied from eight to 15 years.

The connection between solar activity and the earth's climate is an area of ongoing and sometimes controversial research. Time will tell whether the sun will once again go into another 'Maunder Minimum' within the lifetime of the present generation, with very many spotless days. If this happens we're likely to have a much colder climate for a few decades.

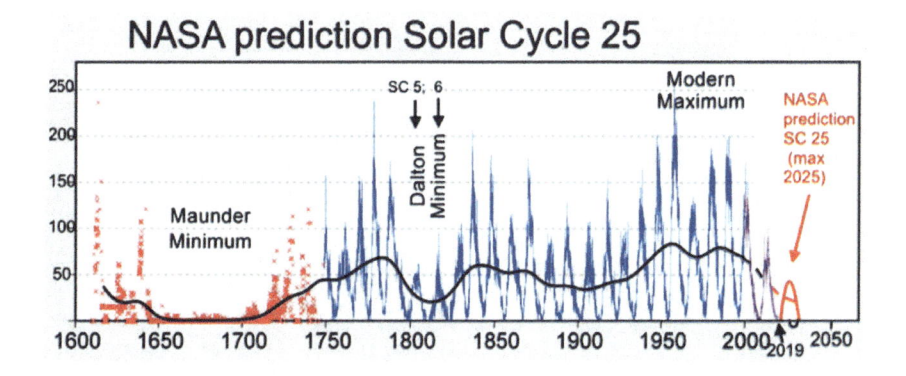

The Sun 117

The Maunder Butterfly

The butterfly diagram, first drawn in 1904 is one of the most powerful representations of the inner workings of the Sun. It describes the cyclic restructuring of the dynamo-driven magnetic fields, as well as the birth of strong field regions, dominating the activity of the Sun. The solar astronomers Annie and Walter Maunder were jointly responsible for its discovery. Many years later Annie Maunder wrote in a letter : "We made this diagram in a week of evenings, one dictating and the other ruling these little lines that show the spots in any given latitude at any time in the sunspot period. Every half hour or so we exchanged the dictating and ruling according as voice or hand got tired… This diagram has three desiccated butterflies on it; it originally had two only, but we added a third cycle when it had gone its 11-12 years complete course." For Annie and Walter Maunder, the discovery of the butterfly diagram was the culmination of decades of work on the observation, cataloguing and analysis of sunspots, which they carried out at the Royal Observatory at Greenwich and at their home.

On 21 May 1940, the Maunders' original butterfly was mailed from London to her friend Stephen Ionides in the United States, to save it from possible destruction during the Blitz. It was then given on indefinite loan to Walter Orr Roberts of Harvard College Observatory (renamed the High Altitude Observatory in 1946 and now part of NCAR in Boulder, Colorado), where it is on display. (Bogdan 2000)

The original Butterfly diagram, covering the period 1877 – 1902, as published by E W Maunder is shown below.

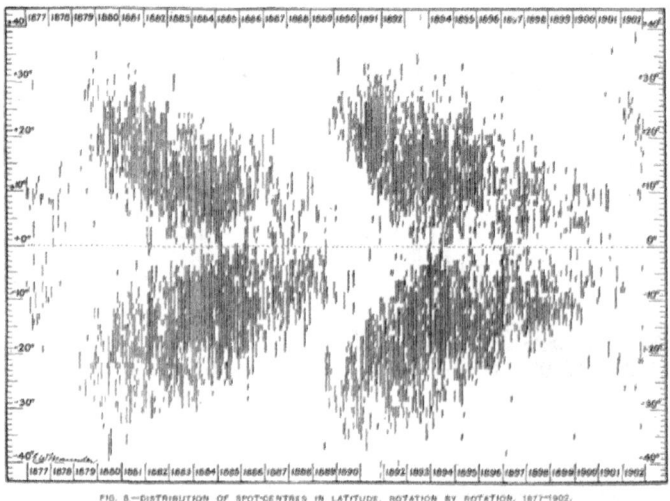

Sunspot numbers 1700 - present

A graph of the sunspot numbers from 1700 to date is shown below. The graph is from a website of the Royal Belgium Observatory.

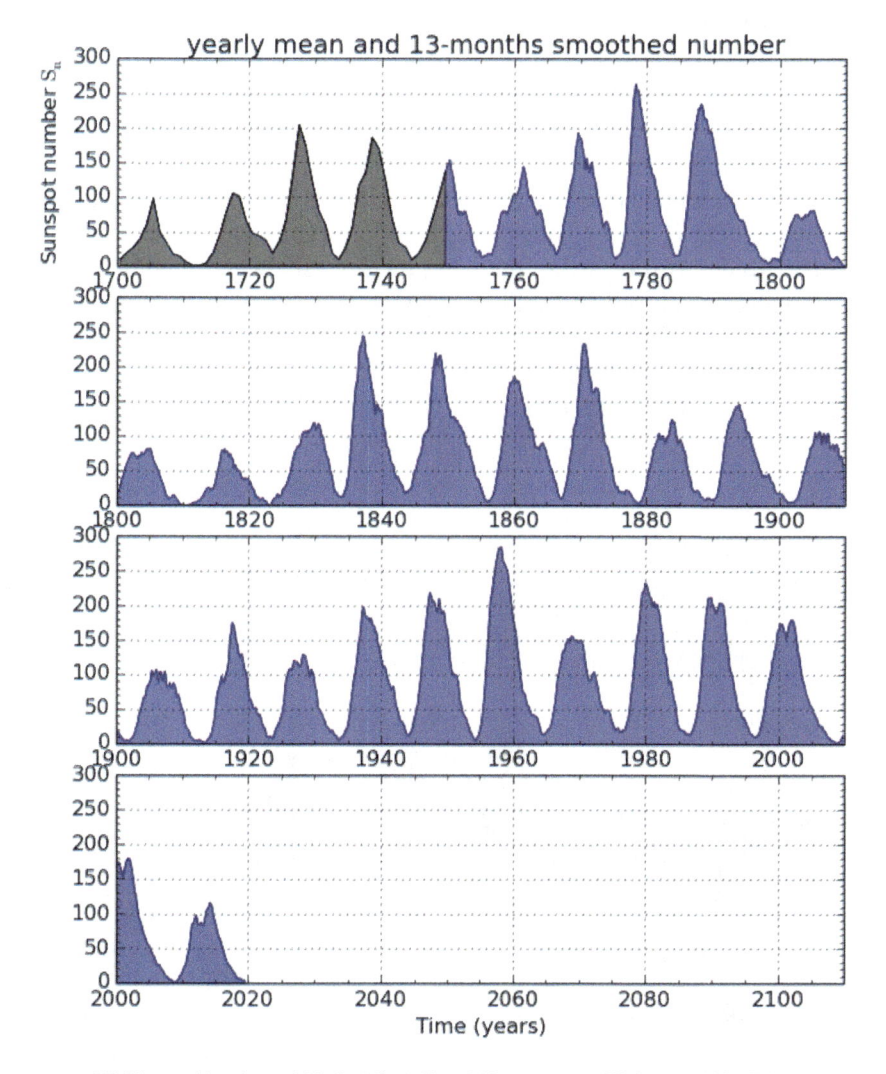

SILSO graphics (http://sidc.be/silso) Royal Observatory of Belgium 2020 February 1

The Sun 119

Sunspot numbers 1950 - present

The "World Data Center for the Production, Preservation and Dissemination of the International Sunspot Number" (WDC-SILSO) is an activity of the Operational Directorate "Solar Physics and Space Weather" also known internationally as the Solar Influences Data analysis Center (SIDC). The SIDC is a department of the Royal Observatory of Belgium. Its mission is to preserve, develop and diffuse the knowledge of the long-term variations of solar activity, as a reference input to studies of the solar cycle mechanism and of the solar forcing on the Earth's climate.

The work realized at WDC-SILSO is under supervision from the International Astronomical Union (IAU), the International Union of Radio Science (URSI), and the International Association of Geomagnetism (IAGA). They provide endorsement of the World Data Center SILSO, with regard to the scientific usefulness and quality of the sunspot data produced and archived by this data centre.

The charts below (Source: SILSO data/image, Royal Observatory of Belgium, Brussels) show the sunspots numbers for three periods: 1955 to date, 2007 to date and 2016 to date.

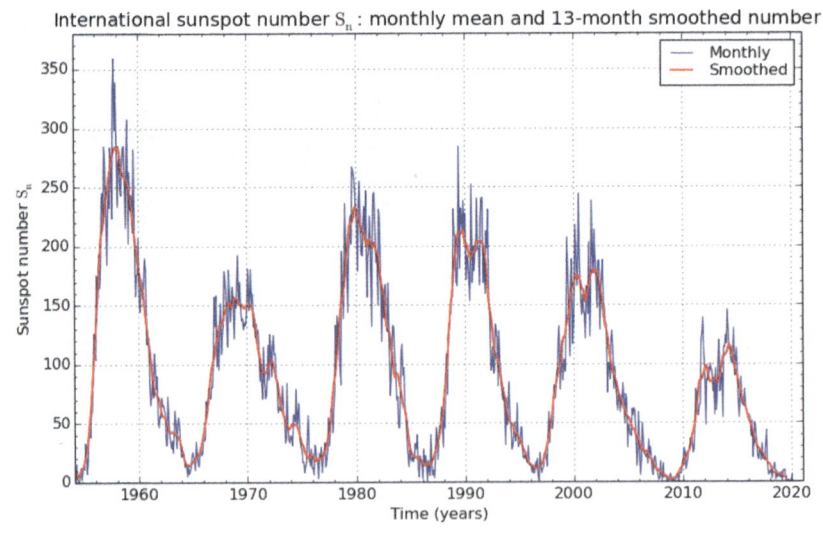

International sunspot number S_n : monthly mean and 13-month smoothed number

SILSO graphics (http://sidc.be/silso) Royal Observatory of Belgium 2020 February 1

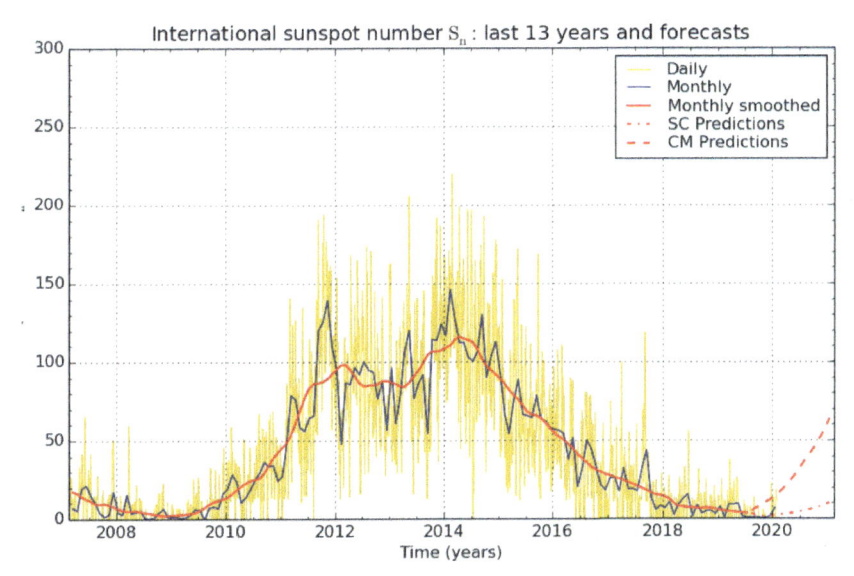

International sunspot number S_n: last 13 years and forecasts

Forecast: Standard Curves method

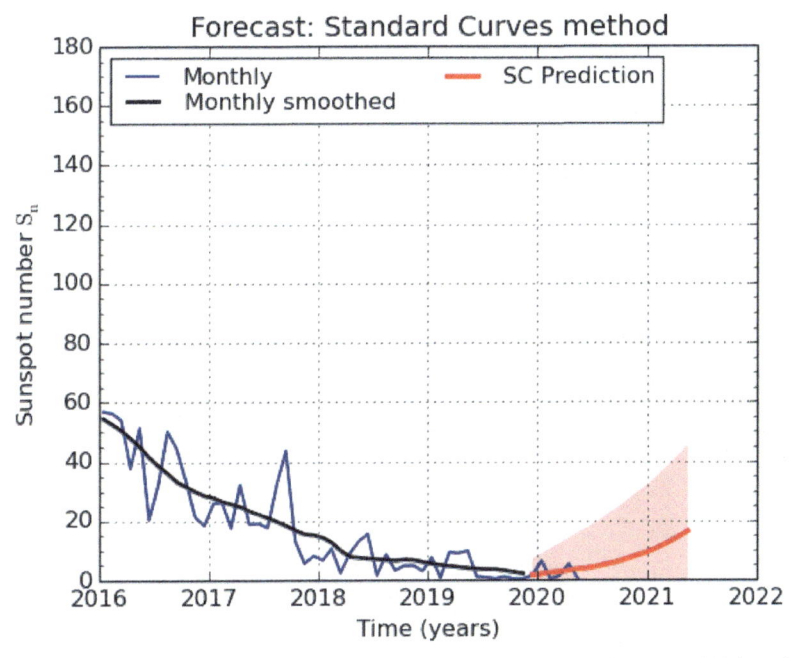

SILSO graphics (http://sidc.be/silso) Royal Observatory of Belgium 2020 June 1

The Sun 121

5
Astronomical causes of climate change

"The laws of physics represent something of beauty in the universe. If you believe in God, then God is responsible for that symmetry and beauty."

Professor Jeff Forshaw, writing in the book *The Quantum Universe: Everything that can happen does happen* by Brian Cox and Jeff Forshaw, Allen Lane, UK, 2011.

Milanković cycles

Milutin Milanković (1879 – 1958) was a Serbian mathematician, astronomer, climatologist, geophysicist, civil engineer and popularizer of science. *Wikipedia* has an excellent description of his contribution to global science. At NASA, in their edition of "On the Shoulders of Giants", Milanković has been ranked among the top fifteen minds of all time in the field of earth sciences.

The following are extracts from *Wikipedia*:

Milanković gave two fundamental contributions to global science. The first contribution is the "Canon of the Earth's Insolation", which characterizes the climates of all the planets of the Solar system. The second contribution is the explanation of Earth's long-term climate changes caused by changes in the position of the Earth in comparison to the Sun, now known as Milanković cycles. This explained the ice ages occurring in the geological past of the Earth, as well as the climate changes on the Earth which can be expected in the future.

Milutin Milanković was born in the village of Dalj, a settlement on the banks of the Danube in what was then part of the Austro-Hungarian Empire (present day Croatia). Milutin and his twin sister were the oldest of seven children. Their father was a merchant, landlord, and a local politician who died when Milutin was eight. As a result, Milutin and his siblings were raised by his mother, grandmother, and an uncle. As his health was fickle, Milutin received his elementary education at home (in "the classroom without walls"), learning from his father Milan, private teachers, and from numerous relatives and friends of the family, some of whom were renowned philosophers, inventors, and poets. He attended secondary school in nearby Osijek, completing it in 1896.

In October 1896, at the age of seventeen, he moved to Vienna to study Civil Engineering at the Vienna University of Technology and graduated in 1902 with the best marks. After graduating and spending his obligatory year in military service, Milanković borrowed money from an uncle to pay for additional schooling at the Technical University in engineering. At age twenty-five, his PhD thesis was entitled *Contribution to the Theory of Pressure Curves* and its implementation allowed assessment of pressure curves' shape and properties when continuous pressure is applied, which is very useful in bridge, cupola and abutment construction. After graduation he then worked for an engineering firm in Vienna, using his knowledge to design structures.

Milanković continued to practice civil engineering in Vienna until 1 October 1909 when he was offered the chair of applied mathematics (rational, celestial mechanics, and theoretical physics) at the University of Belgrade. Though he continued to pursue his investigations of various problems pertaining to the application of reinforced concrete, he decided to concentrate on fundamental research. While studying the works of the contemporaneous climatologist Julius von Hann, Milanković noticed a significant issue, which became one of the major objects of his scientific research: a mystery ice age. The idea of possible astronomically-related climate changes was first considered by astronomers (John Herschel, 1792-1871) and then postulated by geologists (Louis Agassiz, 1807-1873). In parallel, there were also several attempts to explain the climate change by the influence of astronomical forces (the most comprehensive of them was the theory put forward by James Croll in the 1860s).

The works of Joseph Adhemar
Milanković studied the works of Joseph Adhemar whose pioneering theory on the astronomical origins of ice ages were formally rejected by his contemporaries and James Croll whose work was effectively forgotten about even after acceptance by contemporaries such as Charles Darwin. Despite having valuable data on the distribution of ice ages on Alps, climatologists and geologists could not discover the basic causes – that is, the different insolations of the Earth during past ages remained beyond the scope of these sciences. But Milanković decided to follow their path and attempt correctly to calculate the magnitude of such influences.

Milanković sought the solution of these complex problems in the field of spherical geometry, celestial mechanics, and theoretical physics. He began working on it in 1912, after he had realized that *"most of meteorology is nothing but a collection of innumerable empirical findings, mainly numerical data, with traces of physics used to explain some of them... Mathematics was even less applied, nothing more than elementary calculus... Advanced mathematics had no role ..."* His first work described the present climate on Earth and how the Sun's rays determine the temperature on Earth's surface after passing through the atmosphere. He published the first paper on the subject entitled *Contribution to the mathematical theory of climate* in Belgrade on 5 April 1912. His next paper was entitled *Distribution of the sun radiation on the earth's surface* and was published on 5 June 1913. He correctly calculated the intensity of insolation and developed a mathematical theory describing

Earth's climate zones. His aim was an integral, mathematically accurate theory which connects thermal regimes of the planets to their movement around the Sun. He wrote: "...such a theory would enable us to go beyond the range of direct observations, not only in space, but also in time... It would allow reconstruction of the Earth's climate, and also its predictions, as well as give us the first reliable data about the climate conditions on other planets." Then he tried to find a mathematical model of a cosmic mechanism to describe the Earth's climatic and geological history. He published a paper on the subject entitled *About the issue of the astronomical theory of ice ages* in 1914. But the cosmic mechanism was not an easy problem, and Milanković took three decades to develop an astronomical theory.

At the same time, the July Crisis between the Austro-Hungarian empire and Serbia broke and for the duration of the war Milanković was in prison like facilities which are detailed in *Wikipedia*.

"The heavy iron door closed behind me....I sat on my bed, looked around the room and started to take in my new social circumstances... In my hand luggage which I brought with me were my already printed or only started works on my cosmic problem; there was even some blank paper. I looked over my works, took my faithful ink pen and started to write and calculate... When after midnight I looked around in the room, I needed some time to realize where I was. The small room seemed to me like an accommodation for one night during my voyage in the Universe."

Milanković spent almost the entire war using mathematical methods to study the current climate of inner planets of the solar system. He formulated a precise, numerical climatological model with the capacity for reconstruction of the past and prediction of the future, and established the astronomical theory of climate as a generalized mathematical theory of insolation. When these most important problems of the theory were solved, and a firm foundation for further work built, Milanković finished a book which was published in 1920, by the Gauthier-Villars in Paris under the title *Mathematical Theory of Heat Phenomena Produced by Solar Radiation*. Immediately after the publication of this book in 1920, meteorologists recognized it as a significant contribution to the study of contemporary climate.

Orbital variations and ice age cycles

Milanković's works on astronomical explanations of ice ages, especially his curve of insolation for the past 130,000 years, received support from the climatologist Wladimir Köppen and from the geophysicist Alfred Wegener. Köppen noted the usefulness of Milanković's theory for paleoclimatological researchers. Milanković received a letter in September 1922 from Köppen, who asked him to expand his studies from 130,000 years to 600,000 years. They agreed that summer insolation is a crucial factor for climate. After developing the mathematical machinery enabling him to calculate the insolation in any given geographical latitude and for any annual season, Milanković was ready to start the realization of the mathematical description of climate of the Earth in the past. Milanković spent 100 days doing the calculations and prepared a graph of solar radiation changes at geographical latitudes of 55°, 60° and 65° north for the past 650,000 years. These curves showed the variations in insolation which correlated with the series of ice ages. Köppen felt that Milanković's theoretical approach to solar energy was a logical approach to the problem. His solar curve was introduced in a work entitled *Climates of the geological past*, published by Wladimir Köppen and his son-in-law Alfred Wegener in 1924.

Milanković put the sun at the centre of his theory, as the only source of heat and light in the solar system. He considered three cyclical movements of the Earth: eccentricity (100,000-year cycle – Johannes Kepler, 1609); axial tilt (41,000-year cycle – from 22.1° to 24.5° (presently, the Earth's tilt is 23.5°) – Ludwig Pilgrim, 1904); and precession (23,000-year cycle – Hipparchus, 130 BC). Each cycle works on a different time-scale and each affects the amount of solar energy received by the planets. Such changes in the geometry of an orbit lead to the changes in the insolation – the quantity of heat received by any spot at the surface of a planet. These orbital variations, which are influenced by gravity of the Moon, Sun, Jupiter, and Saturn, form the basis of the Milanković cycle. His original contribution to celestial mechanics is called Milanković's system of vector elements of planetary orbits.

In the period from 1935 to 1938 Milanković calculated that ice cover depended on changes in insolation. He succeeded in defining the mathematical relationship between summer insolation and the altitude of the snow line. In this way he defined the increase of snow which would occur as a consequence of any given change in summer insolation. He published his results in the study *New Results of the Astronomic Theory of Climate Changes* in 1938. He showed a graph presenting bordering altitudes of ice covers for any period of time during the last 600,000 years. André Berger and Jacques Laskar later developed this theory further.

Polar wandering
Conversations with Wegener, the author of continental drift theory, got Milanković interested in the interior of the Earth and the movement of the poles, so he told his friend that he would investigate polar wandering. In November 1929, Milanković received an invitation from Professor Beno Gutenberg of Darmstadt to collaborate on a ten volume handbook on geophysics and to publish his views on the problem of the secular variations of the Earth's rotational poles. Wegener presented extensive empirical evidence in his scientific work on the 'great events' during the Earth's past. However, one of the main findings that especially preoccupied Wegener and then Milanković was the discovery of big coal reserves on the Svalbard Islands, in the Arctic Ocean, which could not form at the present latitude of these islands. In the meantime, Wegener died (from hypothermia or heart failure) in November 1930 during his fourth expedition to Greenland. Milanković became convinced that the continents 'float' on a somewhat fluid subsurface and that the positions of the continents with respect to the axis of rotation affect the centrifugal force of the rotation and can throw the axis off balance and force it to move. Wegener's tragedy additionally motivated Milanković to persevere in solving the problem of polar wandering.

Milanković's work on the trajectory of poles was well accepted only by Köppen's associates, because most of the scientific community was skeptical about Wegener and Milanković's new theories. Later, in the 1950s and 1960s, development of the new scientific discipline in geophysics known as palaeomagnetism led to the key evidence on the basis of studying the records of Earth's magnetic field in rocks over geological time. Paleomagnetic evidence, both reversals and polar wandering data, led the revival of the theories of continental drift and its transformation into plate tectonics in the 1960s and 1970s. Unlike Milanković's linear trajectory of poles, palaeomagnetism reconstructed the path of the poles over geological history to show the nonlinear trajectory.

Later life
To collect his scientific work on the theory of solar radiation that was scattered in many books and papers, Milanković began to collate his life's work in 1939. The tome was entitled *Canon of Insolation of the Earth and Its Application to the Problem of the Ice Ages*, which covered his nearly three decades of research, including a large number of formulas, calculations and schemes, but also summarized universal laws through

which it was possible to explain cyclical climate change and the attendant 11 ice ages – his namesake Milanković cycles.

Milanković spent two years arranging and writing the "Canon". The manuscript was submitted to print on 2 April 1941 – four days before the attack of Nazi Germany and its allies on the Kingdom of Yugoslavia. In the bombing of Belgrade on 6 April 1941, the printing house where his work was being printed was destroyed; however, almost all of the printed sheet paper remained undamaged in the printing warehouse. After the successful occupation of Serbia on 15 May 1941, two German officers and geology students came to Milanković in his house and brought greetings from Professor Wolfgang Soergel (de) of Freiburg. Milanković gave them the only complete printed copy of the "Canon" to send to Soergel, to make certain that his work would be preserved. Milanković did not take part in the work of the university during the occupation, and after the war he was reinstated as professor.

The "Canon" was issued in 1941 by the Royal Serbian Academy, 626 pages in quarto, and was printed in German as *Kanon der Erdbestrahlung und seine Anwendung auf das Eiszeitenproblem*.

The titles of the six parts of the book are:
1. "The planets' motion around the Sun and their mutual perturbations"
2. "The rotation of the Earth"
3. "Secular wanderings of the rotational poles of the Earth"
4. "The Earth's insolation and its secular changes"
5. "The connection between insolation and the temperature of the Earth and its atmosphere. The mathematical climate of the Earth"
6. "The ice age, its mechanism, structure and chronology".

History of his life and work
During the German occupation of Serbia from 1941 to 1944, Milanković withdrew from public life and decided to write a *History of his life and work* going beyond scientific matters, including his personal life and the love of his father who died in his youth. His autobiography would be published after the war, entitled *Recollection, Experiences and Vision* in Belgrade in 1952. After the war, Milanković was vice president of the Serbian Academy of Sciences (1948–1958) and became a member of the Commission 7 for celestial mechanics in the International Astronomical Union in 1948. In the same year, he became a member of the Italian Institute of Paleontology. In November 1954, fifty years after receiving

his original diploma, he received the Golden Doctor's diploma from the Technical University of Vienna.

At the same time, Milanković began publishing numerous books on the history of science, including *Isaac Newton and Newton's Principia (1946)*, *The founders of the natural science Pythagoras – Democritus – Aristotle – Archimedes (1947)*, *History of astronomy – from its beginnings up to 1727 (1948)*, *Through empire of science – images from the lives of great scientists (1950)*, *Twenty-two centuries of Chemistry (1953)*, and *Techniques in the ancient times (1955)*. In 1958, Milanković suffered a stroke and died in Belgrade.

After Milanković's death, most of the scientific community came to dispute his "astronomical theory" and no longer recognized the results of his research. But ten years after his death and fifty years from the first publication, Milanković's theory was again taken under consideration. His "book" was translated into English under the title *Canon of Insolation of the Ice-Age Problem* in 1969 by the Israel Program for Scientific Translations, and was published by the U.S. Department of Commerce and the National Science Foundation in Washington, D.C.

In the beginning, recognition came slowly, but later, the theory was proven to be accurate. Project CLIMAP (Climate: Long Range Investigation, Mapping and Production) finally resolved the dispute and proved the theory of Milanković cycles. In 1972, scientists compiled a time scale of climatic events in the past 700,000 years from deep-sea cores. They performed the analysis of the cores and four years later, came to the conclusion that in the past 500,000 years, climate has changed depending on the inclination of the Earth's axis of rotation and its precession. In 1988, a new major project COHMAP (Cooperative Holocene Mapping Project) reconstructed the patterns of global climate change over the last 18,000 years, again demonstrating the key role of astronomical factors. In 1989, the project SPECMAP (Spectral Mapping Project), showed that the climate changes are responses to changes in solar radiation of each of the three astronomical cycles.

In 1999, it was shown that variations in the isotopic composition of oxygen in the sediments at the bottom of the ocean follow Milanković theory. There are other recent studies that indicate the validity of the original Milanković theory. Although orbital forcing of Earth's climate is well accepted, the details of how orbitally-induced changes in insolation affect climate are still debated. He was awarded Order of Saint Sava and Order of the Yugoslav Crown.

Alan Buis of NASA's Jet Propulsion Laboratory has summarised the Milanković theory and says that our lives literally revolve around cycles: series of events that are repeated regularly in the same order. There are hundreds of different types of cycles in our world and in the universe. Some are natural, such as the change of the seasons, annual animal migrations or the circadian rhythms that govern our sleep patterns. Others are human-produced, like growing and harvesting crops, musical rhythms or economic cycles.

Cycles also play key roles in Earth's short-term weather and long-term climate. A century ago, Serbian scientist Milutin Milanković hypothesized the long-term, collective effects of changes in Earth's position relative to the Sun are a strong driver of Earth's long-term climate, and are responsible for triggering the beginning and end of glaciation periods (Ice Ages).

Specifically, he examined how variations in three types of Earth orbital movements affect how much solar radiation (known as insolation) reaches the top of Earth's atmosphere as well as where the insolation reaches. These cyclical orbital movements, which became known as the Milanković cycles, cause variations of up to 25% in the amount of incoming insolation at Earth's mid-latitudes (the areas of our planet located between about 30 and 60 degrees north and south of the equator).

The Milanković cycles include:
1. The shape of Earth's orbit, known as eccentricity;
2. The angle Earth's axis is tilted with respect to Earth's orbital plane, known as obliquity; and
3. The direction Earth's axis of rotation is pointed, known as precession.

Eccentricity
Earth's annual pilgrimage around the Sun isn't perfectly circular, but it's pretty close. Over time, the pull of gravity from our solar system's two largest gas giant planets, Jupiter and Saturn, causes the shape of Earth's orbit to vary from nearly circular to slightly elliptical. Eccentricity measures how much the shape of Earth's orbit departs from a perfect circle. These variations affect the distance between Earth and the Sun.

Eccentricity is the reason why our seasons are slightly different lengths, with Summers in the Northern Hemisphere currently about 4.5 days longer than Winters, and Springs about three days longer than Autumns. As eccentricity decreases, the length of our seasons gradually evens out.

The difference in the distance between Earth's closest approach to the

Sun (known as perihelion), which occurs on or about January 3 each year, and its farthest departure from the Sun (known as aphelion) on or about July 4, is currently about 5.1 million km, a variation of 3.4%. That means each January, about 6.8% more incoming solar radiation reaches Earth than it does each July.

When Earth's orbit is at its most elliptic, about 23% more incoming solar radiation reaches Earth at our planet's closest approach to the Sun each year than does at its farthest departure from the Sun. Currently, Earth's eccentricity is near its most elliptic and is very slowly decreasing, in a cycle that spans about 100,000 years.

The total change in global annual insolation due to the eccentricity cycle is very small. Because variations in Earth's eccentricity are fairly small, they're a relatively minor factor in annual seasonal climate variations.

Obliquity

The angle Earth's axis of rotation is tilted as it travels around the Sun is known as obliquity. Obliquity is why Earth has seasons. Over the last million years, it has varied between 22.1 and 24.5 degrees perpendicular to Earth's orbital plane. The greater Earth's axial tilt angle, the more extreme our seasons are, as each hemisphere receives more solar radiation during its summer, when the hemisphere is tilted toward the Sun, and less during winter, when it is tilted away. Larger tilt angles favour periods of deglaciation (the melting and retreat of glaciers and ice sheets). These effects aren't uniform globally -- higher latitudes receive a larger change in total solar radiation than areas closer to the equator.

Earth's axis is currently tilted 23.4 degrees, or about half way between its extremes, and this angle is very slowly decreasing in a cycle that spans about 41,000 years. It was last at its maximum tilt about 10,700 years ago and will reach its minimum tilt about 9,800 years from now. As obliquity decreases, it gradually helps make our seasons milder, resulting in increasingly warmer winters, and cooler summers that gradually, over time, allow snow and ice at high latitudes to build up into large ice sheets. As ice cover increases, it reflects more of the Sun's energy back into space, promoting even further cooling.

Precession

As Earth rotates, it wobbles slightly upon its axis, like a slightly off-centre spinning toy top. This wobble is due to tidal forces caused by the gravitational influences of the Sun and Moon that cause Earth to bulge at the equator, affecting its rotation. The trend in the direction of this wobble relative to the fixed positions of stars is known as axial precession. The cycle of axial precession spans about 25,771.5 years.

Axial precession makes seasonal contrasts more extreme in one hemisphere and less extreme in the other. Currently perihelion occurs during winter in the Northern Hemisphere and in summer in the Southern Hemisphere. This makes Southern Hemisphere summers hotter and moderates Northern Hemisphere seasonal variations. But in about 13,000 years, axial precession will cause these conditions to flip, with the Northern Hemisphere seeing more extremes in solar radiation and the Southern Hemisphere experiencing more moderate seasonal variations.

Axial precession also gradually changes the timing of the seasons, causing them to begin earlier over time, and gradually changes which star Earth's axis points to at the North Pole (the North Star). Today Earth's North Stars are Polaris and Polaris Australis, but a couple of thousand years ago, they were Kochab and Pherkad.

There's also apsidal precession. Not only does Earth's axis wobble, but Earth's entire orbital ellipse also wobbles irregularly, primarily due to its interactions with Jupiter and Saturn. The cycle of apsidal precession spans about 112,000 years. Apsidal precession changes the orientation of Earth's orbit relative to the elliptical plane.

Apsidal precession
The combined effects of axial and apsidal precession result in an overall precession cycle spanning about 23,000 years on average.

Milanković assumed changes in radiation at some latitudes and in some seasons are more important than others to the growth and retreat of ice sheets. In addition, it was his belief that obliquity was the most important of the three cycles for climate, because it affects the amount of insolation in Earth's northern high-latitude regions during summer (the relative role of precession versus obliquity is still a matter of scientific study).

He calculated that Ice Ages occur approximately every 41,000 years. Subsequent research confirms that they did occur at 41,000-year intervals between one and three million years ago. But about 800,000 years ago, the cycle of Ice Ages lengthened to 100,000 years, matching Earth's eccentricity cycle. While various theories have been proposed to explain this transition, scientists do not yet have a clear answer.

Milanković's work was supported by other researchers of his time, and he authored numerous publications on his hypothesis. But it wasn't until about 10 years after his death in 1958 that the global science community began to take serious notice of his theory. In 1976, a study in the journal *Science* by Hays et al. using deep-sea sediment cores found that Milanković cycles correspond with periods of major climate change over the past 450,000 years, with Ice Ages occurring when Earth was undergoing different stages of orbital variation.

Several other projects and studies have also upheld the validity of Milanković's work, including research using data from ice cores in Greenland and Antarctica that has provided strong evidence of Milanković cycles going back many hundreds of thousands of years. In addition, his work has been embraced by the National Research Council of the U.S. National Academy of Sciences.

Scientific research to better understand the mechanisms that cause changes in Earth's rotation and how specifically Milanković cycles combine to affect climate is ongoing. But the theory that they drive the timing of glacial-interglacial cycles is well accepted.

Solar magnetic variations and the Earth's climate

The Sun has an associated magnetic field known as the interplanetary magnetic field (IMF). When this interacts with the Earth's magnetic field some changes occur in the Earth's atmospheric circulation. From time to time, as it sweeps past the Earth, the direction of the IMF changes from towards the Earth to away from the Earth. The time of this change varies but on average could be regarded as about once every 12 days.

In a study using data for the 21-year period 1997-2017 (published in the *Meteorological Society of New Zealand Newsletter 156: Autumn 2019)*, Graham Ward has found what appear to be significant changes in the Southern Oscillation Index (SOI) at times when the IMF changes direction. These events are known as IMF sector boundary crossings. Data giving the time and direction of these crossings were obtained for this study from the Wilcox Solar Observatory (Svalbard Sector Boundary List 1926 – present).

The Wilcox Solar Observatory (WSO) began collecting daily observations of the Sun's global (or mean) magnetic field in May 1975, with the goal of understanding changes in the Sun and how those changes affect the Earth. That science is now called space weather. Since May 1976 daily low-resolution maps of the Sun's magnetic field have been made at the WSO, along with observations of solar surface motions. The observatory is located in the foothills just west of the Stanford University campus. Current research topics include space weather, the large-scale magnetic field, and the solar cycle.

The Southern Oscillation Index (SOI) is effectively a measure of the barometric pressure difference between Tahiti and Darwin and can be regarded as a key indicator of the overall state of the global climate at the time. The changes in the SOI at the time of each IMF change of direction (sector boundary crossing) were found to be very large on the average during the two extreme El Niño years 1997 and 2015 (accompanied by very low negative values of the SOI), and also during the extreme La Niña years 2010 and 2011 (accompanied by very high positive values of the SOI). Values of the SOI were generally less (positive or negative) in the remaining years of the study and the apparent effect on the SOI at the time of each sector boundary crossing in those years generally smaller, but still noteworthy.

The revelation of these results leaves us with one big question: "As it seems most unlikely that the results are due to pure chance, what exactly is the mechanism causing them?" Are interplanetary/solar magnetic (tidal) forces responsible? Could these influences be largely or at least partly the cause of the global climate changes that we are now witnessing?

A paper by Italian scientists SA Capuano et al. published in 2018 offers a further insight into this subject. The extract from the published paper includes the following:

The debated question on the possible relation between the Earth's magnetic field and climate has been usually focused on direct correlations between different time series representing both systems. However, the physical mechanism able to potentially explain this connection is still an open issue. Finding hints about how this connection could work would suppose an important advance in the search of an adequate physical mechanism. Here, we propose an innovative information-theoretic tool, i.e. the transfer entropy (which is the transfer of information between two random processes) as a good candidate for this scope because it is able to determine, not simply the possible existence of a connection, but even the direction in which the link is produced.

We have applied this new methodology to two real time series, the South Atlantic Anomaly (SAA) area extent at the Earth's surface (representing the geomagnetic field system) and the Global Sea Level (GSL) rise (for the climate system) for the last 300 years, to measure the possible information flow and sense between them. This connection was previously suggested considering only the long-term trend while now we study this possibility also in shorter scales. The new results seem to support this hypothesis, with more information transferred from the SAA to the GSL time series, with about 90% of confidence level.

This result provides new clues on the existence of a link between the geomagnetic field and the Earth's climate in the past and on the physical mechanism involved because, thanks to the application of the transfer entropy, we have determined that the sense of the connection seems to go from the system that produces geomagnetic field to the climate system.

Of course, the connection does not mean that the geomagnetic field is fully responsible for the climate changes, rather that it is an important driving component to the variations of the climate.

6

The role of the oceans

"As we acquire more knowledge, things do not become more comprehensible, but more mysterious."

Albert Schweitzer

Global ocean currents as climate controllers

One way that the world's ocean affects weather and climate is by playing an important role in keeping our planet warm. The majority of radiation from the sun is absorbed by the ocean, particularly in tropical waters around the equator, where the ocean acts like a massive, heat-retaining solar panel. Land areas also absorb some sunlight, and the atmosphere helps to retain heat that would otherwise quickly radiate into space after sunset.

The ocean doesn't just store solar radiation; it also helps to distribute heat around the globe. When water molecules are heated, they exchange freely with the air in a process called evaporation. Ocean water is constantly evaporating, increasing the temperature and humidity of the surrounding air to form rain and storms that are then carried by trade winds. In fact, almost all rain that falls on land starts off in the ocean. The tropics are particularly rainy because heat absorption, and thus ocean evaporation, is highest in this area.

Outside of Earth's equatorial areas, weather patterns are driven largely by ocean currents (*NOAA Ocean Exploration and Research*). Currents are movements of ocean water in a continuous flow, created largely by surface winds but also partly by temperature and salinity gradients, Earth's rotation, and tides. Major current systems typically flow clockwise in the Northern Hemisphere and counter clockwise in the Southern Hemisphere; in circular patterns that often trace the coastlines.

Ocean currents as a conveyor belt

Ocean currents act much like a conveyor belt, transporting warm water and precipitation from the equator toward the poles and cold water from the poles back to the tropics. Thus, ocean currents regulate global climate, helping to counteract the uneven distribution of solar radiation reaching Earth's surface. Without currents in the ocean, regional temperatures would be more extreme–super hot at the equator and frigid toward the poles–and much less of Earth's land would be habitable.

Ocean currents are continuous, directed movements of sea water generated by a number of forces acting upon the water, including wind, the Coriolis effect, breaking waves, cabbeling, and temperature and salinity differences. Depth contours, shoreline configurations, and interactions with other currents influence a current's direction and strength. Ocean currents are primarily horizontal water movements. An ocean current flows, as reported in *Wikipedia*, for great distances and together they create the global conveyor belt, which plays a dominant role in determining the climate of many of Earth's regions. More specifically, ocean currents influence the temperature of the regions through which they travel. Warm currents travelling along more temperate coasts increase the temperature of the area by warming the sea breezes that blow over them. The most striking example is the Gulf Stream, which makes northwest Europe much more temperate than any other region at the same latitude. Another example is Lima, Peru, where the climate is cooler, being sub-tropical, than the tropical latitudes in which the area is located, due to the effect of the Humboldt Current.

From May to September 2016, Susan Lozier and her oceanographic team made five research cruises across the North Atlantic, hauling up dozens of moored instruments that track currents far beneath the surface. The data they retrieve will be the first complete set documenting how North Atlantic waters are shifting – and should help solve the mystery of whether there is a long-term slowdown in ocean circulation. "We have a lot of people very interested in the data," says Lozier, a physical oceanographer at Duke University. The work is reviewed by Nicola Jones writing in *e360.yale.edu* on September 6, 2016.

Atlantic slowdown
Researchers have been worried about an Atlantic slowdown for years. The Atlantic serves as the engine for the planet's conveyor belt of ocean currents: The massive amount of cooler water that sinks in the North Atlantic stirs up that entire ocean and drives currents in the Southern and Pacific oceans, too. "It is the key component in global circulation", says Ellen Martin, a paleoclimate and ocean current researcher at the University of Florida. When the Atlantic turns sluggish, it has worldwide impacts. The entire Northern Hemisphere cools, Indian and Asian monsoon areas dry up, North Atlantic storms get amplified, and less ocean mixing results in less plankton and other life in the sea. A single Atlantic Ocean current system accounts for up to a quarter of the planet's heat flux.

Paleoclimatologists have spotted times in the deep past when the current slowed quickly and dramatically, cooling Europe by 5 to 10 °C and causing far-reaching impacts on climate. Modellers have tried to predict how human-caused climate change might impact the Atlantic current, and how its slowdown might influence the world's weather even more. Years of intensive peering at this question haven't yet provided much clarity. Now, debate is raging about whether the recent Atlantic slowdown has been triggered by climate change, or just part of a normal cycle of fast and slow currents. New studies in the last few years have come out supporting both prospects. The new data from the north, Lozier and others hope, might help to classify things.

The Day After Tomorrow
When the Hollywood blockbuster *The Day After Tomorrow* threw the Atlantic Ocean current into the popular spotlight in 2004, researchers laughed at its portrayal of an ocean current shutdown. In the movie, the world was plunged into a new ice age in a matter of days, with cold fronts literally chasing people at a sprint. However the disaster at the core of the film was based on some reality. A huge amount of heat is moved around our planet by a single ocean current system – the Atlantic Meridional Overturning Circulation (AMOC) – which accounts for up to a quarter of the planet's heat flux. The system is driven by density: waters that are cold or salty are denser and so dive down to the ocean floor. As a result, cold waters sink in the North Atlantic and flow southwards, while warm

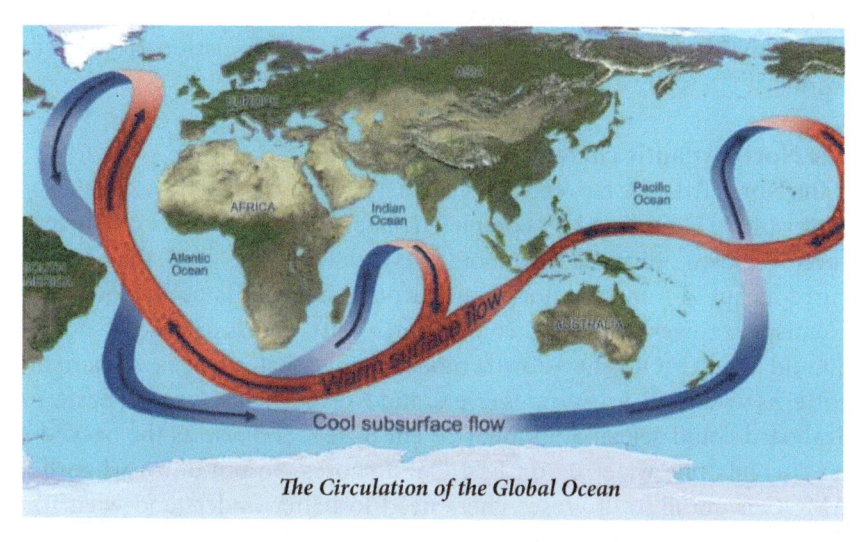

The Circulation of the Global Ocean

tropical waters at the surface flow northwards in the Gulf Stream, making northern Europe unusually mild for its latitude. If northern waters get too warm, or too fresh from melting ice, they then can stop being dense enough to sink. That causes a major traffic jam for the water attempting to move north, and the system grinds to a halt.

Throughout the Atlantic Ocean, the circulation carries warm waters (red arrows) northward near the surface and cold deep waters (blue arrows) southward. Image courtesy of NASA/JPL. This has happened before. Researchers have spotted dramatic AMOC slowdowns of more than 50% during the last glaciation some 100,000 to 10,000 years ago, over a period perhaps as short as decades. The theory - being debated - is that as ice sheets got too big to stay stable, armadas of icebergs broke off, floated out to sea, and melted; even though the waters were chilly, the huge influx of freshwater made them less dense, and so they stopped the currents. Looking further back in time to the last interglacial period about 120,000 years ago, which is more like today's interglacial world, is trickier. A study of some proxy measurements has shown that there may have been rapid slowdowns in the last interglacial, also.

"It seems to be a fairly stable system, until we push it just the right amount and then we're in terrible shape," says Martin, a paleoclimate and ocean current researcher at the University of Florida, "I don't think you want to play with the AMOC." The last review by the IPCC concluded that the AMOC is very likely to slow by the end of the century, perhaps by as much as 54 % in the worst-case scenario, where emissions keep going up and global temperatures rise about 4°C. The range of possible slowdowns in these predictions is huge, starting at just 1% for an emissions-restricted world.

The North Atlantic current
If the North Atlantic current slows dramatically, then the entire Northern Hemisphere would cool. A complete collapse of the current could even reverse global warming for about 20 years; but the heat that ocean currents fail to transport northwards would make parts of the Southern Hemisphere even hotter. A cooler north isn't necessarily good news. Should the AMOC shut down, models show that changes in rainfall patterns would dry up Europe's rivers, and North America's entire Eastern Seaboard could see an additional 76 cm of sea level rise as the backed-up currents pile water up on East Coast shores. To pin down what the AMOC is going to do, researchers need to better understand what it's doing right now. That is proving tricky.

The problem researchers face is that the AMOC is extremely capricious, wobbling around more from year to year than the expected shift to date from global warming. Just like temperature or sea level records, this makes for a very noisy signal in which it's hard to see long-term trends.

"It's analogous to the early difficulty seeing a global warming signature," says Columbia University paleoclimatologist and oceanographer Jerry McManus. "Now that signature is compelling, but it took a while to see it clearly. Now that's happening with AMOC. "

The first string of more than a dozen moorings from Florida to the Canary Islands were deployed in the ocean in 2004 to investigate this current – the so-called RAPID array. They have shown a drop in water flow from 20 sverdrups (or million cubic meters of water per second) to 15 sverdrups over a decade. The variability is huge. In 2009 to 2010, for example, the current was particularly sluggish for some reason, with water transport dropping by about a third. That contributed to make the next winter the coldest for the United Kingdom since 1890, with heavy snowfalls and travel chaos. From New York to Newfoundland, sea levels were boosted by over 12 cm. Lozier's data from the northern part of the ocean – in an array called OSNAP – will add a missing piece to the puzzle of what is happening to the current. A pocket of cold water has formed in the northern Atlantic Ocean from melting Arctic and Greenland ice. Scientists say it has the potential to disrupt ocean circulation.

Sea surface temperature as a proxy for current
Actual measurements of the AMOC across the ocean only date back to 2004; to get a longer-term picture, researchers have to rely on other measurements to infer ocean current. Last year, Stefan Rahmstorf, of the Potsdam Institute for Climate Impact Research in Germany, grabbed media headlines with a paper looking at sea surface temperature as a proxy for current. That study argued that the Atlantic current has slowed more since 1975 than at any point in the last thousand years, creating an obvious chilly area over the North Atlantic – one of the only spots on the planet that's actually cooling. The slowdown started in about the 1930s, Rahmstorf says, strongly suggesting that mankind is to blame.

Others aren't yet convinced. "The jury is still out," says Lozier, who notes that sea surface temperature is a messy proxy for current. "Weakening is a possibility, but it hasn't been proven yet," agrees Laura Jackson of the UK's Met Office, who studies the AMOC. Jackson's own work in a special collection of papers about ocean circulation in *Nature Geoscience* (2016, 2018, 2020) showed that the AMOC has a decadal oscillation that naturally makes it swing from high to low flow. The mechanisms behind that aren't well understood, but the upshot is that the slowdown seen since 2004 could just be due to one of these oscillations. It's also possible that both things are true. There could be a decadal-scale oscillation sitting on top of a longer-term slowdown caused by climate change.

Another paper published in that same issue of *Nature Geoscience*, however, suggests that the amount of meltwater from Greenland isn't yet enough to affect the AMOC, despite the fact that Greenland is shedding nearly 300 billion tons of water a year. "It sounds like a lot of water, but it's going over a big area," says Jackson. Most of the freshwater pouring into the Labrador Sea seems to be swirled off down the Canadian coast by smaller ocean currents or eddies, instead of building up and stopping the AMOC. If the AMOC has really been slowing since about 1930 thanks to humanity's influence on the climate, the exact way that is happening remains unclear. It could simply be the warming of Atlantic waters in critical areas, or the introduction of extra freshwater from increased rain. "We need another decade of observations, at least," says Jackson, who also keenly awaits the OSNAP data. "Knowing what's happening at high latitudes will help us determine which model is right," she says. Meanwhile a third line of moorings in the South Atlantic, from Brazil to South Africa, should start to highlight what's happening at the other end of the ocean.

For now, everyone awaits more data to see whether the AMOC is slowing down and, if so, what that will mean for the planet. "It's complicated because there are feedbacks, and we don't understand them all. Some could be positive; some could be negative," says Jackson.

Climate Change: A Natural Hazard

In 2004, the book *Climate Change: A Natural Hazard* was published. The author William Kininmonth demonstrated that the model of the climate system represented by the IPCC is inadequate as a foundation for future planning. In a recent paper Kininmonth has updated the views he expressed in his earlier book.

There are two competing views on how Earth's climate changes. The first, as espoused by the IPCC, holds that Earth's temperature is primarily a function of the properties and atmospheric concentrations of greenhouse gases, and how these gases interact with atmospheric radiation. The second, as outlined here, is that Earth's temperature is regulated by atmospheric transport of energy from the tropics to polar regions, and how the rate of transport varies with ocean circulations, particularly the millennial period thermohaline circulation.

Poleward transport of energy by the atmosphere circulation is required to sustain high latitude temperatures against net radiation loss, especially during winter months. The data demonstrate that, as equatorial ocean surface temperatures rise and more energy is exchanged with the atmosphere, wintertime temperatures over high latitudes have risen and the melt period for polar ice has extended. The observed temperature rise over the equatorial region has been amplified over high latitudes of winter because the increased latent energy exchange over the warming tropical oceans is realised over higher latitudes as heat.

There is little variation over time in the rate of absorption of solar energy into the tropical ocean layer. Consequently, it is variations in the ocean gyres and the thermohaline circulation that regulate the availability of heat and latent energy for transport to polar regions.

It is estimated that the energy available from the tropical ocean for poleward transport varies by about 8.5 W/m^2 with every 1°C of surface temperature change. This points to a limit to further global warming and debunks the alarmists' scenario of 'runaway global warming'. If the overturning thermohaline circulation were to be stilled, then only about 25 W/m^2 of energy would be made available to the atmosphere, thus limiting the tropical ocean surface temperature rise to about 3°C.

The overturning period of the thermohaline circulation has been variously estimated as of the order of 1,000 years, a period that is consistent with variations in northern polar temperatures as discerned from Greenland ice cores. The period is also consistent with historical accounts of waxing and waning of civilisations over the recent few thousand years, with civilisations seeming to flourish in the warmer phases.

The annual cycle of heating and cooling over middle and higher latitudes is a powerful stimulus to the inertial modes in the ocean circulation. Oscillations associated with the inertial modes are reflected, through equatorial ocean surface temperature, in climate variability on multi-decadal and multi-centennial timescales.

The contemporary warming trend, as Earth emerges from the Little Ice Age, is consistent with a slowing of the thermohaline circulation. The warming is an order of magnitude greater than what might have been expected from the post-industrial increase in atmospheric CO_2.

Indian Ocean Dipole (IOD)

The Indian Ocean Dipole (IOD), also known as the Indian Niño, is an irregular oscillation of sea surface temperatures in which the western Indian Ocean becomes alternately warmer (positive phase) and then colder (negative phase) than the eastern part of the ocean. *Wikipedia* describes the IOD as follows:

The IOD involves an aperiodic oscillation of sea-surface temperatures (SST), between "positive", "neutral" and "negative" phases. A positive phase sees greater-than-average sea-surface temperatures and greater precipitation in the western Indian Ocean region, with a corresponding cooling of waters in the eastern Indian Ocean – which tends to cause droughts in adjacent land areas of Indonesia and Australia. The negative phase of the IOD brings about the opposite conditions, with warmer water and greater precipitation in the eastern Indian Ocean, and cooler and drier conditions in the west. The IOD also affects the strength of monsoons over the Indian subcontinent. A significant positive IOD occurred in 1997–98, with another in 2006. The IOD is one aspect of the general cycle of global climate, interacting with similar phenomena like the El Niño-Southern Oscillation (ENSO) in the Pacific Ocean.

The IOD phenomenon was first identified by climate researchers in 1999. An average of four each positive-negative IOD phases occur during each 30-year period with each phase lasting around 6 months. However, there have been 12 positive IODs since 1980 and no negative phases from 1992 until a strong negative phase in late 2010. The occurrence of consecutive positive IOD phases is extremely rare with only two such events recorded, 1913–1914 and the three consecutive events from 2006 to 2008 which preceded the Australian Black Saturday bushfires. Modelling suggests that consecutive positive phases could be expected to occur twice over a 1,000-year period. The positive IOD in 2007 evolved together with La Niña, which is a very rare phenomenon that has happened only once in the available historical records (1967). A strong negative IOD developed in October 2010, which, coupled with a strong and concurrent La Niña, caused the 2010–2011 Queensland floods and the 2011 Victorian floods.

Coral Dipole Mode Index
In 2008, Nerilie Abram, Australian National University (ANU), Canberra, used coral records from the eastern and western Indian Ocean

to construct a coral Dipole Mode Index extending back to 1846 AD. This extended perspective on IOD behaviour suggested that positive IOD events increased in strength and frequency during the 20th century. A positive IOD is associated with droughts in Southeast Asia and Australia. More extreme positive IOD events are expected.

A 2009 study by Ummenhofer et al. at the University of New South Wales (UNSW), Climate Change Research Centre, has demonstrated a significant correlation between the IOD and drought in the southern half of Australia, in particular the south-east. Every major southern drought since 1889 has coincided with positive-neutral IOD fluctuations including the 1895–1902, 1937–1945, 1995–2009 droughts.

The research shows that when the IOD is in its negative phase, with cool western Indian Ocean waters and warm waters off northwest Australia (Timor Sea), winds are generated that pick up moisture from the ocean and then sweep down towards southern Australia to deliver higher rainfall. In the IOD-positive phase, the pattern of ocean temperatures is reversed, weakening the winds and reducing the amount of moisture picked up and transported across Australia. The consequence is that rainfall in the south-east is well below average during periods of a positive IOD. The study also shows that the IOD has a much more significant effect on the rainfall patterns in south-east Australia than the El Niño-Southern Oscillation (ENSO) in the Pacific Ocean.

A positive IOD is linked to higher than average rainfall during the "East African Short Rains" (EASR) between October and December. Higher rainfall during the EASR are associated with warm SST in the western Indian Ocean and low level westerlies across the equatorial region of the ocean which brings moisture over the East Africa region. The increased rainfall associated with a positive IOD has been found to result in increased flooding over East Africa during the EASR period. During a particularly strong positive IOD at the end of 2019, average rainfall over East Africa was 300% higher than normal. This higher than average rainfall has resulted in a high prevalence of flooding in the countries of Djibouti, Ethiopia, Kenya, Uganda, Tanzania, Somalia and South Sudan. Torrential rainfall and increased risk of landslides over the region during this period often results in widespread destruction and loss of life.

It is expected that the Western Indian ocean will warm at accelerated rates due to climate change, leading to an increasing occurrence of positive IODs. This is likely to result in the increasing intensity of rainfall during the short rain period over East Africa.

The effect of the IOD on El Niño studied by Hameed et al. in 2018 at the University of Aizu, simulated the impact of a positive IOD event on Pacific surface wind and SST variations. They show that IOD-induced surface wind anomalies can produce El Niño-like SST anomalies, with the IOD's impact on SST being the strongest in the far-eastern Pacific. They further demonstrated that IOD-ENSO interaction is a key for the generation of "Super El Niños".

The IOD is related to multiple cyclones that ravaged East Africa in 2019 (killing thousands), aided by warmer than normal waters offshore (starting with Cyclone Idai and continuing on to the 2019–20 South-West Indian Ocean cyclone season), the 2019-20 Australian drought and bushfires (convective IOD cycle brings dry air down on Australia), the 2020 Jakarta floods (convective IOD cycle prevents moist air near tropics from going south to Australia, concentrating it), and the 2019–20 East Africa locust infestation (via number of supportive weather factors).

The IOD is one of the key drivers of Australia's climate and can have a significant impact on agriculture as described by the *Australian Bureau of Meteorology* website. This is because events generally coincide with the winter crop growing season. Neutral, positive, or negative IOD phases usually start around May or June, peak between August and October and then rapidly decay when the monsoon arrives in the Southern Hemisphere around the end of spring.

In the Neutral IOD phase water from the Pacific flows between the islands of Indonesia, keeping seas to Australia's northwest warm. Air rises above this area and falls over the western half of the Indian Ocean basin, blowing westerly winds along the equator.

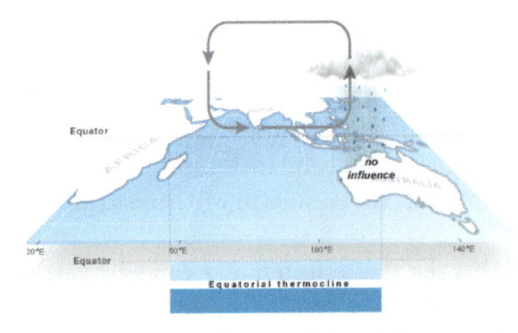

Indian Ocean Dipole (IOD): **Neutral phase**

Temperatures are close to normal across the tropical Indian Ocean, and hence the neutral IOD results in little change to Australia's climate.
In the Positive IOD phase westerly winds weaken along the equator allowing warm water to shift towards Africa. Changes in the winds also allow cool water to rise up from the deep ocean in the east. This sets up a temperature difference across the tropical Indian Ocean with cooler than normal water in the east and warmer than normal water in the west. Generally this means there is less moisture than normal in the atmosphere to the northwest of Australia. This changes the path of weather systems coming from Australia's west, often resulting in less rainfall and higher than normal temperatures over parts of Australia during winter and spring.

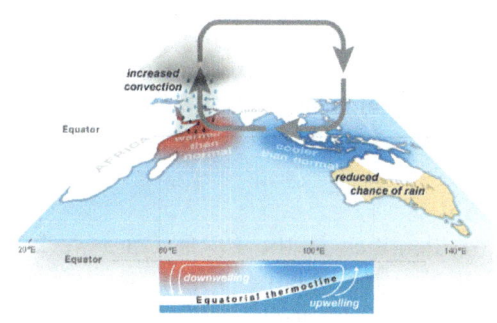

Indian Ocean Dipole (IOD): **Positive phase**

In the Negative IOD phase westerly winds intensify along the equator, allowing warmer waters to concentrate near Australia. This sets up a temperature difference across the tropical Indian Ocean, with warmer than normal water in the east and cooler than normal water in the west. A negative IOD typically results in above-average winter–spring rainfall over parts of southern Australia as the warmer waters off northwest Australia provide more available moisture to weather systems crossing the country.

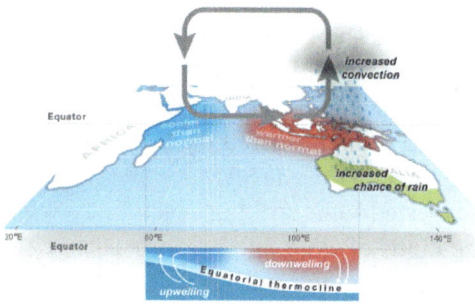

Indian Ocean Dipole (IOD): **Negative phase**

Southern Annular Mode (SAM)

New Zealand's NIWA has an informative review of the Southern Annular Mode (SAM) written by Jim Renwick and David Thompson. The Southern Annular Mode (or SAM) is a ring of climate variability that encircles the South Pole and extends out to the latitudes of New Zealand. (Its counterpart, the NAM, centres on the North Pole and affects climate in the Northern Hemisphere.) The SAM involves alternating changes in windiness and storm activity between the middle latitudes, where New Zealand lies (40-50°S), and higher latitudes, over the southern oceans and Antarctic sea ice zone (50-70°S). In its positive phase, the SAM is associated with relatively light winds and more settled weather over New Zealand latitudes, together with enhanced westerly winds over the southern oceans. In the opposite (negative) phase, the westerlies increase over New Zealand, with more unsettled weather, while windiness and storm activity ease over the southern oceans.

Identifying the SAM
The SAM was first identified in the 1970s. On a week-to-week basis, it flips between states – causing either windier or calmer weather over New Zealand latitudes – in an unpredictable way, apparently at random. Though these phase changes of the SAM cannot be predicted more than a few days in advance, once changed, the phases tend to persist for several weeks. In recent years, scientists have noticed a trend in the SAM towards more periods of the positive phase, with a tendency towards strong westerlies over the southern oceans and lighter winds over the middle latitudes. The trend appears to be related to the Antarctic ozone hole, and the influence of the stratosphere on the weather lower down. The question is: what effect is this having on weather and climate in New Zealand?

During the summer of December 2005-February 2006, Renwick and Thompson examined rainfall and temperature data from stations around New Zealand, looking for days when the SAM was strongly positive or strongly negative. Then they compared daily climate statistics over New Zealand for the two extremes of the SAM.

Initial results suggested some striking effects on New Zealand climate, consistent with the kinds of wind and pressure changes outlined above. The data reveal lower than normal rainfall and higher than normal temperatures throughout western parts of the North and South Islands;

these rainfalls and temperatures are consistent with the weaker than normal westerly winds in those regions. Precipitation was as much as 5 mm less per day over the west coast of the South Island, and temperatures were at least 0.5°C higher in a broad region stretching from Auckland to the western fiords. The negative SAM phase showed the opposite picture, with cooler and wetter conditions in the west of both islands. These temperature and precipitation anomalies in the western half of the country are statistically significant, but the effects along the east coast of the country are weak and are not statistically significant.

Each positive or negative SAM event tends to last for around one to two weeks, though longer periods may also occur. The time frame between positive and negative events is quite random, but typically in the range of a week to a few months. The effect that the SAM has on rainfall varies greatly depending on season and region. In the Australian region (*www.bom.gov.au*) SAM has three phases: neutral, positive and negative.

In a negative SAM phase, the belt of westerly winds expands and is positioned more northwards towards the equator and Australia. This results in stronger than normal westerly winds, lower atmospheric pressure, more cold fronts and more storm systems over southern Australia. Typically this means that there are more rain events in winter for southern Australia. However, in eastern Australia, the northward displacement of the westerly winds means less moist onshore flow from the east, and thus decreases rainfall for eastern Australia.

New Zealand lies mid-way between the tropics and the Southern Ocean, and our day-to-day weather can arrive from either direction. The following are abstracts relating to SAM and ENSO from the website of the New Zealand Meteorological Service.

On a longer time scale (weeks to months), tropical weather is influenced by the state of the El Niño-Southern Oscillation (ENSO). The ENSO climate pattern affects wind flows, rainfall distribution and sea temperatures right across the tropics, from equatorial South America to Indonesia. It also has some effect on New Zealand's climate (winds, temperatures and rainfall patterns), although generally to a lesser degree than in the tropics. This is because weather patterns to the south of the country also play their part. The word 'annular' means 'ring-like', and that is exactly what the SAM does – it controls the ring of westerly winds that circle the South Pole.

The Annual average SAM index from 1887-2016. published by the NZ Department of Statistics is shown below.

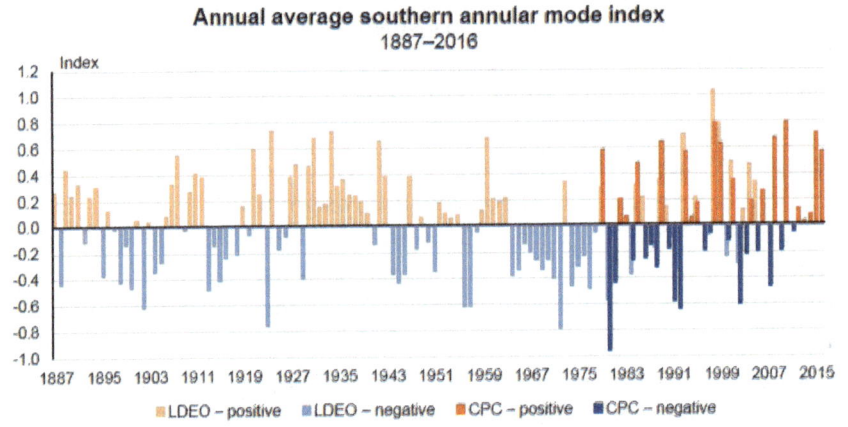

**Annual average southern annular mode index
1887–2016**

Source: GEOMAR, Helmholtz Centre for Ocean Research Kiel (Visbeck LDEO); National Weather Service Climate Prediction Center (CPC)

The SAM produces alternating bands of windiness and storminess between the higher latitudes (the Southern Ocean and Antarctica) and the mid-latitudes (e.g. the New Zealand region). When the SAM is positive, pressures are lower than normal over Antarctica, and westerly winds are stronger than normal over the Southern Ocean. Over New Zealand itself, pressures are higher than usual, particularly over the South Island. Relatively light winds (weaker westerlies) and settled weather prevail over much of New Zealand during the positive phase of the SAM.

Daily values of the Southern Annular Mode, as observed between 1 September 2014 and 1 February 2015 show there was a sustained period of negative SAM in late October and through November 2014, and the strongly positive SAM phase during December 2014 and most of January 2015.

In contrast, during the negative phase of the SAM, pressures are higher than usual over Antarctica, and westerly winds are weaker than normal over the Southern Ocean. Lower pressures dominate over the South Island, and stronger, stormy westerlies affect most of New Zealand. Evidence of the SAM in New Zealand can be seen in the seasonal rainfall and temperature. The response in the positive phase is roughly the reverse of that seen in the negative phase. However, the effects do vary by season and by region, and typically the most significant changes occur in western regions of both Islands. It is, on average, warmer and drier than usual during positive phases of the SAM, and wetter and cooler than usual in the negative phase, for western regions of the country. The response in eastern parts of the country is much less clear-cut. Responses tend to be small, or weakly opposite that seen in the west of the country. Some details are given for the positive phase of the SAM in the text below.

During the positive phase of the Southern Annular Mode (SAM) the following climatic factors prevail:
- Ring of westerly winds contracts towards Antarctica.
- Stormy Southern Ocean.
- Higher pressures over the South Island.
- Warmer summer days for western and inland parts of both Islands, also Southland and Otago; cooler summers elsewhere along the eastern coastline of both Islands.
- Warmer winters right across the country.
- Drier than normal summers for western and inland parts of both Islands, also the eastern South Island south of about Banks Peninsula.
- Risk of wetter than usual summers for Northland.
- No clear signal in summer rainfall for Nelson, Marlborough, Bay of Plenty, or the east of the North Island.
- Drier than normal winters for most regions, excepting Westland and Fiordland (wetter), and Nelson, Bay of Plenty, Gisborne and Hawkes Bay (no clear signal or risk wetter).

There are therefore links between the state of the SAM, and monthly or seasonal pressure, rainfall and temperature patterns in the New Zealand region. An important question is; can the state of the SAM be used to forecast our likely climate variations over the next few weeks? The answer is 'almost'. The phase of the SAM can, and does, flip-flop week to week. But usually, once the SAM has changed phase, the phase tends to last several weeks. There are already operational forecasts of the SAM phase in use, which extend out for the next fortnight.

What are El Niño and La Niña?

El Niño and La Niña are complex weather patterns resulting from variations in ocean temperatures in the Equatorial Pacific. El Niño and La Niña are opposite phases of what is known as the El Niño-Southern Oscillation (ENSO) cycle. La Niña is sometimes referred to as the cold phase of the ENSO cycle, and El Niño as the warm phase of ENSO. These deviations from normal surface temperatures can have large-scale impacts not only on ocean processes, but also on global weather and climate.

El Niño and La Niña episodes typically last nine to 12 months, but some prolonged events may last for years. While their frequency can be quite irregular, El Niño and La Niña events occur on average every two to seven years. Typically, El Niño occurs more frequently than La Niña.

El Niño
El Niño means The Little Boy, or Christ Child in Spanish. El Niño was originally recognized by fishermen off the coast of South America in the 1600's, with the appearance of unusually warm water in the Pacific Ocean. The name was chosen based on the time of year (around December) during which these warm water events tended to occur. The term El Niño refers to the large-scale ocean-atmosphere climate interaction linked to a periodic warming in sea surface temperatures across the central and east-central Equatorial Pacific. The presence of El Niño can significantly influence weather patterns, ocean conditions, and marine fisheries across large portions of the globe for an extended period of time.

La Niña
La Niña means The Little Girl in Spanish. La Niña is also sometimes called El Viejo, anti-El Niño, or simply "a cold event." La Niña episodes represent periods of below-average sea surface temperatures across the east-central Equatorial Pacific. Global climate La Niña impacts tend to be opposite those of El Niño impacts. In the tropics, ocean temperature variations in La Niña also tend to be opposite those of El Niño.

El Niño and La Niña weather influences in New Zealand (Source: NIWA)
During El Niño, New Zealand tends to experience stronger or more frequent winds from the west in summer, typically leading to drought in

east coast areas and more rain in the west. In winter, the winds tend to be more from the south, bringing colder conditions to both the land and the surrounding ocean. In spring and autumn south–westerly winds are more common.

A typical El Niño weather pattern (Source: NIWA):

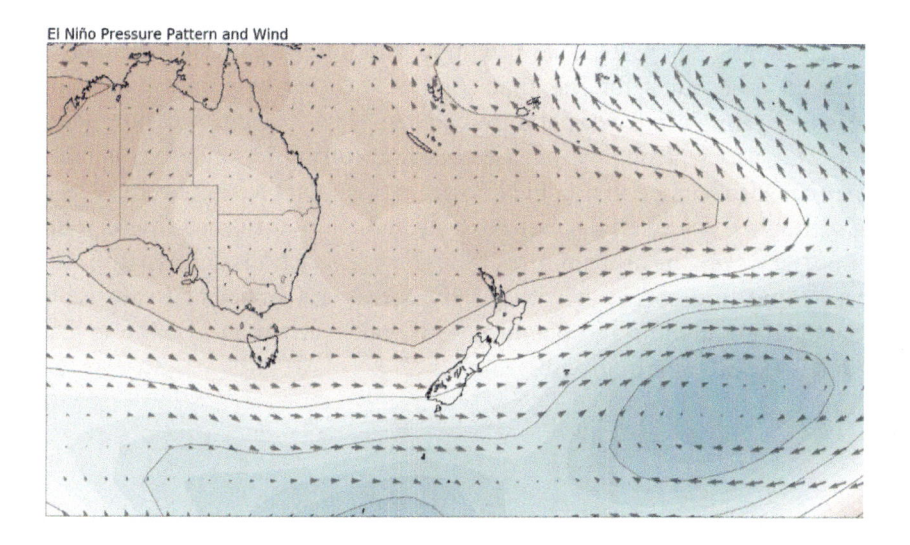

A typical La Niña weather pattern (Source: NIWA):

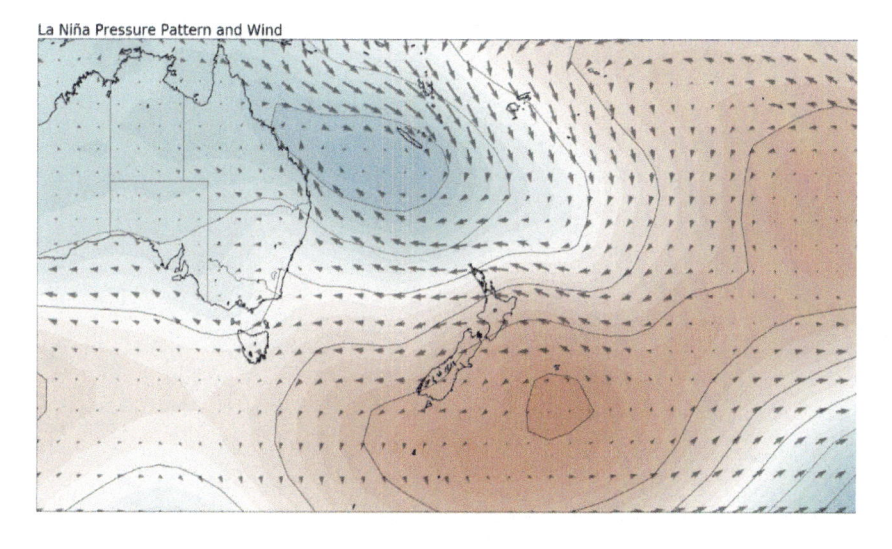

The role of the oceans 157

La Niña events have different impacts on New Zealand's climate. More north-easterly winds are characteristic, which tend to bring moist, rainy conditions to the north-east of the North Island, and reduced rainfall to the south and south-west of the South Island. Therefore, some areas, such as central Otago and South Canterbury, can experience drought in both El Niño and La Niña. Warmer than normal temperatures typically occur over much of the country during La Niña, although there are regional and seasonal exceptions.

Although ENSO events have an important influence on New Zealand's climate, it accounts for less than 25% of the year to year variance in seasonal rainfall and temperature at most New Zealand measurement sites. East coast droughts may be common during El Niño events, but they can also happen in non El Niño years (for example, the severe 1988-89 drought). Also, serious east coast droughts do not occur in every El Niño. However, the probabilities of the climate variations discussed above happening in association with ENSO events are sufficient to warrant management actions and planning to be taken when an El Niño or La Niña is expected or in progress.

7

The climate record over the centuries

"As long as the earth remains, there will be planting and harvest, cold and heat, winter and summer."

Genesis 8:22

Central England temperatures 1700-2018

Yearly mean temperatures have been recorded in Central England since about 1700. It is the longest temperature series in the world derived from instrumental records. It shows an increase in temperature of approximately 1.3°C from the end of the 17th Century to the end of the 20th Century/beginning of 21st Century. Subtle difference in timing between the warming/cooling phases between the Central England record and the other localities may reflect local climate variation, but the similarity in events between continents suggests the Central England Temperature record is recording global temperature patterns.

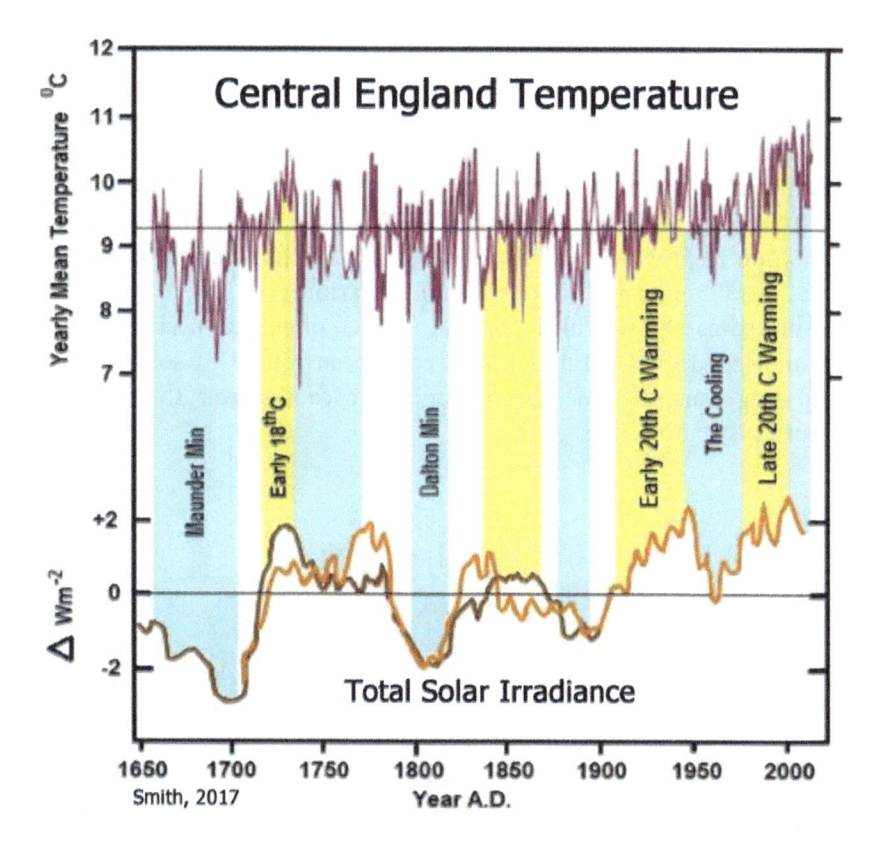

Source: Alan D Smith; *An Analysis of Climate Forcing's from the Central England Temperature Record.* British Journal of Environment & Climate Change 7(2): 113-118, 2017

Records of sunspot numbers began in 1610 such that detailed estimates of solar variation for the years covered by the England temperature record can be made without resort to the use of proxy data.

Reconstructions of total solar radiance (TSR) differ in magnitude, but there is agreement in form with 4 peaks and 4 to 6 troughs occurring over the time-scale of the England temperature record. These are: a minimum in TSR associated with the Maunder Sunspot Minimum in the latter half of the 17th Century; a peak, possibly bi-modal approaching modern TSR values during the 18th Century; a well-defined trough corresponding with the Dalton Sunspot Minimum between 1800-1820; a poorly defined TSR peak in the mid 19th Century; a reduction in TSR during the late 19th Century; increasing TSR during the early 20th Century; a decrease in TSR from around 1950-1975; and a second phase of TSR increase in the late 20th Century.

There is good correspondence with TSR throughout the England temperature record, with warm events correlating with high TSR and cool phases correlating with plateaus or decreases in TSR. However, for temperature increases from the beginning of the Industrial Revolution (Maunder Minimum and Dalton Minimum to end of 20th Century), high TSR models can account for only 63-67% of the temperature increase. This would suggest that one third of Global Warming/Climate Change can be attributed to anthropogenic global warming.

Approximately two-thirds (0.8°C to 0.9°C) of climate warming since the mid-late 18th Century (1.3°C) can be attributed to solar causes, suggesting warming due to anthropogenic causes over the last two centuries is 0.4 to 0.5°C.

Central England surface air temperatures 1660 - present

As noted, the Central England surface air temperature series (below) is the longest existing meteorological record. (Thin lines are the annual values, the thick lines are the running 11 year average).

The graphs for annual, summer and winter temperatures have been prepared using the composite monthly meteorological series originally painstakingly homogenized and published by the late professor Gordon Manley (1974). The data series is now updated by the Hadley Centre.

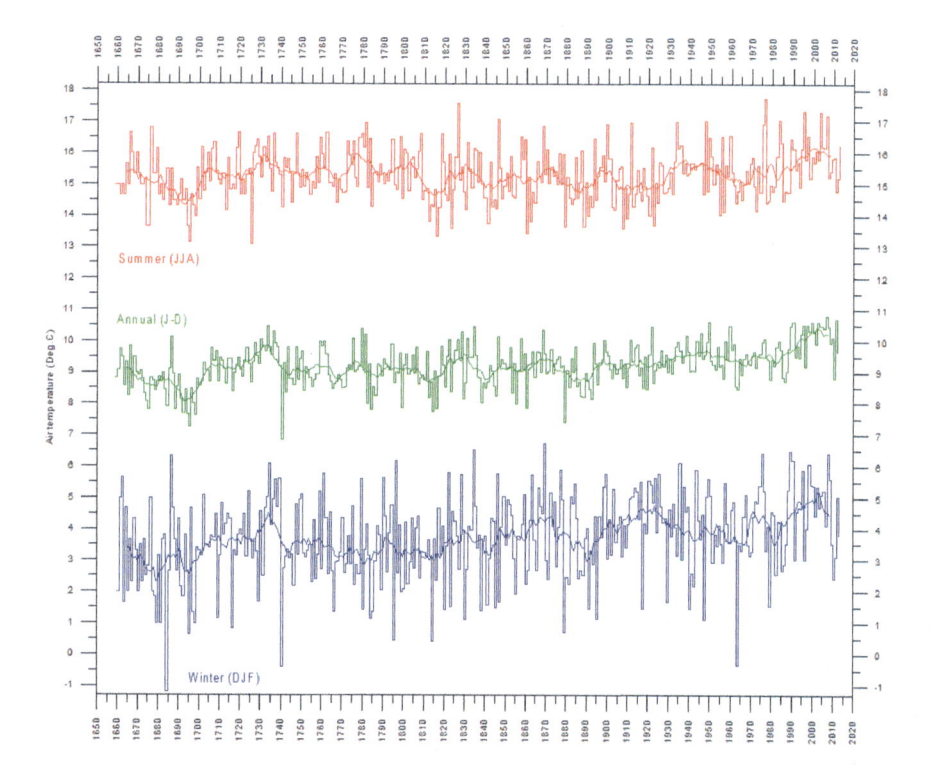

The climate record over the centuries 163

Southern Oscillation Index (SOI)

The Southern Oscillation Index (SOI) is a standardized index based on the observed sea level pressure differences between Tahiti and Darwin, Australia. The SOI is a leading measure of the large-scale fluctuations in air pressure occurring between the western and eastern tropical Pacific (i.e., the state of the Southern Oscillation) during El Niño and La Niña episodes.

El Niño–Southern Oscillation (ENSO) is an irregularly periodic variation in winds and sea surface temperatures over the tropical eastern Pacific Ocean, affecting the climate of much of the tropics and subtropics. The warming phase of the sea temperature is known as El Niño and the cooling phase as La Niña. The Southern Oscillation is the accompanying atmospheric component, coupled with the sea temperature change: El Niño is accompanied by high air surface pressure in the tropical western Pacific and La Niña with low air surface pressure there. The two periods last several months each and typically occur every few years with varying intensity per period.

The two phases relate to the Walker circulation, which was discovered by Gilbert Walker during the early twentieth century. The Walker circulation is caused by the pressure gradient force that results from a high-pressure area over the eastern Pacific Ocean, and a low-pressure system over Indonesia. Weakening or reversal of the Walker circulation (which includes the trade winds) decreases or eliminates the upwelling of cold deep sea water, thus creating an El Niño by causing the ocean surface to reach above average temperatures. An especially strong Walker circulation causes a La Niña, resulting in cooler ocean temperatures due to increased upwelling.

Mechanisms that cause the oscillation remain under study. The extremes of this climate pattern's oscillations cause extreme weather (such as floods and droughts) in many regions of the world. Developing countries dependent upon agriculture and fishing, particularly those bordering the Pacific Ocean, are the most affected.

In general, smoothed time series of the SOI correspond very well with changes in ocean temperatures across the eastern tropical Pacific. The negative phase of the SOI represents below-normal air pressure at Tahiti and above-normal air pressure at Darwin. The positive phase of the SOI represents above-normal air pressure at Tahiti and below-normal air pressure at Darwin.

Prolonged periods of negative SOI values coincide with abnormally warm ocean waters across the eastern tropical Pacific typical of El Niño episodes. In contrast, prolonged periods of positive SOI values coincide with abnormally cold ocean waters across the eastern tropical Pacific typical of La Niña episodes. Sustained negative values of the SOI below −8 often indicate El Niño episodes. These negative values are usually accompanied by sustained warming of the central and eastern tropical Pacific Ocean and a decrease in the strength of the Pacific Trade Winds.

Sustained positive values of the SOI above +8 are typical of a La Niña episode. They are associated with stronger Pacific trade winds and warmer sea temperatures to the north of Australia. Waters in the central and eastern tropical Pacific Ocean become cooler during this time.

The following chart (from the The Australian Bureau of Meteorology) shows monthly values of the SOI from 1880 to April 2020.

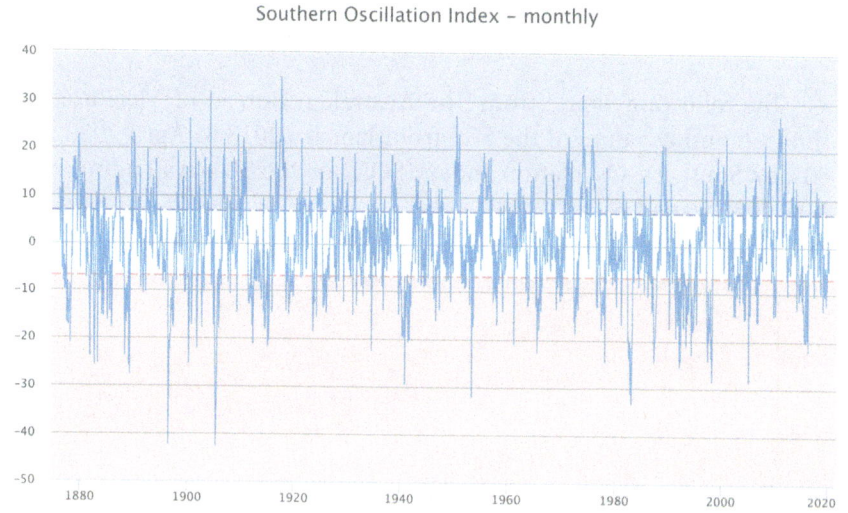

Southern Oscillation Index – monthly

© Copyright Commonwealth of Australia 2020, Bureau of Meteorology

The climate record over the centuries 165

The following chart (from the New Zealand's NIWA) shows values of the SOI from 1880 to 2019.

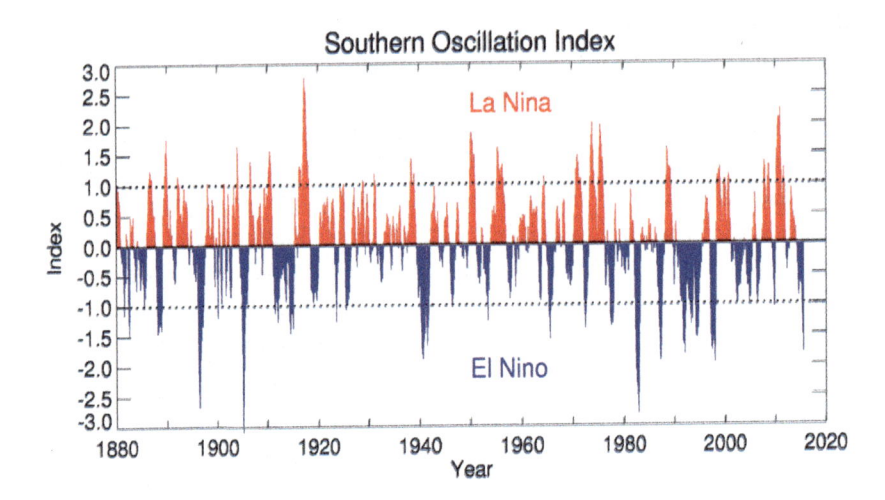

The following chart (from The Australian Bureau of Meteorology) shows monthly values of the SOI from January 2018 to April 2020. The 30-day Southern Oscillation Index (SOI) for the 30 days ending mid-May 2020 was +1.6.

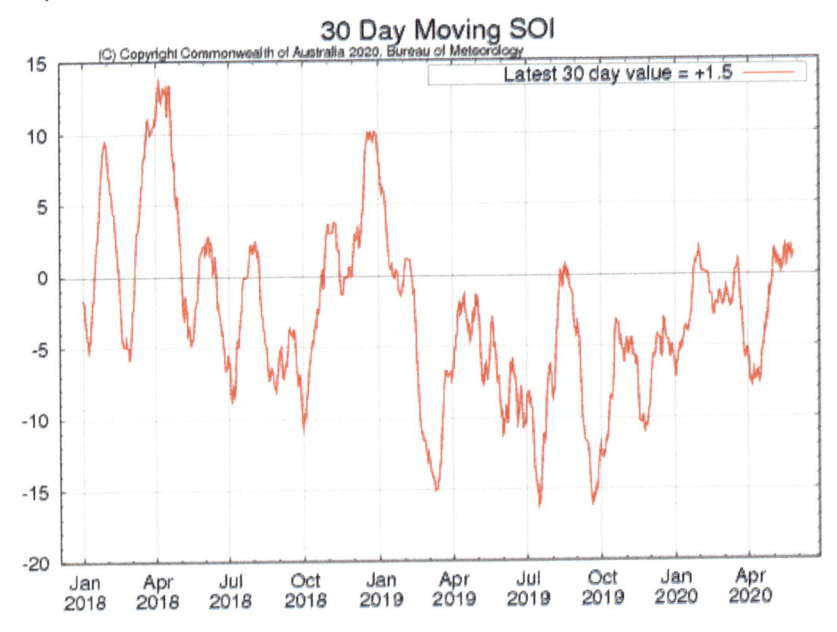

Tropospheric temperatures 1979 to May 2020

The chart below shows that since 1979, when reliable satellite observations became available, there has been little overall trend in the average tropospheric temperatures, apart from milder/warmer temperatures since about 1997, and two significant warm periods associated with the El Niño events in 1998 and 2015-16.

The latest global average temperatures of the troposphere updated to May 2020 - observed from US National Oceanic and Atmospheric Administration satellites – are computed by the University of Alabama at Huntsville in the United States. The data shows variations from the 30 year period 1981-2010.

Since 1979, NOAA satellites have been carrying instruments which measure the natural microwave thermal emissions from oxygen in the atmosphere. The intensity of the signals these microwave radiometers measure at different microwave frequencies is directly proportional to the temperature of different, deep layers of the atmosphere. Every month, researchers at the University of Alabama (Dr John Christy and Dr Roy Spencer) update global temperature datasets that represent the piecing together of the temperature data from a total of fourteen instruments flying on different satellites over the years.

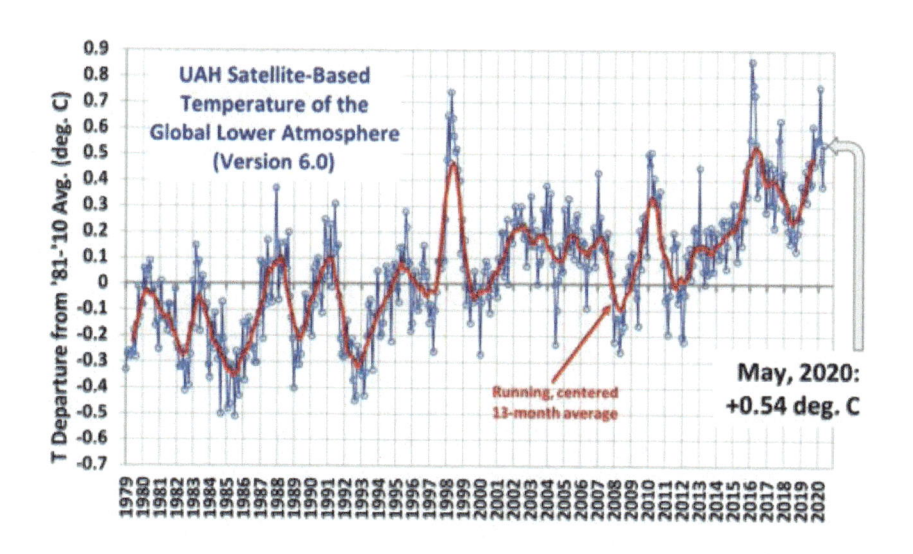

The graph represents the latest update; updates are usually made within the first week of every month. Contrary to some reports, the satellite measurements are not calibrated in any way with the global surface-based thermometer records of temperature. They instead use their own on-board precision redundant platinum resistance thermometers calibrated to a laboratory reference standard before launch.

The troposphere is the lowest layer of Earth's atmosphere. It contains approximately 75% of the atmosphere's mass and 99% of its water vapour and aerosols. The average depth of the troposphere is approximately 17 km in the middle latitudes.

The latest data for May 2020 is +0.54°C.

The coolest months since 1979 were September 1984, with -0.49 °C, and November 1984, with -0.42°C.

The warmest months were February 2016 with +0.83°C, February and April 1998, and February 2020, all +0.76°C, and March 2016 +0.73°C, and April 2016 +0.73°C.

The chart shows the El Niño warming in the 1998 period, and 2015-16, and the Mount Pinatubo, volcanic cooling during 1992-1993.

Global temperatures 1996 - May 2020

Global temperatures are compiled for various areas including global (land-ocean), global (meteorological stations), three latitude bands, and hemispheric, by the Goddard Institute for Space Studies of NASA (see *data.giss.nasa*).

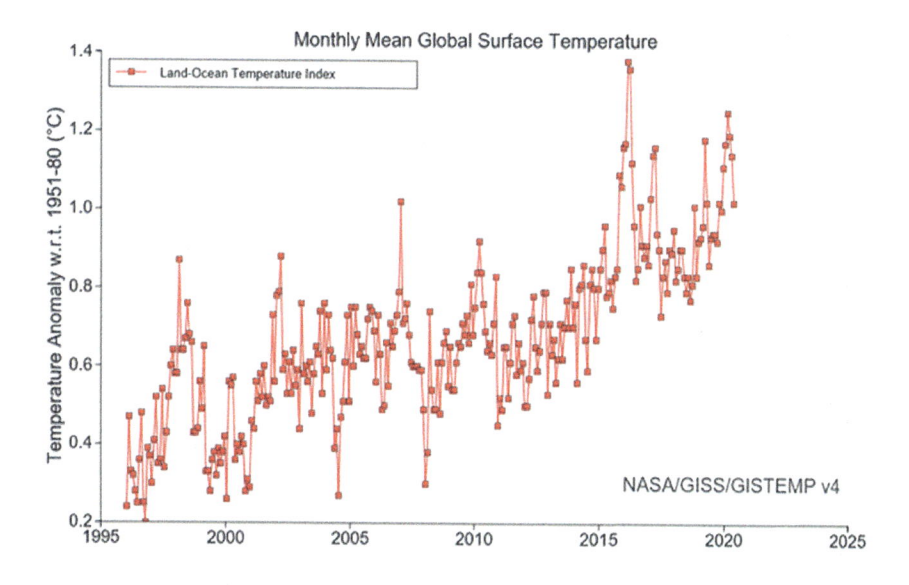

The graph shows the monthly mean global surface temperature anomaly from the base period 1951-1980, for the period 1996 - May 2020.

The GISS Surface Temperature Analysis (GISTEMP) is an estimate of global surface temperature change. Graphs and tables are updated around the middle of every month using current data files from NOAA GHCN v3 (meteorological stations), ERSST v4 (ocean areas), and SCAR (Antarctic stations), combined as described in the December 2010 publication (Hansen et al. 2010). These updated files incorporate reports for the previous month and also late reports and corrections for earlier months.

The basic GISS temperature analysis scheme was defined in the late 1970's when a method of estimating global temperature change was needed for comparison with one-dimensional global climate models. The scheme was based on the finding that the correlation of temperature change was reasonably strong for stations separated by up to 1200 km, especially at middle and high latitudes. This fact proved sufficient to obtain useful estimates for global mean temperature changes.

The chart shows that from 1997 to May 2020 there has been a small warming in the global monthly temperatures, and a relatively warm period associated with the recent El Niño event.

Global annual temperatures 1880 - 2019

Global temperatures for various areas including global (land-ocean), global (meteorological stations), three latitude bands, and hemispheric are compiled by the Goddard Institute for Space Studies.

The chart below shows the annual mean global surface temperature anomaly from the base period 1951-1980, for the period 1880 - 2019. For details see *data.giss.nasa*.

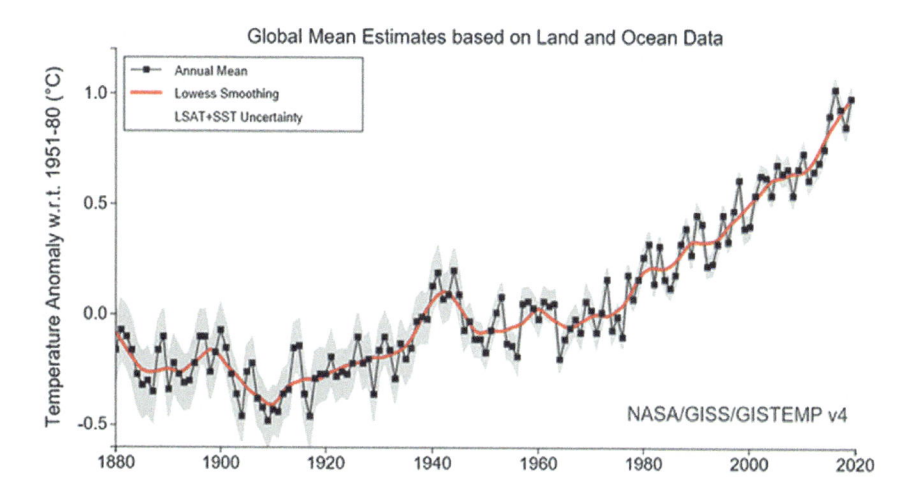

The global temperature shows little change from 1880 to 1910, a general warming from 1910 to the early 1940's, a cooling from the early 1940's to 1980, and a general warming from the 1980s to today.

The basic GISS temperature analysis scheme was defined in the late 1970s by James Hansen when a method of estimating global temperature change was needed for comparison with one-dimensional global climate models. The scheme was based on the finding that the correlation of temperature change was reasonably strong for stations separated by up to 1200 km, especially at middle and high latitudes. This fact proved sufficient to obtain useful estimates for global mean temperature changes.

Temperature analyses were carried out prior to 1980, notably those of Murray Mitchell, but most covered only 20-90°N latitudes. The first published results (Hansen et al. 1981) showed that, contrary to impressions from northern latitudes, global cooling after 1940 was small, and there was net global warming of about 0.4°C between the 1880s and

1970s. The early analysis scheme went through a series of enhancements.

The analysis method was fully documented by Hansen and Lebedeff in 1987 including quantitative estimates of the error in annual and 5-year mean temperature change. This was done by sampling at station locations a spatially complete data set of a long run of a global climate model, which was shown to have realistic spatial and temporal variability. A more complete uncertainty analysis was published by Lenssen et al. in 2019.

As there are other potential sources of error, such as urban warming near meteorological stations, many other methods have been used to verify the approximate magnitude of inferred global warming. These methods include inference of surface temperature change from vertical temperature profiles in the ground (bore holes) at many sites around the world, rate of glacier retreat at many locations, and studies by several groups of the effect of urban and other local human influences on the global temperature record. All of these yield consistent estimates of the approximate magnitude of global warming.

Further affirmation of the reality of the warming is its spatial distribution, which has largest values at locations remote from any local human influence, with a global pattern consistent with that expected for response to global climate forcings (larger in the Northern Hemisphere than the Southern Hemisphere, larger at high latitudes than low latitudes, larger over land than over ocean).

An updated documentation by Hansen et al. in 2010 compares alternative analyses and addresses questions about perception and reality of global warming; various choices for the ocean data are tested. It is also shown that global temperature change is sensitive to estimated temperature change in polar regions, where observations are limited. A multi-year smoothing is applied to fully remove the annual cycle and improve information content in temperature graphs.

Despite large year-to-year fluctuations associated with the El Niño-La Niña cycle of tropical ocean temperature, the conclusion could be made that global temperatures continue to rise in the 21st century. NOAA in their report *Climate Change: Global Temperatures*, dated January 16, 2020 commented on the current state of global temperatures.

- In 2019, the average temperature across global land and ocean surfaces was 0.95°C above the twentieth-century average of 13.9°C, making it the second-warmest year on record.

- The global annual temperature has increased at an average rate of 0.07°C per decade since 1880 and over twice that rate (+0.18°C) since 1981.

- The five warmest years in the 1880–2019 record have all occurred since 2015, while nine of the 10 warmest years have occurred since 2005.

- From 1900 to 1980 a new temperature record was set on average every 13.5 years; since 1981, it has increased to every 3 years.

Arctic and Antarctic temperatures January 1979 to January 2020

Each month Professor Ole Humlum of The University Centre in Svalbard (UNIS), in Norway publishes on his very comprehensive website a large number of charts and related analyses of data from international sources such as NASA. His latest website can be found at *www.climate4you.com*.

One example of what is contained in his web base are the charts of Arctic and Antarctic surface air temperatures from January 1979 to January 2020.

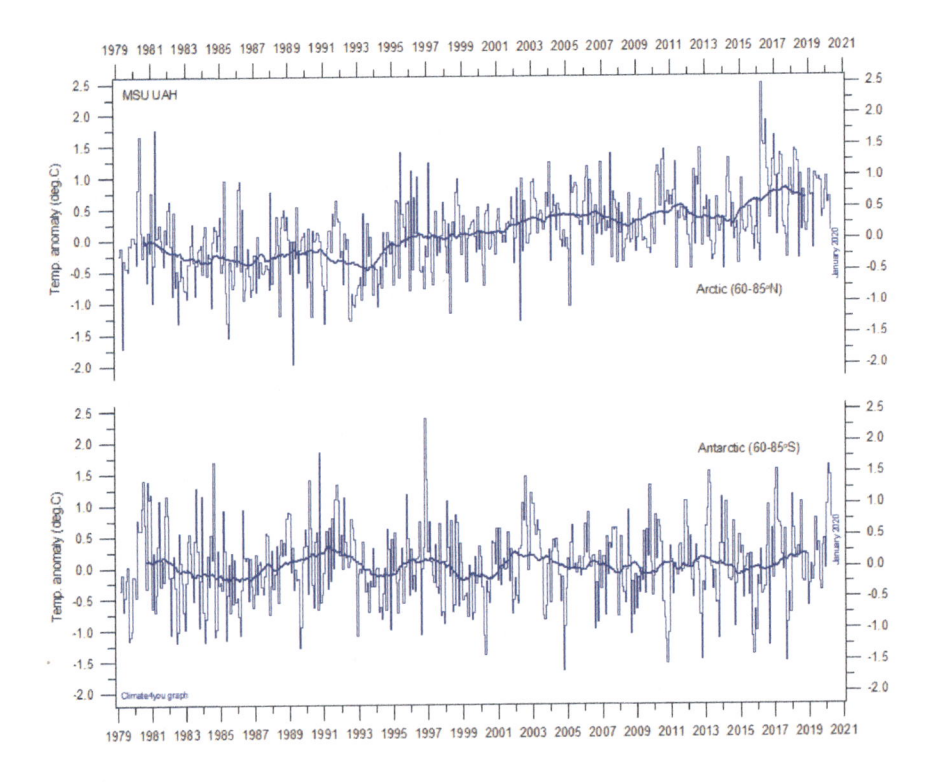

HadCRUT4 is a global temperature dataset, providing gridded temperature anomalies across the world as well as averages for the hemispheres and the globe as a whole. CRUTEM4 and HadSST3 are the land and ocean components of this overall dataset, respectively. These

174 *Climate Change: Nature is in Control*

datasets have been developed by the Climatic Research Unit (University of East Anglia) in conjunction with the Hadley Centre (UK Met Office), apart from the sea surface temperature (SST) dataset which was developed solely by the UK Hadley Centre.

The chart shows area weighted Arctic (70-90 degrees N) monthly surface air temperature anomalies (HadCRUT4) since January 2000, in relation to the WMO normal period 1961-1990. The thin line shows the monthly temperature anomaly, while the thicker line shows the running 37-month (c. 3 year) average.

8

Lessons from history

To know the road ahead, ask those coming back

(Chinese Proverb)

"If we have anything to fear from 'climate change', it is not warming, whose effects are almost wholly beneficial. What we need to fear is a return of the cold, dry, hungry ice ages."

Garth George writing in the *Bay of Plenty Times* on July 7, 2012 on *Cold comfort for global warming*.

Vikings and their explorations in a warmer world

The Greenlandic Vikings' apogee coincided with the Medieval Warm Period (also known as the Medieval Climate Anomaly), generally dated from about 950-1250; their disappearance followed the onset of the Little Ice Age, which ran from about 1300-1850. Both periods according to *Wikipedia* are firmly documented in European and Icelandic historical records. Thus, popular authors and some scientists have fixed on the idea that nice weather drew the settlers to Greenland, and bad weather froze and starved them. But there are no early historical climate records from Greenland. Recently, historians have proposed more complex factors in addition to, or instead of, climate: hostilities with the Inuit, a decline in ivory trade, soil erosion caused by the Vikings' imported cattle, or a migration back to Europe to farms depopulated by the Black Plague.

The Medieval Warm Period (MWP), also called medieval warm epoch or little climatic optimum, was a brief climatic interval that is hypothesized to have occurred from approximately 950 to 1250 (roughly coinciding with the Middle Ages in Europe), in which relatively warm conditions are said to have prevailed in various parts of the world, though predominantly in the Northern Hemisphere from Greenland eastward through Europe and parts of Asia.

The controversial medieval warm period
John Rafferty (*www.brittanica.com*) has commented that the notion of a medieval warm period is highly controversial. Many paleoclimatologists claim that well-documented evidence for the phenomenon appears across the North Atlantic region, while others maintain that the phenomenon was global, occurring all over the world. Still other scientists insist that their data do not show appreciable changes in average temperature anywhere over the course of the interval. Meanwhile, global warming skeptics have used the MWP to bolster their position in the debate over the nature and effects of climate change.

Direct measurements of climate conditions collected by thermometers, barometers, rain gauges, and other equipment have been available since the 19th century. The climatic conditions of older periods, however, have to be "reconstructed" with the help of historical documents (which contain figures on food production, the length of growing seasons, and the duration of ice on bodies of water) and other indirect measures of climate (including "climate proxies" such as tree rings, ice cores, and sediment cores). Many such studies suggest that Europe's Middle Ages did see several multiyear stretches of relatively pleasant conditions and reliable weather. There is little evidence that such conditions prevailed on a global scale, however. Some climate proxies point to several periods of extended drought during the MWP in some locations, such as the Sierra Nevada mountains of North America, parts of Australia, and the Asian steppe, whereas other areas, such as northern China, experienced a mix of heavy rainfall and drought.

Many studies show that the amount of warming occurring during the MWP varied by season and region. Some provide evidence of relatively warm temperatures (most pronounced during the summer months) in several regions, including the North Atlantic, northern Europe, China, and parts of North America, as well as the Andes, Tasmania, and New Zealand. Other studies maintain that the temperature conditions of certain regions, such as the Mediterranean, South America, and other locations in the Southern Hemisphere, were essentially no different from those of the present day.

Only a few studies have attempted to assign a specific value to changes in average global temperatures during the MWP. In 1965 British climatologist Hubert Horace Lamb examined historical records of harvests and precipitation, along with early ice-core and tree-ring data, and concluded that the MWP was probably 1–2 °C (1.8–3.6 °F) warmer than early 20th-century conditions in Europe. Attempts to calculate global temperature changes during the MWP, even using modern instrumental and ice-core sampling techniques, have been inconclusive.

Vikings and their explorations

The website *www.sunnysuffolk.edu* has a very informative paper, written by Scott Mandia on February 3, 2017, on Vikings and their explorations in a warmer world. During the years 800-1200, Iceland and Greenland were settled by the Vikings. These people, also known as the Norse, included Norwegians, Swedes, Danes, and Finns. The warm climate during the MWP allowed this great migration to flourish. Drift ice posed the greatest hazard to sailors but reports of drift ice in old records do not appear until the thirteenth century. The Norse peoples travelled to Iceland for a variety of reasons including a search for more land and resources to satisfy a growing population and to escape raiders and harsh rulers.

One force behind the movement to Iceland in the ninth century was the ruthlessness of Harald Fairhair, a Norwegian King (Bryson, 1977).

Vikings travelling to Iceland from Norway during the MWP were probably encouraged by the sight of pastures with sedges, grasses and dwarf woodlands of birch and willow resembling those at home. Animal bones and other materials collected from archaeological sites reveal Icelandic Vikings had large farmsteads with dairy cattle (a source of meat), pigs, sheep and goats (for wool, hair, milk, and meat). Farmsteads also had ample pastures and fields of barley used for the making of beer and these farms were located near bird cliffs (providing meat, eggs, and eiderdown) and inshore fishing grounds. Fishing was primarily done with hand lines or from small boats that did not venture across the horizon (McGovern and Perdikaris, 2000).

Erik the Red

In 960, Thorvald Asvaldsson of Jaederen in Norway killed a man. He was forced to leave the country so he moved to northern Iceland. He had a ten year old son named Erik, or Erik the Red. Erik too had a violent streak and in 982 he killed two men. Erik the Red was banished from Iceland for three years so he sailed west to find a land that Icelanders had discovered years before but knew little about. Erik searched the coast of this land and found the most hospitable area, a deep fiord on the southwestern coast. Warmer Atlantic currents met the island there and conditions were not much different than those in Iceland (trees and grasses). He called this new land "Greenland" because he "believed more people would go thither if the country had a beautiful name," according to one of the Icelandic chronicles (Hermann, 1954); although Greenland, as a whole, could not be considered "green." Additionally, the land was not very good for farming.

Norse, or Vikings, led by Erik the Red, first sailed from recently settled Iceland to southwestern Greenland around 985, according to Icelandic records. Some 3,000 to 5,000 settlers eventually lived in Greenland, harvesting walrus ivory and raising livestock. But the colonies disappeared between about 1360 and 1460, leaving only ruins, and a longstanding mystery as to what happened. The native Inuit remained, but Europeans did not re-inhabit Greenland until the 1700s.

The Greenland Vikings

The Greenland Vikings lived mostly on dairy produce and meat, primarily from cows. The vegetable diet of Greenlanders included berries, edible grasses, and seaweed, but these were inadequate even during the best harvests. During the MWP, Greenland's climate was so cold that cattle breeding and dairy farming could only be carried on in the sheltered fiords. The growing season in Greenland even then was very short. Frost typically occurred in August and the fiords froze in October. Before the year 1300, ships regularly sailed from Norway and other European countries to Greenland bringing with them timber, iron, corn, salt, and other needed items.

The gift of a cargo of wine
Trade was by barter. Greenlanders offered butter, cheese, wool, and their frieze cloths, which were greatly sought after in Europe, as well as white and blue fox furs, polar bear skins, walrus and narwhal tusks, and walrus skins. In fact, two Greenland items in particular were prized by Europeans: white bears and the white falcon. These items were given as royal gifts. For instance, the King of Norway-Denmark sent a number of Greenland falcons as a gift to the King of Portugal, and received in return the gift of a cargo of wine (Stefansson, 1966). Because of the shortage of adequate vegetables and cereal grains, and a shortage of timber to make ships, the trade link to Iceland and Europe was vital (Hermann, 1954).

One study undercuts the idea that the MWF was global and that Vikings may not have colonized Greenland in nice weather. Vikings colonized Greenland and possibly neighbouring Baffin Island during what has been assumed to be – perhaps mistakenly – a temporary warm period. They disappeared in the 1400s. Southern Greenland's Hvalsey church is the best preserved Viking ruin. (*Wikimedia Commons*).

A new study questions the popular notion that 10th-century Norse people were able to colonize Greenland because of a period of unusually warm weather. Based upon signs left by old glaciers, researchers say the climate was already cold when the Norse arrived–and that climate thus probably played little role in their mysterious demise some 400 years later. On a larger scale, the study adds to building evidence that the so-called MWP, when Europe enjoyed exceptionally clement weather, did not necessarily extend to other parts of the world. "It's becoming clearer that the MWP was patchy, not global," said lead author Nicolás Young, a glacial geologist at Columbia University's Lamont-Doherty Earth Observatory. "The concept is Eurocentric–that's where the best-known observations were made. Elsewhere, the climate might not have been the same." Climate scientists have cited the MWP to explain anomalies in rainfall and temperature in far-flung regions, from the U.S. Southwest to China. The study appears in the journal *Science Advances* in 2015.

Glaciers usually advance during cold times and recede during warm ones. Two glaciers in western Greenland are now retreating from where they may have been when the Vikings arrived (Jason Briner). In the new study, the scientists sampled boulders left by advancing glaciers over the last 1,000-some years in southwest Greenland, and on neighbouring Baffin Island, which the Norse may also have occupied, according to newly uncovered evidence. Glacial advances during the Little Ice Age have wiped out most evidence of where the glaciers were during the Norse settlement. Young and his colleagues were able to find traces of a few moraines–heaps of debris left at glaciers' ends–that, by their layout, they could tell predated the Little Ice Age advances. Using newly precise methods of analyzing chemical isotopes in the rocks, they showed that these moraines had been deposited during the Viking occupation, and that the glaciers had neared or reached their later maximum Little Ice Age positions between 975 and 1275. The strong implication: it was at least as cold when the Vikings arrived as when they left. "If the Vikings travelled to Greenland when it was cool, it's a stretch to say deteriorating climate drove them out," said Young.

The effects of the MWP were not uniform
The findings fit with other recently developed evidence that the effects of the MWP were not uniform; some places, including parts of central Eurasia and northwestern North America, may actually have cooled off. In western Greenland, small outlet glaciers are wasting backward, leaving behind piles of rocks, or moraines, that mark their previous advances, and meltwater has formed a lake (Jason Briner) .

In the Atlantic region, the research includes a 2013 study of ocean-bottom sediments suggesting that temperatures in the western North Atlantic actually went down as the eastern North Atlantic warmed. Other studies of the region suggest a more complex picture. A 2011 study of a core from the Greenland ice sheet shows a strong cooling at the start of Norse occupation, and another in the middle, with interspersed warming. On the other hand, lake-bottom sediments from southwestern Greenland studied in 2011 by Lamont-Doherty paleoclimatologist William D'Andrea, suggest it might indeed have been warm when the Norse arrived, but that climate cooled starting in 1160, well before the Little Ice Age.

The new study may feed recent suggestions by other researchers that the Medieval Warm Period was in part just an extended phase of the North Atlantic Oscillation (NAO). Modern observations show that the NAO is a generally decadal-scale climate cycle, in which warm winds from the west strengthen and boost temperatures in Europe and Iceland, but simultaneously make southwest Greenland and Baffin Island colder, by sucking in more Arctic air. That makes the two regions temperatures seesaw in opposite directions.

In Baffin Island's Naqsaq Valley, University at Buffalo geologist Jason Briner sampled a boulder left by a glacier around the time of early Viking settlement. Measurements of chemical isotopes within the rock suggest settlers in neighbouring Greenland faced cold weather (Nicolás Young). Gifford Miller, a paleoclimatologist at the University of Colorado, called the paper "a coup de grace on the MWP". Miller said it shows "with great clarity of evidence" that "the idea of a consistently warm Medieval period is certainly an oversimplification and of little utility".

Astrid Ogilvie, a climate historian at Iceland's Stefansson Arctic Institute and the University of Colorado's Institute for Arctic and Alpine Research, said the study "shows that the climate is clearly more complicated and variable than people earlier assumed." As for the Vikings, the climate story has been dimming for some time, she said. "I do not like the simplistic argument that the Greenland people went there when it was warm, and then 'it got cold and they died,'" she said. "I think the MWP has been built on many false premises, but it still clings to the popular imagination".

The rocks were analyzed at the University at Buffalo, and at the Lamont-Doherty lab of geochemist and study co-author Joerg Schaefer. The Lamont lab is among a handful that can precisely date such recent rock deposits. The analyses are done by measuring build-ups of small amounts of Beryllium 10, an isotope created when cosmogenic rays strike rock surfaces newly exposed by melting ice. In addition to Young and Schaefer, the paper was co-authored by Avriel Schweinsberg and Jason Briner of the University at Buffalo, who carried out the Greenland portion of the fieldwork.

Building the cathedrals of Europe... the climate factor

When I was in Canada about 30 years ago, I listened to a lecture about Medieval Warming, the building of the Gothic Cathedrals and the freemasons. It appears that there was no theological reason why the cathedrals were built at that time but there is an interesting link between the warmth of Europe in the 11th to 15th centuries, the wine of England and the freemasons and their lodges.

The Medieval Warm Period is an epoch of relatively warm climate which existed in the 10th-13th centuries, following the climatic pessimum of the Great Migration and preceding the so-called Little Ice Age of the 14th-18th centuries. Prior to current theories about man-made global warming - a full 400–700 years before humans began the Industrial revolution - the Medieval warm period's mild winters and relatively warm and even weather allowed for unprecedented crop growth, urban expansion, and the establishment of Scandinavian settlements in Greenland and North America.

Rather than the limiting the Medieval warm period to "Europe and neighbouring regions or the North Atlantic", Willie Soon and Sallie Baliunas of the *Harvard-Smithsonian Center for Astrophysics* found 112 studies containing information about the medieval warm period in Russia, the U.S. Corn Belt, Central Plains and Southwest; much of China and Japan; southern Africa; Argentina, Chile and Peru, America, Australia and Antarctica ... in the Indian Ocean, both central and southern; and in the Central and Western Pacific Ocean. In the Southern Hemisphere, twenty-one of twenty-two studies showed evidence of the Medieval Warming.

Climate became distinctly more benign
Thomas Gale Moore of the Hoover Institution wrote about the Medieval Warm Period: "The three centuries beginning with the eleventh century, during which the climate became distinctly more benign, witnessed a profound revolution which, by the late 1200's had transformed the landscape into an economy filled with merchants, vibrant towns and great fairs. Crop failures became less frequent; new territories were brought under control. With a more clement climate and a more reliable food supply, the population mushroomed.

The historian Charles Van Doren claimed that: "the ... three centuries, from about 1000 to about 1300, became one of the most optimistic, prosperous, and progressive periods in European history." All across Europe, the population went on an unparalleled building spree, erecting at huge cost spectacular cathedrals and public edifices. Ponderous Romanesque churches gave way to soaring Gothic cathedrals. Virtually all the magnificent religious shrines that we visit in awe today were started by the optimistic populations of the eleventh through the thirteenth centuries, although many remained unfinished for centuries.

Many of the Gothic cathedrals of Europe were built or were commenced during the period 1100-1500. This period was a time of warming (in some cases warmer than at present) when abundant crops were available to provide food for the builders of the cathedrals. There appears to be no theological reason why the cathedrals were built at that time, but the development of architectural techniques was a significant factor. Perhaps the main reason why the cathedrals were built was related in whole or in part by the warmer weather.

Masons in Medieval England
Masons in Medieval England were responsible for constructing some of England's most famous buildings. Masons were highly skilled craftsmen and their trade was most frequently used in the building of castles, churches and cathedrals. Masons belonged to a guild. However, a mason's guild was not linked to just one town as the members of the mason's guild had to move to where building was required. The Mason's Guild was an international one and even in Medieval England, the guild was sometimes referred to as the Free Masons. 'Free' stone was the name of the stone commonly used by masons as it was soft and facilitated intricate carvings.

Masons tended to lead nomadic lives. They went where there was employment. Other tradesmen could effectively stay where they were as there was enough trade for their skill to allow them to settle. However, masons had to move on to their next source of employment once a building had been completed – and that could be many miles away.

A mason would have an apprentice working for him. When the mason moved on to a new job, the apprentice would move with him. When a mason felt that his apprentice had learned enough about the trade, he would be examined at a Mason's Lodge. If he passed this examination of his skill, he would be admitted to that lodge as a master mason and given a mason's mark that would be unique to him. Once given this mark, the new master mason would put it on any work that he did so that it could be identified as his work.

A mason at the top of his trade was a master mason. However, a Master Mason, by title, was the man who had overall charge of a building site and master masons would work under this person. A Master Mason also had charge over carpenters, glaziers etc. In fact, everybody who worked on a building site was under the supervision of the Master Mason. He would work in what was known as the Mason's Lodge. All important building sites would have such a building that served as a workshop and a drawing office from which all the work on the building site was organised. Anyone who arrived at the building site and claimed that they were a master mason would be tested by the Master Mason and by master masons already working on the site. By doing this they ensured that quality was maintained – and that they would have a good chance of future building work.

Trademark carvings

When a Master Mason moved on, he took his lodge with him. That does not mean the physical building but the organisation and culture of the Master Mason and those who worked with him. Even the carving of sub-parapet friezes - a very localised phenomenon - suggests a building culture at work amongst the masons, and very certainly amongst one or more Master Masons. Beyond that, however, and most telling of all, is the plethora of "trademark carvings"- notably the mooning man - that are surely products of what we would today call a corporate identity. That identity was surely forged in the closed world of the Lodge.

The word "freemason" does not appear, according to Knoop and Jones, until 1376. That it does so quite late in the medieval period might have something to do with the advance of English at the expense of Latin (and French) in the world of commerce.

In its origin, the word "freemason" would undoubtedly seem connected with "freestone", which is the name given to any fine-grained sandstone or limestone that can be freely worked in any direction and sawn with a toothed saw.

So we can see that the freemason was not defined by his "freedom" as many assume (all masons were equally free or otherwise) but by his ability to work in the finest stone that was used for the most decorative purposes. Nor was he defined by membership of some mystical "order" of masons with hierarchies, secrets and rituals such as characterise the modern (or, as they would prefer to see it, ancient) institution of Freemasonry.

Knoop and Jones uncovered evidence that one of the first tasks of the Master was to prepare templates made of wood or sheet metal. If he needed a cross section of a pillar, for example, he would make a template for his men to copy. Similarly for window tracery. Some of these templates still exist in the roof of York Minster. There were writings and drawings available but they were scarce and expensive. Also the plans for a church would call for an impracticably large canvas. The masons, then, would draw in a box filled with sand or plaster. Again, at York Minster the "drawing floor" still exists.

There can be no doubt that masons in Medieval England were highly skilled craftsmen. Testimony to their work stands today in the numerous cathedrals and castles that still exist.

Economic activity in Europe
Throughout Europe economic activity blossomed during this period of warming. Banking, insurance, and finance developed; a money economy became well entrenched; manufacturing of textiles expanded to levels never seen before. Farmers in medieval England launched a thriving wine industry. Good wines demand warm springs free of frosts, substantial summer warmth and sunshine without too much rain, and sunny days in the autumn. The northern limit for grapes during the Middle Ages was about 500 km north of the current commercial wine areas in France and Germany.

The medieval warm period, which started a century earlier in Asia, benefited the rest of the globe as well. From the ninth through the thirteenth centuries, farming spread into northern portions of Russia. In the Far East, Chinese and Japanese farmers migrated north into Manchuria, the Amur Valley and northern Japan. The Vikings founded colonies in Iceland and Greenland, then actually green. Scandinavian seafarers discovered "Vinland" along the East Coast of North America.

The systematic investigation of a possible medieval climate anomaly - especially in Europe - was initially the field of historical climatology. Long before the beginning of instrumental measurements, a record of climate change could be drawn from historical documents and archaeological finds, leading to conclusions on climatic conditions and their consequences. Thus, for the period from about 1300, there are reasonably complete historical reports of summer and winter weather. It was through the pioneering work in this field, of the British climatologist Hubert Lamb and the French historian Emmanuel Le Roy Ladurie, that the first comprehensive overviews of higher temperatures and social contexts for the North Atlantic and Europe were delivered.

The term "medieval warm period" was then primarily influenced by the work of Hubert Lamb of the University of East Anglia in the 1960s, and later adopted by other fields of research. Lamb called this a global warming, which he stated regionally with an increase up to 1-2°C and whose peak he suspected between the years 1000 and 1300. Lamb found evidence of such warming, especially around the North Atlantic, while there were indications of relatively low temperatures for the North Pacific at about the same time. As a cause, he assumed displacements of the Arctic polar vortex.

The Dust Bowl era in the United States in the 1930's

The Dust Bowl as described in *Wikipedia* was a period of severe dust storms that greatly damaged the ecology and agriculture of the American and Canadian prairies during the 1930s; severe drought and a failure to apply dryland farming methods to prevent wind erosion caused the phenomenon. The low rainfalls and very high temperatures in many areas during the 1930's are unprecedented in modern times. The decade of the 1930s tends to get lumped into a decade of persistent heat and drought, yet, much of the reputation of that decade comes from just two of those years, 1934 and 1936. The summer of 1934 was the culmination of several previous dry summers. 1928 was an exceptionally wet summer for the state, it currently ranks as the 2nd wettest summer of record with a statewide average precipitation of 13.14 inches. Yet, the proverbial faucet was abruptly shut off after that warm season. The summer of 1929 was the exact opposite of the previous summer. Dry conditions continued in 1930, 1931, 1932 and 1933 but those years were not as severe as those recorded in 1929.

By the end of 1935, many farmers, especially in North Dakota thought the dryness that plagued the state was coming to a close, but little did individuals realize that the most extreme year that they would ever experience was about to impact much of the north central United States. The year 1936 started with the most severe cold wave on record. From the middle of January through the middle of February, most of North Dakota did not record a high temperature above 0°F. In fact, Langdon recorded 42 consecutive days during that time frame without the temperature exceeding 0°F. That winter of 1935-1936 was the coldest on record for all of North Dakota and much of the rest of the immediate area. It was toward the end of that horrific cold snap that the coldest observed temperature in North Dakota was recorded. On Saturday, February 15, 1936, cooperative observer Court Shubert recorded a temperature of -60°F. Bismarck reached -42°F that morning, just 3°F shy of the all-time lowest temperature for that location.

NASA scientists have an explanation for one of the worst climatic events in the history of the United States, the "Dust Bowl" drought, which devastated the Great Plains and all but dried up an already depressed American economy in the 1930's. Siegfried Schubert of NASA's Goddard

Space Flight Center, Greenbelt, Md., and colleagues used a computer model developed with modern-era satellite data to look at the climate over the past 100 years. The study found cooler than normal tropical Pacific Ocean surface temperatures combined with warmer tropical Atlantic Ocean temperatures to create conditions in the atmosphere that turned America's breadbasket into a dust bowl from 1931 to 1939. These changes in sea surface temperatures created shifts in the large-scale weather patterns and low level winds that reduced the normal supply of moisture from the Gulf of Mexico and inhibited rainfall throughout the Great Plains.

"The 1930s drought was the major climatic event in the nation's history," Schubert said. "Just beginning to understand what occurred is really critical to understanding future droughts and the links to global climate change issues we're experiencing today." By discovering the causes behind U.S. droughts, especially severe episodes like the Plains' dry spell, scientists may recognize and possibly foresee future patterns that could create similar conditions. For example, La Niñas are marked by cooler than normal tropical Pacific Ocean surface water temperatures, which impact weather globally, and also create dry conditions over the Great Plains.

Dust storms on the Great Plains
The model showed cooler than normal tropical Pacific Ocean temperatures and warmer than normal tropical Atlantic Ocean temperatures contributed to a weakened low-level jet stream and changed its course. The jet stream, a ribbon of fast moving air near the Earth's surface, normally flows westward over the Gulf of Mexico and then turns northward pulling up moisture and dumping rain onto the Great Plains. As the low level jet stream weakened, it travelled farther south than normal. The Great Plains dried up and dust storms formed. The research shed light on how tropical sea surface temperatures can have a remote response and control over weather and climate. It also confirmed droughts can become localized based on soil moisture levels, especially during summer. When rain is scarce and soil dries, there is less evaporation, which leads to even less precipitation, creating a feedback process that reinforces lack of rainfall.

The study also shed light on droughts throughout the 20th century. Analysis of other major U.S. droughts of the 1900s suggests a cool tropical Pacific was a common factor. Schubert said simulating major events like the 1930s drought provides an excellent test for computer models. While the study finds no indication of a similar Great Plains drought in the near future, it is vital to continue studies relating to climate change. NASA's current and planned suite of satellite sensors is uniquely poised to answer related climate questions. (see "On the Cause of the 1930s Dust Bowl," recently published by Siegfried D. Schubert, Max J. Suarez, Philip J. Pegion, Randal D. Koster, and Julio T. Bacmeister in the March 19, 2004 edition of *Science Magazine*).

Homestead on the range
The website *homestead on the range.com* raises the question of the effect of solar cycles. Solar cycles have been observed since 1755, and many scientists have suggested that there is a correlation between the two phenomena. But in relation to the causes of the Dust Bowl the jury is divided. Suffice to say that the Dust Bowl began around 1930 or 1931, depending on where you lived, and ended between 1936 and 1940. The solar minimum (period of least solar activity) occurred in 1933, while the solar maximum (period of most solar activity) appears to have been around 1936 or 1937. The Dust Bowl therefore began as solar activity approached a low and ended about the time solar activity reached a peak (making allowance for regional variation). Some scientists consider that during periods of low solar activity, aerosol particles build up in the earth's atmosphere, instead of being dispersed by solar ejections. These particles in turn become condensation nuclei for clouds. In contrast clouds with large numbers of condensation nuclei tend to produce less precipitation.

History.com has written comprehensively about the Dust Bowl, as the following extracts show.

The Homestead Act of 1862, which provided settlers with 160 acres of public land, was followed by the Kinkaid Act of 1904 and the Enlarged Homestead Act of 1909. These acts led to a massive influx of new and inexperienced farmers across the Great Plains. Many of these late nineteenth and early twentieth century settlers lived by the superstition "rain follows the plough." Emigrants, land speculators, politicians and even some scientists believed that homesteading and agriculture would permanently affect the climate of the semi-arid Great Plains region, making it more conducive to farming.

This false belief was linked to "Manifest Destiny"–an attitude that Americans had a sacred duty to expand west. A series of wet years during the period created further misunderstanding of the region's ecology and led to the intensive cultivation of increasingly marginal lands that couldn't be reached by irrigation. Rising wheat prices in the 1910s and 1920s, and increased demand for wheat from Europe during World War I encouraged farmers to plough up millions of hectares of native grassland to plant wheat, corn and other row crops. But as the United States entered the Great Depression, wheat prices plummeted. Farmers tore up even more grassland in an attempt to harvest a bumper crop and break even. Crops began to fail with the onset of drought in 1931, exposing the bare, over-ploughed farmland. Without deep-rooted prairie grasses to hold the soil in place, it began to blow away. Eroding soil led to massive dust storms and economic devastation – especially in the Southern Plains.

During the Dust Bowl period, severe dust storms, often called "black blizzards" swept the Great Plains. Some of these carried Great Plains topsoil as far East as Washington, D.C. and New York City, and coated ships in the Atlantic Ocean with dust. Billowing clouds of dust would darken the sky, sometimes for days at a time. In many places, the dust drifted like snow and residents had to clear it with shovels. Dust worked its way through the cracks of even well-sealed homes, leaving a coating on food, skin and furniture.

President Franklin D. Roosevelt established a number of measures to help alleviate the plight of poor and displaced farmers. He also addressed the environmental degradation that had led to the Dust Bowl in the first place. Congress established the Soil Erosion Service and the Prairie States Forestry Project in 1935. These programmes put local farmers to work planting trees as windbreaks on farms across the Great Plains. The Soil Erosion Service, now called the Natural Resources Conservation Service (NRCS) implemented new farming techniques to combat the problem of soil erosion.

The Okies

Roughly 2.5 million people left the Dust Bowl states – Texas, New Mexico, Colorado, Nebraska, Kansas and Oklahoma – during the 1930s. It was the largest migration in American history. Oklahoma alone lost 440,000 people to migration. Many of them, poverty-stricken, travelled west looking for work. From 1935 to 1940, roughly 250,000 Oklahoma migrants moved to California. A third settled in the state's agriculturally rich San Joaquin Valley. These Dust Bowl refugees were called "Okies." Okies faced discrimination, menial labour and pitiable wages upon reaching California. Many of them lived in shantytowns and tents along irrigation ditches. "Okie" soon became a term of disdain used to refer to any poor Dust Bowl migrant, regardless of their state of origin. The abandonment of homesteads and financial ruin resulting from catastrophic topsoil loss led to widespread hunger and poverty.

Historian James N. Gregory examined Census Bureau statistics and other records to learn more about the migrants. Based on a 1939 survey of occupation by the Bureau of Agricultural Economics of about 116,000 families who arrived in California in the 1930s, he learned that only 43% of south westerners were doing farm work immediately before they migrated. The poor economy displaced more than just farmers as refugees to California; many teachers, lawyers, and small business owners moved west with their families during this time. After the Great Depression ended, some moved back to their original states. But many others remained where they had resettled and about one-eighth of California's population is of Okie heritage.

The Dust Bowl as described in *Wikipedia* says that with insufficient understanding of the ecology of the plains, farmers had conducted extensive deep ploughing of the virgin topsoil of the Great Plains during the previous decade; this had displaced the native, deep-rooted grasses that normally trapped soil and moisture even during periods of drought and high winds. The rapid mechanization of farm equipment, especially small gasoline tractors, and widespread use of the combine harvester contributed to farmers' decisions to convert arid grassland (much of which received no more than 250 mm of precipitation per year) to cultivated cropland. During the drought of the 1930s, the unanchored soil turned to dust, which the prevailing winds blew away in huge clouds that sometimes blackened the sky.

Black blizzards
These choking billows of dust – named "black blizzards" or "black rollers" – travelled cross country, reaching as far as the East Coast and striking such cities as New York City and Washington, D.C. On the plains, they often reduced visibility to 1 meter or less. *Associated Press* reporter Robert E. Geiger happened to be in Boise City, Oklahoma, to witness the "Black Sunday" black blizzards of April 14, 1935; Edward Stanley, the Kansas City news editor of the *Associated Press*, coined the term "Dust Bowl" while rewriting Geiger's news story.

Patrick Allitt recounts how fellow historian Donald Worster responded to his return visit to the Dust Bowl in the mid-1970s when he revisited some of the worst afflicted counties: Capital-intensive agribusiness had transformed the scene; deep wells into the aquifer, intensive irrigation, the use of artificial pesticides and fertilizers, and giant harvesters were creating immense crops year after year whether it rained or not. According to the farmers he interviewed, technology had provided the perfect answer to old troubles, such that the bad days would not return. In Worster's view, by contrast, the scene demonstrated that America's capitalist high-tech farmers had learned nothing. They were continuing to work in an unsustainable way, devoting far cheaper subsidized energy to growing food than the energy could give back to its ultimate consumers. In contrast with Worster's pessimism, historian Mathew Bonnifield argued that the long-term significance of the Dust Bowl was "the triumph of the human spirit in its capacity to endure and overcome hardships and reverses."

The Dust Bowl also captured the imagination of the nation's artists, photographers, musicians, and authors. John Steinbeck memorialized the plight of the Okies in his 1939 novel *The Grapes of Wrath*. Photographer Dorothea Lange captured what have become classic images of the dust storms and migrant families. Among her most well-known photographs is *Destitute Pea Pickers in California. Mother of Seven Children*, which depicted a gaunt-looking woman, Florence Owens Thompson, holding three of her children. This picture expressed the struggles of people caught by the Dust Bowl and raised awareness in other parts of the country of its reach and human cost. Artist Alexander Hogue painted Dust Bowl landscapes, and Folk musician Woody Guthrie's semi-autobiographical first album Dust Bowl Ballads in 1940, told stories of economic hardship faced by Okies in California.

Sea level changes

Global (or eustatic) sea level change is measured relative to an idealised reference level, the geoid, which is a mathematical model of planet Earth's surface. Global sea level is a function of the volume of the ocean basins and the volume of water they contain. Changes in global sea level are caused by – but not limited to - four main mechanisms:
(Source: *www.climate4you.com*)

1. Changes in local and regional air pressure and wind, and tidal changes introduced by the Moon.

2. Changes in ocean basin volume by tectonic (geological) forces.

3. Changes in ocean water density caused by variations in currents, water temperature and salinity.

4. Changes in the volume of water caused by changes in the mass balance of terrestrial glaciers.

In addition to these there are other mechanisms influencing sea level; such as storage of ground water, storage in lakes and rivers, evaporation, etc.

Mechanism 1 is controlling sea level at many sites on a time scale from months to several years. As an example, many coastal stations show a pronounced annual variation reflecting seasonal changes in air pressures and wind speed. Longer-term climatic changes playing out over decades or centuries will also affect measurements of sea level changes.

Mechanism 2, with the important exception of earthquakes and tsunamis, typically operates over long (geological) time scales, and is not significant on human time scales. It may relate to variations in the sea-floor spreading rate, causing volume changes in mid-ocean mountain ridges, and to the slowly changing configuration of land and oceans.

Mechanism 3 (temperature-driven expansion) only affects the uppermost part of the oceans on human time scales. Usually, temperature-driven changes in density are more important than salinity-driven changes. Seawater is characterised by a relatively small coefficient of expansion, but the effect should however not be overlooked, especially when interpreting satellite altimetry data. Temperature-driven expansion of a column of seawater will not affect the total mass of water within the column considered and will therefore not affect the potential at the top of the water column. Temperature-driven ocean water expansion will therefore not in itself lead to lateral displacement of water, but only lift the ocean surface locally.

Mechanism 4 (changes in glacier mass balance) is an important driver for global sea level changes along coasts, for human time scales. Volume changes of floating glaciers – ice shelves – has no influence on the global sea level, just like volume changes of floating sea ice has no influence. Only the mass-balance of grounded or land-based glaciers is important for the global sea level along coasts.

9

Extreme events

"Nature is a lot stronger than the rest of us (when referring to Hurricane Irene)".

Mayor of New York, Michael Bloomberg (August 27, 2011)

The year without a summer

The 19th Century weather disaster - dubbed "The Year Without a Summer" - happened in 1816, when weather in Europe and North America took a bizarre turn which resulted in widespread crop failures and famine.

On April 10, 1815, Mount Tambora in Indonesia produced the largest eruption known on the planet during the last 10,000 years. The volcano erupted more than 50 cubic kilometres of magma. The eruption produced global climatic effects and killed more than 100,000 people, directly and indirectly. Pyroclastic flows reached the sea on all sides of the peninsula, and heavy tephra fall devastated croplands, causing an estimated 60,000 fatalities. Entire villages were buried under thick pumice deposits. Some of the settlements have recently been brought back to light by archaeological excavations, making a site called 'Pompeii of Indonesia'. While the death toll of people living on Sumbawa and surrounding coastal areas was high enough, even more fatalities can be attributed to an indirect effect of global climate deterioration after the eruption.

These changes turned 1816 into 'The Year without a Summer' for much of Europe, causing widespread famine. The reason for the climatic changes was increased absorption of sunlight due to a veil of aerosols dispersed around both hemispheres by stratospheric currents from the tall eruption column. Global temperatures dropped by as much as 3°C in 1816.

Unprecedented weather in 1816

'The Year without a Summer' was well reported in the United States and Europe, as the following description suggests.

The weather in 1816 was unprecedented. Spring arrived but then everything seemed to turn backward, as cold temperatures returned. The sky seemed permanently overcast. The lack of sunlight became so severe farmers lost their crops and food shortages were reported in Ireland, France, England, and the United States. In Virginia, Thomas Jefferson retired from the presidency and farming at Monticello sustained crop failures that sent him further into debt.

It would be more than a century before anyone understood the reason for the peculiar weather disaster: the eruption of an enormous volcano on a remote island in the Indian Ocean one year earlier had thrown enormous amounts of volcanic ash into the upper atmosphere.

But before the cause was known, in Switzerland, the damp and dismal summer of 1816 led to the creation of a significant literary work. A group of writers, including Lord Byron, Percy Bysshe Shelley, and his future wife, challenged each other to write dark tales inspired by the gloomy and chilly weather. During the miserable weather Mary Shelley wrote her classic novel *Frankenstein*.

The *Albany Advertiser* went on to propose some theories about why the weather was so bizarre.

The mention of sunspots is interesting, as sunspots had been seen by astronomers. What's fascinating is the newspaper article from 1816 proposes such events be studied, so people can learn what is going on. For example:

"Many seem disposed to charge the peculiarities of the season, the present year, upon the spots on the sun. If the dryness of the season has in any measure depended on the latter cause, it has not operated uniformly in different places – the spots have been visible in Europe, as well as in the United States and yet in some parts of Europe, as we have already remarked, they have been drenched with rain."

"Without undertaking to discuss, much less to decide, such a learned subject as this, we should be glad if proper pains were taken to ascertain, by regular journals of the weather from year to year, the state of the seasons in this country and Europe, as well as the general state of health in both quarters of the globe. We think the facts might be collected, and the comparison made, without much difficulty; and when once made, that it would be of great advantage to medical men, and medical science."

Volcanic hazards

Today, in 2020, we now know volcanoes can pose many hazards. One hazard is that volcanic ash can be a threat to jet aircraft where ash particles can be melted by the high operating temperature. The melted particles then adhere to the turbine blades and alter their shape, disrupting the operation of the turbine.

Large volcanic eruptions can affect temperature, as ash and droplets of sulphuric acid obscure the sun and cool the Earth's lower atmosphere, or troposphere. However, they also absorb heat radiated up from the Earth, thereby warming the upper atmosphere, or stratosphere. Historically, so-called volcanic winters have caused catastrophic famines.

And from Wood, Gillen D'Arcy. '1816, The Year without a Summer'. Britain, Representation and Nineteenth-Century History. Ed. Dino Franco Felluga. Extension of Romanticism and Victorianism on the Net, we read the following:

"To be alive in the years 1816-18, almost anywhere in the world, meant to be hungry. Across the globe during the so-called 'Year without a Summer' – which was, in fact, a three-year climate crisis – harvests perished in frost and drought or were washed away by flooding rains. Villagers in Vermont survived on hedgehogs and boiled nettles, while the peasants of Yunnan in China sucked on white clay. Summer tourists travelling in France mistook beggars crowding the roads for armies on the march."

"Famine-friendly diseases cholera and typhus stalked the globe from India to Italy, while the price of bread and rice, the world's staple foods, skyrocketed with no relief in sight. Across a European continent devastated by the Napoleonic wars, tens of thousands of unemployed veterans found themselves unable to feed their families. They gave vent to their desperation in town square riots and military-style campaigns of arson, while governments everywhere feared revolution. In New England, 1816 was nicknamed 'Eighteen-Hundred-and-Froze-to-Death' while Germans called 1817 'The Year of the Beggar'. "

"In the scientific literature, the 1816's cold summer was the most significant meteorological event of the nineteenth century. The global climate emergency period of 1816-18, as a whole, offers us a clear window onto a world convulsed by weather anomalies, with human communities everywhere struggling to adapt to sudden, radical shifts in weather patterns, and to a consequent tsunami of famine, disease, dislocation and unrest."

Volcanic eruptions

Volcanic eruptions are responsible for releasing molten rock, or lava, from deep within the Earth, forming new rock on the Earth's surface. Eruptions also impact the atmosphere. The gases and dust particles thrown into the atmosphere during volcanic eruptions have influences on climate. UCAR (*ucar.edu*) says that most of the particles spewed from volcanoes cool the planet by shading incoming solar radiation. The cooling effect can last for months to years depending on the characteristics of the eruption. Volcanoes have also caused global warming over millions of years during times in Earth's history when extreme amounts of volcanism occurred, releasing greenhouse gases into the atmosphere.

Even though volcanoes are in specific places on Earth, their effects can be more widely distributed as gases, dust, and ash get into the atmosphere. Because of atmospheric circulation patterns, eruptions in the tropics can have an effect on the climate in both hemispheres while eruptions at mid or high latitudes only have impact on the hemisphere they are within. Materials that make their way from volcanic eruptions into the atmosphere: are particles of dust and ash, sulphur dioxide, and greenhouse gases like water vapour and CO_2.

Volcanic ash and dust
Volcanic ash and dust released into the atmosphere during an eruption shade sunlight and cause temporary cooling. Larger particles of ash have little effect because they fall out of the air quickly. Small ash particles form a dark cloud in the troposphere that shades and cools the area directly below. Most of these particles fall out of the atmosphere within rain a few hours or days after an eruption. The smallest particles of dust get into the stratosphere and are able to travel vast distances, often worldwide. These tiny particles are so light that they can stay in the stratosphere for months, blocking sunlight and causing cooling over large areas of the Earth.

Often, erupting volcanoes emit sulphur dioxide into the atmosphere. Sulphur dioxide is much more effective than ash particles at cooling the climate. The sulphur dioxide moves into the stratosphere and combines with water to form sulphuric acid aerosols. The sulphuric acid makes a haze of tiny droplets in the stratosphere that reflects incoming solar radiation, causing cooling of the Earth's surface. The aerosols can stay in the stratosphere for up to three years, moved around by winds and causing significant cooling worldwide. Eventually, the droplets grow large enough to fall to Earth.

Volcanoes also release large amounts of greenhouse gases such as water vapour and CO_2. The amounts put into the atmosphere from a large eruption doesn't change the global amounts of these gases very much. However, there have been times during Earth's history when intense volcanism has significantly increased the amount of CO_2 in the atmosphere and caused global warming.

During major explosive eruptions, the US Geological Survey (*usgs.gov*) says that huge amounts of volcanic gas, aerosol droplets, and ash are injected into the stratosphere. Injected ash falls rapidly from the stratosphere – most of it is removed within several days to weeks – and has little impact on climate change. But volcanic gases like sulphur dioxide can cause global cooling, while volcanic CO_2, a greenhouse gas, has the potential to promote global warming.

Krakatoa and Tambora

Several eruptions during the past century have caused a decline in the average temperature at the Earth's surface of up to 0.5°C for periods of 1 to 3 years. *Wikipedia* says that the climactic eruption of Mount Pinatubo on June 15, 1991, was one of the largest eruptions of the twentieth century and injected a 20-million ton sulphur dioxide cloud into the stratosphere at an altitude of more than 30 km. The Pinatubo cloud was the largest sulphur dioxide cloud ever observed in the stratosphere since the beginning of such observations by satellites in 1978. It caused what is believed to be the largest aerosol disturbance of the stratosphere in the twentieth century, though probably smaller than the disturbances from eruptions of Krakatau in 1883 and Tambora in 1815. Consequently, it was a standout in its climate impact and cooled the Earth's surface for three years following the eruption, by as much as 1.1°C at the height of the impact.

The large 1783-1784 Laki fissure eruption in Iceland released a staggering amount more sulphur dioxide than Pinatubo (approximately 120-million ton vs. 20). Although the two eruptions were significantly different in length and style, the added atmospheric sulphur dioxide caused regional cooling of Europe and North America by similar amounts for similar periods of time.

CO_2 is a greenhouse gas and is the primary gas blamed for climate change. While sulphur dioxide released in contemporary volcanic

Extreme events 205

eruptions has occasionally caused detectable global cooling of the lower atmosphere, the CO_2 released in contemporary volcanic eruptions has never caused detectable global warming of the atmosphere. In 2015, human activities were responsible for a projected 32.3 billion metric tons (gigatonnes) of CO_2 emissions. All studies to date of global volcanic CO_2 emissions indicate that present-day subaerial and submarine volcanoes release less than a percent of the CO_2 released currently by human activities. While it has been proposed that intense volcanic release of CO_2 in the deep geologic past did cause global warming, and possibly some mass extinctions, this is a topic of scientific debate at present.

Mount St. Helens
There is no question that very large volcanic eruptions can inject significant amounts of CO_2 into the atmosphere. The 1980 eruption of Mount St. Helens vented approximately 10 million tons of CO_2 into the atmosphere in only 9 hours. However, it currently takes humanity only 2.5 hours to put out the same amount. While large explosive eruptions like this are rare and only occur globally every 10 years or so, humanity's emissions are ceaseless and increasing every year.

New Zealand
In a case study in New Zealand, M.J. Salinger writing in *Weather and Climate 1998* says that major volcanic eruptions which inject significant amounts of dust and sulphate aerosols into the atmosphere produce discernible climate signals in the New Zealand region. A superimposed epoch (compositing) method was used to determine the effects on regional temperatures of the six major volcanic eruptions since the 1880s that have been likely to have affected New Zealand climate. Regional atmospheric circulation anomalies during the three significant late twentieth century volcanic eruption events were examined. As El Niño - Southern Oscillation (ENSO) events significantly effect temperature and circulation anomalies, these climatic effects were removed.

The results showed that the effects on temperature and atmospheric circulation in the New Zealand region commenced rapidly, in the first few months after the volcanic eruption event, and lasted 24 months. These events were found to depress surface temperatures in the region by 0.3°C to 0.4°C from 1 to 21 months after the eruption. Atmospheric circulation anomaly patterns were very distinct and showed more surface southerlies and troughs near the Chatham Islands (east of New Zealand) in the first two seasons (1-6 months) after the eruption, followed by stronger west to south west flow anomalies in seasons 3 to 5 (7 to 15 months) over the region. Finally, a period of more troughs over the North Island of New Zealand occurred in seasons 6 to 8 (16 to 24 months) after the eruption episode. The magnitude of the volcanic signal in the New Zealand region is consistent with previous larger-scale global studies.

Tropical Cyclones

A tropical cyclone is a rapidly rotating storm system characterized by a low-pressure centre, a closed low-level atmospheric circulation, strong winds, and a spiral arrangement of thunderstorms that produce heavy rain or squalls. Depending on its location and strength, a tropical cyclone is referred to by different names, including hurricane, typhoon, tropical storm, cyclonic storm, tropical depression, tropical cyclone and cyclone. A hurricane is a tropical cyclone that occurs in the Atlantic Ocean and north-eastern Pacific Ocean, a typhoon occurs in the north-western Pacific Ocean; and in the south Pacific or Indian Ocean, comparable storms are referred as "tropical cyclones" or "severe cyclonic storms", or simply cyclones. *Wikipedia* has a comprehensive review of tropical cyclones.

In the most recent and reliable records, most tropical cyclones which attained a pressure of 900 hPa or less have occurred in the Western North Pacific Ocean. The strongest tropical cyclone recorded worldwide, as measured by minimum central pressure, was Typhoon *Tip*, which reached a pressure of 870 hPa on October 12, 1979. On October 23, 2015, Hurricane *Patricia* attained the strongest 1-minute sustained winds on record at 345 km/h.

"Tropical" refers to the geographical origin of these systems, which form almost exclusively over tropical seas. "Cyclone" refers to their winds moving in a circle, whirling round their central clear eye, with their winds blowing anticlockwise in the Northern Hemisphere and clockwise in the Southern Hemisphere. The opposite direction of the circulation is due to the Coriolis effect. Tropical cyclones typically form over large bodies of relatively warm water. They derive their energy through the evaporation of water from the ocean surface, which ultimately recondenses into clouds and rain when moist air rises and cools to saturation.

The strong rotating winds of a tropical cyclone are a result of the conservation of angular momentum imparted by the Earth's rotation as air flows inwards toward the axis of rotation. As a result, they rarely form within 5° of the equator. Tropical cyclones are almost unknown in the South Atlantic due to a consistently strong wind shear and a weak Intertropical Convergence Zone. The African easterly jet and areas of atmospheric instability which give rise to cyclones in the Atlantic Ocean and Caribbean Sea, along with the Asian monsoon and Western Pacific Warm Pool, are features of the Northern Hemisphere and Australia.

Coastal regions are particularly vulnerable to the impact of a tropical cyclone, compared to inland regions. The primary energy source for these storms is warm ocean waters. These storms are therefore typically strongest when over or near water, and weaken quite rapidly over land. Coastal damage may be caused by strong winds and rain, high waves (due to winds), storm surges (due to wind and severe pressure changes), and the potential of spawning tornadoes. Tropical cyclones also draw in air from a large area–which can be a vast area for the most severe cyclones– and concentrate the precipitation of the water content in that air (made up from atmospheric moisture and moisture evaporated from water) into a much smaller area. This continual replacement of moisture-bearing air by new moisture-bearing air after its moisture has fallen as rain, may cause extremely heavy rain and river flooding up to 40 kilometres from the coastline, far beyond the amount of water that the local atmosphere holds at any one time.

Effects on human populations
Though their effects on human populations are often devastating, tropical cyclones can relieve drought conditions. In fact when I was writing my first book in 1970 (*The Value of the Weather*) the first section I wrote was related to the "benefits of tropical cyclones" which I recall my graduate students of the day were happy to critically evaluate. Tropical cyclones also carry heat energy away from the tropics and transport it toward temperate latitudes, which plays an important role in modulating regional and global climate.

At the outer edge of the storm, air may be nearly calm; however, due to the Earth's rotation, the air has non-zero absolute angular momentum. As air flows radially inward, it begins to rotate cyclonically to conserve angular momentum. At an inner radius, air begins to ascend to the top of the troposphere. This radius is typically coincident with the inner radius of the eyewall, and has the strongest near-surface winds of the storm; consequently, it is known as the *radius of maximum winds*. Once aloft, air flows away from the storm's centre, producing a shield of cirrus clouds.

At the centre of a mature tropical cyclone, air sinks rather than rises. For a sufficiently strong storm, air may sink over a layer deep enough to suppress cloud formation, thereby creating a clear "eye". Weather in the eye is normally calm and free of clouds, although the sea may be extremely violent. The eye is normally circular and is typically 30–65 km in diameter, though eyes as small as 3 km and as large as 370 km have been observed.

The cloudy outer edge of the eye is called the "eyewall". The eyewall typically expands outward with height, resembling an arena football stadium; this phenomenon is sometimes referred to as the "stadium effect". The eyewall is where the greatest wind speeds are found, air rises most rapidly, clouds reach their highest altitude, and precipitation is the heaviest. The heaviest wind damage occurs where a tropical cyclone's eyewall passes over land.

Metrics used to measure tropical cyclones
There are a variety of metrics commonly used to measure tropical cyclone size. The most common metrics include the radius of maximum wind, the radius of 34-knot wind (i.e. gale force), the radius of outermost closed isobar (ROCI), and the radius of vanishing wind.

Size plays an important role in modulating damage caused by a storm. All else equal, a larger storm will impact a larger area for a longer period of time. The passage of a tropical cyclone over the ocean causes the upper layers of the ocean to cool substantially, which can influence subsequent cyclone development. This cooling is primarily caused by wind-driven mixing of cold water from deeper in the ocean with the warm surface waters. This effect results in a negative feedback process that can inhibit further development or lead to weakening. Additional cooling may come in the form of cold water from falling raindrops (this is because the atmosphere is cooler at higher altitudes).

There are six Regional Specialized Meteorological Centres (RSMCs) worldwide. These organizations are designated by the World Meteorological Organization and are responsible for tracking and issuing bulletins, warnings, and advisories about tropical cyclones in their designated areas of responsibility. Also, there are six Tropical Cyclone Warning Centres (TCWCs) that provide information to smaller regions.

The RSMCs and TCWCs are not the only organizations that provide information about tropical cyclones to the public. The Joint Typhoon Warning Center (JTWC) issues advisories in all basins except the Northern Atlantic for the United States Government. The Philippine Atmospheric, Geophysical and Astronomical Services Administration (PAGASA) issues advisories and names for tropical cyclones that approach the Philippines in the Northwestern Pacific to protect the life and property of its citizens. The Canadian Hurricane Centre (CHC) issues advisories on hurricanes and their remnants for Canadian citizens when they affect Canada.

On March 26, 2004, Hurricane *Catarina* became the first recorded South Atlantic cyclone, striking southern Brazil with winds equivalent to Category 2 on the Saffir-Simpson Hurricane Scale. As the cyclone formed outside the authority of another warning center, Brazilian meteorologists initially treated the system as an extra tropical cyclone, but later on, classified it as tropical.

In the Northern Atlantic Ocean, a distinct cyclone season occurs from June 1 to November 30, sharply peaking from late August through September. The statistical peak of the Atlantic hurricane season is September 10. The Northeast Pacific Ocean has a broader period of activity, but in a similar time frame to the Atlantic. The Northwest Pacific sees tropical cyclones year-round, with a minimum in February and March and a peak in early September. In the North Indian basin, storms are most common from April to December, with peaks in May and November. In the Southern Hemisphere, the tropical cyclone year begins on July 1 and runs all year-round encompassing the tropical cyclone seasons, which run from November 1 until the end of April, with peaks in mid-February to early March.

Tropical cyclone formation

The formation of tropical cyclones is the topic of extensive ongoing research and is still not fully understood. While six factors appear to be generally necessary, tropical cyclones may occasionally form without meeting all of the following conditions. In most situations, water temperatures of at least 26.5 °C are needed down to a depth of at least 50 m. Waters of this temperature cause the overlying atmosphere to be unstable enough to sustain convection and thunderstorms. Another factor is rapid cooling with height, which allows the release of the heat of condensation that powers a tropical cyclone. High humidity is needed, especially in the lower-to-mid troposphere; when there is a great deal of moisture in the atmosphere, conditions are more favourable for disturbances to develop. Low amounts of wind shear are needed, as high shear is disruptive to the storm's circulation.

Tropical cyclones generally need to form more than 555 km or five degrees of latitude away from the equator, allowing the Coriolis effect to deflect winds blowing towards the low pressure centre and creating a circulation. Lastly, a formative tropical cyclone needs a pre-existing system of disturbed weather. Tropical cyclones will not form spontaneously. Low-latitude and low-level westerly wind bursts associated with the

Madden–Julian oscillation can create favourable conditions for tropical cyclogenesis by initiating tropical disturbances.

The movement or track of a tropical cyclone is typically approximated as the sum of two terms: "steering" by the background environmental wind and "beta drift". Environmental steering is the dominant term. Conceptually, it represents the movement of the storm due to prevailing winds and other wider environmental conditions, similar to "leaves carried along by a stream". Physically, the winds, or flow field, in the vicinity of a tropical cyclone may be treated as having two parts: the flow associated with the storm itself, and the large-scale background flow of the environment in which the storm takes place. In this way, tropical cyclone motion may be represented to first-order simply as advection of the storm by the local environmental flow. This environmental flow is termed the "steering flow".

Inter-tropical Convergence Zone
Climatologically, tropical cyclones are steered primarily westward by the east-to-west trade winds on the equatorial side of the subtropical ridge–a persistent high-pressure area over the world's subtropical oceans. In the tropical North Atlantic and Northeast Pacific oceans, the trade winds steer tropical easterly waves westward from the African coast toward the Caribbean Sea, North America, and ultimately into the central Pacific Ocean before the waves dampen out. These waves are the precursors to many tropical cyclones within this region. In contrast, in the Indian Ocean and Western Pacific in both hemispheres, tropical cyclogenesis is influenced less by tropical easterly waves and more by the seasonal movement of the Inter-tropical Convergence Zone and the monsoon trough. Additionally, tropical cyclone motion can be influenced by transient weather systems, such as extratropical cyclones.

Though a tropical cyclone typically moves from east to west in the tropics, its track may shift poleward and eastward either as it moves west of the subtropical ridge axis or else if it interacts with the mid-latitude flow, such as the jet stream or an extratropical cyclone. This motion, termed "recurvature", commonly occurs near the western edge of the major ocean basins, where the jet stream typically has a poleward component and extratropical cyclones are common.

The landfall of a tropical cyclone occurs when a storm's surface centre moves over a coastline. Storm conditions may be experienced on the coast and inland hours before landfall; in fact, a tropical cyclone can launch its strongest winds over land, yet not make landfall. NOAA uses the term "direct hit" to describe when a location (on the left side of the eye) falls within the radius of maximum winds (or twice that radius if on the right side), whether or not the hurricane's eye made landfall.

Most tropical cyclones form on the side of the subtropical ridge closer to the equator, then move poleward past the ridge axis before recurving into the main belt of the westerlies. When the subtropical ridge position shifts due to El Niño, so will the preferred tropical cyclone tracks. Areas west of Japan and Korea tend to experience much fewer September–November tropical cyclone impacts during El Niño and neutral years. During El Niño years, the break in the subtropical ridge tends to lie near 130°E which would favour the Japanese archipelago. During El Niño years, Guam's chance of a tropical cyclone impact is one-third more likely than of the long-term average. The tropical Atlantic Ocean experiences depressed activity due to increased vertical wind shear across the region during El Niño years. During La Niña years, the formation of tropical cyclones, along with the subtropical ridge position, shifts westward across the western Pacific Ocean, which increases the landfall threat to China and much greater intensity in the Philippines.

A tropical cyclone can cease to have tropical characteristics in several different ways. One such way is if it moves over land, thus depriving it of the warm water it needs to power itself, quickly losing strength. Most strong storms lose their strength very rapidly after landfall and become disorganized areas of low pressure within a day or two, or evolve into extratropical cyclones. There is a chance a tropical cyclone could regenerate if it managed to get back over open warm water, such as with Hurricane *Ivan*. If it remains over mountains for even a short time, weakening will accelerate. Many storm fatalities occur in mountainous terrain, when diminishing cyclones unleash their moisture as torrential rainfall. This rainfall may lead to deadly floods and mudslides, as was the case with Hurricane *Mitch* around Honduras in October 1998. Without warm surface water, the storm cannot survive.

Human dimensions of weather modification

In the 1960s and 1970s, the United States government attempted to weaken hurricanes through Project Storm fury by seeding selected storms with silver iodide. It was thought that the seeding would cause supercooled water in the outer rain bands to freeze, causing the inner eyewall to collapse and thus reducing the winds. The winds of Hurricane

Debbie – a hurricane seeded in Project Storm Fury – dropped as much as 31%, but *Debbie* regained its strength after each of two seeding forays. In an earlier episode in 1947, disaster struck when a hurricane east of Jacksonville, Florida promptly changed its course after being seeded, and smashed into Savannah, Georgia. Because there was so much uncertainty about the behaviour of these storms, the federal government would not approve seeding operations unless the hurricane had a less than 10% chance of making landfall within 48 hours, greatly reducing the number of possible test storms. The project was dropped after it was discovered that eyewall replacement cycles occur naturally in strong hurricanes, casting doubt on the result of the earlier attempts. Today, it is known that silver iodide seeding is not likely to have an effect because the amount of supercooled water in the rain bands of a tropical cyclone is too low.

Other approaches have been suggested over time, including cooling the water under a tropical cyclone by towing icebergs into the tropical oceans. Other ideas range from covering the ocean in a substance that inhibits evaporation, dropping large quantities of ice into the eye at very early stages of development (so that the latent heat is absorbed by the ice, instead of being converted to kinetic energy that would feed the positive feedback loop), or blasting the cyclone apart with nuclear weapons. Project Cirrus even involved throwing dry ice on a cyclone. These approaches all suffer from one flaw above many others: tropical cyclones are simply too large and long-lived for any of the weakening techniques to be practical.

During the Project Storm Fury period two important conferences were held at the National Center for Atmospheric Research (NCAR) in 1965/68. The first was *Human Dimensions of Weather Modification* in connection with a Symposium on the Economic and Social Aspects of Weather Modification held from July 1-3, 1965. The conference was chaired by W. R. Derrick Sewell, Department of Geography, University of Chicago, and the University of Victoria, BC, Canada. This conference, the first of its kind in the world was held partially in response to questions being asked about the non-scientific aspects of weather modification (such as cloud-seeding, the steering of hurricanes, and fog discernment at airports) and it brought together experts from politics, law, sociology, economics, geography, and ecology.

The 1965 conference was followed in 1968 by a second conference on the *Human Dimensions of the Atmosphere*. I was one of the invited participants, and as with the 1965 conference it was a pioneer conference during which the non-scientific aspects of the atmosphere were discussed, including the legal, social, political and ecological aspects of modifying a hurricane. The key question is "assuming it is possible to steer a hurricane", under whose authority should it be done, and if something goes wrong and the hurricane heads to South Carolina instead of Maryland, who will pay for the damage to homes in South Carolina, and what are the overriding legal and political consequences of the decision. As a result of the conference, it was considered that the likelihood of the President of the US directing the US Airforce to attempt to steer or modify a hurricane in the future was minimal.

Further aspects of the legal implications of the atmospheric resource are given in my 1970 book *The Value of the Weather,* pages 349 to 360. This book was reproduced in 2019 as a Routledge Library Edition.

A report on these conferences in given in a paper *Human Response to Weather and Climate* by W R D Sewell, R W Kates, and L E Philips. *Geographical Review* 68:262-280. They comment that despite its charm and wit, the oft-quoted aphorism attributed to Mark Twain, "Everybody talks about the weather but nobody does anything about it," is hardly accurate. People, do, in fact, do something about the weather. They adapt to it or adjust to it, they move toward certain climatic regimes or away from them, and they have long contemplated weather modification. However, although geographers undoubtedly recognize that weather and climate have pervasive effects on human activity, there appears to have been a general decline in their interest in these relationships and in their ability to answer certain fundamental questions. These questions have become more and more important in recent years as man's ability to predict and modify the weather increases.

Human responses to weather and climate

Traditionally, human responses to weather and climate has consisted in adaptation, adjustments, and movement. In a broad spectrum of human activity, weather and climate have little perceptible effect on the activity pursued or on the rhythm of its pursuit. Other activities people can try to adjust to are variations of weather and climate. This response functions on several levels. At a minimum level man changes his clothing to adjust to daily changes in the weather. At a more permanent level he insulates his home and installs a furnace or air conditioning to adjust to seasonal fluctuations; he builds storm-proof structures to resist high winds; he develops weather-resistant crop varieties to withstand droughts or floods. In his definition movement and modification would presumably be a part of adjustment.

Tropical cyclones out at sea cause large waves, heavy rain, flood and high winds, disrupting international shipping and, at times, causing shipwrecks. Tropical cyclones stir up water, leaving a cool wake behind them, which causes the region to be less favourable for subsequent tropical cyclones. On land, strong winds can damage or destroy vehicles, buildings, bridges, and other outside objects, turning loose debris into deadly flying projectiles. The storm surge, or the increase in sea level due to the cyclone, is typically the worst effect from land-falling tropical cyclones, historically resulting in 90% of tropical cyclone deaths. The broad rotation of a land-falling tropical cyclone, and vertical wind shear at its periphery, spawns tornadoes. Tornadoes can also be spawned as a result of eyewall meso-vortices, which persist until landfall.

Over the past two centuries, tropical cyclones have been responsible for the deaths of about 1.9 million people worldwide. Large areas of standing water caused by flooding lead to infection, as well as contributing to mosquito-borne illnesses. Crowded evacuees in shelters increase the risk of disease propagation. Tropical cyclones significantly interrupt infrastructure, leading to power outages, bridge destruction, and the hampering of reconstruction efforts. On average, the Gulf and east coasts of the United States suffer over US$5 billion in hurricane damage every year. The majority (83%) of tropical cyclone damage is caused by severe hurricanes, category 3 or greater. However, category 3 or greater hurricanes only account for about one-fifth of cyclones that make landfall every year.

Although cyclones take an enormous toll in lives and personal property, they may be important factors in the precipitation regimes of places they impact, as they may bring much-needed precipitation to otherwise dry regions. Tropical cyclones also help maintain the global heat balance by moving warm, moist tropical air to the middle latitudes and polar regions, and by regulating the thermohaline circulation through upwelling. The storm surge and winds of hurricanes may be destructive to human-made structures, but they also stir up the waters of coastal estuaries, which are typically important fish breeding locales. Tropical cyclone destruction spurs redevelopment, greatly increasing local property values.

When hurricanes surge upon shore from the ocean, salt is introduced to many freshwater areas and raises the salinity levels too high for some habitats to withstand. Some are able to cope with the salt and recycle it back into the ocean, but others cannot release the extra surface water quickly enough or do not have a large enough freshwater source to replace it. Because of this, some species of plants and vegetation die due to the excess salt. In addition, hurricanes can carry toxins and acids onto shore when they make landfall. The flood water can pick up the toxins from different spills and contaminate the land that it passes over. The toxins are very harmful to the people and animals in the area, as well as the environment around them. The flooding water can also spark many dangerous oil spills.

Hurricane preparedness
Hurricane preparedness encompasses the actions and planning taken before a tropical cyclone strikes to mitigate damage and injury from the storm. Knowledge of tropical cyclone impacts on an area helps plan for future possibilities. Preparedness may involve preparations made by individuals as well as centralized efforts by governments or other organizations. Tracking storms during the tropical cyclone season helps individuals know current threats. Regional Specialized Meteorological Centres and Tropical Cyclone Warning Centres provide current information and forecasts to help individuals make the best decision possible.

Global Tropical Cyclone Landfalls at Hurricane Strength 1970 to 2019
Black = S/S Category 1 &2; Grey = S/S Category 3+

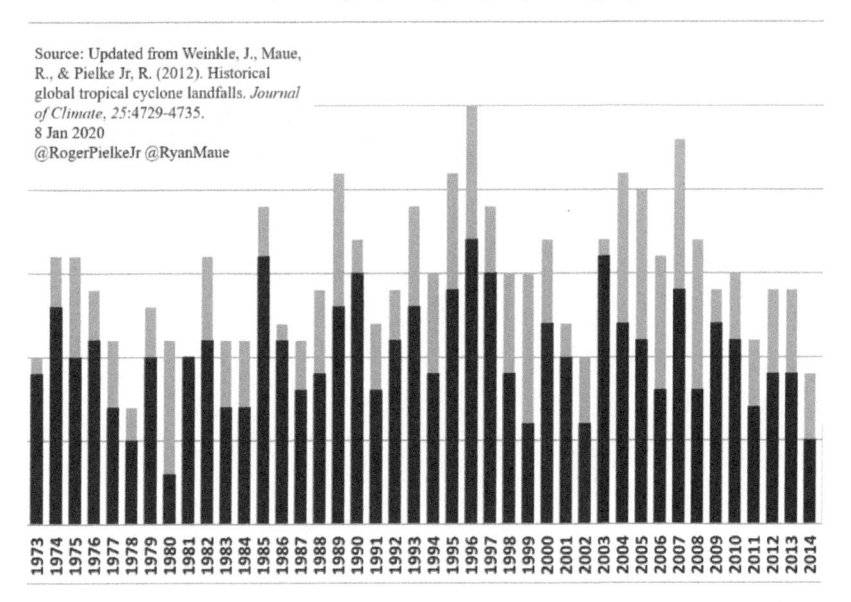

Source: Updated from Weinkle, J., Maue, R., & Pielke Jr, R. (2012). Historical global tropical cyclone landfalls. *Journal of Climate, 25*:4729-4735.
8 Jan 2020
@RogerPielkeJr @RyanMaue

10

Anthropogenic influences on the climate

"Cleaning up the environment is fine, but whether we can control the climate by doing so is quite another matter."

A comment on the G8 Meeting in L'Aquila, Italy in July 2009 (and also what was expressed at the Copenhagen Climate Conference in December 2009).

The Greenhouse effect

The greenhouse effect (from the website of NIWA New Zealand) is a warming of the earth's surface and lower atmosphere caused by substances such as CO_2 and water vapour which let the sun's energy through to the ground but impede the passage of energy from the earth back into space. Energy emitted from the sun (solar radiation) is concentrated in a region of short wavelengths including visible light. Much of the short wave solar radiation travels down through the Earth's atmosphere to the surface virtually unimpeded. Some of the solar radiation is reflected straight back into space by clouds and by the earth's surface. Much of the solar radiation is absorbed at the earth's surface, causing the surface and the lower parts of the atmosphere to warm.

The warmed Earth emits radiation upwards. In the absence of any atmosphere, the upward radiation from the Earth would balance the incoming energy absorbed from the Sun at a mean surface temperature of around -18°C, 33° colder than the observed mean surface temperature of the Earth. The presence of "greenhouse" gases in the atmosphere accounts for the temperature difference.

Infra-red radiation emitted by the Earth is concentrated at long wavelengths and is strongly absorbed by greenhouse gases in the atmosphere, such as water vapour, CO_2 and methane. Absorption of heat causes the atmosphere to warm and emit its own infra-red radiation. The Earth's surface and lower atmosphere warm until they reach a temperature where the infra-red radiation emitted back into space, plus the directly reflected solar radiation, balance the absorbed energy coming in from the sun. As a result, the surface temperature of the globe is around 15°C on average, 33 °C warmer than it would be if there were no atmosphere. This is called the "natural greenhouse effect".

The effect of increased greenhouse gas concentrations is related to the premise that if extra amounts of greenhouse gases are added to the atmosphere, such as from human activities, then they will absorb more of the infra-red radiation. The Earth's surface and the lower atmosphere will warm further until a balance of incoming and outgoing radiation is reached again (the emission of infra-red radiation increases as the temperature of the emitting body rises). This extra warming is called the "enhanced greenhouse effect".

Natural Greenhouse Effect

Human Enhanced Greenhouse Effect

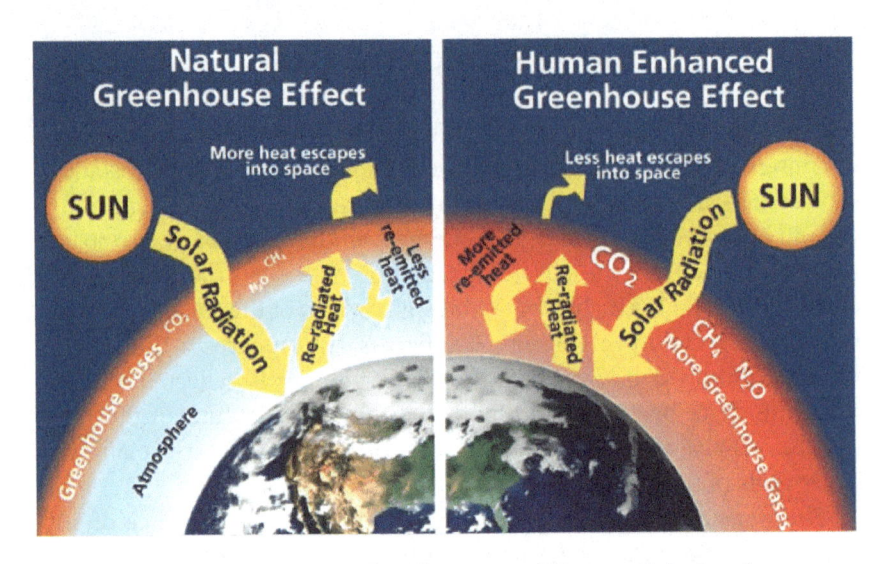

(Source: Center for Climate and Energy Solutions)

The magnitude of the enhanced greenhouse effect is influenced by various complex interactions in the earth-ocean-atmosphere system. For example, as the temperature of the earth's surface increases more water vapour is evaporated. Since water vapour is itself a strong greenhouse gas this is a positive feedback which will tend to amplify the warming effect of (for example) CO_2 emissions. Clouds tend both to cool the Earth because they reflect incoming sunlight, and to warm it by trapping outgoing infra-red radiation. The net result over the Earth of clouds is a cooling, but it is still uncertain whether this overall cooling will increase or decrease as greenhouse gas concentrations increase. Heat is distributed vertically in the atmosphere by motion, turbulence and evaporation and condensation of moist air, as well as by the radiative processes.

Thus many processes and feedbacks must be accounted for in order to realistically predict climate changes resulting from particular greenhouse gas emission scenarios. These complications are the source of much of the debate which has occurred about the likely magnitude and timing of climate changes due to enhanced greenhouse gas emissions.

A greenhouse gas as reviewed by *Wikipedia* is a gas that absorbs and emits radiant energy within the thermal infrared range. Greenhouse gases cause the greenhouse effect on planets. The primary greenhouse gases in Earth's atmosphere are water vapour (H_2O), carbon dioxide (CO_2), methane (CH_4), nitrous oxide (N_2O), and ozone (O_3). Human activities since the beginning of the Industrial Revolution (around 1750) have produced a 45% increase in the atmospheric concentration of CO_2, from 280 ppm in 1750 to 420 ppm in 2020. The last time the atmospheric concentration of CO_2 was this high was over 3 million years ago. The current increase has occurred despite the uptake of more than half of the emissions by various natural "sinks" involved in the carbon cycle. The vast majority of anthropogenic CO_2 emissions come from combustion of fossil fuels, principally coal, oil, and natural gas, with additional contributions coming from deforestation, changes in land use, soil erosion and agriculture (including livestock).The leading source of anthropogenic methane emissions is animal agriculture, followed by fugitive emissions from gas, oil, coal and other industry, solid waste, wastewater and rice production. At current emission rates, temperatures could increase by 2°C , which the IPCC designated as the upper limit to avoid "dangerous" levels, by 2036.

Non-greenhouse gases

The major constituents of Earth's atmosphere are, nitrogen (N_2)(78%), oxygen (O_2)(21%), and argon (Ar)(0.9%). These gases are not greenhouse gases because molecules containing two atoms of the same element such as N_2 and O_2 have no net change in the distribution of their electrical charges when they vibrate, and monatomic gases such as Ar do not have vibrational modes. Hence they are almost totally unaffected by infrared radiation. Some molecules containing just two atoms of different elements, such as carbon monoxide (CO) and hydrogen chloride (HCl), do absorb infrared radiation, but these molecules are short-lived in the atmosphere owing to their reactivity or solubility. Therefore, they do not contribute significantly to the greenhouse effect and often are omitted when discussing greenhouse gases.

In contrast, greenhouse gases are those that absorb and emit infrared radiation in the wavelength range emitted by Earth. CO_2 (0.04%), nitrous oxide, methane and ozone are trace gases that account for almost one tenth of 1% of Earth's atmosphere and have an appreciable greenhouse effect. As previously noted these gases in order of magnitude are water vapour, CO_2, methane, nitrous oxide, ozone, chlorofluorocarbons, and hydrofluorocarbons.

Atmospheric concentrations are determined by the balance between sources (emissions of the gas from human activities and natural systems) and sinks (the removal of the gas from the atmosphere by conversion to a different chemical compound or absorption by bodies of water). The proportion of an emission remaining in the atmosphere after a specified time is the "airborne fraction" (AF). The annual airborne fraction is the ratio of the atmospheric increase in a given year to that year's total emissions. As of 2006 the annual airborne fraction for CO_2 was about 0.45. The *annual airborne fraction* increased at a rate of 0.25 ± 0.21% per year over the period 1959–2006.

The major non-gas contributor to Earth's greenhouse effect, clouds, also absorb and emit infrared radiation and thus have an effect on greenhouse gas radiative properties. Clouds are water droplets or ice crystals suspended in the atmosphere. The contribution of each gas to the greenhouse effect is determined by the characteristics of that gas, its abundance, and any indirect effects it may cause. For example, the direct radiative effect of a mass of methane is about 84 times stronger than the same mass of CO_2 over a 20 year time frame but it is present in much smaller concentrations so that its total direct radiative effect has so far been smaller. This is in part due to its shorter atmospheric lifetime in the absence of additional carbon sequestration. On the other hand, in addition to its direct radiative impact, methane has a large, indirect radiative effect because it contributes to ozone formation.

Clearly the greenhouse effect is very complex: perhaps the jury is already out and it may be prudent not to base policies about the totality of the atmospheric resource until the full role of the greenhouse effect is understood.

Urban heat island effect

An urban heat island (UHI) is an urban area or metropolitan area that is significantly warmer than its surrounding rural areas due to human activities. The temperature difference is usually larger at night than during the day, and is most apparent when winds are weak. UHI is most noticeable during the summer and winter. A brief summary of the UHI by *Wikipedia* highlights a phenomena which has been known for many decades, and is good example of how human influences sometimes inadvertently affect the environment where we live. UHI was first investigated and described by Luke Howard in the 1810s, although he was not the one to name the phenomenon.

The main cause of the urban heat island effect is from the modification of land surfaces. Waste heat generated by energy usage is a secondary contributor. As a population centre grows, it tends to expand its area and increase its average temperature. The term heat island is also used; the term can be used to refer to any area that is relatively hotter than the surroundings, but generally refers to human-disturbed areas.

Monthly rainfall is greater downwind of cities, partially due to the UHI. Increases in heat within urban centres increases the length of growing seasons, and decreases the occurrence of weak tornadoes in some areas. The UHI decreases air quality by increasing the production of pollutants such as ozone, and decreases water quality as warmer waters flow into area streams and put stress on their ecosystems.

Not all cities have a distinct urban heat island, and the heat island characteristics depend strongly on the background climate of the area in which the city is located. Mitigation of the urban heat island effect can be accomplished through the use of green roofs and the use of lighter-coloured surfaces in urban areas, which reflect more sunlight and absorb less heat.

Concerns have been raised about possible contribution from urban heat islands to global warming. While some lines of research have not detected a significant impact, other studies have concluded that heat islands can have measurable effects on climate phenomena at the global scale.

Wikipedia says that there are several causes of an urban heat island (UHI); for example, dark surfaces absorb significantly more solar radiation, which causes urban concentrations of roads and buildings to heat more than suburban and rural areas during the day. Materials commonly used in urban areas for pavement and roofs, such as concrete and asphalt, have significantly different thermal bulk properties (including heat capacity and thermal conductivity) and surface radiative properties (albedo and emissivity) than the surrounding rural areas. This causes a change in the energy budget of the urban area, often leading to higher temperatures than surrounding rural areas. Another major reason is the lack of evapotranspiration (through lack of vegetation) in urban areas. The U.S. Forest Service found in 2018 that cities in the United States are losing 36 million trees each year.

Other causes of an UHI are due to geometric effects. The tall buildings within many urban areas provide multiple surfaces for the reflection and absorption of sunlight, increasing the efficiency with which urban areas are heated. This is called the "urban canyon effect". Another effect of buildings is the blocking of wind, which also inhibits cooling by convection and prevents pollutants from dissipating. Waste heat from automobiles, air conditioning, industry, and other sources also contributes to the UHI. High levels of pollution in urban areas can also increase the UHI, as many forms of pollution change the radiative properties of the atmosphere. UHI not only raises urban temperatures but also increases ozone concentrations because ozone is a greenhouse gas whose formation will accelerate with the increase of temperature.

The difference in temperature between an inner city and its surrounding suburbs is frequently mentioned in weather reports, as in "20°C downtown, 18°C in the suburbs". The annual mean air temperature of a city with 1 million people or more can be 1.0–3.0°C warmer than its surroundings.

The IPCC stated that "it is well-known that compared to non-urban areas urban heat islands raise night-time temperatures more than daytime temperatures." For example, Barcelona, Spain is 0.2°C cooler for daily maximum and 2.9°C warmer for minimum temperatures than a nearby rural station. A description of the very first report of the UHI by Luke Howard in the late 1810s said that the urban centre of London was warmer at night than the surrounding countryside by 2.1°C . Though the warmer air temperature within the UHI is generally most apparent at night, urban heat islands exhibit significant and somewhat paradoxical diurnal behaviour. The air temperature difference between the UHI and the surrounding environment is large at night and small during the day.

Throughout the daytime, particularly when the skies are cloudless, urban surfaces are warmed by the absorption of solar radiation. Surfaces in the urban areas tend to warm faster than those of the surrounding rural areas. By virtue of their high heat capacities, urban surfaces act as a giant reservoir of heat energy. For example, concrete can hold roughly 2,000 times as much heat as an equivalent volume of air.

At night, the situation reverses. The absence of solar heating leads to the decrease of atmospheric convection and the stabilization of the urban boundary layer. If enough stabilization occurs, an inversion layer is formed. This traps urban air near the surface, and keeping surface air warm from the still-warm urban surfaces, resulting in warmer night time air temperatures within the UHI. Other than the heat retention properties of urban areas, the night time maximum in urban canyons could also be due to the blocking of "sky view" during cooling. Surfaces lose heat at night principally by radiation to the comparatively cool sky, and this is blocked by the buildings in an urban area.

Predicting the effects of the urban heat island
Leonard O. Myrup published the first comprehensive numerical treatment to predict the effects of the urban heat island (UHI) in December 1969 (*Journal of Applied Meteorology*). His paper surveys UHI and criticizes then-existing theories as being excessively qualitative. A general purpose, numerical energy budget model is described and applied to the urban atmosphere. Calculations for several special cases as well as a sensitivity analysis are presented. The model is found to predict the correct order of magnitude of the urban temperature excess. The heat island effect is found to be the net result of several competing physical processes. In general, reduced evaporation in the city centre and the thermal properties of the city building and paving materials are the dominant parameters. It is suggested that such a model could be used in engineering calculations to improve the climate of existing and future cities.

Aside from the effect on temperature, UHIs can produce secondary effects on local meteorology, including the altering of local wind patterns, the development of clouds and fog, the humidity, and the rates of precipitation. The extra heat provided by the UHI leads to greater upward motion, which can induce additional shower and thunderstorm activity. In addition, the UHI creates during the day a local low pressure area where relatively moist air from its rural surroundings converges, possibly leading to more favourable conditions for cloud formation. Rainfall rates downwind of cities are increased between 48% and 116%. Partly as a result of this warming, monthly rainfall is about 28% greater between

30 km to 65 km downwind of cities, compared with upwind. Some cities show a total precipitation increase of 51%.

Health and welfare of urban residents
UHIs have the potential to directly influence the health and welfare of urban residents. Within the United States alone, an average of 1,000 people die each year due to extreme heat. As UHIs are characterized by increased temperature, they can potentially increase the magnitude and duration of heat waves within cities. Research has found that the mortality rate during a heat wave increases exponentially with the maximum temperature, an effect that is exacerbated by the UHI. The night time effect of UHIs can be particularly harmful during a heat wave, as it deprives urban residents of the cool relief found in rural areas during the night.

Research in the United States suggests that the relationship between extreme temperature and mortality varies by location. Heat is more likely to increase the risk of mortality in cities in the northern part of the country than in the southern regions of the country. For example, when Chicago, Denver, or New York experience unusually hot summertime temperatures, elevated levels of illness and death are predicted. In contrast, parts of the country that are mild to hot year-round have a lower public health risk from excessive heat. Research shows that residents of southern cities, such as Miami, Tampa, Los Angeles, and Phoenix, tend to be acclimated to hot weather conditions and therefore less vulnerable to heat related deaths. However, as a whole, people in the United States appear to be adapting to hotter temperatures further north each decade. However, this might be due to better infrastructure, more modern building design, and better public awareness.

The US Center for Disease Control and Prevention notes that it "is difficult to make valid projections of heat-related illness and death under varying climate change scenarios" and that "heat–related deaths are preventable, as evidenced by the decline of all-cause mortality during heat events over the past 35 years". However, some studies suggest that the effects of UHIs on health may be disproportionate, since the impacts may be unevenly distributed based on a variety of factors such as age, ethnicity and socioeconomic status. This raises the possibility of health impacts from UHIs being an environmental justice issue.

Mitigation strategies include:
- White roofs: Painting rooftops white has become a common strategy to reduce the heat island effect. In cities, there are many dark coloured surfaces that absorb the heat of the sun in turn lowering the albedo of the city. White rooftops allow high solar reflectance and high solar emittance, increasing the albedo of the city or area where the effect is occurring.
- Green roofs: Green roofs are another method of decreasing the urban heat island effect. Green roofery is the practice of having vegetation on a roof; such as having trees or a garden. The plants that are on the roof increase the albedo and decreases the urban heat island effect. This method has been studied and criticized for the fact that green roofs are affected by climatic conditions, green roof variables are hard to measure, and are very complex systems.
- Planting trees in cities: Planting trees around the city can be another way of increasing albedo and decreasing the urban heat island effect. It is recommended to plant deciduous trees because they can provide many benefits such as more shade in the summer and not blocking warmth in winter.
- Green parking lots: Green parking lots use surfaces other than asphalt and vegetation to limit the urban heat island effect.

Cities providing climate solutions
Dr. Mittul Vahanvati, RMIT; Dr. Adriana Keating, Centre for Urban Research; Helen Cheng of The Fifth Estate write on the *Greenroofs.com* website June 2019 that most of the time we discuss climate change as affecting cities and the people who live in them. Less well known is that cities – specifically their planning and design – also create climate change through the UHI (Urban Heat Island). Encouragingly, this means that cities can provide climate solutions.

There is a myriad of strategies being adopted by cities across the world to reduce Urban Heat Island (UHI) and adapt to climate change:

Green roofs and walls, increasing green space and canopy cover, urban farms, storing stormwater and increasing groundwater percolation, and expansion of highly reflective pavements are just some of the strategies being used, globally.

Decisions must be evidence-based and be supported by political goodwill to allow for change to happen.

- Concerted action is required from state and local governments (especially amongst planners and urban designers), the private sector (especially architects and developers), researchers, the not-for-profit sector, and finally from city residents themselves.
- UHI and outdoor air quality (OAQ) are complex problems that require resilience thinking to understand how and where to make positive change.
- For example, addressing the UHI effect requires understanding the interrelations between urban morphology (grey infrastructure), green-blue infrastructure, local climatic conditions, and economic and political conditions and trends.
- A third key principle is the massive potential for nature-based solutions for reducing the UHI effect.
- These initiatives include green infrastructure such as street trees, parks and backyard gardens, and blue infrastructure such as water sensitive urban design and allowing rainwater to percolate in the soil. Not only does more green and blue space reduce heat, it has significant other benefits for city residents and local biodiversity.

Australian forest fires and climate

Bushfires in Australia are a widespread and regular occurrence that have contributed significantly to shaping the nature of the continent over millions of years. Eastern Australia is one of the most fire-prone regions of the world, and its predominant eucalyptus forests have evolved to thrive on the phenomenon of bushfire. However the fires can cause significant property damage and loss of both human and animal life. Bushfires have killed approximately 800 people in Australia since 1851 and billions of animals.

The most destructive fires are usually preceded by extreme high temperatures, low relative humidity and strong winds, which combine to create ideal conditions for the rapid spread of fire. Severe fire storms are often named according to the day on which they peaked, including the five most deadly blazes: Black Saturday 2009 in Victoria (173 people killed, 2000 homes lost); Ash Wednesday 1983 in Victoria and South Australia (75 people dead, nearly 1900 homes lost); Black Friday 1939 in Victoria (71 people dead, 650 houses destroyed); Black Tuesday 1967 in Tasmania (62 people dead and almost 1300 homes); and the Gippsland fires and Black Sunday of 1926 in Victoria (60 people killed over a two-month period). Other major conflagrations include the 1851 Black Thursday bushfires, the 2006 December bushfires, the 1974-75 fires that affected 15% of Australia, and the 2019–20 bushfires. In January 2020, it was estimated that over 1.25 billion animals died in the 2019-2020 Australian bushfire season.

The gradual drying of the Australian continent over the last 15 million years has produced an ecology and environment prone to fire, which has resulted in many specialised adaptations amongst flora and fauna. Some of the country's flora has evolved to rely on bushfires for reproduction. Aboriginal Australians used to use fire to clear grasslands for hunting and to clear tracks through dense vegetation, and European settlers have also had to adapt to using fire to enhance agriculture and forest management since the 19th century. Fire and forest management has evolved again through the 20th and 21st centuries with the spread of national parks and nature reserves, while human-caused global warming is predicted to continue increasing the frequency of blazes.

According to Tim Flannery (*The Future Eaters*), fire is one of the most important forces at work in the Australian environment. Some plants have evolved a variety of mechanisms to survive or even require bushfires (possessing epicormic shoots or lignotubers that sprout after a fire, or developing fire-resistant or fire-triggered seeds), or even encourage fire (eucalypts contain flammable oils in the leaves) as a way to eliminate competition from less fire-tolerant species. Early European explorers of the Australian coastline noted extensive bushfire smoke. Abel Janszoon Tasman's expedition saw smoke drifting over the coast of Tasmania in 1642 and noted blackened trunks and baked earth in the forests. While charting the east coast in 1770, Captain Cook's crew saw autumn fires in the bush burning on most days of the voyage.

Flannery writes that "The use of fire by Aboriginal people was so widespread and constant that virtually every early explorer in Australia makes mention of it. It was Aboriginal fire that prompted James Cook to call Australia 'This continent of smoke'. " However, he goes on to say: "When control was wrested from the Aborigines and placed in the hands of Europeans, disaster resulted." Fire suppression became the dominant paradigm in fire management leading to a significant shift away from traditional burning practices. A 2001 study found that the disruption of traditional burning practices and the introduction of unrestrained logging meant that many areas of Australia were now prone to extensive wildfires especially in the dry season. A similar study in 2017 found that the removal of mature trees by Europeans since they began to settle in Australia may have triggered extensive shrub regeneration which presents a much greater fire fuel hazard. Another factor was the introduction of gamba grass imported into Queensland as a pasture grass in 1942, and planted on a large scale from 1983. This can fuel intense bushfires, leading to loss of tree cover and long-term environmental damage.

Australia's hot, arid climate and wind-driven bushfires were a new and frightening phenomenon to the European settlers of the colonial era. The devastating Victorian bushfires of 1851, remembered as the Black Thursday bushfires, burned in a chain from Portland to Gippsland, and sent smoke billowing across the Bass Strait to north west Tasmania, where terrified settlers huddled around candles in their huts under a blackened afternoon sky. The fires covered five million hectares (around one quarter of what is now the state of Victoria). Around twelve lives were recorded lost, along with one million sheep and thousands of cattle.

New arrivals from the wetter climes of Britain and Ireland learned painful lessons in fire management and the European farmers slowly began to adapt – growing green crops around their haystacks and burning fire breaks around their pastures, and becoming cautious about burn offs of wheatfield stubble and ringbarked trees. But major fire events persisted, including South Gippsland's 1898 Red Tuesday bushfires that burned 260,000 hectares and claimed twelve lives and more than 2,000 buildings. Large bushfires continued throughout the 20th century. With increasing population and urban spread into bushland came increasing death tolls and property damage during large fires.

During the 1925-26 Victorian bushfire season, large areas of Gippsland in Victoria caught fire, leading to the Black Sunday fires on 14 February, when 31 people were killed in Warburton, near Melbourne. These fires remain the fifth most deadly bushfires recorded, with 60 people killed over two months.

Black Friday bushfires
The 1939 fire season was one of the worst on record for Australia, peaking with Victoria's devastating Black Friday bushfires of 13 January, but enduring for the full summer, with fires burning the urban fringes of Sydney, Melbourne and Canberra, and ash falling as far away as New Zealand. The Black Friday fires were the third deadliest on record, with some 71 people killed and 650 houses destroyed. They followed years of drought and a series of extreme heatwaves that were accompanied by strong northerly winds, after a very dry six months. Melbourne hit 45.6 °C and Adelaide 46.1°C . In NSW, Bourke suffered 37 consecutive days above 38 degrees and Menindee hit a record 49.7°C on 10 January 1939. The state of Victoria was hardest hit, with an area of almost two million hectares burned, 71 people killed, and whole townships wiped out, along with many sawmills and thousands of sheep, cattle and horses. Fires had been burning through December, but linked up with devastating force on Friday 13 January, plunging many areas of the state into midday blackness.

After the bushfires, Victoria convened a Royal Commission. Judge Leonard Stretton was instructed to inquire into the causes of the fires, and consider the measures taken to prevent the fires and to protect life and property. He made seven major recommendations to improve forest and fire management, and planned burning became an official fire management practice.

The Stretton Royal Commission later wrote:

"On 13 January it appeared that the whole State was alight. At midday, in many places, it was dark as night. Men carrying hurricane lamps, worked to make safe their families and belongings. Travellers on the highways were trapped by fires or blazing fallen trees, and perished. Throughout the land there was daytime darkness... Steel girders and machinery were twisted by heat as if they had been of fine wire. Sleepers of heavy durable timber, set in the soil, their upper surfaces flush with the ground, were burnt through... Where the fire was most intense the soil was burnt to such a depth that it may be many years before it shall have been restored..."

In the summer of 1967, Tasmania suffered its most destructive fire season, and Australia's fourth most deadly on record. A verdant spring had added higher than usual fuel to the state's forest floors, and strong northerly winds and high temperatures drove at least 80 different fires across the south-east, burning to within 2 kilometres of the centre of Hobart, the state capital. The infernos killed 62 people and destroyed almost 1300 homes.

From 27 December 1993 to 16 January 1994, over 800 severe fires burned along the coastal areas of New South Wales, affecting the state's most populous regions. Blazes emerged from the Queensland border down the north and central coast, through the Sydney basin and down the south coast to Batemans Bay. The 800,000-hectare spread of fires were generally contained within less than 100 kilometres from the coast, and many burned through rugged and largely uninhabited country in national parks or nature reserves. Dramatic scenes of the city of Sydney shrouded in thick bushfire smoke, and bushland suburbs on fire were broadcast around the world.

On 29 December 1993, the Dept of Bushfire Services was monitoring more than a dozen fires around the state, and homes were threatened in Turramurra by a fire in the Lane Cove River reserve, and a scrub fire had briefly cut off the holiday village of Bundeena in the Royal National Park, south of Sydney. *The Age* reported on 7 January 1994 that one quarter of NSW was under threat in the worst fires seen in the state for nearly fifty years, as hundreds of firefighters from interstate joined 4000 NSW firefighters battling blazes from Batemans Bay to Grafton. Deputy Prime Minister Brian Howe, ordered 100 soldiers to join firefighting efforts, and placed a further 100 on standby. Some 20,000 firefighters were deployed against around 800 fires mainly along the coast and ranges. The fires caused mass evacuations, claimed four lives, destroyed some 225 homes and burnt 800,000 hectares (2,000,000 acres) of bushland. They were met with one of the largest firefighting efforts in Australian history. A lengthy Coronial inquest followed the fires, leading to the formation of the New

South Wales Rural Fire Service. The *Rural Fires Act 1997* was proclaimed on 1 September 1997.

From September 2019 until March 2020, when the final fire was extinguished, Australia had experienced one of the worst bush fires in history. 2019 had been the hottest record year for Australia, with the bushfire season starting in June 2019. This caused mass damage all around the country with fires in each state and territory. The east coast had widespread destruction from the mega-blaze.

Many fires are as a result of either deliberate arson or carelessness, however these fires normally happen in readily accessible areas and are rapidly brought under control. Man-made events include arcing from overhead power lines, arson, accidental ignition in the course of agricultural clearing, grinding and welding activities, campfires, cigarettes and dropped matches, sparks from machinery and controlled burn escapes. They spread based on the type and quantity of fuel that is available. Fuel can include everything from trees, underbrush and dry grassy fields to homes. Wind supplies the fire with additional oxygen pushing the fire across the land at a faster rate. Electric power lines being brought down or arcing in high winds have also caused fires.

Dry lightning

In recent times most major bush fires have been started in remote areas by dry lightning. Some reports indicate that a changing climate could also be contributing to the ferocity of the 2019–20 fires with hotter, drier conditions making the country's fire season longer and much more dangerous. Strong winds also promote the rapid spread of fires by lifting burning embers into the air. This is known as spotting and can start a new fire up to 40 kilometres downwind from the fire front. In New South Wales, dry Föhn-like winds originating from the Great Dividing Range abruptly raise air temperatures in the lee of that mountain range and reduce atmospheric moisture, thus elevating fire danger. This occurs because of the partial orographic obstruction of comparatively damp low-level air and the sinking of drier upper-level air in leeward of the mountains, which is heated because of the adiabatic compression.

Large, violent wildfires can generate winds of their own, called fire whirls. Fire whirls are like tornadoes and result from the vortices created by the fire's heat. When these vortices are tilted from horizontal to vertical, this creates fire whirls. These whirls have been known to hurl flaming logs and burning debris over considerable distances. In the Northern

Territory fires can also be spread by black kites, whistling kites and brown falcons. These birds have been spotted picking up burning twigs, flying to areas of unburned grass and dropping them to start new fires there. This exposes their prey attempting to flee the blazes: small mammals, birds, lizards, and insects.

Months of severe drought and record-breaking temperatures fuelled a series of massive bush fires across Australia during the 2019-2020 summer. Hot and windy conditions had authorities of Australian Capital Territory declare a state of emergency.

Heatwaves and droughts
Australia's climate has warmed by more than 1°C over the past century, causing an increase in the frequency and intensity of heatwaves and droughts. Eight of Australia's ten warmest years on record have occurred since 2005. A study in 2018 conducted at Melbourne University found that the major droughts of the late 20th century and early 21st century in southern Australia are "likely without precedent over the past 400 years". Across the country, the average summer temperatures have increased leading to record-breaking hot weather, with the early summer of 2019 the hottest on record. 2019 was also Australia's driest ever year since 1900 with rainfall 40% lower than average.

Heatwaves and droughts dry out the undergrowth and create conditions that increase the risk of bushfires. This has become worse in the last 30 years. Since the mid-1990s, southeast Australia has experienced a 15% decline in late autumn and early winter rainfall and a 25% decline in average rainfall in April and May. Rainfall for January to August 2019 was the lowest on record in the Southern Downs (Queensland) and Northern Tablelands (New South Wales) with some areas 77% below the long term average. But as almost always happens, rains do come again, and the following map of rainfalls in Australia for the cumulative months of February to April 2020 shows that Nature is still in control.

In the 2000s IPCC concluded that ongoing anthropogenic climate change was virtually certain to increase the intensity and frequency of fires in Australia – a conclusion that has been endorsed in numerous reports since. In November 2019, the Australian Climate Council published a report titled *This is Not Normal* which also found the catastrophic bushfire conditions affecting NSW and Queensland in late 2019 have been aggravated by climate change. According to Nerilie Abram writing in *Scientific American* "the link between the current extremes and anthropogenic climate change is scientifically indisputable".

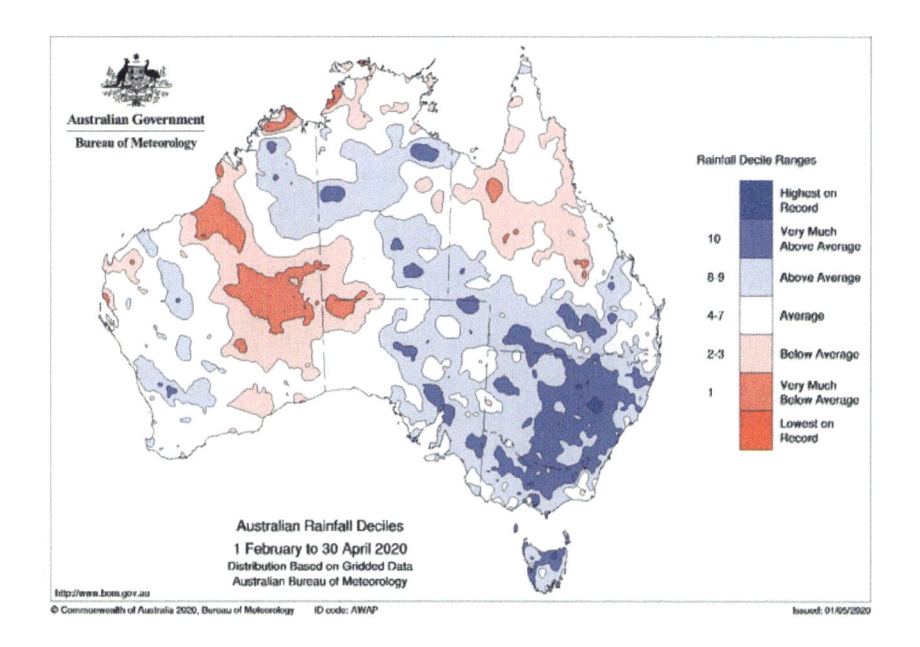

Australian Rainfall Deciles
1 February to 30 April 2020
Distribution Based on Gridded Data
Australian Bureau of Meteorology

Until the 2019–2020 Australian bushfire season, the forests in Australia were thought to reabsorb all the carbon released in bushfires across the country. This would mean the forests achieved net-zero emissions. However, scientists now say that global warming is making bushfires burn more intensely and frequently and believe the 2019-2020 fires have already released approximately 350 million tonnes of CO_2 – as much as two-thirds of Australia's average annual CO_2 emissions (530 million tonnes) in 2017 in just the past three months. David Bowman, professor of pyrogeography and fire science at the University of Tasmania warned that so much damage has been done that Australian forests may take more than 100 years to re-absorb the carbon that has been released so far this fire season. In January 2020, the UK Met Office said Australia's bushfires in 2019-2020 were expected to contribute 2% to the increase in the atmospheric concentration of major greenhouse gases, one of the largest annual increases in atmospheric CO_2 on record. Climate studies show that conditions which promote extreme bushfires in Australia will only get worse as more greenhouse gases are added to the atmosphere.

Bush fires kill animals directly and also destroy local habitats, leaving the survivors vulnerable even once the fires have passed. Professor Chris Dickman at Sydney University estimates that in the first three months of the 2019–2020 bushfires, over 800 million animals died in NSW, and

Anthropogenic influences on the climate 237

more than one billion nationally. This figure includes mammals, birds, and reptiles but does not include insects, bats or frogs. Many of these animals were burnt to death in the fires, with many others dying later due to the depletion of food and shelter resources and predation by feral cats and red foxes. Dickman adds that Australia has the highest rate of species loss of any area in the world, with fears that some of Australia's native species, like the Kangaroo Island dunnart, may even become extinct because of the current fires.

Koalas are perhaps the most vulnerable because they are slow-moving. In extreme fires, koalas tend to climb up to the top of a tree and curl into a ball where they become trapped. In January 2020 it was reported that half of the 50,000 koalas on Kangaroo Island off Australia's southern coast, which are kept separate to those on the mainland as insurance for the species' future, are thought to have died in the previous few weeks. The island is renowned for its mixture of animal species, and fears that it may never recover its population. Tens of thousands of farm animals, mostly sheep, were also killed in the fire on Kangaroo Island.

During the 2019-2020 bushfire season at least 33 people have been killed, 4 of which were firefighters. About 2,000 homes were destroyed, which has forced thousands to seek shelter elsewhere. Two people also died on Kangaroo Island in South Australia. More than 80 homes were destroyed in South Australia near Adelaide Hills, as well as one-third of the vineyards that provide grapes for the wine industry.

Smoke and air pollution
As a result of intense smoke and air pollution stemming from the fires, in January 2020 Canberra measured the worst air quality index of any major city in the world. The orange-tinged smoke entered homes and offices buildings across the capital making breathing outside very difficult, forcing businesses and institutions to shut their doors. Prof David Bowman, director of the Fire Centre Research Hub at the University of Tasmania, referred to the 2019–2020 fires as "absolutely transformative and unprecedented" in scale and stated, "It's pretty much a third of the Australian population that has been impacted, with prolonged, episodic exposure and sometimes extreme health impacts." Since September 2019, close to 3,000 firefighters have been out every day in NSW battling blazes. The NSW RFS stated that close to 90% of those are unpaid volunteers. David McBride, associate professor of occupational and environmental medicine at the University of Otago stated, "They push themselves to the

limit – they can suffer heat stress, which is a life-threatening injury, and end up with chronic bronchitis and asthma".

Economic damage from 2009's Black Saturday fires, the costliest in Australia's history, reached an estimated A$4.4 billion. *Moody's Analytics* says the cost of the 2019–2020 bushfires is likely to exceed even that figure and will cripple consumer confidence and harm industries such as farming and tourism. Medical bills from the current fires and smoke haze are expected to reach hundreds of millions of dollars with one analysis suggesting disruptions caused by the fire and smoke haze could cost Sydney as much as A$50 million a day. The Insurance Council of Australia estimated that claims for damage from the fires would be more than A$700 million, with claims expected to jump when more fire-hit areas became accessible. In response to the current (2019-20) fires, the federal government announced that compensation would be paid to volunteer firefighters, military personnel would be deployed to assist, and an A$2 billion bush fire recovery fund would be established. New South Wales, which has been hardest hit by the crisis, has pledged A$1 billion focused on repairing infrastructure.

After many major bushfires, state and federal governments have initiated inquiries to see what could be done to address the problem. A report published in 2015 stated there have been 51 inquiries into wildfires and wildfire management since 1939. The authors noted that Royal Commissions were not the most effective way to learn from past bushfire events. Many of the inquiries into bushfires have recommended "hazard reduction burning" intended to reduce the available fuel and have set targets to burn a certain percentage of forest each year to reduce risk. Planned burns are difficult to do safely and many of the investigations and Royal Commissions have found these targets are seldom met. At the same time, fire management experts disagree on how effective planned burning is.

During the fire season, the Bureau of Meteorology (BOM) provides fire weather forecasts. Fire agencies determine the appropriate Fire Danger Rating by considering the predicted weather including temperature, relative humidity, wind speed and dryness of vegetation. These Fire Danger Ratings are a feature of weather forecasts and alert the community to the actions they should take in preparation for the day. Ratings are broadcast via newspapers, radio, TV, and the internet.

In 2009, a standardised *Fire Danger Rating* (FDR) was adopted by all Australian states. This included a whole new level – catastrophic fire danger. The first time this level of danger was forecast for Sydney was in November 2019 during the 2019-2020 bushfire season. In 2010, following a national review of the bush fire danger ratings, new trigger points for each rating were introduced for grassland areas in most jurisdictions.

Bushfires have accounted for over 800 deaths in Australia since 1851 and, in 2012, the total accumulated cost was estimated at $1.6 billion. In terms of monetary cost however, they rate behind the damage caused by drought, severe storms, hail and cyclones, perhaps because they most commonly occur outside highly populated urban areas. However, the severe fires of the summer of 2019-2020 affected densely populated areas, including holiday destinations, leading NSW Rural Fire Services Commissioner, Shane Fitzsimmons, to claim it was "absolutely" the worst bushfire season on record.

Methane

In 1859, John Tyndall determined that coal gas, a mix of methane (CH_4) and other gases, strongly absorbed infrared radiation. Methane was subsequently detected in the atmosphere in 1948, and in the 1980s scientists realized that human emissions were having a substantial impact. Methane is gas that is found in small quantities in Earth's atmosphere. Methane is the simplest hydrocarbon, consisting of one carbon atom and four hydrogen atoms. Methane is a powerful greenhouse gas. Methane is flammable, and is used as a fuel worldwide. It is a principal component of natural gas. Burning methane in the presence of oxygen releases CO_2 and water vapour.

Although the concentration of methane in Earth's atmosphere is small (around 1.8 parts per million), it is an important greenhouse gas because it is such a potent heat absorber. The concentration of methane in our atmosphere has risen by about 150% since 1750, apparently largely due to human activities. Methane accounts for about 20% of the heating effects by all of the greenhouse gases combined. Both natural and human sources supply methane to Earth's atmosphere. Major natural sources of methane include emissions from wetlands and oceans, and from the digestive processes of termites. Sources related to human activities include rice production, landfills, raising cattle and other ruminant animals (cow burps!), and energy generation.

Methane and ruminant livestock
The release of methane gas from ruminant livestock (sheep and cattle) amounts to almost 30% of New Zealand's greenhouse gas emissions, and it is the largest contributor of greenhouse gases in the country, and hence it is especially important in looking at New Zealand's contribution to the world's greenhouse gases. Methane also accounts for over 40% of all emissions in terms of global warming potential. However, internationally the dominant sources of methane are rice paddies and wetlands, not farm animals. New Zealand therefore has a special interest in the measurement and mitigation of methane emissions from livestock. The inventory of New Zealand's greenhouse gas emissions is calculated annually by the New Zealand Ministry for the Environment and reported internationally. According to this inventory, methane emissions from ruminants have increased by 10% since 1990. (Over the same period, CO_2 emissions from

road transport have grown by 62%, and nitrous oxide emissions from agricultural soils by 25%.)

Measurements of methane emission rates on sheep and dairy cows have repeatedly shown that the variability of emissions between individual animals is large (e.g. for young sheep grazing the same pasture, emission rates varied from 9 to 35 g/day per sheep). While this variability may one day be exploited to reduce methane release by selecting for low-emitting animals, it is not well understood. It also leads to uncertainty in the national inventory calculations, which are based on measurements at the "animal scale", i.e. from small samples of animals (typically 20). In order to quantify this uncertainty, data representative for larger numbers of animals under typical farm management practice are needed, in other words, measurements at the "farm scale" or "paddock scale" are required.

Johannes Laubach and Frank Kelliher of *Landcare Research* have developed micro-meteorological techniques for measuring paddock-scale rates of net methane emissions from herds or flocks of freely grazing animals. "Micro-meteorological" means that wind transport of the emitted gas, away from the animals, is used as a vehicle to determine the emission rates. To this end, wind speed, direction and turbulence parameters are measured, as well as the air's methane concentration. For the animals, these techniques are unobtrusive, and are thus representative of normal behaviour and physiology. The techniques have been successfully used on commercially-managed farms.

When applying these techniques, Johannes and Frank collaborate with *AgResearch* colleagues who make measurements on selected animals from the herd or flock under investigation. This allows them to compare paddock-scale data to animal-scale data; so far there has always been good agreement. The work is currently focused on dairy cattle. On dairy farms in Canterbury, with herds of 270 to 550 cows, seasonal methane emission rates ranged from 284 to 427 g/day per cow.

Methane is a very effective greenhouse gas. While its atmospheric concentration is much less than that of CO_2, methane is 28 times more effective (averaged over 100 years) at trapping infrared radiation. The atmospheric residence time of methane is approximately 9 years. Residence time is the average time it takes for a molecule to be removed from the atmosphere. In this case, every molecule of methane that goes into the atmosphere remains there for 8 years until it is removed by oxidization into CO_2 and water (H_2O). This implies that providing the population of dairy cows in New Zealand does not increase, the total methane contribution of dairy cows to the atmosphere will not be beyond what is released today. However, it is difficult to quantify methane emissions since sources are spread out over large areas and emission values are small and variable in time and space.

It is estimated that up to 60% of the current methane flux from land to the atmosphere is the result of human activities. Some of these activities include emissions from fermentation processes associated with livestock, from cultivated rice paddies, from fossil fuel use and biomass burning, and from landfills.

Methane concentrations have been increasing steadily for the past 200 years, and despite a decline from 1983-2006, it increased again in 2007. Over this time period, atmospheric methane concentrations have more than doubled. As with CO_2, human activity is increasing the methane concentration faster than natural sinks can offset it. Future trends are particularly difficult to anticipate, partly due to an incomplete understanding of the climate feedbacks related to methane emissions. It is also difficult to predict how, as human populations grow, possible changes in livestock raising, rice cultivation, and energy utilization will influence methane emissions.

Atmospheric methane and climate change – an alternative viewpoint
W. A. van Wijngaarden and W. Happer of the Department of Physics and Astronomy, York University, Canada, and the Department of Physics, Princeton University, USA, respectively, in a report on the CO_2 Coalition website (*CO2coalition.org*) on November 22, 2019, comments that "proposals to place harsh restrictions on methane emissions because of warming fears are not justified by facts."

The editor of the CO_2 website notes that this paper is a contribution to the "*CO_2 Coalition's Climate Issues in Depth*" series. The series is designed for readers who desire greater scientific detail than is provided by our White Papers for general audiences. The Happer-van Wijngaarden paper is a summary of an extensive paper, *Infrared Forcing of Greenhouse Gases*, that they are preparing for publication in a technical journal. Using measurements of hundreds of thousands of individual "line strengths" of the major greenhouse gases in Earth's atmosphere, they show that methane is nearly irrelevant to global warming. Adding a methane molecule to the atmosphere hinders radiative cooling 30 times more than adding a CO_2 molecule. But CO_2 molecules are being added 300 times faster than methane molecules. So methane contributes only about 30/300 or 1/10 of the already small warming from CO_2.

This paper served as the scientific backing for a November 2019 submission to the *US Environmental Protection Agency* by the Life: Powered project of the Texas Public Policy Foundation. The policy implication of the paper is that methane emissions should not be regulated because of any concern about global warming. Cows and pipelines can rest easy.

In the Abstract to the paper, the authors state atmospheric methane contributes to the radiative forcing of Earth's atmosphere. Radiative forcing is the difference in the net upward thermal radiation from the Earth through a transparent atmosphere and radiation through an otherwise identical atmosphere with greenhouse gases. Radiative forcing, normally specified in units of W/m^2, depends on latitude, longitude and altitude, but it is often quoted for a representative temperate latitude, and for the altitude of the tropopause, or for the top of the atmosphere.

For current concentrations of greenhouse gases, the radiative forcing at the tropopause, per added methane molecule, is about 30 times larger than the forcing per added molecule of CO_2. This is due to the heavy saturation of the absorption band of the abundant greenhouse gas, CO_2. But the rate of increase of CO_2 molecules, about 2.3 ppm/year (ppm = part per million by mole), is about 300 times larger than the rate of increase of methane molecules, which has been around 0.0076 ppm/year since the year 2008. So the contribution of methane to the annual increase in forcing is one tenth (30/300) that of CO_2. The net forcing increase from methane and CO_2 increases is about 0.05 W/m^2/year.

Other things being equal, this will cause a temperature increase of about 0.012°C/year. Their conclusion that "Proposals to place harsh restrictions on methane emissions because of warming fears are not justified by facts". This is contrary to much of the current literature on the role of atmospheric methane in global warming.

Why are New Zealand cows emitting so much methane?
Graham Shepherd of *BioAgriNomics* is a New Zealand soil scientist and independent farm advisor. The following are extracts from his *Opinion* webpage.

The answer lies in the poor quality of pasture the animal is consuming. Thus there is now a reliance on supplements to fill the shortcomings of the pasture, a limitation that comes at a hefty economic cost to the farmer. Cows by and large are fed nitrate-rich, crude protein-rich pastures that are low in carbohydrates, sugars and starch. The microbes in the rumen therefore lack the energy to efficiently convert the plant material into milk, meat and fibre. Instead, more than 80% is converted to ammonia (NH$_3$), methane and CO$_2$. The production of these gases could be significantly reduced by simply presenting the animal with energy-rich, species diverse pasture.

While methane is reported as a major GHG accounting for over 40% of NZ emissions in its global warming potential, it's a gas that's rapidly broken down in the atmosphere by hydroxyl radicals photo-oxidising methane, methyl (CH$_3$, a non-GHG), and CO$_2$.

Moist air above pastures in fact photo-oxidises far more methane than is able to be produced by the soil or animals grazing that area. CO$_2$ should be seen as a critically important resource where its associated carbon can be sequestered into the soil by promoting the capacity and rate of photosynthesis, the density and length of the root system, and the biomass and activity of soil microbes.

We can more than offset all our emissions by simply sequestering sufficient carbon from the atmosphere, but more importantly we need to reduce our overall emissions. Despite commonly held perceptions, this can easily be achieved by simply changing to management practices that address the root cause of our high emissions rather than attempting to mitigate them by applying the many band-aids now developed. This has significant implications for the Zero Carbon Bill now before a parliamentary select committee. Unless New Zealand implements those farm management practices that enable the sequestration of soil carbon by the drawdown of atmospheric CO$_2$ and minimise the emissions of methane, New Zealand will continue to fall short of the emission targets set.

Methane is also a necessary requirement of methanotrophic bacteria in the soil which takes up methane from the atmosphere as its energy source and oxidises it. Soils act as a major sink for atmospheric methane, converting it to CO$_2$ and moisture. The amount of methane emitted by one cow is equivalent to the amount of methane the methanotrophic bacteria can consume on 3.4 ha of land.

In addition, it has been shown that methane emissions can be slashed by more than 80% by adding seaweed (*Asparagopsis taxiformis*) to the cow's diet, highlighting the importance of diet in mitigating methane emissions. At a GHG workshop at New Zealand's Massey University a few years ago I asked, "how would improving a cow's diet affect the emissions of methane?" The answer given was no more than 10%. How wrong they were. Like us the animal responds to what it eats.

The real concern with methane is its vast storage and emissions from formerly frozen methane hydrates on many continental shelves. This of course is outside the realm and influence of NZ's agriculture.

We need to use our grey matter more to think about what's in the dry matter. If we don't, the public and politicians' perception that agriculture is destructive to the environment will continue and our markets will turn more towards plant based and synthetic milk and meat products. Unawareness, vested interests and groups that lobby for something similar to the status quo are a concern because they come with a high economic and environmental cost. Because our total emissions have increased 800% since 1990 (Statistics NZ) one must ask whether their focus on implementing band-aids to offset our high environmental footprint has worked for us.

11

Adaptation to climate

".. for all our clever inventions, technology and science, natural forces will always have the final say."

Kerre Woodham, writing in the "Herald on Sunday" on 18 April 2010.

Emission Trading Schemes (ETS)

An Emissions Trading Scheme for global greenhouse gas emissions (GHGs) works by establishing property rights for the atmosphere. The atmosphere is considered to be a global public good, and GHG emissions are an international externality. The emissions from all sources of GHGs contribute to the overall stock of GHGs in the atmosphere. In the cap-and-trade variant of emissions trading, a limit on access to a resource (the cap) is defined and then allocated among users in the form of permits. Compliance is established by comparing actual emissions with permits surrendered including any permits traded within the cap. The environmental integrity of emissions trading depends on the setting of the cap, not the decision to allow trading.

For the purposes of analysis, it is possible to separate efficiency (achieving a given objective at lowest cost) and equity (fairness). Economists generally agree that to regulate emissions efficiently, all polluters need to face the full costs of their actions (ie, the full marginal social costs of their actions). Regulation of emissions that is applied only to one economic sector or region drastically reduces the efficiency of efforts to reduce global emissions. There is, however, no scientific consensus over how to share the costs and benefits of reducing future climate change (mitigation of climate change), or the costs and benefits of adapting to any future climate change.

The *World Resources Institute* (WRI) in a review paper by Kelly Vevin and Chantal Davis published in September 2019 says that to avoid the worst climate impacts, global greenhouse gas (GHG) emissions will not only need to drop by half in the next 10 years, they will then have to reach net-zero around mid-century. Recognizing this urgency, the UN Secretary General recently asked national leaders to come to the UN Climate Action Summit in September 2019 with announcements of targets for "net-zero emissions" by 2050. Several countries have already committed to do so, along with some states, cities and companies.

Net-zero emissions will be achieved when any remaining human-caused GHG emissions are balanced out by removing GHGs from the atmosphere (a process known as carbon removal). First and foremost, human-caused emissions – like those from fossil-fuelled vehicles and factories – should be reduced as close to zero as possible. Any remaining GHGs would be balanced with an equivalent amount of carbon removal, by restoring forests or through direct air capture and storage (DACS) technology. The concept of net-zero emissions is akin to "climate neutrality."

Under the Paris Agreement, countries agreed to limit warming well below 2°C and ideally 1.5°C. Climate impacts that are already unfolding around the world, even with only 1.1°C warming, from melting ice to devastating heat waves and more intense storms show the urgency of minimizing temperature increase to no more than 1.5°C.

Special Report on Global Warming
The Special Report on Global Warming of 1.5°C, from the Intergovernmental Panel on Climate Change (IPCC), finds that if the world reaches net-zero emissions one decade sooner, by 2040, the chance of limiting warming to 1.5°C is considerably higher. The sooner emissions peak, and the lower they are at that point, the more realistic it is that net-zero is achieved in time. There would also be less need to rely on carbon removal in the second half of the century.

Importantly, the time frame for reaching net-zero emissions differs significantly if one is referring to CO_2 alone, or referring to all major GHGs (including methane, nitrous oxide, and "F gases" such as hydrofluorocarbons, commonly known as HFCs). For non-CO_2 emissions, the net-zero date is later because some of these emissions – such as methane from agricultural sources – are considered somewhat more difficult to phase out. However, these gases will drive temperatures higher in the near-term, potentially pushing temperature change past the 1.5°C threshold much earlier. Because of this, it's important for countries to specify whether their net-zero targets cover only CO_2 or all major GHGs. A comprehensive net-zero emissions target would include all major GHGs, ensuring that non-CO_2 gases are also reduced.

Because countries' economies and stages of development vary widely, there is no one-size-fits-all timeline for individual countries. There are, however, hard physical limits to the total emissions the atmosphere can support while limiting global temperature increase to the agreed goals of the Paris Agreement. At the very least, major emitters (such as the United States, the European Union and China) should reach net-zero GHG emissions by 2050, or the emissions will not reduce quickly enough regardless of what other countries do. Ideally, major emitters will reach net-zero much earlier, given that the largest economies play an outsize role in determining the trajectory of global emissions.

Fifteen countries, as of early 2020, have now adopted net-zero targets – Bhutan, Costa Rica, Denmark, Fiji, Finland, France, Iceland, Japan, the Marshall Islands, Norway, Portugal, Sweden, Switzerland, the United Kingdom and Uruguay. While there are new announcements every month, the percentage of global emissions covered by some form of a net-zero target still only hovers around 5%. Some of these targets are in law, and some are in other policy documents. Some net-zero targets have been incorporated directly into countries' long-term, low-emissions development strategies, while other countries have adopted net-zero targets before submitting a long-term strategy.

New Zealand Emissions Trading Scheme
One country example of an Emission Trading Scheme is the New Zealand Emissions Trading Scheme (NZ ETS). The scheme is a partial-coverage all-free allocation uncapped highly internationally linked emissions trading scheme. The NZ ETS was first legislated in the NZ Climate Change Response (Emissions Trading) Amendment Act 2008 in September 2008 under the Fifth Labour Government of New Zealand and then amended (November 2009 and November 2012) by the Fifth National Government.

The NZ ETS covers forestry (a net sink), energy (42% of total emissions in 2012), industry (7%), and waste (5%), but not pastoral agriculture (46% of 2012 total emissions). Participants in the NZ ETS must surrender one emission unit (either an international 'Kyoto' unit or a New Zealand-issued unit) for every two tonnes of CO_2 equivalent emissions reported or they may choose to buy NZ units from the government at a fixed price of NZ$25. The one-for-two transitional measure has been phased out evenly across relevant sectors over three years from 1 January 2017. The old 50% surrender obligation increased to 67% from 1 January 2017, and increased to 83% from 1 January 2018. There was a full surrender obligation from 1 January 2019 for all sectors in the NZ ETS. This phased approach was intended to allow businesses time to plan and adjust, and therefore to support a more stable market.

Individual sectors of the economy have different entry dates when their obligations to report emissions and surrender emission units took effect. Forestry, which contributed 19% of NZ's 2008 emissions, entered the NZ ETS on 1 January 2008. The stationary energy, industrial processes and liquid fossil fuel sectors entered the NZ ETS on 1 July 2010. The waste sector (landfill operators) entered on 1 January 2013. From November 2009, methane and nitrous oxide emissions from pastoral agriculture were scheduled to be included in the NZ ETS from 1 January 2015. However, agriculture was indefinitely excluded from the NZ ETS in 2013.

The NZ ETS is highly linked to international carbon markets as it allows the importing of most of the Kyoto Protocol emission units. It also creates a specific domestic unit; the 'New Zealand Unit' (NZU), which will be issued by free allocation to emitters, with no auctions intended in the short term. The NZU is equivalent to 1 tonne of CO_2. Free allocation of NZUs will vary by sector. The commercial fishery sector (who are not participants) will receive a free allocation of units on a historic basis. Owners of pre-1990 forests will receive a fixed free allocation of units. Free allocation to emissions-intensive industry, will be provided on an output-intensity basis. For this sector, there is no set limit on the number of units that may be allocated. The number of units allocated to eligible emitters will be based on the average emissions per unit of output within a defined 'activity'. Bertram and Terry in a 2010 book *The Carbon Challenge* state that as the NZ ETS does not 'cap' emissions, the NZ ETS is not a cap and trade scheme as understood in the economics literature.

Stakeholders criticism
Some stakeholders have criticised the New Zealand Emissions Trading Scheme for its generous free allocations of emission units and the lack of a carbon price signal (the Parliamentary Commissioner for the Environment), and for being ineffective in reducing emissions (*Greenpeace Aotearoa New Zealand*). Several NZ media commentators have also made comments on the scheme and the following are comments made in the early 2010's. Rod Oram commented in a *Sunday Star Times* column that the National Government's changes to the ETS were "a giant step backwards" which would "drive up emissions, perpetuate old technology, necessitate ever-greater subsidies and reduce New Zealand's international competitiveness and reputation." Oram considered that the amendments to the NZ ETS destroyed its effectiveness. His examples were: removing limits on emissions by adopting intensity-based allocation of free carbon credits, slavishly following climate-laggard Australia, minimising the price incentive by extending the free allocation of credits for 75 years, muting the price signal with a $NZ25 per tonne of carbon cap, forcing forestry holders of credits to sell them overseas because of the $NZ25 per tonne cap, cancelling complementary measures such as fuel efficiency standards, giving in to special pleading via subsidies, and creating uncertainty for business.

The *New Zealand Herald's* economics editor Brian Fallow said: "Clearly emissions will peak higher and later than they would have done under the existing scheme. But the higher and later the peak in emissions, the steeper and more economically costly the subsequent decline will have to be".

Building sea walls to combat rising sea levels

Seawalls are very widespread around the world's coasts and many ad-hoc seawalls are found in developing countries. Seawalls are hard engineered structures with a primary function to prevent further erosion of the shoreline. They are built parallel to the shore and aim to hold or prevent sliding of the soil, while providing protection from wave action (UNFCCC, 1999). Although their primary function is erosion reduction, they have a secondary function as coastal flood defences. The physical form of these structures is highly variable; seawalls can be vertical or sloping and constructed from a wide variety of materials. They may also be referred to as revetments. The description of this technology originates from Linham and Nicholls (2010). The following information is based on the item in *Wikipedia* and analyses by French (2001).

Seawalls form a defining line between sea and land. They are frequently used in locations where further shore erosion will result in excessive damage, e.g. when roads and buildings are about to fall into the sea. Seawalls are typically, heavily engineered, inflexible structures and are generally expensive to construct and require proper design and construction supervision. The shape of the seaward face is important in the deflection of incoming wave energy; smooth surfaces reflect wave energy while irregular surfaces scatter the direction of wave reflection.

The main advantage of a seawall is that it provides a high degree of protection against coastal flooding and erosion. A well maintained and appropriately designed seawall will also fix the boundary between the sea and land to ensure no further erosion will occur – this is beneficial if the shoreline is home to important infrastructure or other buildings of importance. As well as fixing the boundary between land and sea, seawalls also provide coastal flood protection against extreme water levels. Provided they are appropriately designed to withstand the additional forces, seawalls will provide protection against water levels up to the seawall design height. In the past the design height of many seawalls was based on the highest known flood level (van der Meer, 1998).

Seawalls also have a much lower space requirement than other coastal defences such as dikes, especially if vertical seawall designs are selected. In many areas land in the coastal zone is highly sought-after; by reducing the space requirements for coastal defence the overall costs of construction may fall. The increased security provided by seawall construction also maintains hinterland values and may promote investment and development of the area (Nicholls et al., 2007). Moreover, if appropriately designed, seawalls have a high amenity value – in many countries, seawalls incorporate promenades which encourage recreation and tourism. Provided they are adequately maintained, seawalls are potentially long-lived structures. The seawall in Galveston, Texas was constructed in 1903 and continues to provide coastal flood and erosion protection to the city to this day (Dean & Dalrymple, 2002).

Seawalls are subjected to significant loadings, as a result of wave impact. These loadings increase with water depth in front of the structure because this enables larger waves close to the shoreline. Seawalls are designed to dissipate or reflect incoming wave energy and as such, must be designed to remain stable under extreme wave loadings. The effects of sea level rise, increased wave heights and increased storminess caused by climate change must all be taken into account. Sediment availability is also affected by seawall construction. The problem is caused by replacing soft, erodible shorelines with hard, non-erodible ones. While this protects the valuable hinterland, it causes problems in terms of sediment starvation; erosion in front of the seawall will continue at historic or faster rates but the sediment is not replaced through the erosion of the hinterland (French, 2001). This can cause beach lowering, which reduces beach amenity value and increases wave loadings on the seawall by allowing larger waves close to the shore.

In the absence of a seawall, natural shoreline erosion would supply adjacent stretches of coastline with sediment, through a process known as longshore drift. Once a seawall is constructed however, the shoreline is protected from erosion and the supply of sediment is halted. This causes sediment starvation at sites located along the shore, in the direction of longshore drift and this has the capacity to induce erosion at these sites.

Although seawalls prevent erosion of protected shorelines, where the seawall ends, the coast remains free to respond to natural conditions. This means that undefended areas adjacent to the wall could move inland causing a stepped appearance to the coast (French, 2001). The downdrift end of the seawall is also typically subjected to increased erosion as a result of natural processes. This flanking effect can cause undermining and instability of the wall in extreme cases.

Because seawalls are immovable defences, they can also interfere with natural processes such as habitat migration which is naturally induced by sea level change. Seawalls obstruct the natural inland migration of coastal systems in response to sea level rise, therefore causing coastal squeeze. This process causes a reduction in the area of intertidal habitats such as sandy beaches and saltmarshes because these environments are trapped between a rising sea level and unmoving, hard defences. A potential problem is overtopping. This occurs when water levels exceed the height of the seawall, resulting in water flow into areas behind the structure. Overtopping is not a continuous process but usually occurs when individual high waves attack the seawall, causing a temporary increase in water level which exceeds the structure height (Goda, 2000). If the structure is too low, excessive overtopping can remove considerable amounts of soil or sand from behind the wall, thus weakening it.

By encouraging development, hard defences necessitate continued investment in maintenance and upgrades, effectively limiting future coastal management options. Although authorities may not have a responsibility to continue providing protection, the removal of defences is likely to be both costly and politically controversial (Nicholls et al., 2007). Seawalls also reduce beach access for handicapped people and for emergency services. This can be problematic if the beach fronting such structures is to be used for recreation. The appearance of seawalls can be aesthetically displeasing which can further negatively affect beaches dependent upon a tourist economy.

A study by Linham et al. (2010) indicates that the unit cost of constructing 1 km of vertical seawall is in the range of US$0.4 to 27.5 million. The study found seawall costs for around ten countries. Most were developed country examples, although a number of newly developed and developing countries, such as Egypt, Singapore and South Africa were also found. Problems arise in the reporting of unit costs for vertical seawalls as the effect of height on unit costs is rarely considered. As such, these costs are likely to relate to seawalls of various heights; this explains some of the significant variation in costs between projects.

Some of the best unit cost information is given by the English Environment Agency (2007), for unit costs relevant to the UK. This source gives an average construction cost for seawalls of US$2.65 million (at 2009 price levels). This cost includes direct construction costs, direct overheads, costs of associated construction works, minor associated work, temporary works, compensation events and delay costs. This does not include external costs such as consultants, land and compensation payments.

Seawall construction on a community scale
Seawall construction is possible on a community scale. There are many examples of ad-hoc construction to protect individual properties and communities. However, ad-hoc seawalls are likely to give much less consideration to the water levels, wave heights and wave loadings during an extreme event. This is largely because these events are hard to foresee without a well-developed science and technology base. For example, traditional seawall construction methods in Fiji involved poking sticks into the ground to create a fence, behind which logs, sand and refuse would be piled to pose a barrier to the sea. This type of traditional construction has shown to have low effectiveness against significant events, however, and in many cases, these defences are washed away during extreme events.

A case study from the Pacific island of Fiji (Mimura & Nunn, 1998) shows seawall construction to be very costly even when local materials were utilised in conjunction with other materials supplied by the government. Seawall construction in Fiji consumed the villagers' time and also required significant time and money to be spent on the provision of catering services for workers. The availability of experience, materials, labour and specialised machinery for the construction of seawalls may also pose a barrier to the implementation of this technology.

French (2001) recommends proactive construction of seawalls at some distance inland. This reduces interference with coastal processes and creates a buffer zone to protect against coastal flooding and erosion. A key barrier to this type of approach lies in convincing and educating landowners of the necessity for, and benefits of, these measures (Mimura & Nunn, 1998). Seawalls can also be implemented as part of a wider coastal zone management plan which employs other technologies such as beach nourishment and managed realignment. Placement of seawalls inland, following managed retreat, reduces interference with coastal zone processes and creates a buffer zone to protect against coastal flooding and erosion (French, 2001). The seawall therefore acts as a last line of defence. Use of seawalls in conjunction with beach nourishment can also address some of the negative impacts of seawall construction, such as beach lowering and downdrift erosion.

Impacts on New Zealand's coastal areas
Likely impacts of climate change on New Zealand's coastal areas and how central and local government are preparing for these impacts is discussed

in a paper prepared by New Zealand's *Ministry for the Environment*. What is discussed is relevant to many countries.

The global average sea level rose about 19 cm between 1901 and 2010, at an average rate of 1.7 mm per year. From 1993 to 2016 the global average sea level rose at an average rate of about 3.4 mm per year using IPCC data. Due to the influence of regional climate trends and gravitational effects, sea level does not rise uniformly around the globe. Much of New Zealand's urban development and infrastructure is located in coastal areas. This makes it vulnerable to coastal hazards such as coastal erosion, inundation (flooding) by the sea and sea level rise.

Climate change is likely to bring the following changes:
- increased frequency, duration and extent of coastal flooding
- coastal defences are overtopped by waves or high tides more often
- severe storms increase in intensity and storm surge levels rise
- some sandy beaches may continue to accrete, but more slowly
- some gravel beaches are more likely to erode
- the potential for saltwater to enter underground freshwater aquifers increases.

New Zealand's *Ministry for the Environment* says that it is important that New Zealand (and most if not all coastal areas) start planning for future sea level rise. The Ministry recommends developing flexible adaptation plans, rather than relying on a single sea level rise value or scenario. This is because there is a wide range of possible coastal futures with ongoing sea level rise, particularly heading into next century. The Ministry's Coastal Hazards and Climate Change guidance provides four scenarios of future sea level rise to use in conducting hazard and risk assessments. It also provides minimum transitional sea level rise values for use in planning processes for two out of four broad categories of development.

Category A – Coastal subdivision, greenfield developments and major new infrastructure
The New Zealand Coastal Policy Statement 2010 emphasises locating such development away from areas prone to coastal hazard risks (including climate change) and avoiding increasing the risk. Therefore, councils considering coastal subdivision, greenfield developments and major new infrastructure should avoid the hazard risk by considering sea level rise over more than 100 years and using the highest sea level rise scenario.

Category B – Changes in land use and redevelopment (intensification)
When considering changes in land use and redevelopment (intensification), councils should conduct a risk assessment using all four sea level rise scenarios and the adaptive pathways planning approach.

Category C – Existing coastal development and asset planning
For planning and decision timeframes out to 2120, councils should use a minimum transitional value for sea level rise of 1 metre relative to the 1986-2005 baseline.

Category D – Non-habitable short-lived assets
For planning and decision timeframes out to 2120, councils should use a minimum transitional value for sea level rise of 0.65 metres relative to the 1986-2005 baseline.

Many local authorities in New Zealand have already started to plan for sea level rise. Some councils have completed coastal hazard assessments and have developed maps showing areas which are expected to be affected over the next 50-100 years. Other activities being undertaken by local government include:
- restricting development in coastal erosion areas
- planning for managed retreat
- rejecting consents for alterations or extensions to existing buildings in the coastal zone
- discouraging the construction of defences such as sea walls.

Defending vulnerable infrastructure
Researchers have estimated the cost of defending vulnerable infrastructure within portions of shoreline that could be at least 15% underwater by 2040. Defending against rising seas could cost US communities $416bn in the next 20 years, according to a report on *guardian.com*. Spending on seawalls alone could total almost as much as the initial investment in the US interstate highway system, the authors said. And the billions involved will represent just a fraction of adaptation efforts governments in coastal states will have to fund if they do not want to simply retreat.

"I don't think anybody's thought about the magnitude of this one small portion of overall adaptation costs and it's a huge number," said Richard Wiles, executive director of the *Center for Climate Integrity* (CCI), which published the report. Estimates of how much sea level rise will cost often focus on impacts by 2100, Wiles said, adding that people will be paying for the climate crisis much earlier. "You're looking at close to half a trillion spent over the next 20 years and no one has thought about that. So the question is, who's going to pay for that? Is it really going to be taxpayers? The current position of climate polluters is that they should pay nothing, and that's just not tenable."

The CCI published the report with analysis by lead scientist Paul Chinowksy, director of the environmental design programme at the University of Colorado Boulder and chief executive of the firm *Resilient Analytics*. The cost figures in the CCI report are based on localized projections for sea level rise under the UN Intergovernmental Panel on Climate Change (IPCC) scenario for moderate levels of pollution. In that scenario, called RCP 4.5, emissions would peak around 2040 and then begin to decline. The projections in the report were calculated by the climate science and news organization *Climate Central*.

Not all studies are pessimistic
Low-lying Pacific islands regarded as "poster child" examples of the threat from rising sea levels are expanding not sinking, a new study has revealed. Scientists have been surprised by the findings, which show that some islands have grown by almost one-third over the past 60 years. Paul Chapman writing in *www.telegraph.co.uk* on 3 June 2010 reports that among the island chains to have increased in land area are Tuvalu and neighbouring Kiribati, both of which attracted attention at 2009 Copenhagen climate summit.

In the study, researchers compared aerial photographs and high-resolution satellite images of 27 islands taken since the 1950s. Only four islands, mostly uninhabited, had decreased in area despite local sea level rises of almost five inches in that time, while 23 stayed the same or grew. Seven islands in Tuvalu grew, one by 30%, although the study did not include the most populous island.

In Kiribati, the three of the most densely populated islands, Betio, Bairiki and Nanikai, also grew by between 12.5 and 30%. Professor Paul Kench, of the University of Auckland, who co-authored the study with Dr Arthur Webb, a Fiji-based expert on coastal processes, said the study challenged the view that the islands were sinking as a result of global warming. "80% of the islands we've looked at have either remained about the same or, in fact, got larger. Some have got dramatically larger," he said. "We've now got evidence the physical foundations of these islands will still be there in 100 years," he told *New Scientist* magazine.

He said the study suggested the islands had a natural ability to respond to rising seas by accumulating coral debris from the outlying reefs that surround them. "It has long been thought that as the sea level goes up, islands will sit there and drown. But they won't," Professor Kench said. The trend is largely explained by the fact that the islands comprise mostly coral debris eroded from encircling reefs, which is pushed up on to the islands by wind and waves. Because coral is a living organism, it continues to grow and establish itself in its new home, so the process becomes continuous.

Land reclamation and deposition of other sediment also contribute to the process. "These islands are so low lying that in extreme events waves crash straight over the top of them," Professor Kench said. "In doing that they transport sediment from the beach or adjacent reef platform and they throw it on to the top of the island."

But the two scientists warn that people living on the islands still face serious challenges from climate change, particularly if the pace of sea level rises were to overtake that of sediment build-up. The fresh groundwater that sustains villagers and their crops could be destroyed. "The land may be there but will they still be able to support human habitation?" he said. Naomi Thirobaux, a student from Kiribati who has studied the islands for a PhD, said "No one should be lulled into thinking erosion and inundation were not taking their toll on the islands. In a populated place, people can't move back or inland because there's hardly any place to move into, so that's quite dramatic."

Of course not everyone is overly concerned with rising sea levels including the Maldives. Sea level rise, a trend that predates the Industrial Revolution, is being blamed on CO_2 emissions and has become one of the most potent harangues used to guilt-trip the populace of major industrial countries over the use of carbon-based energy. These comments by Thomas Lifson writing on November 4, 2019 on the website *climatechangedispatch.com* says that the Maldives are building seaside airports despite predictions of sea level doom.

As the flattest country on Earth, the Republic of Maldives is extremely vulnerable to rising sea level and faces the very real possibility that the majority of its land area will be underwater by the end of this century. Today, the white sand beaches and extensive coral reefs of the Maldives' 1,190 islands draw more than 600,000 tourists annually.

Sea level rise is likely to worsen existing environmental stresses in the Maldives, such as periodic flooding from storm surge, and a scarcity of fresh water for drinking and other purposes.

Adaptation to climate

Given mid-level scenarios for global warming emissions, the Maldives is projected to experience sea level rise of the order of half a metre – and to lose some 77% of its land area – by around the year 2100. If sea level were instead to rise by one metre, the Maldives could be almost completely inundated by about 2085.

The Maldivian government has identified many potential strategies for adapting to rising seas but is also considering relocating its people to a new homeland. Yet, one of the strategies of the Maldives is the construction of 5 airports to bring in tourists.

The *Maldives Insider* comments: "The airport being developed in Kulhudhuffushi, a key population zone in the north, and in Maafaru, a proposed ultra-luxury tourism zone, had earlier welcomed test flights. However, delays in the construction of the terminal and other support facilities had pushed back commercial operations. Six hectares off the southern coast of Kulhudhuffushi and another nine hectares from the island's wetlands were reclaimed for the airport, which has a runway measuring 1,200 metres in length and 60 metres in width. Glenn Reynolds of *Instapundit* has coined an immortal rejoinder for "warmists" who talk a good line about the global warming threat, but live their lives as if it doesn't exist (Al Gore's multiple energy-consuming mansions, Robert F. Kennedy's private jet use, for example) but applies only to nations like the Maldives."

Declaring Climate Emergencies

Oxford Dictionaries has declared "climate emergency" the word of the year for 2019, following a hundred-fold increase in usage that it says demonstrated a "greater immediacy" in the way we talk about the climate. The *guardian.com* website reports that *climate emergency* is defined as "a situation in which urgent action is required to reduce or halt climate change and avoid potentially irreversible environmental damage resulting from it", *Oxford* said the words soared from "relative obscurity" to "one of the most prominent – and prominently debated – terms of 2019." According to the dictionary's data, usage of "climate emergency" soared 10,796%.

Oxford said the choice was reflective, not just of the rise in climate awareness, but the focus specifically on the language we use to discuss it. The rise of "climate emergency" reflected a conscious push towards language of immediacy and urgency. The dictionary said that in 2019, "climate" became the most common word associated with "emergency", three times more than "health emergency" in second. In May 2019 *The Guardian* updated its style guide to clarify that "climate emergency" or "global heating" would be favoured over "climate change" or "global warming" (although the original terms are not banned) – to better reflect the scientific consensus that this was "a catastrophe for humanity".

What follows is a "time history" of the declarations of "climate emergencies" from the first declaration in the City of Darebin, Melbourne, Australia on 5 December 2016 to today. Whether the declarations of such "emergencies" is justified, time will tell.

A climate emergency declaration or *declaring a climate emergency* is an action taken by governments and scientists to acknowledge humanity is in a climate emergency. *Wikipedia* states the first such declaration was made in December 2016. Since then over 1,400 local governments in 28 countries have made climate emergency declarations (as of 23 February 2020).

Once a government makes a declaration the next step, at least in theory, is for the declaring government to set priorities to mitigate climate change, prior to ultimately entering a state of emergency or equivalent. In declaring a climate emergency, a government admits that global warming exists and that the measures taken up to this point are not enough to limit the changes brought by it. The decision stresses the need for the government and administration to devise measures that try and stop human-caused global warming.

Adaptation to climate

The declarations can be made on different levels, for example at a national or local government level, and they can differ in depth and detail in their guidelines. The term *climate emergency* does not only describe formal decisions, but also includes actions to avert climate breakdown. This is supposed to justify and focus them. The specific term "emergency" is used to assign priority to the topic, and to generate a mind-set of urgency. The term "climate emergency" has been promoted by climate activists and pro-climate action politicians to add a sense of urgency for responding to a long-term problem.

Climate Emergency Declaration petition
Encouraged by the campaigners behind a Climate Emergency Declaration petition, which had been launched in Australia in May 2016, the first governmental declaration of a climate emergency in the world was put forward by Trent McCarthy, an Australian Greens Councillor at the City of Darebin in Melbourne, Australia. The city declared a climate emergency on 5 December 2016. In August 2017, Darebin decided upon a catalogue of actions in a "Darebin Climate Emergency Plan". Darebin's declaration was followed by Hoboken in New Jersey and Berkeley, California.

Following these developments, in 2018, UK Green Party politician Carla Denyer, then a member of Bristol City Council, took the lead role in bringing about Bristol City Council's declaration of a climate emergency. This was the first such declaration in Europe, and has been widely credited as a breakthrough moment for cities and national parliaments beginning to declare climate emergency. Denyer's motion was described in the UK newspaper *The Independent* as 'the historic first motion' which by July 2019 had been 'copied by more than 400 local authorities and parliaments'. On 28th April 2019, the Scottish Parliament declared a climate emergency, making Scotland the first country to do so. This was quickly followed by the National Assembly for Wales on the 29th April and then the Parliament of the United Kingdom for the UK as whole on 1st May 2019.

Pope Francis declared a climate emergency in June 2019. The Pope also called for a "radical energy transition" away from fossil fuels towards renewable energy sources, and urged leaders to "hear the increasingly desperate cries of the earth and its poor." He also argued against "the continued search for new fossil fuel reserves" and stated that "fossil fuels should remain underground."

On 10 July 2019, more than 7,000 higher and further education institutions from six continents announced that they were declaring a Climate Emergency, and agreed to undertake a three-point plan to address the crisis through their work with students. In June 2019, Councillor Trent McCarthy of the City of Darebin brought together councillors and parliamentarians in Australia and around the world for two online link-ups to connect the work of climate emergency-declared councils and governments. Following these link-ups and a successful motion at the National General Assembly of Local Government, McCarthy announced the formation of Climate Emergency Australia, a new network of Australian governments and councils advocating for a climate emergency response. Representative Earl Blumenauer of Oregon believes the US government should declare a climate emergency. Blumenauer's proposed legislation is supported by 2020 US Presidential candidate Bernie Sanders, as well as Congresswoman Alexandria Ocasio-Cortez.

In 2019, according to an eight-country poll, a majority of the public recognise the climate crisis as an "emergency" and say politicians are failing to tackle the problem, backing the interests of big oil over the wellbeing of ordinary people. The survey found that climate breakdown is viewed as the most important issue facing the world in seven out of the eight countries surveyed.

The Australian Greens Party is calling on the federal Parliament to declare a climate emergency. Greens MP for Melbourne, Adam Bandt, welcomed the UK Parliament's declaration of a climate emergency and argued that Australia should follow their lead. In October 2019, an official e-petition to the Australian Parliament calling for the declaration of a climate emergency, received more than 400,000 signatories. (This is the single most popular online Parliamentary petition in Australia.) In October 2019, the Australian Labor Party supported the Greens Party's policy to declare a climate emergency, however the proposition failed with the rejection of the Morrison Government.

First National Climate Emergency Summit
On 5 November 2019, the journal *BioScience* published an article endorsed by further 11,000 scientists from 153 nations, that states Climate Emergency ("We declare clearly and unequivocally that planet Earth is facing a climate emergency") and that the world's people face "untold suffering due to the climate crisis" unless there are major transformations to global society. On 14-15 February 2020 the first National Climate Emergency Summit was held at the city hall in Melbourne, Australia.

It was a sold out event with 2,000 attendees and 100 speakers. On 28 November 2019, the European Parliament declared a climate emergency.

United Nations Environment Programme (UNEP) has outlined the facts you need to know about why we need the Climate Emergency. Of course, time will tell whether the "Declarations" were necessary and what affect they had in policy decisions.

- Climate change is real and human activities are the main cause. (IPCC)
- The concentration of greenhouse gases in the earth's atmosphere is directly linked to the average global temperature on Earth. (IPCC)
- The concentration has been rising steadily, and mean global temperatures along with it, since the time of the Industrial Revolution. (IPCC)
- The most abundant greenhouse gas, accounting for about two-thirds of greenhouse gases, CO_2, is largely the product of burning fossil fuels. (IPCC)

Impacts of a 1.1°C increase are here today in the increased frequency and magnitude of extreme weather events from heatwaves, droughts, flooding, winter storms, hurricanes and wildfires. (IPCC)

What do we need to do to limit global warming and act on climate change?

- The UNEP Emissions Gap Report 2019 shows that we are on the brink of missing the 1.5°C target and condemning humanity to a future of serious climate change impacts. Countries cannot wait until they submit their updated Paris pledges in one year's time to act.
- To prevent warming beyond 1.5°C, we need to reduce emissions by 7.6% every year from this year to 2030. (EGR, 2019)
- 10 years ago, if countries had acted on this science, governments would have needed to reduce emissions by 3.3% each year. Every year we fail to act, the level of difficulty and cost to reduce emissions goes up. (EGR, 2019)
- Nations agreed to a legally binding commitment in Paris to limit global temperature rise to no more than 2°C above pre-industrial levels, but also offered national pledges to cut or curb their greenhouse gas emissions by 2030. This is known as the Paris Agreement. The initial pledges of 2015 are insufficient to meet the target, and governments are expected to review and increase these pledges as a key objective this year, 2020.
- This review of the Paris Agreement commitments will take place at the 2020 climate change conference known at COP26 in Glasgow,

UK in November 2020. This conference was expected to be the most important inter-governmental meeting on the climate crisis since the Paris agreement was passed in 2015 but has been postponed because of COVID-19.
- The success or otherwise of this conference will have stark consequences for the world. If countries cannot agree on sufficient pledges, in another 5 years, the emissions reduction necessary will leap to a near-impossible -15.5% every year. The unlikelihood of achieving this far steeper rate of decarbonization, means the world faces a global temperature increase that will rise above 1.5°C. Every fraction of additional warming above 1.5°C will bring worsening impacts, threatening lives, food sources, livelihoods and economies worldwide.
- Countries are not on track to fulfill the promises they have made.
- Increased commitments can take many forms but overall they must serve to shift countries and economies onto a path of decarbonization, setting targets for net zero carbon, and timelines of how to reach that target, most typically through a rapid acceleration of energy sourced from renewables and a rapid deceleration of fossil fuel dependency.

While there will still be serious climate impacts at 1.5°C, this is the level scientists say is associated with less devastating impacts than higher levels of global warming.

Climate emergency warning exposed as fraud
In contrast with the above there are of course other viewpoints as to whether the "declaration of climate emergencies" is necessary. In a review in the March 3, 2020 edition of the *Manila Times* Yen Makabenta featured two articles: 1. "Climate emergency warning exposed as fraud" by Bob Adelmann, *New American*, Nov. 12 2019; and 2. "The biggest lie ever told – man-made global warming" by Tom Harris, *America Out Loud*, March 29, 2019.

Bob Adelmann exposed the lie about 11,000 scientists approving and supporting the warning of a climate emergency. He wrote:

"When the American Institute of Biological Sciences (AISB) released its warning of a climate emergency last week, the mainstream media reported it without checking its veracity. After all, the AISB is a prestigious non-profit with goals that sound honourable. This is being sorely tested now that it was learned that many of the 11,000 'scientists' who approved of and supported the climate warning weren't scientists

Adaptation to climate 267

after all. But none of this deterred august members of the Fourth Estate from reporting favourably on the warning as its recommendations lined up with the standard global-warning demands being pushed by climate alarmists.

The *Washington Post* breathlessly headlined: "More than 11,000 scientists from around the world declare a 'climate emergency' – and then further tarnished its image by declaring that it marks the first time a large group of scientists has formally come out in favour of labelling climate change an 'emergency.' " On the other hand, Ezra Levant, a Canadian media personality and political activist, called the whole thing a joke: "I'm sorry, but that's a joke… I wonder, are there even 11,000 climate scientists in the world?"

Tom Harris' article in *America Out Loud* is even more devastating. It destroys the claim that CO_2 causes climate change.

Mr. Harris wrote:"Today's climate change is well within the range of natural climate variability through Earth's 4.5-billion-year history. In fact, it is within the range of the climate change of the last 10,000 years, a period known as the Holocene, 95% of which was warmer than today. Indeed, it is now cooler than the Holocene Optimum, which spanned a period from about 9,000 to 5,000 years ago. The Optimum was named at a time when warming was understood to be a good thing in contrast to the miserable cold times that periodically cripple mankind. A small group fooled the world into believing that warming is bad and that today's weather is warmer than ever before, all caused by the human addition of a relatively trivial amount of CO_2 to the atmosphere. It is the biggest lie ever told, and that reason alone caused many to believe."

The ultimate lie is that members of the IPCC community are telling us the truth about the dangers of man-made climate change. In 1998, Kyoto Protocol supporter professor Tom Wigley estimated that, even if we met all the Kyoto reduction targets, it would only lower temperatures by 0.05°C by 2050. After the Paris Agreement, Danish statistician Bjorn Lomborg calculated that, if fully implemented, Paris would reduce the global temperature by 0.048°C by 2100.

Climate refugees

Climate refugees according to *Wikipedia* are people who are forced to leave their home region due to sudden or long-term changes to their local environment. These are changes which compromise their secure livelihood. Such changes may include increased droughts, desertification, sea level rise, and disruption of seasonal weather patterns (i.e. monsoons). Climate refugees may choose to flee to or migrate to another country, or they may migrate internally within their own country.

Despite problems in formulating a uniform and clear-cut definition of environmental migration, such a concept has increased as an issue of concern in the 2000s as policy-makers, environmental and social scientists attempt to conceptualize the potential societal effects of climate change and general environmental degradation. "Unless it is assumed" in order to consider a person a climate refugee, nature or the environment could be considered the persecutor.

Climate refugees do not really fit into any of the legal definitions of a refugee. Not all climate refugees migrate from their home country, on occasion they are just displaced within their country of origin. Moreover, the refugees aren't leaving their homes because of fear they will be persecuted, or because of "generalized violence or events seriously disturbing public order." Even though the definition of who is a refugee was expanded since its first international and legally binding definition in 1951; people who are forced to flee due to environmental change are still not offered the same legal protection as refugees.

The term "environmental refugee" was first proposed by Lester Brown in 1976. *The International Organization for Migration* (IOM) proposes the following definition for environmental migrants:

"Environmental migrants are persons or groups of persons who, for compelling reasons of sudden or progressive changes in the environment that adversely affect their lives or living conditions, are obliged to leave their habitual homes, or choose to do so, either temporarily or permanently, and who move either within their country or abroad."

Climate refugees or climate migrants are a subset of environmental migrants who were forced to flee "due to sudden or gradual alterations in the natural environment related to at least one of three impacts of climate change: sea level rise, extreme weather events, and drought and water scarcity."

IOM proposes three major types of environmental migrants:
- *Environmental emergency migrants:* people who flee temporarily due to an environmental disaster or sudden environmental event. (Examples: someone forced to leave due to a hurricane, tsunami, earthquake, etc.)
- *Environmental forced migrants:* people who have to leave due to deteriorating environmental conditions. (Example: someone forced to leave due to a slow deterioration of their environment such as deforestation, coastal deterioration, etc.)
- *Environmental motivated migrants* also known as *environmentally induced economic migrants:* people who choose to leave to avoid possible future problems. (Example: someone who leaves due to declining crop productivity caused by desertification). "Those displaced temporarily due to local disruption such as an avalanche or earthquake; those who migrate because environmental degradation has undermined their livelihood or poses unacceptable risks to health; and those who resettle because land degradation has resulted in desertification or because of other permanent and untenable changes in their habitat".

Other categorisations include:
- *Pressured environmental migrants – slow onset.* This type of migrant is displaced from their environment when an event is predicted prior to when it would be imperative for the inhabitants to leave. Such events could be desertification or prolonged drought, where the people of the region are no longer able to maintain farming or hunting to provide a hospitable living environment.
- *Imperative environmental migrants – gradual onset.* These are migrants that have been or will be "permanently displaced" from their homes due to environmental factors beyond their control.
- *Temporary environmental migrants – short term, sudden onset.* This includes migrants suffering from a single event (e.g. Hurricane *Katrina*). This does not mean that their status of being temporary is any less severe than other groups, it simply means that they are able to go back to the place they fled from (though it may be undesirable to do so) granted that they are able to rebuild what was broken, and go on to maintain a similar quality of life to the one prior to the natural disaster. This type of migrant is displaced from their home state when their environment rapidly changes. They are displaced when disastrous events occur, such as tsunamis, hurricanes, tornadoes, and other natural disasters occur.

In 2017, *Wikipedia* noted that there was no standard definition of a climate refugee in international law. However, an article in the UN Dispatch noted that "people who have been uprooted because of climate change exist all over the world – even if the international community has been slow to recognize them as such."

Environmental migrants
Experts have suggested that due to the difficulty of rewriting the UN's 1951 convention on refugees, it may be preferable to treat these refugees as "environmental migrants." In January 2020, the UN Human Rights Committee ruled that "refugees fleeing the effects of the climate crisis cannot be forced to return home by their adoptive countries."

There have been a number of attempts over the decades to enumerate environmental migrants and refugees. Jodi Jacobson (1988) is cited as the first researcher to enumerate the issue, stating that there were already up to 10 million 'Environmental Refugees'. Drawing on 'worst-case scenarios' about sea level rise, she argued that all forms of 'Environmental Refugees' would be six times as numerous as political refugees. By 1989, Mustafa Tolba, Executive Director of UNEP, was claiming that 'as many as 50 million people could become environmental refugees' if the world did not act to support sustainable development. In 1990, the Intergovernmental Panel on Climate Change (IPCC 1990: 20) declared that the greatest single consequence of climate change could be migration, 'with millions of people displaced by shoreline erosion, coastal flooding and severe drought'.

In the mid-1990s, British environmentalist, Norman Myers, became the most prominent proponent of this 'maximalist' school (Suhrke 1993), noting that "environmental refugees will soon become the largest group of involuntary refugees". Additionally, he stated that there were 25 million environmental refugees in the mid-1990s, further claiming that this figure could double by 2010, with an upper limit of 200 million by 2050 (Myers 1997). Myers argued that the causes of environmental displacement would include desertification, lack of water, salination of irrigated lands and the depletion of biodiversity. He also hypothesised that displacement would amount to 30m in China, 30m in India, 15m in Bangladesh, 14m in Egypt, 10m in other delta areas and coastal zones, 1m in island states, and with otherwise agriculturally displaced people totalling 50m by 2050. More recently, Myers has suggested that the figure by 2050 might be as high as 250 million.

Adaptation to climate

These claims have gained significant currency, with the most common projection being that the world will have 150–200 million climate change refugees by 2050. Variations of this claim have been made in influential reports on climate change by the IPCC (Brown 2008: 11) and the *Stern Review on the Economics of Climate Change* (Stern et al. 2006: 3), as well as by NGOs such as *Friends of the Earth, Greenpeace* Germany (Jakobeit and Methmann 2007) and Christian Aid; and inter-governmental organisations such as the Council of Europe, UNESCO, IOM and UNHCR.

Norman Myers is the most cited researcher in this field, who found that 25 million environmental migrants existed in 1995 in his work (Myers & Kent 1995), which drew upon over 1000 sources. However, Vikram Kolmannskog has stated that Myers' work can be 'criticized for being inconsistent, impossible to check and failing to take proper account of 'opportunities to adapt' (2008: 9). Furthermore, Myers himself has acknowledged that his figures are based upon 'heroic extrapolation' (Brown 2008: 12). More generally, Brown has argued that there is 'surprisingly little scientific evidence' that indicates that the world is 'filling-up with environmental refugees' (1998: 23). Indeed, Francois Gemenne has stated that: 'When it comes to predictions, figures are usually based on the number of people living in regions at risk, and not on the number of people actually expected to migrate. Estimates do not account for adaptation strategies (or) different levels of vulnerability' (Gemenne 2009: 159).

In the first half of the year 2019, *Wikipedia* said that 7 million people were internally (e.g. in their country) displaced by events of extreme weather, according to the *Internal Displacement Monitoring Centre*. This was a record at that time and the number is twice the number displaced by violence and conflicts.

In Asia and the Pacific, the *Internal Displacement Monitoring Centre* noted that more than 42 million people were displaced in Asia and the Pacific during 2010 and 2011. This figure includes those displaced by storms, floods, and heat and cold waves. Still others were displaced by drought and sea level rise. Most of those compelled to leave their homes eventually returned when conditions improved, but an undetermined number became migrants, usually within their country, but also across national borders.

Climate-induced migration
Climate-induced migration is a highly complex issue which needs to be understood as part of global migration dynamics. Migration typically has multiple causes, and environmental factors are intertwined with other social and economic factors, which themselves can be influenced by environmental changes. Environmental migration should not be treated solely as a discrete category, set apart from other migration flows. A 2012 *Asian Development Bank* study argues that climate-induced migration should be addressed as part of a country's development agenda, given the major implications of migration on economic and social development. The report recommends interventions both to address the situation of those who have migrated, as well as those who remain in areas subject to environmental risk. It says: "To reduce migration compelled by worsening environmental conditions, and to strengthen the resilience of at-risk communities, governments should adopt policies and commit financing to social protection, livelihoods development, basic urban infrastructure development, and disaster risk management."

Additionally, it is maintained that it is the poor populate areas that are most at risk for environmental destruction and climate change, including coastlines, flood-lines, and steep slopes. As a result, climate change threatens areas already suffering from extreme poverty. "The issue of equity is crucial. Climate affects us all, but does not affect us all equally," UN Secretary-General Ban Ki-moon told delegates at a climate conference in Indonesia. Africa is also one of the world regions where environmental displacement is critical largely due to droughts and other climate-related eventualities.

Due to rising sea levels, as many as 70,000 people will be displaced in the Sundarbans as early as 2020 according to an estimate by the *School of Oceanographic Studies* at *Jadavpur University*. One expert calls for restoring the Sundarbans' original mangrove habitats to both mitigate the impacts of rising seas and storm surges, and to serve as a carbon sink for greenhouse gas emissions.

Climate change refugee
In what turned out to be a test case, a Kiribati man, Loane Teitiota, in 2013, sought to claim that he was a "climate change refugee" under the Convention relating to the Status of Refugees (1951). This was determined by the *High Court of New Zealand* to be untenable. In commenting on the case, *Wikipedia* said that *The Refugee Convention* did not apply

Adaptation to climate

as there is no persecution or serious harm related to any of the five stipulated convention grounds. The Court rejected the argument that the international community itself (or countries which can be said to have been historically high emitters of CO_2 or other greenhouse gases) were the "persecutor" for the purposes of the *Refugee Convention*. This analysis of the need for the person to identify persecution of the type described in the *Refugee Convention* does not exclude the possibility that people in countries experiencing severe impacts of climate change can come to the *Refugee Convention*. However, it is not the climate change event itself, rather the social and political response to climate change, which is likely to create the pathway for a successful claim.

The New Zealand Immigration and Protection Tribunal and the High Court, said that there is a complex inter-relationship between natural disasters, environmental degradation and human vulnerability. Sometimes a tenable pathway to international protection under the *Refugee Convention* can result. Environmental issues sometimes lead to armed conflict. There may be ensuing violence towards or direct repression of an entire section of a population. Humanitarian relief can become politicised, particularly in situations where some group inside a disadvantaged country is the target of direct discrimination.

The New Zealand Court of Appeal also rejected the claim in a 2014 decision. On further appeal, the *New Zealand Supreme Court* confirmed the earlier adverse rulings against the application for refugee status, with the *Supreme Court* also rejecting the proposition "that environmental degradation resulting from climate change or other natural disasters could never create a pathway into the *Refugee Convention* or protected person jurisdiction". Teitiota appealed to the UN. In January 2020, the *UN Human Rights Committee* "ruled against Teitiota on the basis that his life was not at imminent risk," but also said that it was a human rights violation to force refugees to return "to countries where climate change poses an immediate threat."

12

Energy

> We simply must balance our demand for energy with our shrinking resources. By acting now we can control our future instead of letting the future control.
>
> President Jimmy Carter

Fossil fuels

A fossil fuel is a fuel formed by natural processes, such as anaerobic decomposition of buried dead organisms, containing energy originating in ancient photosynthesis. Such organisms and their resulting fossil fuels typically have an age of millions of years, and sometimes more than 650 million years. Fossil fuels contain high percentages of carbon and include petroleum, coal, and natural gas. Commonly used derivatives of fossil fuels include kerosene and propane. Fossil fuels range from volatile materials with low carbon-to-hydrogen ratios (like methane), to liquids (like petroleum), to non-volatile materials composed of almost pure carbon, like anthracite coal. Methane can be found in hydrocarbon fields either alone, associated with oil, or in the form of methane clathrates.

As of 2018, *Wikipedia* says that the world's primary energy sources consisted of petroleum (34%), coal (27%), natural gas (24%), amounting to an 85% share for fossil fuels in primary energy-consumption in the world. In contrast, non-fossil sources included nuclear (4.4%), hydroelectric (6.8%), and other renewables (4.0%, including geothermal, solar, tidal, wind, wood, waste). Although natural processes continually form fossil fuels, such fuels are generally classified as non-renewable resources because they take millions of years to form and the known viable reserves are being depleted much faster than new ones are being made.

Most air pollution deaths are due to fossil fuels, and fossil fuel phase-out, as estimated by *Wikipedia*, would save 3.6 million lives each year. Because of the importance of greenhouse gases on the earth's climate, it is natural that other non greenhouse gas sources of energy are sought after. These include nuclear, nuclear fusion, hydroelectric, geothermal, solar, wind, biomass, wood, tidal, and waste.

The use of fossil fuels raises serious environmental concerns. The burning of fossil fuels produces around 21.3 billion tonnes (21.3 gigatonnes) of CO_2 per year. It is estimated that natural processes can only absorb about half of that amount, so there is a net increase of 10.65 billion tonnes of atmospheric CO_2 per year. CO_2 is a greenhouse gas that increases radiative forcing and contributes to global warming along with ocean acidification. A global movement towards the generation of low-carbon renewable energy is underway to help reduce global greenhouse gas emissions. Nevertheless, attempts to reduce fossil fuels and replace them with the "cleaner" forms of energy production, do present significant difficulties. These problems, particularly in regards to wind, biomass, electric cars, and wind energy are well exposed in the 2019 film *Planet of the Humans* by Michael Moore.

The theory that fossil fuels formed from the fossilized remains of dead plants by exposure to heat and pressure in the Earth's crust over millions of years was first introduced, as noted in *Wikipedia*, (by Andreas Libavius "in his 1597 Alchemia (Alchymia)" and later by Mikhail Lomonosov "as early as 1757 and certainly by 1763". The first use of the term "fossil fuel" occurs in the work of the German chemist Caspar Neumann, in English translation in 1759. The Oxford English Dictionary notes that in the phrase "fossil fuel" the adjective "fossil" means "obtained by digging; found buried in the earth", which dates to at least 1652, before the English noun "fossil" came to refer primarily to long-dead organisms in the early 18th century.

Aquatic phytoplankton and zooplankton that died and sedimented in large quantities under anoxic conditions millions of years ago began forming petroleum and natural gas as a result of anaerobic decomposition. Over geological time this organic matter, mixed with mud, became buried under further heavy layers of inorganic sediment. The resulting high levels of heat and pressure caused the organic matter to chemically alter, first into a waxy material known as kerogen which is found in oil shales, and then with more heat into liquid and gaseous hydrocarbons in a process known as catagenesis. Despite these heat driven transformations (which may increase the energy density compared to typical organic matter), the embedded energy is still photosynthetic in origin.

Terrestrial plants, on the other hand, tended to form coal and methane. Many of the coal fields date to the Carboniferous period of Earth's history. Terrestrial plants also form type III kerogen, a source of natural gas. There is a wide range of organic, or hydrocarbon, compounds in any given fuel mixture. The specific mixture of hydrocarbons gives a fuel its characteristic properties, such as boiling point, melting point, density, viscosity, etc. Some fuels like natural gas, for instance, contain only very low boiling, gaseous components. Others such as gasoline or diesel contain much higher boiling components.

Commercial exploitation of petroleum began in the 19th century, largely to replace oils from animal sources (notably whale oil) for use in oil lamps. Natural gas, once flared-off as an unneeded by-product of petroleum production, is now considered a very valuable resource. Natural gas deposits are also the main source of the element helium.

Heavy crude oil, which is much more viscous than conventional crude oil, and oil sands, where bitumen is found mixed with sand and clay, began to become more important as sources of fossil fuel as of the early 2000s. Oil shale and similar materials are sedimentary rocks containing kerogen, a complex mixture of high-molecular weight organic compounds, which yield synthetic crude oil when heated (pyrolyzed). With additional processing, they can be employed in lieu of other already established fossil fuel deposits. More recently, there has been disinvestment from exploitation of such resources due to their high carbon cost, relative to more easily processed reserves.

Prior to the latter half of the 18th century, windmills and watermills provided the energy needed for industry such as milling flour, sawing wood or pumping water, and burning wood or peat provided domestic heat. The wide scale use of fossil fuels, coal at first and petroleum later, to fire steam engines enabled the Industrial Revolution. At the same time, gas lights using natural gas or coal gas were coming into wide use. The invention of the internal combustion engine and its use in automobiles and trucks greatly increased the demand for gasoline and diesel oil, both made from fossil fuels. Other forms of transportation, railways and aircraft, also required fossil fuels. The other major use for fossil fuels is in generating electricity and as feedstock for the petrochemical industry. Tar, a leftover of petroleum extraction, is used in construction of roads.

Supply and demand

The principle of supply and demand holds that as hydrocarbon supplies diminish, prices will rise. Therefore, higher prices will lead to increased alternative, renewable energy supplies as previously uneconomic sources become sufficiently economical to exploit. Artificial gasolines and other renewable energy sources currently require more expensive production and processing technologies than conventional petroleum reserves, but may become economically viable in the near future. Different alternative sources of energy include nuclear, hydroelectric, solar, wind, and geothermal.

One of the more promising energy alternatives is the use of inedible feed stocks and biomass for CO_2 capture as well as biofuel. While these processes are not without problems, they are currently in practice around the world. Biodiesels are being produced by several companies and the source of great research at several universities. Some potential processes for conversion of renewable lipids into usable fuels is through hydro treating and decarboxylation. Combustion of fossil fuels generates sulphuric, carbonic, and nitric acids, which fall to Earth as acid rain, impacting both natural areas and the built environment. Monuments and sculptures made from marble and limestone are particularly vulnerable, as the acids dissolve calcium carbonate.

Fossil fuels also contain radioactive materials, mainly uranium and thorium, which are released into the atmosphere. In 2000, about 12,000 tonnes of thorium and 5,000 tonnes of uranium were released worldwide from burning coal. It is estimated that during 1982, US coal burning released 155 times as much radioactivity into the atmosphere as the Three Mile Island accident. Burning coal also generates large amounts of bottom ash and fly ash. These materials are used in a wide variety of applications, utilizing, for example, about 40% of the US production.

Harvesting, processing, and distributing fossil fuels can also create environmental concerns. Coal mining methods, particularly mountaintop removal and strip mining, have negative environmental impacts, and offshore oil drilling poses a hazard to aquatic organisms. Fossil fuel wells can contribute to methane production via fugitive gas emissions. Oil refineries also have negative environmental impacts, including air and water pollution. Transportation of coal requires the use of diesel-powered locomotives, while crude oil is typically transported by tanker ships, each of which requires the combustion of additional fossil fuels.

Environmental regulation uses a variety of approaches to limit these emissions, such as command-and-control (which mandates the amount of pollution or the technology used), economic incentives, or voluntary programmes. These environmental pollutions impact on human beings because particles of the fossil fuel in the air cause negative health effects when inhaled. These health effects include premature death, acute respiratory illness, aggravated asthma, chronic bronchitis and decreased lung function. The poor, undernourished, very young and very old, and people with pre-existing respiratory disease and other ill health, are more at risk.

Geothermal energy

To produce power from geothermal energy, wells are dug about 1 to 2km deep into underground reservoirs to access the steam and hot water there, which can then be used to drive turbines connected to electricity generators. There are three types of geothermal power plants: dry steam, flash and binary. Dry steam is the oldest form of geothermal technology and takes steam out of the ground and uses it to directly drive a turbine. Flash plants use high-pressure hot water into cool, low-pressure water, whilst binary plants pass hot water through a secondary liquid with a lower boiling point, which turns to vapour to drive the turbine.

Geothermal electricity generation is currently used in 26 countries while geothermal heating is in use in 70 countries. *Wikipedia* reviews this important source of energy. As of 2020, worldwide geothermal power capacity amounts to 12.8 gigawatts (GW), of which 28% or 3.55 GW are installed in the United States. International markets grew at an average annual rate of 5% over the three years to 2015, and global geothermal power capacity is expected to reach 14.5–17.6 GW by 2020. Based on current geologic knowledge and technology, the Geothermal Energy Association (GEA) publicly estimates that only 6.9% of total global potential has been tapped so far, while the IPCC reported geothermal power potential to be in the range of 35 GW to 2 TW. Countries generating more than 15% of their electricity from geothermal sources include El Salvador, Kenya, the Philippines, Iceland, New Zealand, and Costa Rica.

Geothermal power is considered to be a sustainable, renewable source of energy because the heat extraction is small compared with the Earth's heat content. The greenhouse gas emissions of geothermal electric stations are on average 45 g CO_2/Kw hr of electricity, or less than 5% of that of conventional coal-fired plants. As a source of renewable energy for both power and heating, geothermal has the potential to meet 3-5% of global demand by 2050. With economic incentives, it is estimated that by 2100 it will be possible to meet 10% of global demand.

In the 20th century, demand for electricity led to the consideration of geothermal power as a generating source. Prince Piero Ginori Conti tested the first geothermal power generator on 4 July 1904 in Larderello, Italy. It successfully lit four light bulbs. Later, in 1911, the world's first commercial geothermal power station was built there. Experimental generators were built in Beppu, Japan and The Geysers, California, in the 1920s, but Italy was the world's only industrial producer of geothermal electricity until 1958.

In 1958, New Zealand became the second major industrial producer of geothermal electricity in the world when its Wairakei station was commissioned. This was the first station to use flash steam technology. Over the past 60 years, net fluid production has been in excess of 2.5 km^3. In 1960, Pacific Gas and Electric began operation of the first successful geothermal electric power station in the United States at The Geysers in California. The original turbine lasted for more than 30 years and produced 11 MW net power.

The binary cycle power station was first demonstrated in 1967 in the Soviet Union and later introduced to the United States in 1981, following the 1970s energy crisis and significant changes in regulatory policies. This technology allows the use of much lower temperature resources than were previously recoverable. In 2006, a binary cycle station in Chena Hot Springs, Alaska, came on-line, producing electricity from a record low fluid temperature of 57°C.

Geothermal electric stations have until recently been built exclusively where high-temperature geothermal resources are available near the surface. The development of binary cycle power plants and improvements in drilling and extraction technology may enable enhanced geothermal systems over a much greater geographical range. Demonstration projects are operational in Landau-Pfalz, Germany, and Soultz-sous-Forêts, France, while an earlier effort in Basel, Switzerland was shut down after it triggered earthquakes. Other demonstration projects are under construction in Australia, the United Kingdom, and the United States of America.

Thermal efficiency

The thermal efficiency of geothermal electric stations is low, around 7–10%, because geothermal fluids are at a low temperature compared with steam from boilers. By the laws of thermodynamics this low temperature limits the efficiency of heat engines in extracting useful energy during the generation of electricity. Exhaust heat is wasted, unless it can be used directly and locally, for example in greenhouses, timber mills, and district heating. The efficiency of the system does not affect operational costs as it would for a coal or other fossil fuel plant, but it does factor into the viability of the station. In order to produce more energy than the pumps consume, electricity generation requires high-temperature geothermal fields and specialized heat cycles. Because geothermal power does not rely on variable sources of energy, unlike, for example, wind or solar, its capacity factor can be quite large – up to 96% has been demonstrated. However, the global average capacity factor was 74.5% in 2008, according to the IPCC.

The *Power Technology* organisation says that geothermal energy has been a consistent and expanding source of energy in recent years. According to the International Renewable Energy Agency (IRENA), geothermal energy has grown steadily from around 10GW worldwide in 2010 to 13.3GW in 2018.

Geothermal energy is used in over 20 countries. The United States is the largest producer of geothermal energy in the world, and hosts the largest geothermal field. Known as "The Geysers" in California, the field is spread over 117 square kilometres and formed of 22 power plants, with an installed capacity of over 1.5GW. Geothermal energy is also prevalent in Iceland, where it has been used since 1907. Describing itself as a 'pioneer' of geothermal power, the country produces 25% of its energy from five geothermal power plants. This is due to the 600 hot springs and 200 volcanoes in the country.

The British Geological Survey describes geothermal thermal energy as a "carbon-free, renewable, sustainable form of energy that provides a continuous, uninterrupted supply of heat that can be used to heat homes and office buildings and to generate electricity." Geothermal energy only produces one-sixth of the CO_2 produced by a natural gas plant and it is not affected by weather conditions like wind or solar.

However, there are some drawbacks to this energy source. Despite low CO_2 production geothermal has been associated with other emissions like sulphur dioxide and hydrogen sulphide. Similar to fracking, geothermal power plants have been the cause of mini tremors in the area they operate in and also have a high initial cost to build.

New Zealand has an abundant supply of geothermal energy because the country is located on the boundary between two tectonic plates. This means that the Earth's crust is thinner and the hot mantle below is much closer to the surface. Centuries before New Zealand's European settlers began turning geothermal energy into electricity, the Māori population were cooking, washing and warming themselves with heat directly from the earth's core. Today, according to New Zealand's *Energy Efficiency and Conservation Authority* (EECA) geothermal energy provides 17% of New Zealand's electricity and about 8 PJ directly as heat.

For producing electricity, geothermal fluid (a mixture of high pressure water and steam) from wells several kilometres deep is piped to a central generation plant where it is turned into steam or commonly used to vaporise another fluid in organic Rankine cycle (ORC) systems. The steam or vapour then drives the turbine generators producing electricity. Used geothermal fluid is re-injected through wells back into the geothermal field to maintain its pressure and structure although some fluid is still discharged into rivers by older plants. New Zealand uses hot water and steam directly for industrial processes including pulp and paper-making, wood processing, dairy manufacturing and heating greenhouses.

Geothermal energy supply isn't dependent on weather conditions, making it consistent and reliable. It's a renewable resource, but it needs careful management and monitoring to control reservoir water and pressure levels and prevent land subsidence and depletion. Geothermal fluids also contain gases and minerals, though amounts vary from field to field, and the amount released depends on the design of power station. While electricity generated from geothermal energy produces some greenhouse gas emissions, the overall emissions intensity of geothermal electricity is about one-quarter of that of the cleanest natural gas-fuelled power station.

Total geothermal electricity capacity in New Zealand in 2020 stands at over 900 MW. It has been estimated that there is sufficient geothermal resource for about another 1,000 MW of electricity generation. New Zealand could also use more geothermal energy directly, for example as industrial process heat, or by finding uses for waste heat from geothermal power stations.

Nuclear Energy

The International Atomic Energy Association (IAEA) states that nuclear energy is essential for sustainable economic growth and improved human welfare. Nuclear energy provides access to clean, reliable and affordable energy, mitigating the negative impacts of climate change. It is a significant part of the world energy mix and its use is expected to grow in the coming decades. The IAEA fosters the efficient and safe use of nuclear power by supporting existing and new nuclear programmes around the world, catalysing innovation and building capacity in energy planning, analysis, and nuclear information and knowledge management. The Agency helps countries meet growing energy demand for development, while improving energy security, reducing environmental and health impacts, and mitigating climate change.

The IAEA assists countries in all aspects of the nuclear fuel cycle, from uranium mining, to spent fuel and radioactive waste management, fostering technical information exchange between countries. It also supports the broad use of peaceful nuclear technology through research reactors and non-electric applications, as well as the development of fusion.

The US Energy Information Administration (EIA) website says that atoms are the tiny particles in the molecules that make up gases, liquids, and solids. Atoms themselves are made up of three particles called protons, neutrons, and electrons. An atom has a nucleus (or core) containing protons and neutrons, which is surrounded by electrons. Protons carry a positive electrical charge, and electrons carry a negative electrical charge. Neutrons do not have an electrical charge. Enormous energy is present in the bonds that hold the nucleus together. This nuclear energy can be released when those bonds are broken. The bonds can be broken through nuclear fission, and this energy can be used to produce electricity.

In nuclear fission, atoms are split apart, which releases energy. All nuclear power plants use nuclear fission, and most nuclear power plants use uranium atoms. During nuclear fission, a neutron collides with a uranium atom and splits it, releasing a large amount of energy in the form of heat and radiation. More neutrons are also released when a uranium atom splits. These neutrons continue to collide with other uranium atoms, and the process repeats itself over and over again. This process is called a nuclear chain reaction. This reaction is controlled in nuclear power plant reactors to produce a desired amount of heat.

Nuclear energy can also be released in nuclear fusion, where atoms are combined or fused together to form a larger atom. Fusion is the source of energy in the sun and stars. Developing technology to harness nuclear fusion as a source of energy for heat and electricity generation is the subject of ongoing research, but whether or not it will be a commercially viable technology is not yet clear because of the difficulty in controlling a fusion reaction. The sun is basically a giant ball of hydrogen gas undergoing fusion and giving off vast amounts of energy in the process.

Uranium is the fuel most widely used by nuclear plants for nuclear fission. Uranium is considered a non-renewable energy source, even though it is a common metal found in rocks worldwide. Nuclear power plants use a certain kind of uranium, referred to as U-235, for fuel because its atoms are easily split apart. Although uranium is about 100 times more common than silver, U-235 is relatively rare. Most U.S. uranium is mined in the western United States. Once uranium is mined, the U-235 must be extracted and processed before it can be used as a fuel.

The first commercial nuclear power stations started operation in the 1950s, and nuclear energy now provides about 10% of the world's electricity from about 440 power reactors. Of course nuclear technology extends well beyond the provision of low-carbon energy. It helps control the spread of disease, assists doctors in their diagnosis and treatment of patients, and powers our most ambitious missions to explore space. These varied uses position nuclear technologies at the heart of the world's efforts to achieve sustainable development.

The World Nuclear Association in a February 2020 report comments that nuclear energy was first developed in the 1940s, and during the Second World War research initially focused on producing bombs. In the 1950s attention turned to the peaceful use of nuclear fission, controlling it for power generation. Nuclear power has now more than 17,000 reactor years of experience, and nuclear power plants are operational in 30 countries worldwide. In fact, through regional transmission grids, many more countries depend in part on nuclear-generated power; Italy and Denmark, for example, get almost 10% of their electricity from imported nuclear power.

The *Greenpeace* View

Although nuclear power is generated by many countries, there is some, and in some countries, considerable opposition to it. The *Greenpeace* website says that nuclear energy has no place in a safe, clean, sustainable future. Nuclear energy is both expensive and dangerous, and they say that because nuclear pollution is invisible doesn't mean it's clean. Renewable energy is better for the environment, the economy, and doesn't come with the risk of a nuclear meltdown.

Greenpeace got its start protesting nuclear weapons testing back in 1971. They have been fighting against nuclear weapons and nuclear power ever since. High profile disasters in Chernobyl, Ukraine 1986 and Fukushima, Japan 2011 have raised public awareness of the dangers of nuclear power. Consequently, zeal for nuclear energy has fizzled. The catastrophic risks of nuclear energy – like the meltdowns of nuclear reactors in Japan or Ukraine – far outweigh, according to *Greenpeace* the potential benefits. Clearly this is not a view shared by all.

For example, *politico.com* notes that when *Greenpeace* co-founder Patrick Moore first began second-guessing his opposition to nuclear power, he did what any good environmentalist would do: He buried it. The activist had already helped spearhead *Greenpeace's* fight against nuclear testing and had gained international recognition after being arrested for shielding a baby seal from a hunter's club.

"I had always been afraid of nuclear waste," he said in an interview. "I thought if I got anywhere near it, it would kill me. But deep down, intellectually, I knew it could work." As global warming grew from scientific theory to public concern in the late 1980s, Moore left *Greenpeace* in 1986, aiming to prove to the environmental community that pro-nuclear environmentalism was not an oxymoron. Today, he Co-chairs the Nuclear Energy Institute's Clean and Safe Energy Coalition and is a harsh critic of what he calls an "extremist" anti-nuclear environmental movement – his former *Greenpeace* colleagues and others who are unwilling to consider nuclear energy as a solution to global warming.

"Anybody taking a realistic view of our country's energy requirements knows nuclear has to be a big part of the global warming equation," Moore said. "These environmental groups are not doing that." Moore's critiques of the *Sierra Club* and *Friends of the Earth* have not been well-received. He's been called a traitor, a prostitute, and has even been branded the "eco Judas" by former colleagues.

The nuclear debate has already caused a number of small cracks in the green framework. Both the *Environmental Defense Fund* and the *Wildlife Habitat Council* believe nuclear energy must at least be considered as a potential solution.

New nuclear plants are more expensive and take longer to build than renewable energy sources like wind or solar. If we are to avoid the most damaging impacts of climate change, we need solutions that are fast and affordable. Nuclear power is neither. *Greenpeace* also comments that "We can do better than trading off one disaster for another. The nuclear age is over and the age of renewables has begun."

Greenpeace further comments that there is still no safe, reliable solution for dealing with the radioactive waste produced by nuclear plants. Every waste dump in the U.S. leaks radiation into the environment, and nuclear plants themselves are running out of ways to store highly radioactive waste on site. The site selected to store the U.S.'s radioactive waste – Yucca Mountain in Nevada – is both volcanically and seismically active. Beyond the risks associated with nuclear power and radioactive waste, the threat of nuclear weapons looms large.

"Bet the farm" risk
Nuclear energy isn't just bad for the environment, it's bad for our economy says *Greenpeace*. They further comment that nuclear power plants are expensive to build, prompting Wall Street to call new nuclear a "bet the farm" risk. Every nuclear plant under construction in the United States is well behind schedule and at least $1 billion over budget. This is even before taking into account the astounding clean-up and health costs caused by radioactive waste pollution and nuclear meltdowns. Cleaning up Fukushima, if ever possible, will cost at least $100 billion and could be more than double that. So, *Greenpeace* asks why invest money in a dangerous, unsustainable form of energy when we can have clean, renewable energy for less?

Some of the answers to this question are given in the sections of this book on wind energy, solar energy, geothermal energy, and hydro energy. Clearly there will be many countries like Australia who suggest that some countries should be utilising nuclear energy in a much more positive way.

A viable and safe nuclear-fuel alternative to uranium is thorium, but is it an impractical and overly expensive option that could never be adopted by the nuclear industry? Advocates of using thorium as a nuclear fuel instead of uranium point out that it solves many of the problems associated with nuclear energy?

David Sims writing in *thomasnet.com* says that the waste from thorium reactions is dangerous for (only) a few hundred years, instead of the 10,000 or so years for uranium waste, and a thorium reactor could even consume much of the existing uranium waste. India is the market leader in trying to harness thorium for the energy grid. It has the largest proven thorium reserves and the world's only operating thorium reactor, Kakrapar-1, a converted conventional pressurized water reactor. China is working to develop the technology as well, while the United States, France and Britain are studying its viability. Proponents of renewable energy concede that thorium is preferable to uranium, but argue that the millions in subsidies thorium will require to become commercially viable would be better spent on solar, wind and other alternative energy sources. Sims writes that thorium could be part of the answer to the world's energy needs, but it currently lacks a track record of cost-effective energy generation. In the meantime, nations like China and India are taking the lead in developing thorium-based nuclear systems.

Solar energy

Solar power is the conversion of energy from sunlight into electricity, either directly using photovoltaics (PV), indirectly using concentrated solar power, or a combination. Concentrated solar power systems use lenses or mirrors and solar tracking systems to focus a large area of sunlight into a small beam. Photovoltaic cells convert light into an electric current using the photovoltaic effect. One drawback of solar panels which provide an intermittent source of energy, is the need for battery storage or backup on the grid, and the creation of a lot of toxic waste (both during production and at the end of their usable life). Of course, if the world is going to get colder and snowier in the future due to a solar minimum, then solar panels alone, are unlikely to provide the energy we need to keep us warm.

Photovoltaics were initially solely used as a source of electricity for small and medium-sized applications, from the calculator powered by a single solar cell, to remote homes powered by an off-grid rooftop PV system. Commercial concentrated solar power plants were first developed in the 1980s. As the cost of solar electricity has fallen, the number of grid-connected solar PV systems has grown into the millions and utility-scale photovoltaic power stations with hundreds of MW are being built. Solar PV is rapidly becoming an inexpensive, low-carbon technology to harness renewable energy from the Sun. The current (as at February 2020) largest photovoltaic power station in the world is the Pavagada Solar Park, Karnataka, India with a generation capacity of 2050 MW.

The International Energy Agency projected in 2014 that under its "high renewables" scenario, by 2050, solar photovoltaics and concentrated solar power would contribute about 16 and 11%, respectively, of the worldwide electricity consumption, and solar would be the world's largest source of electricity. Most solar installations would be in China and India. In 2017, solar power provided 1.7% of total worldwide electricity production, growing 35% from the previous year. As of 2018, the unsubsidised levelised cost of electricity for utility-scale solar power is around $US43/ MWh.

Many industrialized nations have installed significant solar power capacity into their grids to supplement or provide an alternative to conventional energy sources while an increasing number of less developed nations have turned to solar to reduce dependence on expensive imported fuels. Long distance transmission allows remote renewable energy resources to displace fossil fuel consumption. The array of a photovoltaic power system, or PV system, produces direct current (DC) power which fluctuates with the sunlight's intensity. For practical use this usually requires conversion to certain desired voltages or alternating current (AC), through the use of inverters. Multiple solar cells are connected inside modules. Modules are wired together to form arrays, then tied to an inverter, which produces power at the desired voltage, and for AC, the desired frequency/phase.

Many residential PV systems are connected to the grid wherever available, especially in developed countries with large markets. In these grid-connected PV systems, use of energy storage is optional. In certain applications such as satellites, lighthouses, or in developing countries, batteries or additional power generators are often added as back-ups. Such stand-alone power systems permit operations at night and at other times of limited sunlight.

Development and deployment
The early development of solar technologies starting in the 1860s was driven by an expectation that coal would soon become scarce. Charles Fritts installed the world's first rooftop photovoltaic solar array, on a New York City roof in 1884, using 1% efficient selenium cells. However, development of solar technologies stagnated in the early 20th century in the face of the increasing availability, economy, and utility of coal and petroleum. In 1974 it was estimated that only six private homes in all of North America were entirely heated or cooled by functional solar power systems. The 1973 oil embargo and 1979 energy crisis caused a reorganization of energy policies around the world and brought renewed attention to developing solar technologies. Deployment strategies focused on incentive programmes such as the Federal Photovoltaic Utilization Program in the US and the Sunshine Programme in Japan. Other efforts included the formation of research facilities in the United States (SERI, now NREL), Japan (NEDO), and Germany (Fraunhofer–ISE). Between 1970 and 1983 installations of photovoltaic systems grew rapidly, but falling oil prices in the early 1980s moderated the growth of photovoltaics from 1984 to 1996.

In the mid-1990s development of both, residential and commercial rooftop solar as well as utility-scale photovoltaic power stations began to accelerate again due to supply issues with oil and natural gas, global warming concerns, and the improving economic position of PV relative to other energy technologies. In the early 2000s, the adoption of feed-in tariffs–a policy mechanism, that gives renewables priority on the grid and defines a fixed price for the generated electricity–led to a high level of investment security and to a soaring number of PV deployments in Europe.

In recent years, worldwide growth of solar PV was driven by European deployment, but has since shifted to Asia, especially China and Japan, and to a growing number of countries and regions all over the world, including, but not limited to, Australia, Canada, Chile, India, Israel, Mexico, South Africa, South Korea, Thailand, and the United States.

Worldwide growth of photovoltaics has averaged 40% per year from 2000 to 2013 and total installed capacity reached 303 GW at the end of 2016 with China having the most cumulative installations (78 GW) and Honduras having the highest theoretical percentage of annual electricity usage which could be generated by solar PV (12.5%). The largest manufacturers are located in China. Concentrated solar power (CSP) also started to grow rapidly, increasing its capacity nearly tenfold from 2004 to 2013, albeit from a lower level and involving fewer countries than solar PV. As of the end of 2013, worldwide cumulative CSP-capacity reached 3,425 MW.

In 2010, the International Energy Agency predicted that global solar PV capacity could reach 3,000 GW or 11% of projected global electricity generation by 2050–enough to generate 4,500 TWh of electricity. Four years later, in 2014, the agency projected that, under its "high renewables" scenario, solar power could supply 27% of global electricity generation by 2050 (16% from PV and 11% from CSP).

Photovoltaic power stations
The Desert Sunlight Solar Farm is a 550 MW power plant in Riverside County, California, that uses thin-film CdTe solar modules made by First Solar. As of November 2014, the 550 MW Topaz Solar Farm was the largest photovoltaic power plant in the world. This was surpassed by the 579 MW Solar Star complex. As previously noted, the current largest photovoltaic power station in the world is the Pavagada Solar Park, Karnataka, India with a generation capacity of 2050 MW.

Concentrating solar power stations
Commercial concentrating solar power (CSP) plants, also called "solar thermal power stations", were first developed in the 1980s. The 377 MW

Ivanpah Solar Power Facility, located in California's Mojave Desert, is the world's largest solar thermal power plant project. Other large CSP plants include the Solnova Solar Power Station (150 MW), the Andasol solar power station (150 MW), and Extresol Solar Power Station (150 MW), all in Spain. The principal advantage of CSP is the ability to efficiently add thermal storage, allowing the dispatching of electricity over a 24-hour period. Since peak electricity demand typically occurs at about 5 pm, many CSP power plants use 3 to 5 hours of thermal storage.

Economics of solar energy
The typical cost factors for solar power include the costs of the modules, the frame to hold them, wiring, inverters, labour cost, any land that might be required, the grid connection, maintenance and the solar insolation that location will receive. Adjusting for inflation, it cost $US96 /W for a solar module in the mid-1970s. Process improvements and a very large boost in production have brought that figure down to 68 cents /W in February 2016, according to data from Bloomberg New Energy Finance. Palo Alto California signed a wholesale purchase agreement in 2016 that secured solar power for 3.7 cents/Kwh. In sunny Dubai large-scale solar generated electricity sold in 2016 for just 2.99 cents/Kwh which Bloomberg notes is "competitive with any form of fossil-based electricity – and cheaper than most." However, *Energy central.com* comments that roof-top solar panels really don't make sense, and in many parts of the world there are significant financial incentives for homeowners to install roof-top solar panels. This can include capital grants for the equipment, tax write-offs and/or Feed-In-Tariffs that guarantee that electricity produced by the solar panel will be purchased by the local utility at above-market prices.

Photovoltaic systems use no fuel, and modules typically last 25 to 40 years. Thus, capital costs make up most of the cost of solar power. Operations and maintenance costs for new utility-scale solar plants in the US are estimated to be 9% of the cost of photovoltaic electricity, and 17% of the cost of solar thermal electricity. Governments have created various financial incentives to encourage the use of solar power, such as feed-in tariff programmes. Also, Renewable Portfolio Standards (RPS) impose a government mandate that utilities generate or acquire a certain percentage of renewable power regardless of increased energy procurement costs. In most states, RPS goals can be achieved by any combination of solar, wind, biomass, landfill gas, ocean, geothermal, municipal solid waste, hydroelectric, hydrogen, or fuel cell technologies.

The PV industry has adopted levelized cost of electricity (LCOE) as the unit of cost. The electrical energy generated is sold in units of kilowatt-hours (kWh). As a rule of thumb, and depending on the local insolation, 1 watt-peak of installed solar PV capacity generates about 1 to 2 kWh of electricity per year. This corresponds to a capacity factor of around 10–20%. The product of the local cost of electricity and the insolation determines the break-even point for solar power. The International Conference on Solar Photovoltaic Investments, organized by EPIA, has estimated that PV systems will pay back their investors in 8 to 12 years. As a result, since 2006 it has been economical for investors to install photovoltaics for free in return for a long term power purchase agreement. Fifty percent of commercial systems in the United States were installed in this manner in 2007 and over 90% in 2009.

Grid parity
Grid parity, the point at which the cost of photovoltaic electricity is equal to or cheaper than the price of grid power, is more easily achieved in areas with abundant sun and high costs for electricity such as in California and Japan. In 2008, the levelized cost of electricity for solar PV was $0.25/kWh or less in most of the OECD countries. By late 2011, the fully loaded cost was predicted to fall below $0.15/kWh for most of the OECD and to reach $0.10/kWh in sunnier regions. These cost levels are driving three emerging trends: vertical integration of the supply chain, origination of power purchase agreements (PPAs) by solar power companies, and unexpected risk for traditional power generation companies, grid operators and wind turbine manufacturers. Grid parity was first reached in Spain in 2013. Hawaii and other islands that otherwise use fossil fuel (diesel fuel) to produce electricity, and most of the US is expected to reach grid parity by 2015.

Productivity by location
The productivity of solar power in a region depends on solar irradiance, which varies through the day and is influenced by latitude and climate. The locations with highest annual solar irradiance lie in the arid tropics and subtropics. Deserts lying in low latitudes usually have few clouds, and can receive sunshine for more than ten hours a day. These hot deserts form the *Global Sun Belt* circling the world. This belt consists of extensive swathes of land in Northern Africa, Southern Africa, Southwest Asia, Middle East, and Australia, as well as the much smaller deserts of North

and South America. Africa's eastern Sahara Desert, also known as the Libyan Desert, has been observed to be the sunniest place on Earth according to NASA.

Wind power

Wind is an intermittent energy source, which cannot make electricity nor be dispatched on demand. It also, because of the local weather conditions, provides variable power, which is generally consistent from year to year but varies greatly over shorter time scales. Therefore, it must be used together with other electric power sources or storage to give a reliable supply. As the proportion of wind power in a region increases, more conventional power sources are needed to back it up (such as fossil fuel power and nuclear power), and the grid may need to be upgraded.

Power-management techniques such as having dispatchable power sources, enough hydroelectric power, excess capacity, geographically distributed turbines, exporting and importing power to neighbouring areas, energy storage, or reducing demand when wind production is low, can in many cases overcome these problems. Weather forecasting permits the electric-power network to be readied for the predictable variations in production that occur.

Wind is the movement of air across the surface of the Earth, affected by areas of high pressure and of low pressure. The global wind kinetic energy averaged approximately 1.50 MJ/m^2 over the period from 1979 to 2010, 1.31 MJ/m^2 in the Northern Hemisphere with 1.70 MJ/m^2 in the Southern Hemisphere. The atmosphere acts as a thermal engine, absorbing heat at higher temperatures, releasing heat at lower temperatures. The process is responsible for production of wind kinetic energy at a rate of 2.46 W/m^2 sustaining thus the circulation of the atmosphere against frictional dissipation.

Wind power or wind energy is the use of wind to provide the mechanical power through wind turbines to turn electric generators and traditionally to do other work, like milling or pumping. Wind power is a sustainable and renewable energy, and has a much smaller impact on the environment compared to burning fossil fuels.

Visual Pollution
Wind farms consist of many individual wind turbines, which are connected to the electric power transmission network. Onshore wind is an inexpensive source of electric power, competitive with or in many places cheaper than coal or gas plants. Onshore wind farms also have an impact on the landscape, as typically they need to be spread over more land than other power stations and need to be built in wild and rural

areas. This can lead to "industrialization of the countryside" and habitat loss which some have called "visual pollution". Offshore wind is steadier and stronger than on land and offshore farms have less visual impact, but construction and maintenance costs are higher. Small onshore wind farms can feed some energy into the grid or provide electric power to isolated off-grid locations.

A transmission line is required to bring the generated power to (often remote) markets. For an off-shore station this may require a submarine cable. Construction of a new high-voltage line may be too costly for the wind resource alone, but wind sites may take advantage of lines installed for conventionally fuelled generation.

The UK's investments in offshore wind power have resulted in a rapid decrease of the usage of coal as an energy source between 2012 and 2017, as well as a drop in the usage of natural gas as an energy source in 2017. In 2012, 1,662 turbines at 55 offshore wind farms in 10 European countries produced 18 TWh, enough to power almost five million households. As of September 2018 the Walney Extension in the United Kingdom is the largest offshore wind farm in the world at 659 MW.

In 2015 there were over 200,000 wind turbines operating worldwide, with a total nameplate capacity of 432 GW. The European Union passed 100 GW nameplate capacity in September 2012, while the United States surpassed 75 GW in 2015 and China's grid connected capacity passed 145 GW in 2015. In 2015 wind power constituted 15.6% of all installed power generation capacity in the European Union and it generated around 11.4% of its power.

In 2018, global wind power capacity grew 9.6% to 591 GW and yearly wind energy production grew 10%, reaching 4.8% of worldwide electric power usage, and providing 14% of the electricity in the European Union. Wind power supplied 15% of the electricity consumed in Europe in 2019. Denmark is the country with the highest penetration of wind power, with 43.4% of its consumed electricity from wind in 2017. At least 83 other countries are using wind power to supply their electric power grids.

World wind generation capacity more than quadrupled between 2000 and 2006, doubling about every 3 years. The United States pioneered wind farms and led the world in installed capacity in the 1980s and into the 1990s. In 1997 installed capacity in Germany surpassed the United States and led until once again overtaken by the United States in 2008. China has been rapidly expanding its wind installations in the late 2000s and passed the United States in 2010 to become the world leader. As of 2011,

83 countries around the world were using wind power on a commercial basis.

One of the biggest current challenges to wind power grid integration in the United States is the necessity of developing new transmission lines to carry power from wind farms, usually in remote lowly populated states in the middle of the country due to availability of wind, to high load locations, usually on the coasts where population density is higher. The current transmission lines in remote locations were not designed for the transport of large amounts of energy. However, resistance from state and local governments makes it difficult to construct new transmission lines. These are important issues that need to be solved, as when the transmission capacity does not meet the generation capacity, wind farms are forced to produce below their full potential or stop running all together, in a process known as curtailment. While this leads to potential renewable generation left untapped, it prevents possible grid overload or risk to reliable service.

South Australia generation
In Australia, the state of South Australia generates around half of the nation's wind power capacity. By the end of 2011 wind power in South Australia, championed by then Premier Mike Rann, reached 26% of the State's electric power generation, edging out coal for the first time. At this stage South Australia, with only 7.2% of Australia's population, had 54% of Australia's installed capacity. Further, there appears to be a direct correlation between the cost of electricity in countries around the world, and the amount of renewable energy. South Australia is one of the worst examples. The state government decided to become the largest producer of wind energy in Australia - and as a result, they now have the most expensive, and unreliable, electricity in the world. A quote from Senator Matt Canavan is relevant : "Each wind turbine in Australia gets $AU 600,000 in taxpayer subsidies per year. They only run at 40% capacity and 77% are foreign-owned. Some of these renewable energy types are the biggest dole bludgers in the country, and they're also the biggest paid dole bludgers." It seems that when the subsidies are taken away, renewable energy struggles to be economic at all. The public do not realise the amount of fossil fuels required to even make a wind turbine.

Now that so many wind turbines are reaching the end of their 20 year lifetime, the amount of toxic waste to deal with is another huge problem. So many of those huge turbine blades will just be ending up in a landfill.

Another argument against wind farms is the number of birds, bats and insects being killed by their blades. The greenies argue that these numbers are not that high but the real issue is that they are killing the predator birds at the top of the food chain - like the American Eagle - and that this is the biggest problem. There is also evidence that the acoustic pollution from offshore wind farms interferes with communication and navigation in whales and dolphins.

History
Wind power has been used as long as humans have put sails into the wind. Wind-powered machines used to grind grain and pump water, the windmill and wind pump, were developed in what is now Iran, Afghanistan and Pakistan by the 9th century. Wind power was widely available and not confined to the banks of fast-flowing streams, or later, requiring sources of fuel. Wind-powered pumps drained the polders of the Netherlands, and in arid regions such as the American mid-west or the Australian outback, wind pumps provided water for livestock and steam engines.

The first windmill used for the production of electric power according to *Wikipedia* was built in Scotland in July 1887 by Prof James Blyth of Anderson's College, Glasgow (the precursor of Strathclyde University). Blyth's 10 metre high, cloth-sailed wind turbine was installed in the garden of his holiday cottage at Marykirk in Kincardineshire and was used to charge accumulators developed by the Frenchman Camille Alphonse Faure, to power the lighting in the cottage, thus making it the first house in the world to have its electric power supplied by wind power. Blyth offered the surplus electric power to the people of Marykirk for lighting the main street, however, they turned down the offer as they thought electric power was "the work of the devil." Although he later built a wind turbine to supply emergency power to the local Lunatic Asylum, Infirmary and Dispensary of Montrose, the invention never really caught on as the technology was not considered to be economically viable.

In Cleveland, Ohio, a larger and heavily engineered machine was designed and constructed in the winter of 1887-1888 by Charles F. Brush. This was built by his engineering company at his home and operated from 1886 until 1900. The Brush wind turbine had a rotor 17 metres in diameter and was mounted on an 18 metres tower.

With the development of electric power, wind power found new applications in lighting buildings remote from centrally-generated power. Throughout the 20th century parallel paths developed small wind stations suitable for farms or residences. The 1973 oil crisis triggered investigation in Denmark and the United States that led to larger utility-scale wind generators that could be connected to electric power grids for remote use of power. By 2008, the U.S. installed capacity had reached 25.4 gigawatts, and by 2012 the installed capacity was 60 gigawatts. Today, wind powered generators operate in every size range from tiny stations for battery charging at isolated residences, up to near-gigawatt sized offshore wind farms that provide electric power to national electrical networks.

Maximum level of wind penetration
There is no generally accepted maximum level of wind penetration. The limit for a particular grid will depend on the existing generating plants, pricing mechanisms, capacity for energy storage, demand management and other factors. An interconnected electric power grid will already include reserve generating and transmission capacity to allow for equipment failures. This reserve capacity can also serve to compensate for the varying power generation produced by wind stations.

A wind energy penetration figure can be specified for a different duration of time, but is often quoted annually. To obtain 100% from wind annually requires substantial long term storage or substantial interconnection to other systems which may already have substantial storage. On a monthly, weekly, daily, or hourly basis–or less–wind might supply as much as or more than 100% of current use, with the rest stored or exported. Seasonal industry might then take advantage of high wind and low usage times such as at night when wind output can exceed normal demand. Such industry might include production of silicon, aluminum, steel, or of natural gas, and hydrogen, and using future long term storage to facilitate 100% energy from variable renewable energy. Homes can also be programmed to accept extra electric power on demand, for example by remotely turning up water heater thermostats.

Variability of wind generation
Electric power generated from wind power can be highly variable at several different timescales: hourly, daily, or seasonally. Annual variation also exists, but is not as significant as for the shorter time scales. Because instantaneous electrical generation and consumption must remain in balance to maintain grid stability, this variability can present substantial

challenges to incorporating large amounts of wind power into a grid system. Fluctuations in load and allowance for failure of large fossil-fuel generating units requires operating reserve capacity, which can be increased to compensate for variability of wind generation.

In the UK there were 124 separate occasions from 2008 to 2010 when the nation's wind output fell to less than 2% of installed capacity. A report on Denmark's wind power noted that their wind power network provided less than 1% of average demand on 54 days during the year 2002. Wind power advocates argue that these periods of low wind can be dealt with by simply restarting existing power stations that have been held in readiness, or interlinking with HVDC. Electrical grids with slow-responding thermal power plants and without ties to networks with hydroelectric generation may have to limit the use of wind power. According to a 2007 Stanford University study published in the *Journal of Applied Meteorology and Climatology*, interconnecting ten or more wind farms can allow an average of 33% of the total energy produced (i.e. about 8% of total nameplate capacity) to be used as reliable, base load electric power which can be relied on to handle peak loads, as long as minimum criteria are met for wind speed and turbine height.

Conversely, on particularly windy days, even with penetration levels of 16%, wind power generation can surpass all other electric power sources in a country. In Spain, in the early hours of 16 April 2012 wind power production reached the highest percentage of electric power production till then, at 60% of the total demand. In Denmark, which had power market penetration of 30% in 2013, over 90 hours, wind power generated 100% of the country's power, peaking at 122% of the country's demand at 2 am on 28 October.

Solar power tends to be complementary to wind. On daily to weekly timescales, high pressure areas tend to bring clear skies and low surface winds, whereas low pressure areas tend to be windier and cloudier. On seasonal timescales, solar energy peaks in summer, whereas in many areas wind energy is lower in summer and higher in winter. Thus the seasonal variation of wind and solar power tend to cancel each other somewhat. In 2007, the Institute for Solar Energy Supply Technology of the University of Kassel pilot-tested a combined power plant linking solar, wind, biogas and hydro storage to provide load-following power around the clock and throughout the year, entirely from renewable sources.

Wind power forecasting methods are used, but predictability of any particular wind farm is low for short-term operation. For any particular generator there is an 80% chance that wind output will change less than 10% in an hour and a 40% chance that it will change 10% or more in 5 hours. However, studies by Graham Sinden (2009) suggest that, in practice, the variations in thousands of wind turbines, spread out over several different sites and wind regimes, are smoothed. Thus, while the output from a single turbine can vary greatly and rapidly as local wind speeds vary, as more turbines are connected over larger and larger areas the average power output becomes less variable and more predictable.

Wind power hardly ever suffers major technical failures, since failures of individual wind turbines have hardly any effect on overall power, so that the distributed wind power is reliable and predictable, whereas conventional generators, while far less variable, can suffer major unpredictable outages.

Energy storage

Typically, conventional hydroelectricity complements wind power very well. When the wind is blowing strongly, nearby hydroelectric stations can temporarily hold back the water. When the wind drops they can, provided they have the generation capacity, rapidly increase production to compensate. This gives a very even overall power supply and virtually no loss of energy and uses no more water. Alternatively, where a suitable head of water is not available, pumped-storage hydroelectricity or other forms of grid energy storage such as compressed air energy storage and thermal energy storage can store energy developed by high-wind periods and release it when needed.

The type of storage needed depends on the wind penetration level – low penetration requires daily storage, and high penetration requires both short and long term storage – as long as a month or more. Stored energy increases the economic value of wind energy since it can be shifted to displace higher cost generation during peak demand periods. The potential revenue from this arbitrage can offset the cost and losses of storage. For example, in the UK, the 1.7 GW Dinorwig pumped-storage plant evens out electrical demand peaks, and allows base-load suppliers to run their plants more efficiently. Although pumped-storage power systems are only about 75% efficient, and have high installation costs, their low running costs and ability to reduce the required electrical base-load can save both fuel and total electrical generation costs.

In particular geographic regions, peak wind speeds may not coincide with peak demand for electrical power. In California and Texas, for example, hot days in summer may have low wind speed and high electrical demand due to the use of air conditioning. Some utilities subsidize the purchase of geothermal heat pumps by their customers, to reduce electric power demand during the summer months by making air conditioning up to 70% more efficient; widespread adoption of this technology would better match electric power demand to wind availability in areas with hot summers and low summer winds.

Germany has an installed capacity of wind and solar that can exceed daily demand, and has been exporting peak power to neighbouring countries, with exports which amounted to some 14.7 billion kWh in 2012. A more practical solution is the installation of thirty days storage capacity able to supply 80% of demand, which will become necessary when most of Europe's energy is obtained from wind power and solar power. Just as the EU requires member countries to maintain 90 days strategic reserves of oil it can be expected that countries will provide electric power storage, instead of expecting to use their neighbours for net metering.

According to *BusinessGreen*, wind turbines reached grid parity (the point at which the cost of wind power matches traditional sources) in some areas of Europe in the mid-2000s, and in the US around the same time. Falling prices continue to drive the levelized cost down and it has been suggested that it had reached general grid parity in Europe in 2010, and will reach the same point in the US around 2016 due to an expected reduction in capital costs of about 12%. According to *PolitiFact*, it is difficult to predict whether wind power would remain viable in the United States without subsidies.

Capital intensive

Wind power is capital intensive, but has no fuel costs. The price of wind power is therefore much more stable than the volatile prices of fossil fuel sources. The marginal cost of wind energy once a station is constructed is usually less than 1-cent per kW·h. However, the estimated average cost per unit of electric power must incorporate the cost of construction of the turbine and transmission facilities, borrowed funds, return to investors (including cost of risk), estimated annual production, and other components, averaged over the projected useful life of the equipment, which may be in excess of twenty years. Energy cost estimates are highly dependent on these assumptions so published cost figures can differ substantially.

A British Wind Energy Association report in 2005 gives an average generation cost of onshore wind power of around US (5 to 6 cents) per kW·h. The cost per unit of energy produced was estimated in 2006 to be 5 to 6% above the cost of new generating capacity in the US for coal and natural gas: wind cost was estimated at $55.80/MW·h, coal at $53.10/MW·h and natural gas at $52.50. Similar comparative results with natural gas were obtained in a governmental study in the UK in 2011. It is expected that wind power will be the cheapest form of energy generation in the future. The cost has reduced as wind turbine technology has improved. There are now longer and lighter wind turbine blades, improvements in turbine performance and increased power generation efficiency. Also, wind project capital and maintenance costs have continued to decline. For example, the wind industry in the US in 2014 was able to produce more power at lower cost by using taller wind turbines with longer blades, capturing the faster winds at higher elevations.

A number of initiatives are working to reduce costs of electric power from offshore wind. It has been suggested that innovation at scale could deliver 25% cost reduction in offshore wind by 2020. Henrik Stiesdal, former Chief Technical Officer at Siemens Wind Power, has stated that by 2025 energy from offshore wind will be one of the cheapest, saleable solutions in the UK, compared to other renewables and fossil fuel energy sources, if the true cost to society is factored into the cost of energy equation. He calculates the cost at that time to be 43 EUR/MWh for onshore, and 72 EUR/MWh for offshore wind.

The wind industry
The wind industry in the United States generates tens of thousands of jobs and billions of dollars of economic activity. Wind projects provide local taxes, or payments in lieu of taxes and strengthen the economy of rural communities by providing income to farmers with wind turbines on their land. Wind energy in many jurisdictions receives financial or other support to encourage its development. Wind energy also benefits from subsidies in many jurisdictions, either to increase its attractiveness, or to compensate for subsidies received by other forms of production which have significant negative externalities.

Secondary market forces also provide incentives for businesses to use wind-generated power, even if there is a premium price for the electricity. For example, socially responsible manufacturers pay utility companies a premium that goes to subsidize and build new wind power infrastructure.

Companies use wind-generated power, and in return they can claim that they are undertaking strong "green" efforts. In the US the organization Green-e monitors business compliance with these renewable energy credits. Turbine prices have fallen significantly in recent years due to tougher competitive conditions such as the increased use of energy auctions, and the elimination of subsidies in many markets.

Small-scale wind power is the name given to wind generation systems with the capacity to produce up to 50 kW of electrical power. Isolated communities, that may otherwise rely on diesel generators, may use wind turbines as an alternative. Individuals may purchase these systems to reduce or eliminate their dependence on grid electric power for economic reasons, or to reduce their carbon footprint. Wind turbines have been used for household electric power generation in conjunction with battery storage over many decades in remote areas.

Recent examples of small-scale wind power projects in an urban setting can be found in New York City, where, since 2009, a number of building projects have capped their roofs with Gorlov-type helical wind turbines. Although the energy they generate is small compared to the overall consumption of the building, they help to reinforce the building's 'green' credentials in ways that "showing people your high-tech boiler" cannot. Some of the projects also receive the direct support of the New York State Energy Research and Development Authority.

Grid-connected domestic wind turbines may use grid energy storage, thus replacing purchased electric power with locally produced power when available. The surplus power produced by domestic micro generators can, in some jurisdictions, be fed into the network and sold to the utility company, producing a retail credit for the micro generators' owners to offset their energy costs. Off-grid system users can either adapt to intermittent power or use batteries, photovoltaic or diesel systems to supplement the wind turbine. Equipment such as parking meters, traffic warning signs, street lighting, or wireless Internet gateways may be powered by a small wind turbine, possibly combined with a photovoltaic system, that charges a small battery replacing the need for a connection to the power grid.

A Carbon Trust study into the potential of small-scale wind energy in the UK, published in 2010, found that small wind turbines could provide up to 1.5 terawatt hours (TW·h) per year of electric power (0.4% of total UK electric power consumption), saving 0.6 million tonnes of CO_2 emission savings. This is based on the assumption that 10% of households would install turbines at costs competitive with grid electric power, around 12 pence (US 19 cents) a kW·h. A report prepared for the UK's government-sponsored Energy Saving Trust in 2006, found that home power generators of various kinds could provide 30 to 40% of the country's electric power needs by 2050.

The environmental impact of wind power is considered to be relatively minor compared to that of fossil fuels. However, onshore wind farms can have a significant visual impact and impact on the landscape. Their network of turbines, access roads, transmission lines and substations can result in "energy sprawl". Wind farms typically need to cover more land and be more spread out than other power stations. To power major cities by wind alone would require building wind farms bigger than the cities themselves. A report by the Mountaineering Council of Scotland concluded that wind farms have a negative impact on tourism in areas known for natural landscapes and panoramic views.

Industrialization of the countryside
Wind farms are typically built in wild and rural areas, which can lead to "industrialization of the countryside" and habitat loss. Habitat loss and habitat fragmentation are the greatest impact of wind farms on wildlife. There are also reports of higher bird and bat mortality at wind turbines than there are around other artificial structures. The scale of the ecological impact may or may not be significant, depending on specific circumstances. Prevention and mitigation of wildlife fatalities, and protection of peat bogs, affect the siting and operation of wind turbines.

Wind turbines also generate noise. At a residential distance of 300 metres this may be around 45 dB, which is slightly louder than a refrigerator. At 1.5 km distance they become inaudible. There are anecdotal reports of negative health effects from noise on people who live very close to wind turbines, but research has generally not supported these claims.

Before 2019, many wind turbine blades had been made of fiberglass with designs that only provided a service lifetime of 10 to 20 years. As of February 2018 there was no market for recycling these old blades, and they are commonly disposed of in landfills. Because blades are designed to be hollow, they take up large volume compared to their mass. Landfill operators have therefore started requiring operators to crush the blades before they can be landfilled.

Nuclear power and fossil fuels are subsidized by many governments, and wind power and other forms of renewable energy are also often subsidized. According to the International Energy Agency (IEA) report in 2011, energy subsidies artificially lower the price of energy paid by consumers, raise the price received by producers or lower the cost of production. "Fossil fuels subsidies costs generally outweigh the benefits. Subsidies to renewables and low-carbon energy technologies can bring long-term economic and environmental benefits". In November 2011, an IEA report entitled *Deploying Renewables* 2011 said "subsidies in green energy technologies that were not yet competitive are justified in order to give an incentive to investing into technologies with clear environmental and energy security benefits". The IEA's report disagreed with claims that renewable energy technologies are only viable through costly subsidies and not able to produce energy reliably to meet demand.

However, IEA's views are not universally accepted. Between 2010 and 2016, subsidies for wind were between 1.3¢ and 5.7¢ per kWh. Subsidies for coal, natural gas and nuclear are all between 0.05¢ and 0.2¢ per kWh over all years. On a per-kWh basis, wind is subsidized 50 times as much as traditional sources. In the United States, the wind power industry has recently increased its lobbying efforts considerably, spending about $5 million in 2009 after years of relative obscurity in Washington. By comparison, the U.S. nuclear industry alone spent over $650 million on its lobbying efforts and campaign contributions during a ten-year period ending in 2008.

Following the 2011 Japanese nuclear accidents, Germany's federal government is working on a new plan for increasing energy efficiency and renewable energy commercialization, with a particular focus on offshore wind farms. Under the plan, large wind turbines will be erected far away from the coastlines, where the wind blows more consistently than it does on land, and where the enormous turbines won't bother the inhabitants. The plan aims to decrease Germany's dependence on energy derived from coal and nuclear power plants.

Public Surveys

Surveys of public attitudes across Europe and in many other countries show strong public support for wind power. About 80% of EU citizens support wind power. In Germany, where wind power has gained very high social acceptance, hundreds of thousands of people have invested in citizens' wind farms across the country and thousands of small and medium-sized enterprises are running successful businesses in a new sector that in 2008 employed 90,000 people and generated 8% of

Germany's electric power. Bakker et al. in 2012 found in their study that when residents did not want the turbines located "next to them", their annoyance was significantly higher than those "that benefited economically from wind turbines".

Although wind power is a popular form of energy generation, the construction of wind farms is not universally welcomed, often for aesthetic reasons. In Spain, with some exceptions, there has been little opposition to the installation of inland wind parks. However, the projects to build offshore parks have been more controversial. In particular, the proposal of building the biggest offshore wind power production facility in the world in south-western Spain in the coast of Cádiz, on the spot of the 1805 Battle of Trafalgar has been met with strong opposition from those who fear for tourism and fisheries in the area, and because the area is a war grave.

In a survey conducted by Angus Reid Strategies in October 2007, 89% of respondents said that using renewable energy sources like wind or solar power was positive for Canada, because these sources were better for the environment. Only 4% considered using renewable sources as negative since they can be unreliable and expensive. According to a Saint Consulting survey in April 2007, wind power was the alternative energy source most likely to gain public support for future development in Canada, with only 16% opposed to this type of energy. By contrast, three out of four Canadians opposed nuclear power developments.

A 2003 survey of residents living around Scotland's 10 existing wind farms found high levels of community acceptance and strong support for wind power, with much support from those who lived closest to the wind farms. The results of this survey support those of an earlier Scottish Executive survey "Public attitudes to the Environment in Scotland 2002", which found that the Scottish public would prefer the majority of their electric power to come from renewables, and which rated wind power as the cleanest source of renewable energy. A further survey conducted in 2005 showed that 74% of people in Scotland agree that wind farms are necessary to meet current and future energy needs. When people were asked the same question in a Scottish renewables study conducted in 2010, 78% agreed. The increase is significant as there were twice as many wind farms in 2010 as there were in 2005. The 2010 survey also showed that 52% disagreed with the statement that wind farms are "ugly and a blot on the landscape". 59% agreed that wind farms were necessary and that how they looked was unimportant. Regarding tourism, query responders consider power pylons, cell phone towers, quarries and plantations more negatively than wind farms. Scotland is planning to obtain 100% of electric power from renewable sources by 2020.

Hydroelectricity

Hydroelectricity is electricity produced from hydropower. *Wikipedia* has a very comprehensive analysis of this form of energy.

In 2015, hydropower generated 16.6% of the world's total electricity and 70% of all renewable electricity. This was expected to increase by about 3.1% each year for the next 25 years. Hydropower is produced in 150 countries, with the Asia-Pacific region generating 33% of global hydropower in 2013. China is the largest hydroelectricity producer, with 920 TWh of production in 2013, representing 16.9% of domestic electricity use.

The cost of hydroelectricity is relatively low, making it a competitive source of renewable electricity. The hydro station consumes no water, unlike coal or gas plants. The typical cost of electricity from a hydro station larger than 10 megawatts is 3 to 5 U.S. cents per kilowatt hour. With a dam and reservoir it is also a flexible source of electricity, since the amount produced by the station can be varied up or down very rapidly (in as little as a few seconds) to adapt to changing energy demands. Once a hydroelectric complex is constructed, the project produces no direct waste, and it generally has a considerably lower output level of greenhouse gases than photovoltaic power plants and certainly fossil fuel powered energy plants.

Hydropower has been used since ancient times to grind flour and perform other tasks. In the mid-1770s, French engineer Bernard Forest de Bélidor published *Architecture Hydraulique,* which described vertical- and horizontal-axis hydraulic machines. By the late 19th century, the electrical generator was developed and could be coupled with hydraulics. The growing demand arising from the Industrial Revolution would drive development as well. In 1878, the world's first hydroelectric power scheme was developed at Cragside in Northumberland, England by William Armstrong. It was used to power a single arc lamp in his art gallery. The old Schoelkopf Power Station No. 1, USA, near Niagara Falls, began to produce electricity in 1881. The first Edison hydroelectric power station, the Vulcan Street Plant, began operating September 30, 1882, in Appleton, Wisconsin, with an output of about 12.5 kilowatts. By 1886 there were 45 hydroelectric power stations in the United States and Canada; and by 1889 there were 200 in the United States alone.

At the beginning of the 20th century, many small hydroelectric power stations were being constructed by commercial companies in mountains near metropolitan areas. By 1920, when 40% of the power produced in the United States was hydroelectric, the US Federal Power Act was enacted into law. The Act created the *Federal Power Commission* to regulate hydroelectric power stations on federal land and water. As the power stations became larger, their associated dams developed additional purposes, including flood control, irrigation and navigation. Federal funding became necessary for large-scale development, and federally owned corporations, such as the Tennessee Valley Authority (1933) and the Bonneville Power Administration (1937) were created. Additionally, the US Bureau of Reclamation which had begun a series of western U.S. irrigation projects in the early 20th century, was now constructing large hydroelectric projects such as the 1928 Hoover Dam. The U.S. Army Corps of Engineers was also involved in hydroelectric development, completing the Bonneville Dam in 1937 and being recognized by the Flood Control Act of 1936 as the premier federal flood control agency.

Hydropower as white coal

Hydroelectric power stations continued to become larger throughout the 20th century. Hydropower was sometimes referred to as *white coal*. The Hoover Dam's initial 1,345 MW power station was the world's largest hydroelectric power station in 1936; it was eclipsed by the 6,809 MW Grand Coulee Dam in 1942. The Itaipu Dam opened in 1984 in South America as the largest, producing 14 GW, but was surpassed in 2008 by the Three Gorges Dam in China at 22.5 GW. Hydroelectricity would eventually supply some countries, including Norway, Democratic Republic of the Congo, Paraguay, New Zealand, and Brazil, with over 85% of their electricity. The United States currently has over 2,000 hydroelectric power stations that supply 6.4% of its total electrical production output, which is 49% of its renewable electricity.

Of significance, the technical potential for hydropower development around the world is much greater than the actual production: the percent of potential hydropower capacity that has not been developed is 71% in Europe, 75% in North America, 79% in South America, 95% in Africa, 95% in the Middle East, and 82% in Asia-Pacific. Due to the political and green policy realities of new reservoirs in western countries, and economic limitations in the third world, as well as the lack of a transmission system in undeveloped areas, perhaps only 25% of the remaining technically exploitable potential can be developed before 2050, with the bulk of that being in the Asia-Pacific area. However, some countries have highly developed their hydropower potential and have very little room for growth: Switzerland produces 88% of its potential and Mexico 80%.

The major advantage of conventional hydro-electric dams with reservoirs is their ability to store water at low cost for dispatch later as high value clean electricity. When used as peak power to meet demand, hydroelectricity has a higher value than base power and a much higher value compared to intermittent energy sources.

One important advantage of hydroelectric stations is that they have long economic lives, with some plants still in service after 50–100 years. Operating labour cost is also usually low, as plants are automated and have few personnel on site during normal operation. Where a dam serves multiple purposes, a hydroelectric station may be added with relatively low construction cost, providing a useful revenue stream to offset the costs of dam operation. It has been calculated that the sale of electricity from the Three Gorges Dam will cover the construction costs after five to eight years of full generation. However, some data shows that in most countries large hydropower dams will be too costly and take too long to build to deliver a positive risk adjusted return, unless appropriate risk management measures are put in place.

Dedicated hydroelectric projects

While many hydroelectric projects supply public electricity networks, some are created to serve specific industrial enterprises. For example, dedicated hydroelectric projects are often built to provide the substantial amounts of electricity needed for aluminium electrolytic plants. The Grand Coulee Dam switched to support Alcoa Aluminium in Bellingham, Washington, United States for American World War II airplanes before it was allowed to provide irrigation and power to citizens (in addition to aluminium power) after the war. In Suriname, the Brokopondo Reservoir was constructed to provide electricity for the Alcoa aluminium industry, and New Zealand's Manapouri Power Station was constructed to supply electricity to the aluminium smelter at Tiwai Point.

Since hydroelectric dams do not use fuel, power generation does not produce CO_2. While CO_2 is initially produced during construction of the project, and some methane is given off annually by reservoirs, hydro generally has the lowest lifecycle greenhouse gas emissions for power generation. According to a comparative study by the Paul Scherrer Institute and the University of Stuttgart, hydroelectricity in Europe produces the least amount of greenhouse gases and externality of any energy source. In second place was wind, third was nuclear energy, and fourth was solar photovoltaic. The low greenhouse gas impact of hydroelectricity is found especially in temperate climates. However, greater greenhouse gas emission impacts are found in the tropical regions because the reservoirs of power stations in tropical regions produce a larger amount of methane than those in temperate areas. Like other non-fossil fuel sources, hydropower also has no emissions of sulphur dioxide, nitrogen oxides, or other particulates.

Reservoirs created by hydroelectric schemes often provide facilities for water sports, and become tourist attractions themselves. In some countries, aquaculture in reservoirs is common. Multi-use dams installed for irrigation support agriculture with a relatively constant water supply. Large hydro dams can also control floods, which would otherwise affect people living downstream of the project. However, large reservoirs associated with traditional hydroelectric power stations can result in submersion of extensive areas upstream of the dams, sometimes destroying biologically rich and productive lowland and riverine valley forests, marshland and grasslands. Damming also interrupts the flow of rivers and can harm local ecosystems, and building large dams and reservoirs often involves displacing people and wildlife. The loss of land is often exacerbated by habitat fragmentation of surrounding areas caused by the reservoir.

Hydroelectric projects can also be disruptive to surrounding aquatic ecosystems both upstream and downstream of the plant site. Generation of hydroelectric power changes the downstream river environment. Water exiting a turbine usually contains very little suspended sediment, which can lead to scouring of river beds and loss of riverbanks. Since turbine gates are often opened intermittently, rapid or even daily fluctuations in river flow are observed. Another disadvantage of hydroelectric dams is the need to relocate the people living where the reservoirs are planned. In 2000, the World Commission on Dams estimated that dams had physically displaced 40-80 million people worldwide.

Because large conventional dammed-hydro facilities hold back large volumes of water, a failure due to poor construction, natural disasters or sabotage can be catastrophic to downriver settlements and infrastructure. For example, during Typhoon *Nina* in 1975, the Banqiao Dam failed in Southern China when more than a year's rain fell within 24 hours. The resulting flood resulted in the deaths of 26,000 people, and another 145,000 from epidemics. Millions were left homeless.

Tidal Power

Judging by the sheer force of the waves during a day at the beach, the ocean, as Kristin Majcher writing in the *MIT Technology Review* in the edition of May 20, 2015 says, seems like an abundant source of renewable energy. Indeed, more than 70 companies have developed technologies to generate electricity from the changing height of the tides or the kinetic power of waves. Other companies are exploring novel methods of generating electricity from the ocean's salt content or temperature. Ocean energy has the potential to provide hundreds of gigawatts of power worldwide; the U.K. and U.S. have said that these technologies could provide 20% and 15% of their electricity consumption, respectively. But even though companies and governments have invested millions in these technologies over the years, the power generated from the ocean is miniscule, as a 2013 Ernst & Young report showed.

Tidal power or tidal energy is the form of hydropower that converts the energy obtained from tides into useful forms of power, mainly electricity. Although not yet widely used, tidal energy has the potential for future electricity generation as noted by *Wikipedia*. Tides are more predictable than the wind and the sun. Among sources of renewable energy, tidal energy has traditionally suffered from relatively high cost and limited availability of sites with sufficiently high tidal ranges or flow velocities, thus constricting its total availability. However, many recent technological developments and improvements, both in design (e.g. dynamic tidal power, tidal lagoons) and turbine technology (e.g. new axial turbines, cross flow turbines), indicate that the total availability of tidal power may be much higher than previously assumed and that economic and environmental costs may be brought down to competitive levels.

Historically, tide mills have been used both in Europe and on the Atlantic coast of North America. The incoming water was contained in large storage ponds, and as the tide went out, it turned waterwheels that used the mechanical power it produced to mill grain. The earliest occurrences date from the Middle Ages, or even from Roman times. The process of using falling water and spinning turbines to create electricity was introduced in the U.S. and Europe in the 19th century.

The world's first large-scale tidal power plant was the Rance Tidal Power Station in France, which became operational in 1966. It was the largest tidal power station in terms of output until Sihwa Lake Tidal

Power Station opened in South Korea in August 2011. The Sihwa station uses sea wall defense barriers complete with 10 turbines generating 254 MW.

Earth's oceanic tides

Tidal power is taken from the Earth's oceanic tides. Tidal forces are periodic variations in gravitational attraction exerted by celestial bodies. These forces create corresponding motions or currents in the world's oceans. Due to the strong attraction to the oceans, a bulge in the water level is created, causing a temporary increase in sea level. As the Earth rotates, this bulge of ocean water meets the shallow water adjacent to the shoreline and creates a tide. This occurrence takes place in an unfailing manner, due to the consistent pattern of the moon's orbit around the earth. The magnitude and character of this motion reflects the changing positions of the Moon and Sun relative to the Earth, the effects of Earth's rotation, and local geography of the seafloor and coastlines.

Tidal power is the only technology that draws on energy inherent in the orbital characteristics of the Earth–Moon system, and to a lesser extent in the Earth–Sun system. Other natural energies exploited by human technology originate directly or indirectly with the Sun, including fossil fuel, conventional hydroelectric, wind, biofuel, wave and solar energy. Nuclear energy makes use of Earth's mineral deposits of fissionable elements, while geothermal power utilizes the Earth's internal heat, which comes from a combination of residual heat from planetary accretion (about 20%) and heat produced through radioactive decay (80%).

A tidal generator converts the energy of tidal flows into electricity. Greater tidal variation and higher tidal current velocities can dramatically increase the potential of a site for tidal electricity generation. Because the Earth's tides are ultimately due to gravitational interaction with the Moon and Sun and the Earth's rotation, tidal power is practically inexhaustible and classified as a renewable energy resource.

Tidal power can be classified into four generating methods. Tidal stream generators make use of the kinetic energy of moving water to power turbines, in a similar way to wind turbines that use the wind to power turbines. Some tidal generators can be built into the structures of existing bridges or are entirely submersed, thus avoiding concerns over the impact on the natural landscape. Land constrictions such as straits or inlets can create high velocities at specific sites, which can be captured with the use of turbines. These turbines can be horizontal, vertical, open, or ducted.

Stream energy can be used at a much higher rate than wind turbines due to water being denser than air. Using similar technology to wind turbines converting the energy in tidal energy is much more efficient. Close to 10 mph (about 8.6 knots) ocean tidal current would have an energy output equal or greater than a 90 mph wind speed for the same size of the turbine system.

Tidal barrages make use of the potential energy in the difference in height (or hydraulic head) between high and low tides. When using tidal barrages to generate power, the potential energy from a tide is seized through strategic placement of specialized dams. When the sea level rises and the tide begins to come in, the temporary increase in tidal power is channelled into a large basin behind the dam, holding a large amount of potential energy. With the receding tide, this energy is then converted into mechanical energy as the water is released through large turbines that create electrical power through the use of generators. Barrages are essentially dams across the full width of a tidal estuary.

Dynamic tidal power (or DTP) is a theoretical technology that would exploit an interaction between potential and kinetic energies in tidal flows. It proposes that very long dams (30–50 km length) be built from coasts straight out into the sea or ocean, without enclosing an area. Tidal phase differences are introduced across the dam, leading to a significant water-level differential in shallow coastal seas – featuring strong coast-parallel oscillating tidal currents such as found in the UK, China, and Korea.

A new tidal energy design option is to construct circular retaining walls embedded with turbines that can capture the potential energy of tides. The created reservoirs are similar to those of tidal barrages, except that the location is artificial and does not contain a pre-existing ecosystem. The cancelled build of the Tidal Lagoon Swansea Bay in Wales, United Kingdom would have been the first tidal power station of this type.

Large scale tidal power plants

The first study of large scale tidal power plants was by the US Federal Power Commission in 1924 which if built would have been located in the northern border area of the US state of Maine and the southeastern border area of the Canadian province of New Brunswick, with various dams, powerhouses, and ship locks enclosing the Bay of Fundy and

Passamaquoddy Bay. In 1956, utility Nova Scotia Light and Power of Halifax commissioned a pair of studies into the feasibility of commercial tidal power development on the Nova Scotia side of the Bay of Fundy. The two studies, by Stone & Webster of Boston and by Montreal Engineering Company of Montreal independently concluded that millions of horsepower could be harnessed from Fundy but that development costs would be commercially prohibitive at that time.

A study was commissioned by the Canadian, Nova Scotian and New Brunswick governments (Reassessment of Fundy Tidal Power) to determine the potential for tidal barrages at Chignecto Bay and Minas Basin – at the end of the Fundy Bay estuary. There were three sites determined to be financially feasible: Shepody Bay (1550 MW), Cumberland Basin (1085 MW), and Cobequid Bay (3800 MW). These were never built despite their apparent feasibility in 1977.

The world's first marine energy test facility was established in 2003 to start the development of the wave and tidal energy industry in the UK. Based in Orkney, Scotland, the European Marine Energy Centre (EMEC) has supported the deployment of more wave and tidal energy devices than at any other single site in the world. EMEC provides a variety of test sites in real sea conditions. Its grid connected tidal test site is located at the Fall of Warness, off the island of Eday, in a narrow channel which concentrates the tide as it flows between the Atlantic Ocean and North Sea. This area has a very strong tidal current, which can travel up to 4 m/s (8 knots) in spring tides.

Current and future tidal power schemes include the following.
- The Rance tidal power plant built over a period of 6 years from 1960 to 1966 at La Rance, France. It has 240 MW installed capacity.
- 254 MW Sihwa Lake Tidal Power Plant in South Korea is the largest tidal power installation in the world. Construction was completed in 2011.
- The first tidal power site in North America is the Annapolis Royal Generating Station, Annapolis Royal, Nova Scotia, which opened in 1984 on an inlet of the Bay of Fundy. It has 20 MW installed capacity.
- A 1.2 MW SeaGen system became operational in late 2008 on Strangford Lough in Northern Ireland.
- The Scottish Government has approved plans for a 10 MW array of tidal stream generators near Islay, Scotland, costing 40 million pounds, and consisting of 10 turbines – enough to power over 5,000 homes. The

first turbine was expected to be in operation by 2013.
- The Indian state of Gujarat is planning to host South Asia's first commercial-scale tidal power station. The company Atlantis Resources planned to install a 50 MW tidal farm in the Gulf of Kutch on India's west coast, with construction started in 2012.
- Construction of a 320 MW tidal lagoon power plant outside the city of Swansea in the UK was granted planning permission in June 2015 and work was expected to start in 2016. Once completed, it will generate over 500 GWh of electricity per year, enough to power roughly 155,000 homes.
- The largest tidal energy project entitled MeyGen (398 MW) is currently in construction in the Pentland Firth in northern Scotland.

In terms of Global Warming Potential (i.e. carbon footprint), the impact of tidal power generation technologies ranges between 15 and 37g CO_2-eq/kWhe, with a median value of 23.8g CO_2-eq/kWhe. This is in line with the impact of other renewables like wind and solar power, and significantly better than fossil-based technologies.

Tidal energy has an expensive initial cost which may be one of the reasons tidal energy is not a popular source of renewable energy. It is important to realize that the methods for generating electricity from tidal energy use relatively new technology. It is projected that tidal power will be commercially profitable within 2020 with better technology and larger scales. Tidal energy is however still very early in the research process and the ability to reduce the price of tidal energy is an option. The cost-effectiveness depends on each site tidal generators are being placed. To figure out the cost-effectiveness they use the Gilbert ratio, which is the length of the barrage in metres to the annual energy production in kilowatt hours.

Tidal energy reliability
With tidal energy reliability, the expensive upfront cost of the generators will slowly be paid off. The success of a greatly simplified design, the orthogonal turbine offers considerable cost savings. As a result, the production period of each generating unit is reduced, lower metal consumption is needed and technical efficiency is greater. Scientific research has the capability to have a renewable resource like tidal energy that is affordable as well as profitable.

According to a report from the *World Energy Council and Bloomberg New Energy Finance*, electricity generated from the movements of the ocean costs 2 to 9 times as much as the highest average price for wind energy in Europe. Because these cost estimates only come from a handful of plants, however, it is hard to gauge how much these technologies could cost in the future.

The high cost comes largely from the extensive engineering work necessary to build the power plants, install them, and connect them to the power grid. Many companies have proposed technologies that might more affordably harness energy from waves or tides, but many are still undergoing testing and a clear leading technology hasn't emerged yet, says Alexis Gazzo, an Ernst & Young partner in France. The lack of developed supply chains for any one technology means that components are very expensive. Even at plants that are already built, the variability of tidal patterns can lower the efficiency of the turbines, according to a brief from the International Renewable Energy Association. Project planners also have to consider additional costs for maintenance and monitoring the plant's impact on the environment.

The U.K. passed on commissioning a tidal range power station near Cardiff, Wales, after determining it could have adverse effects on wildlife, in addition to finding it would take between 4 and 9 years to build at a cost of up to £34 billion. A study found that the barrage would cause even more water to flow into an estuary, altering habitats for birds and fish.

However, the U.K. is still pursuing other tidal projects. The country approved the MeyGen array off the Scottish coast. That array uses another design to generate power from the tides. Instead of being part of a barrage structure as in the Rance River plant, these windmill-like turbines are placed in an array underwater. The design looks like a submerged version of an offshore wind farm. The water's current moves the turbines, which generate electricity transmitted to the grid through an underwater cable. So far, the U.K. government and turbine maker Atlantis have secured £51 million in initial funding for the project, which is expected to add nearly 400 megawatts of generating capacity by the early 2020s.

Many of the prime spots for tidal or wave technologies are not near the grid, which means new undersea cables would be required. An ocean research centre in the Bay of Fundy, home of the biggest tides in the world, recently finished laying down 11 km of undersea cables to create the world's biggest transmission line for underwater turbines. The cables will carry enough electricity to power 20,000 homes at peak capacity.

Despite investments in tidal or wave power from the U.K. and other countries, the technologies have developed very slowly. Two manufacturers of wave power equipment, Oceanlinx and Wavebob, went out of business last year and Siemens recently sold its tidal power unit. It is still hard to gauge how much ocean-power technologies would really cost if implemented at scale.

13
Official viewpoints

"The physicist Leo Szilard once announced to his friend Hans Bethe that he was thinking of keeping a diary: 'I don't intend to publish, I am merely going to record the facts for the information of God.' 'Don't you think God knows the facts?' Bethe asked. 'Yes' said Szilard. 'He knows the facts, but he does not know THIS version of the facts'."

From Hans Christian von Baeyer, *Taming the Atom* (from the preface paragraph in *A Short History of Nearly Everything*, by Bill Bryson, A Black Swan Book, 2004)

Intergovernmental Panel on Climate Change (IPCC)

The Intergovernmental Panel on Climate Change (IPCC) is an intergovernmental body of the United Nations that is dedicated to providing the world with objective, scientific information relevant to understanding the scientific basis of the risk of human-induced climate change, its natural, political, and economic impacts and risks, and possible response options. *Wikipedia* has a very comprehensive summary of the IPCC since its inception but for a full description of the IPCC refer to the official documents issued by the IPCC.

The IPCC was established in 1988 by the World Meteorological Organization (WMO) and the United Nations Environment Programme (UNEP) and was later endorsed by the United Nations General Assembly. Membership is open to all members of the WMO and UN. The IPCC produces reports that contribute to the work of the United Nations Framework Convention on Climate Change (UNFCCC), the main international treaty on climate change. The objective of the UNFCCC is to "stabilize greenhouse gas concentrations in the atmosphere at a level that would prevent dangerous anthropogenic (human-induced) interference with the climate system".

It should be noted that the UNFCCC and the IPCC does not cover all aspects of the climate system and in particular does not, with few exceptions, cover the non-human induced causes of climate change such as the impact of the sun, oceans, and volcanoes.

The IPCC's (most recent 2015) Fifth Assessment Report was a critical scientific input into the UNFCCC's Paris Agreement in 2015. IPCC reports cover the "scientific, technical and socio-economic information relevant to understanding the scientific basis of risk of human-induced climate change, its potential impacts and options for adaptation and mitigation". The IPCC does not carry out original research, nor does it monitor climate or related phenomena itself. Rather, it assesses published literature, including peer-reviewed and non-peer-reviewed sources. However, the IPCC can be said to stimulate research in climate science. Chapters of IPCC reports often close with sections on limitations and knowledge or research gaps. The announcement of an IPCC special report can catalyse research activity in that area.

Thousands of scientists and other experts contribute on a voluntary

Official viewpoints 323

basis to writing and reviewing reports, which are then reviewed by governments. IPCC reports contain a "Summary for Policymakers", which is subject to line-by-line approval by delegates from all participating governments. Typically, this involves the governments of more than 120 countries. The IPCC provides an internationally accepted authority on climate change, producing reports that have the agreement of leading climate scientists and consensus from participating governments. The 2007 Nobel Peace Prize was shared between the IPCC and Al Gore.

Following the election of a new Bureau in 2015, the IPCC embarked on its sixth assessment cycle. Besides the Sixth Assessment Report, to be completed in 2022, the IPCC released the Special Report on Global Warming of 1.5°C in October 2018, released an update to its 2006 Guidelines for National Greenhouse Gas Inventories—the 2019 Refinement, and delivered two further special reports in 2019: the Special Report on Climate Change and Land (SRCCL), published online on 7 August 2019, and the Special Report on the Ocean and Cryosphere in a Changing Climate (SROCC), released on 25 September 2019. This makes the sixth assessment cycle the most ambitious in the IPCC's 30-year history. The IPCC also decided to prepare a special report on cities and climate change in the seventh assessment cycle and held a conference in March 2018 to stimulate research in this area.

Advisory Group on Greenhouse Gases

The IPCC developed from an international scientific body, the Advisory Group on Greenhouse Gases set up in 1986 to ensure adequate follow-up of the recommendations of the 1985 Villach Conference (where I was an invited participant) by the International Council of Scientific Unions, the United Nations Environment Programme (UNEP), and the World Meteorological Organization (WMO) to provide recommendations based on current research. This small group of scientists lacked the resources to cover the increasingly complex interdisciplinary nature of climate science. The United States Environmental Protection Agency and State Department wanted an international convention to agree restrictions on greenhouse gases, and the conservative Reagan Administration was concerned about unrestrained influence from independent scientists or from United Nations bodies including UNEP and the WMO. The U.S. government was the main force in forming the IPCC as an autonomous intergovernmental body in which scientists took part both as experts on the science and as official representatives of their governments, to produce reports which had the firm backing of all the leading scientists worldwide researching the topic. This then had to gain consensus agreement from every one of the participating governments. In this way, it was formed as a hybrid between a scientific body and an intergovernmental political organisation.

Principles Governing IPCC Work
The IPCC has adopted and published "Principles Governing IPCC Work", which states that the IPCC will assess:
- the risk of human-induced climate change,
- its potential impacts, and
- possible options for prevention.

This document also states that IPCC will do this work by assessing "on a comprehensive, objective, open and transparent basis the scientific, technical and socio-economic information relevant to understanding the scientific basis" of these topics. The Principles also state that "IPCC reports should be neutral with respect to policy, although they may need to deal objectively with scientific, technical and socio-economic factors relevant to the application of particular policies".

Korean economist Hoesung Lee has been the Chair of the IPCC since 8 October 2015, with the election of the new IPCC Bureau. Before this election, the IPCC was led by Vice Chair Ismail El Gizouli, who was designated acting Chair after the resignation of Rajendra K. Pachauri in February 2015. The previous Chairs were Rajendra K. Pachauri, elected in May 2002; Robert Watson in 1997; and Bert Bolin in 1988. The Chair is assisted by an elected bureau including Vice Chairs and working group Co Chairs, and by a secretariat. The Panel itself is composed of representatives appointed by governments. Participation of delegates with appropriate expertise is encouraged. Plenary sessions of the IPCC and IPCC Working Groups are held at the level of government representatives.

Non-Governmental and Intergovernmental Organizations admitted as observer organizations may also attend. Sessions of the Panel, IPCC Bureau, workshops, expert and lead authors meetings are by invitation only. About 500 people from 130 countries attended the 48th Session of the Panel in Incheon, Republic of Korea, in October 2018, including 290 government officials and 60 representatives of observer organizations. The opening ceremonies of sessions of the Panel and of Lead Author Meetings are open to media, but otherwise IPCC meetings are closed.

There are several major groups:
- IPCC Panel: Meets in plenary session about once a year. It controls the organization's structure, procedures, and work programme, and accepts and approves IPCC reports. The Panel is the IPCC corporate entity.
- Working Groups: Each has two Co Chairs, one from the developed and one from the developing world, and a technical support unit. Sessions of the Working Group approve the Summary for Policymakers of special reports and working group contributions to an assessment report. Each Working Group has a Bureau comprising its Co Chairs and Vice Chairs, who are also members of the IPCC Bureau.
  - Working Group I: Assesses scientific aspects of the climate system and climate change.
  - Working Group II: Assesses vulnerability of socio-economic and natural systems to climate change, consequences, and adaptation options.
  - Working Group III: Assesses options for limiting greenhouse gas emissions and otherwise mitigating climate change.
- Task Force on National Greenhouse Gas Inventories.

The IPCC receives funding through the IPCC Trust Fund, established in 1989 by the United Nations Environment Programme (UNEP) and the World Meteorological Organization (WMO). Costs of the Secretary and of housing the secretariat are provided by the WMO, while UNEP meets the cost of the Deputy Secretary. Annual cash contributions to the Trust Fund are made by the WMO, by UNEP, and by IPCC Members. Payments and their size are voluntary. The Panel is responsible for considering and adopting by consensus the annual budget. The organization is required to comply with the Financial Regulations and Rules of the WMO.

Assessment reports

The IPCC has published five comprehensive assessment reports reviewing the latest climate science, as well as a number of special reports on particular topics. These reports are prepared by teams of relevant researchers selected by the Bureau from government nominations. Expert reviewers from a wide range of governments, IPCC observer organizations and other organizations are invited at different stages to comment on various aspects of the drafts.

The IPCC published its First Assessment Report (FAR) in 1990, a supplementary report in 1992, a Second Assessment Report (SAR) in

1995, a Third Assessment Report (TAR) in 2001, a Fourth Assessment Report (AR4) in 2007 and a Fifth Assessment Report (AR5) in 2014. The IPCC is currently preparing the Sixth Assessment Report (AR6), which will be completed in 2022. Each assessment report is in three volumes, corresponding to Working Groups I, II, and III. It is completed by a synthesis report that integrates the working group contributions and any special reports produced in that assessment cycle.

Scope and preparation of the reports
The IPCC does not carry out research nor does it monitor climate related data. Lead authors of IPCC reports assess the available information about climate change based on published sources. According to IPCC guidelines, authors should give priority to peer-reviewed sources. Authors may refer to non-peer-reviewed sources (the "grey literature"), provided that they are of sufficient quality. Examples of non-peer-reviewed sources include model results, reports from government agencies and non-governmental organizations, and industry journals. Each subsequent IPCC report notes areas where the science has improved since the previous report and also notes areas where further research is required.

There are generally three stages in the review process:
- Expert review (6–8 weeks)
- Government/expert review
- Government review of:
  - Summaries for Policymakers
  - Overview Chapters
  - Synthesis Report

Review comments are in an open archive for at least five years.

First assessment report
The IPCC First Assessment Report (FAR) was completed in 1990, and served as the basis of the UNFCCC.

The executive summary of the WG I Summary for Policymakers report says they are certain that emissions resulting from human activities are substantially increasing the atmospheric concentrations of the greenhouse gases, resulting on average in an additional warming of the Earth's surface. They calculate with confidence that CO_2 has been responsible for over half the enhanced greenhouse effect. They predict that under a "business as usual" (BAU) scenario, global mean temperature will increase by about 0.3 °C per decade during the 21st century. They judge that global mean surface air temperature has increased by 0.3 to 0.6

°C over the last 100 years, broadly consistent with prediction of climate models, but also of the same magnitude as natural climate variability. The unequivocal detection of the enhanced greenhouse effect is not likely for a decade or more.

Second assessment report
Climate Change 1995, the IPCC Second Assessment Report (SAR), was completed in 1996. It is split into four parts:
- A synthesis to help interpret UNFCCC article 2.
- *The Science of Climate Change* (WG I)
- *Impacts, Adaptations and Mitigation of Climate Change* (WG II)
- *Economic and Social Dimensions of Climate Change* (WG III)

Each of the last three parts was completed by a separate Working Group (WG), and each has a Summary for Policymakers (SPM) that represents a consensus of national representatives. The SPM of the WG I report contains headings:

1. Greenhouse gas concentrations have continued to increase.
2. Anthropogenic aerosols tend to produce negative radiative forcings.
3. Climate has changed over the past century (air temperature has increased by between 0.3 and 0.6°C since the late 19th century; this estimate has not significantly changed since the 1990 report).
4. The balance of evidence suggests a discernible human influence on global climate (considerable progress since the 1990 report in distinguishing between natural and anthropogenic influences on climate, because of including aerosols, coupled models, and pattern-based studies).
5. Climate is expected to continue to change in the future (increasing realism of simulations increases confidence; important uncertainties remain but are taken into account in the range of model projections).
6. There are still many uncertainties (estimates of future emissions and biogeochemical cycling; models; instrument data for model testing, assessment of variability, and detection studies).

Third assessment report
The Third Assessment Report (TAR) was completed in 2001 and consists of four reports, three of them from its Working Groups:
- Working Group I: The Scientific Basis
- Working Group II: Impacts, Adaptation and Vulnerability
- Working Group III: Mitigation
- Synthesis Report

A number of the TAR's conclusions are given quantitative estimates of how probable it is that they are correct, e.g., greater than 66% probability of being correct. These are "Bayesian" probabilities, which are based on an expert assessment of all the available evidence.

"Robust findings" of the TAR Synthesis Report include:

- "Observations show Earth's surface is warming. Globally, 1990s very likely warmest decade in instrumental record". Atmospheric concentrations of anthropogenic (i.e., human-emitted) greenhouse gases have increased substantially.
- Since the mid-20th century, most of the observed warming is "likely" (greater than 66% probability, based on expert judgement) due to human activities.
- Projections based on the *Special Report on Emissions Scenarios* suggest warming over the 21st century at a more rapid rate than that experienced for at least the last 10,000 years.
- "Projected climate change will have beneficial and adverse effects on both environmental and socio-economic systems, but the larger the changes and the rate of change in climate, the more the adverse effects predominate."
- "Ecosystems and species are vulnerable to climate change and other stresses (as illustrated by observed impacts of recent regional temperature changes) and some will be irreversibly damaged or lost".
- "Greenhouse gas emission reduction (mitigation) actions would lessen the pressures on natural and human systems from climate change".
- "Adaptation (to the effects of climate change) has the potential to reduce adverse effects of climate change and can often produce immediate ancillary benefits, but will not prevent all damages". An example of adaptation to climate change is building levees in response to sea level rise.

Comments on the TAR

IPCC author Richard Lindzen has made a number of criticisms of the TAR. Among his criticisms, Lindzen has stated that the WGI Summary for Policymakers (SPM) does not faithfully summarize the full WGI report. For example, Lindzen states that the SPM understates the uncertainty associated with climate models. John Houghton, who was a Co Chair of TAR WGI, has responded to Lindzen's criticisms of the SPM. Houghton has stressed that the SPM is agreed upon by delegates from many of the world's governments, and that any changes to the SPM must be supported by scientific evidence. IPCC author Kevin Trenberth has also commented on the WGI SPM. Trenberth has stated that during the drafting of the WGI SPM, some government delegations attempted to "blunt, and perhaps obfuscate, the messages in the report". However, Trenberth concludes that the SPM is a "reasonably balanced summary".

US NRC (2001) concluded that the WGI SPM and Technical Summary are "consistent" with the full WGI report. US NRC (2001) stated:

"The full WGI report is adequately summarized in the Technical Summary. The full WGI report and its Technical Summary are not specifically directed at policy. The Summary for Policymakers reflects less emphasis on communicating the basis for uncertainty and a stronger emphasis on areas of major concern associated with human-induced climate change. This change in emphasis appears to be the result of a summary process in which scientists work with policy makers on the document. Written responses from U.S. coordinating and lead scientific authors to the committee indicate, however, that (a) no changes were made without the consent of the convening lead authors (this group represents a fraction of the lead and contributing authors) and (b) most changes that did occur lacked significant impact."

Fourth assessment report
The Fourth Assessment Report (AR4) was published in 2007. Like previous assessment reports, it consists of four reports:
- Working Group I: The Physical Science Basis
- Working Group II: Impacts, Adaptation and Vulnerability
- Working Group III: Mitigation
- Synthesis Report

People from over 130 countries contributed to the IPCC Fourth Assessment Report, which took 6 years to produce. Contributors to AR4 included more than 2500 scientific expert reviewers, more than 800 contributing authors, and more than 450 lead authors.

"Robust findings" of the Synthesis report include:
- "Warming of the climate system is unequivocal, as is now evident from observations of increases in global average air and ocean temperatures, widespread melting of snow and ice and rising global average sea level".
- Most of the global average warming over the past 50 years is "very likely" (greater than 90% probability, based on expert judgement) due to human activities.
- "Impacts (of climate change) will very likely increase due to increased frequencies and intensities of some extreme weather events".

- "Anthropogenic warming and sea level rise would continue for centuries even if GHG emissions were to be reduced sufficiently for GHG concentrations to stabilise, due to the time scales associated with climate processes and feedbacks". Stabilization of atmospheric greenhouse gas concentrations is discussed in climate change mitigation.
- "Some planned adaptation (of human activities) is occurring now; more extensive adaptation is required to reduce vulnerability to climate change".
- "Unmitigated climate change would, in the long term, be likely to exceed the capacity of natural, managed and human systems to adapt".
- "Many impacts (of climate change) can be reduced, delayed or avoided by mitigation".

Fifth assessment report
The IPCC's Fifth Assessment Report (AR5) was completed in 2014. AR5 followed the same general format as of AR4, with three Working Group reports and a Synthesis report.
Conclusions of AR5 are summarized below:
Working Group I
- "Warming of the climate system is unequivocal, and since the 1950s, many of the observed changes are unprecedented over decades to millennia".
- "Atmospheric concentrations of carbon dioxide, methane, and nitrous oxide have increased to levels unprecedented in at least the last 800,000 years".
- Human influence on the climate system is clear. It is extremely likely (95-100% probability) that human influence was the dominant cause of global warming between 1951–2010.

Working Group II
- "Increasing magnitudes of (global) warming increase the likelihood of severe, pervasive, and irreversible impacts".
- "A first step towards adaptation to future climate change is reducing vulnerability and exposure to present climate variability".
- "The overall risks of climate change impacts can be reduced by limiting the rate and magnitude of climate change".

Working Group III
- Without new policies to mitigate climate change, projections suggest an increase in global mean temperature in 2100 of 3.7°C to 4.8°C, relative to pre-industrial levels (median values; the range is 2.5°C to 7.8°C including climate uncertainty).

- The current trajectory of global greenhouse gas emissions is not consistent with limiting global warming to below 1.5 °C or 2°C, relative to pre-industrial levels. Pledges made as part of the Cancún Agreements are broadly consistent with cost-effective scenarios that give a "likely" chance (66-100% probability) of limiting global warming (in 2100) to below 3°C, relative to pre-industrial levels.

Special Reports on Specific Topics

In addition to climate assessment reports, the IPCC publishes Special Reports on specific topics. The preparation and approval process for all IPCC Special Reports follows the same procedures as for IPCC Assessment Reports. In the year 2011 two IPCC Special Reports were finalized. The Special Report on Renewable Energy Sources and Climate Change Mitigation (SRREN) and the Special Report on Managing Risks of Extreme Events and Disasters to Advance Climate Change Adaptation (SREX). Both Special Reports were requested by governments. Recently additional special reports have been prepared.
- Special Report on Emissions Scenarios (SRES)
- Special Report on renewable energy sources and climate change mitigation (SRREN)
- Special Report on managing the risks of extreme events and disasters to advance climate change adaptation (SREX)
- Special Report on Global Warming of 1.5 °C (SR15)
- Special Report on climate change and land (SRCCL)
- Special Report on the Ocean and Cryosphere in a Changing Climate (SROCC)

Criticisms of the IPCC

There is widespread support for the IPCC in the scientific community, which is reflected in publications by other scientific bodies and experts. However, criticisms of the IPCC have been made. Since 2010 the IPCC has come under yet unparalleled public and political scrutiny. The global IPCC consensus approach has been challenged internally and externally, for example, during the 2009 Climatic Research Unit email controversy ("Climategate"). It is contested by some as an information monopoly with results for both the quality and the impact of the IPCC work as such. This includes the projected date of melting of Himalayan glaciers. A paragraph in the 2007 Working Group II report (*"Impacts, Adaptation and Vulnerability"*, chapter 10) included a projection that Himalayan glaciers could disappear by 2035.

"Glaciers in the Himalaya are receding faster than in any other part of the world and, if the present rate continues, the likelihood of them disappearing by the year 2035 and perhaps sooner is very high if the Earth keeps warming at the current rate. Its total area will likely shrink from the present 500,000 to 100,000 km² by the year 2035."

This projection was not included in the final summary for policymakers. The IPCC has since acknowledged that the date is incorrect, while reaffirming that the conclusion in the final summary was robust. They expressed regret for "the poor application of well-established IPCC procedures in this instance". The date of 2035 has been correctly quoted by the IPCC from the WWF report, which has misquoted its own source, an ICSI report "Variations of Snow and Ice in the past and at present on a Global and Regional Scale".

Former IPCC chairman Robert Watson, regarding the Himalayan glaciers estimation, said that "The mistakes all appear to have gone in the direction of making it seem like climate change is more serious by overstating the impact. That is worrying. The IPCC needs to look at this trend in the errors and ask why it happened". Martin Parry, a climate expert who had been Co Chair of the IPCC working group II, said that "What began with a single unfortunate error over Himalayan glaciers has become a clamour without substance" and the IPCC had investigated the other alleged mistakes, which were "generally unfounded and also marginal to the assessment".

Emphasis of the "hockey stick" graph

The third assessment report (TAR) prominently featured a graph labelled "Millennial Northern Hemisphere temperature reconstruction" based on a 1999 paper by Michael E. Mann, Raymond S. Bradley and Malcolm K. Hughes (MBH99), which has been referred to as the "hockey stick graph". This graph extended the similar graph (Figure 3.20 from the IPCC Second Assessment Report of 1995), and differed from a schematic in the first assessment report that lacked temperature units, but appeared to depict larger global temperature variations over the past 1000 years, and higher temperatures during the Medieval Warm Period than the mid 20th century. The schematic was not an actual plot of data, and was based on a diagram of temperatures in central England, with temperatures increased on the basis of documentary evidence of Medieval vineyards in England. Even with this increase, the maximum it showed for the Medieval Warm Period did not reach temperatures recorded in central England in 2007.

These studies were widely presented as demonstrating that the current warming period is exceptional in comparison to temperatures between 1000 and 1900, and the MBH99 based graph featured in publicity. Even at the draft stage, this finding was disputed by contrarians: in May 2000 Fred Singer's Science and Environmental Policy Project held a press event on Capitol Hill, Washington, D.C., featuring comments on the graph. Wibjörn Karlén and Singer argued against the graph at a United States Senate Committee on Commerce, Science and Transportation hearing on 18 July 2000. Contrarian John Lawrence Daly featured a modified version of the IPCC 1990 schematic, which he mis-identified as appearing in the IPCC 1995 report, and argued that "Overturning its own previous view in the 1995 report, the IPCC presented the 'Hockey Stick' as the new orthodoxy with hardly an apology or explanation for the abrupt U-turn since its 1995 report".

Criticism of the MBH99 reconstruction in a review paper, which was quickly discredited in the Soon and Baliunas controversy, was picked up by the Bush administration, and a Senate speech by US Republican Senator James Inhofe alleged that "man-made global warming is the greatest hoax ever perpetrated on the American people". The data and methodology used to produce the "hockey stick graph" was criticized in papers by Stephen McIntyre and Ross McKitrick, and in turn the criticisms in these papers were examined by other studies and comprehensively refuted by Wahl & Ammann 2007, which showed errors in the methods used by McIntyre and McKitrick.

On 23 June 2005, Rep. Joe Barton, chairman of the House Committee on Energy and Commerce wrote joint letters with Ed Whitfield, chairman of the Subcommittee on Oversight and Investigations demanding full records on climate research, as well as personal information about their finances and careers, from Mann, Bradley and Hughes. Sherwood Boehlert, chairman of the House Science Committee, said this was a "misguided and illegitimate investigation" apparently aimed at intimidating scientists, and at his request the U.S. National Academy of Sciences arranged for its National Research Council to set up a special investigation. The National Research Council's report agreed that there were some statistical failings, but these had little effect on the graph, which was generally correct. In a 2006 letter to *Nature*, Mann, Bradley, and Hughes pointed out that their original article had said that "more widespread high-resolution data are needed before more confident conclusions can be reached" and that the uncertainties were "the point of the article".

The IPCC Fourth Assessment Report (AR4) published in 2007 featured a graph showing 12 proxy based temperature reconstructions, including the three highlighted in the 2001 Third Assessment Report (TAR); Mann, Bradley & Hughes 1999 as before. Jones et al. 1998 and Briffa 2000 had both been calibrated by newer studies. In addition, analysis of the Medieval Warm Period cited reconstructions by Crowley & Lowery 2000 (as cited in the TAR) and Osborn & Briffa 2006. Ten of these 14 reconstructions covered 1,000 years or longer. Most reconstructions shared some data series, particularly tree ring data, but newer reconstructions used additional data and covered a wider area, using a variety of statistical methods. The section discussed the divergence problem affecting certain tree ring data.

Conservative nature of IPCC reports
Some critics, on the other hand, have contended that the IPCC reports tend to be conservative by consistently underestimating the pace and impacts of global warming, and report only the "lowest common denominator" findings.

On the eve of the publication of IPCC's Fourth Assessment Report in 2007 another study was published suggesting that temperatures and sea levels have been rising at or above the maximum rates proposed during IPCC's 2001 Third Assessment Report. The study compared IPCC 2001 projections on temperature and sea level change with observations. Over the six years studied, the actual temperature rise was near the top end of the range given by IPCC's 2001 projection, and the actual sea level rise was above the top of the range of the IPCC projection.

Another example of scientific research which suggests that previous estimates by the IPCC, far from overstating dangers and risks, have actually understated them is a study on projected rises in sea levels. When the researchers' analysis was "applied to the possible scenarios outlined by the IPCC, the researchers found that in 2100 sea levels would be 0.5–1.4 m above 1990 levels. These values are much greater than the 9–88 cm as projected by the IPCC itself in its Third Assessment Report, published in 2001". This may have been due, in part, to the expanding human understanding of climate.

Greg Holland from the National Center for Atmospheric Research, who reviewed a multi-meter sea level rise study by Jim Hansen, noted *"There is no doubt that the sea level rise, within the IPCC, is a very conservative number, so the truth lies somewhere between IPCC and*

Hansen".

In reporting criticism by some scientists that IPCC's then-impending January 2007 report understates certain risks, particularly sea level rises, an *Associated Press* story quoted Stefan Rahmstorf, professor of physics and oceanography at Potsdam University as saying "In a way, it is one of the strengths of the IPCC to be very conservative and cautious and not overstate any climate change risk".

In his December 2006 book, *Hell and High Water: Global Warming*, and in an interview on *Fox News* on 31 January 2007, energy expert Joseph Romm noted that the IPCC Fourth Assessment Report is already out of date and omits recent observations and factors contributing to global warming, such as the release of greenhouse gases from thawing tundra.

Political influence on the IPCC has been documented by the release of a memo by ExxonMobil to the Bush administration, and its effects on the IPCC's leadership. The memo led to strong Bush administration lobbying, evidently at the behest of ExxonMobil, to oust Robert Watson, a climate scientist, from the IPCC chairmanship, and to have him replaced by Pachauri, who was seen at the time as more mild-mannered and industry-friendly.

IPCC processes
Michael Oppenheimer, a long-time participant in the IPCC and coordinating lead author of the Fifth Assessment Report conceded in *Science Magazine's State of the Planet 2008–2009* some limitations of the IPCC consensus approach and asks for concurring, smaller assessments of special problems instead of the large scale approach as in the previous IPCC assessment reports. It has become more important to provide a broader exploration of uncertainties. Others see as well mixed blessings of the drive for consensus within the IPCC process and ask to include dissenting or minority positions or to improve statements about uncertainties.

The IPCC process on climate change and its efficiency and success has been compared with dealings with other environmental challenges (compare Ozone depletion and global warming). In case of the Ozone depletion, global regulation based on the Montreal Protocol has been successful. In case of Climate Change, the Kyoto Protocol failed. The Ozone case was used to assess the efficiency of the IPCC process. The lockstep situation of the IPCC is having built a broad science consensus while states and governments still follow different, if not opposing goals. The underlying linear model of policy-making of *the more knowledge we have, the better the political response will be* is being doubted.

According to Sheldon Ungar's comparison with global warming, the actors in the Ozone depletion case had a better understanding of scientific ignorance and uncertainties (Ungar, 2003). The Ozone case communicated to lay persons "with easy-to-understand bridging metaphors derived from the popular culture" and related to "immediate risks with everyday relevance", while the public opinion on climate change sees no imminent danger. The stepwise mitigation of the Ozone layer challenge was based as well on successfully reducing regional burden sharing conflicts. In case of the IPCC conclusions and the failure of the Kyoto Protocol, varying regional cost-benefit analysis and burden-sharing conflicts with regard to the distribution of emission reductions remain an unsolved problem. In the UK, a report for a House of Lords committee asked to urge the IPCC to involve better assessments of costs and benefits of climate change, but the Stern Review, ordered by the UK government, made a stronger argument in favour to combat human-made climate change.

Outdatedness of reports

Since the IPCC does not carry out its own research, it operates on the basis of scientific papers and independently documented results from other scientific bodies, and its schedule for producing reports requires a deadline for submissions prior to the report's final release. In principle, this means that any significant new evidence or events that change our understanding of climate science between this deadline and publication of an IPCC report cannot be included. In an area of science where our scientific understanding is rapidly changing, this has been raised as a serious shortcoming in a body which is widely regarded as the ultimate authority on the science. However, there has generally been a steady evolution of key findings and levels of scientific confidence from one assessment report to the next.

The submission deadlines for the Fourth Assessment Report (AR4) differed for the reports of each Working Group. Deadlines for the Working Group I report were adjusted during the drafting and review process in order to ensure that reviewers had access to unpublished material being cited by the authors. The final deadline for cited publications was 24 July 2006 The final WG I report was released on 30 April 2007 and the final AR4 Synthesis Report was released on 17 November 2007. Rajendra

Pachauri, the IPCC Chair, admitted at the launch of this report that since the IPCC began work on it, scientists have recorded "much stronger trends in climate change", like the unforeseen dramatic melting of polar ice in the summer of 2007, and added, "that means you better start with intervention much earlier".

Burden on participating scientists
Scientists who participate in the IPCC assessment process do so without any compensation other than the normal salaries they receive from their home institutions. The process is labour-intensive, diverting time and resources from participating scientists' research programmes. Concerns have been raised that the large uncompensated time commitment and disruption to their own research may discourage qualified scientists from participating.

Reframing of scientific research
The 2018 report *What Lies Beneath* by the Breakthrough - National Centre for Climate Restoration, with contributions from Kevin Anderson, James Hansen, Michael E. Mann, Michael Oppenheimer, Naomi Oreskes, Stefan Rahmstorf, Eric Rignot, Hans Joachim Schellnhuber, Kevin Trenberth, and others, urges the IPCC, the wider UNFCCC negotiations, and national policy makers to change their approach. The authors note, "We urgently require a reframing of scientific research within an existential risk-management framework".

InterAcademy Council review
In March 2010, at the invitation of the United Nations Secretary-General and the chair of the IPCC, the InterAcademy Council (IAC) was asked to review the IPCC's processes for developing its reports. The IAC panel, chaired by Harold Tafler Shapiro, convened on 14 May 2010 and released its report on 1 September 2010.

The IAC found that, "The IPCC assessment process has been successful overall". The panel, however, made seven formal recommendations for improving the IPCC's assessment process, including:
1. establish an executive committee;
2. elect an executive director whose term would only last for one assessment;
3. encourage review editors to ensure that all reviewer comments are adequately considered and genuine controversies are adequately reflected in the assessment reports;

4. adopt a better process for responding to reviewer comments;
5. working groups should use a qualitative level-of-understanding scale in the Summary for Policy Makers and Technical Summary;
6. "Quantitative probabilities (as in the likelihood scale) should be used to describe the probability of well-defined outcomes only when there is sufficient evidence"; and
7. implement a communications plan that emphasizes transparency and establish guidelines for who can speak on behalf of the organization.

The panel also advised that the IPCC avoid appearing to advocate specific policies in response to its scientific conclusions. Commenting on the IAC report, *Nature News* noted that "The proposals were met with a largely favourable response from climate researchers who are eager to move on after the media scandals and credibility challenges that have rocked the United Nations body during the past nine months.

Endorsements of the IPCC
Various scientific bodies have issued official statements endorsing and concurring with the findings of the IPCC.
- Joint science academies' statement of 2001. "The work of the Intergovernmental Panel on Climate Change (IPCC) represents the consensus of the international scientific community on climate change science. We recognise IPCC as the world's most reliable source of information on climate change and its causes, and we endorse its method of achieving this consensus".
- Canadian Foundation for Climate and Atmospheric Sciences. "We concur with the climate science assessment of the Intergovernmental Panel on Climate Change (IPCC) in 2001 ... We endorse the conclusions of the IPCC assessment...".
- Canadian Meteorological and Oceanographic Society. "CMOS endorses the process of periodic climate science assessment carried out by the Intergovernmental Panel on Climate Change and supports the conclusion, in its Third Assessment Report, which states that the balance of evidence suggests a discernible human influence on global climate".
- European Geosciences Union. "The Intergovernmental Panel on Climate Change is the main representative of the global scientific community. The IPCC third assessment report represents the state-of-the-art of climate science supported by the major science academies

around the world and by the vast majority of scientific researchers and investigations as documented by the peer-reviewed scientific literature".
- International Council for Science (ICSU). "...the IPCC 4th Assessment Report represents the most comprehensive international scientific assessment ever conducted. This assessment reflects the current collective knowledge on the climate system, its evolution to date, and its anticipated future development".
- National Oceanic and Atmospheric Administration (USA). "Internationally, the Intergovernmental Panel on Climate Change (IPCC)... is the most senior and authoritative body providing scientific advice to global policy makers".
- United States National Research Council. "The IPCC Third Assessment Report conclusion that most of the observed warming of the last 50 years is likely to have been due to the increase in greenhouse gas concentrations accurately reflects the current thinking of the scientific community on this issue".
- Network of African Science Academies. "The IPCC should be congratulated for the contribution it has made to public understanding of the nexus that exists between energy, climate and sustainability".
- Royal Meteorological Society, in response to the release of the Fourth Assessment Report, referred to the IPCC as "The world's best climate scientists".
- Stratigraphy Commission of the Geological Society of London. "The most authoritative assessment of climate change in the near future is provided by the Inter-Governmental Panel for Climate Change".

As previously noted, the UNFCCC and the IPCC does not cover all aspects of the climate system and in particular does not, with few exceptions, cover the non-human induced causes of climate change such as the impact of the sun, oceans, and volcanoes. Time will tell whether this "overemphasis on the role of greenhouses gases" on the climate system is justified.

World Climate Programme

The First World Climate Conference was held on 12-23 February 1979 in Geneva and sponsored by the WMO. It was one of the first major international meetings on climate change. Essentially a scientific conference, it was attended by scientists from a wide range of disciplines. I was one was of those who was invited and I Co-chaired several of the sessions

The Declaration of the Conference called for the urgent development of a common strategy for a greater understanding of the climate system and a rational use of climate information, and proposed the establishment of the World Climate Programme (WCP). Consequently, the World Meteorological Congress, at its Eighth Session in 1979, established WCP as an authoritative international scientific programme with goals to improve understanding of the climate system and to apply that understanding for the benefit of societies coping with climate variability and change.

The four main objectives adopted in 1979 for the WCP were to:
- Determine the physical basis of the climate system that would allow increasingly skilful climate forecasts;
- Develop evermore useful applications of climate information benefitting economic efficiency, the human health of communities, food production and the prudent use of water resources;
- Determine socio-economic impacts and national vulnerabilities to climate variations and change; and
- Develop and maintain an essential global observing system fully capable of supporting the other three objectives.

WCP was established as an interagency, interdisciplinary effort, with WMO, ICSU and United Nations Environment Programme (UNEP) initially as the co-sponsors. When established it comprised of four components:
1. The World Climate Data Programme (WCDP)
2. The World Climate Applications Programme (WCAP)
3. The World Climate Impacts Programme (WCIP)
4. The World Climate Research programme (WCRP)

Leadership of the individual components was assigned to agencies according to their primary mandates. WMO took lead responsibility for

WCDP and WCAP, and UNEP for WCIP. WCRP was co-sponsored by the WMO and ICSU until 1993, when Intergovernmental Oceanographic Commission (IOC) of UNESCO also joined the sponsorship. After the Second World Climate Conference in 1991, World Meteorological Congress, at its Eleventh Session, reoriented the four components and renamed them as follows:
1. World Climate Data and Monitoring Programme (WCDMP)
2. World Climate Applications and Services Programme (WCASP)
3. World Climate Impact Assessment and Response Strategies Programme (WCIRP)
4. World Climate Research Programme (WCRP)

The contributions of the WCP through these four components can be primarily framed under following core areas:
1. Climate observations, monitoring and data management
2. Operational climate information, prediction and analysis systems including user liaison
3. World Climate Programme Impact assessment and response systems
4. Climate research, modelling and tools

WCP, along with WMO's co-sponsored programmes including the Intergovernmental Panel on Climate Change (IPCC) and the Global Climate Observing System (GCOS), have constituted the framework for WMO's climate activities.

Following the establishment of the Global Framework for Climate Services (GFCS) as an overarching outcome of World Climate Conference-3 held in 2009, the World Meteorological Congress, at its Sixteenth Session in 2011, considered the need for restructuring the WCP. Congress agreed to the request of UNEP for the formal closure of WCIRP component of WCP. In order to optimally support the implementation and operation of the various components of GFCS, Congress decided that the new WCP would include GCOS, WCRP and a new World Climate Services Programme (WCSP), merging the existing activities under WCDMP, WCASP including its Climate Information and Prediction Services (CLIPS) project.

Taking note of UNEP's request to replace WCIRP with their new Programme of Research on Climate Change Vulnerability, Impacts and Adaptation (PROVIA), Congress authorized WMO Executive Council to assess its scope, governance structure, funding arrangements, priorities vis-à-vis its relation with GFCS, and make appropriate decisions.

Given the growing awareness about the climate sensitivity of society across a wide range of socio-economic sectors, and increased focus on the need for adaptation and risk management that is implemented at local level and requires climate information and services available at global to regional, national and local scales, the objectives of the refocused WCP are:
- To improve the understanding of climate processes for determining the predictability of climate, including its variability and change, identifying the extent of human influence on climate and developing the capability for climate prediction and projection;
- To promote comprehensive observation of the global climate system and facilitate the effective collection and management of climate data and monitoring, including the detection and assessment of climate variability and changes from global to local scales;
- To enhance and promote the availability of and access to user-targeted climate services, especially prediction, by providing an international framework and establishing the operational elements of production and delivery systems for climate services;
- To foster the effective application of climate knowledge and information for the better management of the risks of climate variability and change into planning, policy and practice and the provision of the required climate services;
- To promote capacity development, particularly in developing and least developed countries, to enable them to contribute to the operation of GFCS and at the same time benefit from it.

The current (2020) components of this restructuring are as follows:

The World Climate Research Programme (WCRP)
The objective of WCRP is to have "a better understanding of the climate system and the causes of climate variability and change" and "to determine the predictability of climate; and to determine the effect of human activities on climate". In practice, the programme aims to foster initiatives in climate research which require or benefit from international coordination and which are unlikely to emerge from national efforts alone. The programme does not fund climate research directly, but may at times exchange views with research funding agencies on global research priorities.

The largest group of contributors to WCRP are several thousands of climate scientists from around the world who offer their expertise and time as volunteers to, for example, help organize workshops in key areas of research, lay out avenues for future research in white paper articles, and serve on WCRP science or advisory boards. Official scientific guidance for the programme is provided by a Joint Scientific Committee (JSC) consisting of 18 volunteer scientists selected by mutual agreement between the three sponsoring organizations. Everyday operations are supported by a secretariat of around 8 full-time staff, hosted by the World Meteorological Organization in Geneva.

WCRP's largest activities are its four "Core Projects" (called SPARC, CLIVAR, CliC, and GEWEX), which support climate research on the global atmosphere, oceans, the cryosphere, and the land surface (together constituting the Earth's physical climate system) as well as interactions and exchanges between them. Each Core Project again has a structure similar to that of WCRP itself, namely contributing scientists, a scientific steering group, and a secretariat ("international project office") hosted by individual countries.

The programme further maintains topical working groups and advisory councils on climate data, climate modelling, subseasonal-to-decadal climate prediction, and regional climate modelling. Additional "Grand Challenges" target specific questions of societal interest within climate science.

One particular output by a WCRP task team is the Coupled Model Intercomparison Project, which standardizes and coordinates regular comparisons of the world's climate models and which provides an important basis for the IPCC Assessment Reports' climate projections.

Global Climate Observing System

The Global Climate Observing System (GCOS) is a WMO-led co-sponsored programme of WMO, the IOC of UNESCO, UNEP and ICSU. The GCOS is built on existing operational and scientific observing, data management and information distribution systems. It is based upon an improved World Weather Watch Global Observing System, the Global Ocean Observing System, the Global Terrestrial Observing System, the WMO global observing systems and the maintenance and enhancement of programmes monitoring other key components of the climate system, such as the distribution of important atmospheric constituents (including the Global Atmosphere Watch).

The vision of the GCOS programme is that all users have access to the climate observations, data records and information which they require to address pressing climate-related concerns. GCOS users include individuals, national and international organizations, institutions and agencies. The role of GCOS is to work with partners to ensure the sustained provision of reliable physical, chemical and biological observations and data records for the total climate system – across the atmospheric, oceanic and terrestrial domains, including hydrological and carbon cycles and the cryosphere.

World Climate Services Programme
The scope of World Climate Services Programme WCSP spans across four inter-related areas:
- Climate data and analysis;
- Climate monitoring, watch and prediction;
- Climate system operation and infrastructure;
- Climate adaptation and risk management;

thereby serving as the Climate Services Information System and a part of the User Interface Platform components of the GFCS. These areas are implemented in two main streams:
- Climate Data and Monitoring
- Climate Applications and Services

WCSP contributes to improve the availability and access to reliable data, advancement of the knowledge in the area of climate data management and climate analysis, definition of the technical and scientific standards, and development of activities to support them in countries. Climate data management will include data rescue, development and coordination of a global climate data management system compatible with the WMO Information System (WIS).

The Global Programme of Research on Climate Change Vulnerability, Impacts and Adaptation (PROVIA)
The Global Programme of Research on Climate Change Vulnerability, Impacts and Adaptation (PROVIA) represents an interface between the research community and decision makers and other stakeholders to improve policy-relevant research on vulnerability, impacts and adaptation (VIA), allowing scientists to coordinate and facilitate the dissemination and practical application of their research.

PROVIA helps the international community of practice share practical experiences and research findings by improving the availability and accessibility of knowledge to the people that need it most. PROVIA aims to do so together with collaborative partners, knowledge networks, and the larger VIA community, by identifying research needs and gaps. It helps the scientific community to mobilize and communicate the growing knowledge-based on VIA so that governments and other main stakeholders are able to solicit scientific knowledge into their decision making processes.

The Paris Climate Agreement

The Paris Agreement builds upon the *UN Convention on Climate Change* and for the first time brings all nations into a common cause to undertake ambitious efforts to combat climate change and adapt to its effects, with enhanced support to assist developing countries to do so. As such, it charts a new course in the global climate effort.

The Paris Agreement's central aim is to strengthen the global response to the threat of climate change by keeping a global temperature rise this century well below 2°C above pre-industrial levels and to pursue efforts to limit the temperature increase even further to a lower 1.5°C. Additionally, the Agreement aims to strengthen the ability of countries to deal with the impacts of climate change. To reach these ambitious goals, appropriate financial flows, a new technology framework and an enhanced capacity building framework will be put in place, thus supporting action by developing countries and the most vulnerable countries, in line with their own national objectives. The Agreement also provides for enhanced transparency of action and support through a more robust transparency framework.

As of January 2020 the only countries with over 1% share of global emissions which have not ratified the Agreement, and so are not parties to the Agreement, are Iran and Turkey. However, on November 4, 2019 the US Secretary of State Michael R Pompeo in a press statement said that the United States began the process to withdraw from The Paris Agreement. Per the terms of the Agreement, the United States accordingly submitted formal notification of its withdrawal to the United Nations. The withdrawal will take effect one year from delivery of the notification, that is November 4, 2020 which is prior to the US Presidential election. President Trump in his early remarks on June 11, 2017 said that the decision to withdraw from The Paris Agreement was because of the unfair economic burden imposed on American workers, businesses, and taxpayers by U.S. pledges made under the Agreement.

President Trump said in his statement that: "The United States has reduced all types of emissions, even as the US grow our economy and ensure our citizens' access to affordable energy. Our results speak for themselves: U.S. emissions of criteria air pollutants that impact human health and the environment declined by 74% between 1970 and 2018. U.S. net greenhouse gas emissions dropped 13% from 2005-2017, even as our economy grew over 19%. The U.S. approach incorporates the reality of the global energy mix and uses all energy sources and technologies cleanly and efficiently, including fossil fuels, nuclear energy, and renewable energy. In international climate discussions, we will continue to offer a realistic and pragmatic model – backed by a record of real world results – showing innovation and open markets to lead to greater prosperity, fewer emissions, and more secure sources of energy. We will continue to work with our global partners to enhance resilience to the impacts of climate change and prepare for and respond to natural disasters. Just as we have in the past, the United States will continue to research, innovate, and grow our economy while reducing emissions and extending a helping hand to our friends and partners around the globe."

The Paris Agreement requires all Parties to put forward their best efforts through nationally determined contributions (NDCs) and to strengthen these efforts in the years ahead. This includes requirements that all Parties report regularly on their emissions and on their implementation efforts.

Problems with The Paris Agreement
Although acclaimed by many people and most countries, several problems with The Paris Agreement can be based on at least four factors: (a) There are no emission reduction commitments for countries such as China and India; (b) Many countries' mitigation commitments are conditionally stated on the foreign aid from the rich countries which may or may not eventuate; (c) There is no legal binding force, that is, all commitments are voluntary; and (d) There is no international monitoring of any of the national commitments and the progress to achieve them.

Chloe Corbyn, of the National Assembly for Wales Research Service, in April 2016 has a succinct summary of The Paris Agreement. In November and December 2015, the 21st Conference of the Parties to the United Nations Framework Convention on Climate Change (UNFCC COP21) took place in Paris. UNFCC is an international environmental agreement on climate change, of which there are 195 Parties, including the UK. The UN Intergovernmental Panel on Climate Change (IPCC) has warned of the consequences of failing to limit global temperature rise to at least 2°C (above pre-industrial times), highlighting that the impacts would pose a threat to humanity and could lead to irreversible climate change.

The meeting in Paris was hailed as a make-or-break opportunity to secure an international agreement on approaches to tackling climate change, a commitment to a longer-term goal of near zero net emissions in the second half of the century, and supporting a transition to a clean economy and low carbon society. The key points of The Paris Agreement are summarised below. The Agreement is due to come into force in 2020.

Governments agreed:
- A long-term goal of keeping the increase in global average temperature to well below 2°C above pre-industrial levels;
- To aim to limit the increase to 1.5°C, since this would significantly reduce risks and the impacts of climate change;
- On the need for global emissions to peak as soon as possible, recognising that this will take longer for developing countries;
- To undertake rapid reductions thereafter in accordance with the best available science.

Before and during the Paris conference, countries submitted comprehensive national climate action plans (INDCs). These are not yet enough to keep global warming below 2°C, but the agreement traces the way to achieving this target.

Governments agreed to:
- Come together every 5 years to set more ambitious targets as required by science;
- Report to each other and the public on how well they are doing to implement their targets;
- Track progress towards the long-term goal through a robust transparency and accountability system;
- Strengthen societies' ability to deal with the impacts of climate change;
- Provide continued and enhanced international support for adaptation to developing countries.

The Agreement also:
- Recognises the importance of averting, minimising and addressing loss and damage associated with the adverse effects of climate change;
- Acknowledges the need to cooperate and enhance the understanding, action and support in different areas such as early warning systems, emergency preparedness and risk insurance.

Support
- The EU and other developed countries will continue to support climate action to reduce emissions and build resilience to climate change impacts in developing countries.
- Other countries are encouraged to provide or continue to provide

such support voluntarily.
- Developed countries intend to continue their existing collective goal to mobilise USD 100 billion per year until 2025 when a new collective goal will be set.

Effectiveness of the Treaty
As reported in *Wikipedia* two studies in the journal *Nature* have said that, as of 2017, none of the major industrialized nations were implementing the policies they had envisioned and have not met their pledged emission reduction targets, and even if they had, the sum of all member pledges (as of 2016) would not keep global temperature rise "well below 2°C". According to UNEP the emission cut targets in November 2016 will result in temperature rise by 3°C above pre-industrial levels, far above the 2°C of the Paris climate agreement.

In addition, an MIT News article written on 22 April 2016 discussed recent MIT studies on the true impact that The Paris Agreement had on global temperature increase. Using their Integrated Global System Modelling (IGSM) to predict temperature increase results in 2100, they used a wide range of scenarios that included no effort towards climate change past 2030, and full extension of The Paris Agreement past 2030. They concluded that The Paris Agreement would cause temperature decrease by about 0.6 to 1.1°C compared to a no-effort-scenario, with only a 0.1°C change in 2050 for all scenarios. They concluded that, although beneficial, there was strong evidence that the goal provided by The Paris Agreement could not be met in the future; under all scenarios, warming would be at least 3.0°C by 2100.

The Legal and Economic Case against the Paris Climate Treaty: An alternative viewpoint
In a report (Issue Analysis 2017, No 6) written for the *Competitive Enterprise Institute* (CEI), Christopher C. Horner, and Marlo Lewis, examined the Paris Treaty and say that President Trump should keep his two-part campaign promise to cancel U.S. participation in the Paris Climate Agreement and stop all payments to United Nations global warming programmes. They say the report says that The Paris Agreement is a costly and ineffectual solution to the alleged climate crisis. It is also plainly a treaty, despite President Obama's attempt to implement it without the Senate's advice and consent. Failure to withdraw from the Agreement would entrench a constitutionally damaging precedent, set

President Trump's domestic and foreign policies in conflict, and ensure decades of diplomatic blowback. For those and other reasons, The Paris Agreement imperils both America's economic future and capacity for self-government.

The Paris Agreement and the 1992 treaty it purports to modify, the United Nations Framework Convention on Climate Change, both contain provisions for withdrawal. There are concerns about diplomatic blowback if President Trump withdraws from the Agreement or submits it for the Senate's advice and consent actually confirms the wisdom of exercising one of those options. The Paris Agreement is designed to institutionalize a running campaign of diplomatic blowback unless the U.S. submits to ever-tightening constraints, ratcheting up every five years. If President Trump withdraws, any diplomatic blowback would largely be a muted one-off event, without the economic, political, and security costs that staying in The Paris Agreement entails.

To safeguard America's economic future and capacity for self-government, President Trump should pull out of The Paris Agreement. There are several options for doing so, and regardless of which option Trump selects, his administration should make the case for withdrawal based on the following key points:

1. The Paris Climate Agreement is a treaty by virtue of its costs and risks, ambition compared to predecessor climate treaties, dependence on subsequent legislation by Congress, intent to affect state laws, U.S. historic practice with regard to multilateral environmental agreements, and other common-sense criteria.
2. In America's constitutional system, treaties must obtain the advice and consent of the Senate before the United States may lawfully join them. President Obama deemed The Paris Agreement to not be a treaty in order to evade constitutional review, which the Agreement almost certainly would not have survived.
3. Allowing Obama's climate coup to stand will set a dangerous precedent that will undermine one of the Constitution's important checks and balances. It will allow a future president to adopt any treaty he and foreign elites want, without Senate ratification, just by deeming it "not a treaty."
4. The Agreement endangers America's capacity for self-government. It empowers one administration to make legislative commitments for decades to come, without congressional authorization, and regardless of the outcome of future elections. It would also make

U.S. energy policies increasingly unaccountable to voters, and increasingly beholden to the demands of foreign leaders, U.N. bureaucrats, and international pressure groups.

The key aspects of The Paris Agreement
The Paris Agreement opened for signature on 22 April 2016 – Earth Day – at UN Headquarters in New York. It entered into force on 4 November 2016, 30 days after the so-called "double threshold" (ratification by 55 countries that account for at least 55% of global emissions) had been met. Since then, more countries have ratified and continue to ratify the Agreement, reaching a total of 125 Parties in early 2017.

In order to make the Paris Agreement fully operational, a work programme was launched in Paris to develop modalities, procedures and guidelines on a broad array of issues. Since 2016, Parties have worked together in the subsidiary bodies (APA, SBSTA and SBI) and various constituted bodies. The Conference of the Parties serving as the meeting of the Parties to the Paris Agreement (CMA) met for the first time in conjunction with COP 22 in Marrakesh (in November 2016) and adopted its first two decisions.

The Paris Agreement, adopted through Decision 1/CP.21, addresses crucial areas necessary to combat climate change. Some of the key aspects of the Agreement are set out below:

- **Long-term temperature goal** (Art. 2) – The Paris Agreement, in seeking to strengthen the global response to climate change, reaffirms the goal of limiting global temperature increase to well below 2°C, while pursuing efforts to limit the increase to 1.5°C.
- **Global peaking and 'climate neutrality'** (Art. 4) – To achieve this temperature goal, Parties aim to reach global peaking of greenhouse gas emissions (GHGs) as soon as possible, recognizing peaking will take longer for developing country Parties, so as to achieve a balance between anthropogenic emissions by sources and removals by sinks of GHGs in the second half of the century.
- **Mitigation** (Art. 4) – The Paris Agreement establishes binding commitments by all Parties to prepare, communicate and maintain a nationally determined contribution (NDC) and to pursue domestic measures to achieve them. It also prescribes that Parties shall communicate their NDCs every 5 years and provide information necessary for clarity and transparency. To set a firm foundation for higher ambition, each successive NDC will represent a progression

beyond the previous one and reflect the highest possible ambition. Developed countries should continue to take the lead by undertaking absolute economy-wide reduction targets, while developing countries should continue enhancing their mitigation efforts, and are encouraged to move toward economy-wide targets over time in the light of different national circumstances.
- **Sinks and reservoirs** (Art.5) –The Paris Agreement also encourages Parties to conserve and enhance, as appropriate, sinks and reservoirs of GHGs as referred to in Article 4, paragraph 1(d) of the Convention, including forests.
- **Voluntary cooperation/Market- and non-market-based approaches** (Art. 6) – The Paris Agreement recognizes the possibility of voluntary cooperation among Parties to allow for higher ambition and sets out principles – including environmental integrity, transparency and robust accounting – for any cooperation that involves internationally transferral of mitigation outcomes. It establishes a mechanism to contribute to the mitigation of GHG emissions and support sustainable development, and defines a framework for non-market approaches to sustainable development.
- **Adaptation** (Art. 7) – The Paris Agreement establishes a global goal on adaptation – of enhancing adaptive capacity, strengthening resilience and reducing vulnerability to climate change in the context of the temperature goal of the Agreement. It aims to significantly strengthen national adaptation efforts, including through support and international cooperation. It recognizes that adaptation is a global challenge faced by all. All Parties should engage in adaptation, including by formulating and implementing National Adaptation Plans, and should submit and periodically update an adaptation communication describing their priorities, needs, plans and actions. The adaptation efforts of developing countries should be recognized.
- **Loss and damage** (Art. 8) – The Paris Agreement recognizes the importance of averting, minimizing and addressing loss and damage associated with the adverse effects of climate change, including extreme weather events and slow onset events, and the role of sustainable development in reducing the risk of loss and damage. Parties are to enhance understanding, action and support, including through the Warsaw International Mechanism, on a cooperative and facilitative basis with respect to loss and damage associated with the adverse effects of climate change.

- **Finance, technology and capacity-building support** (Art. 9, 10 and 11) – The Paris Agreement reaffirms the obligations of developed countries to support the efforts of developing country Parties to build clean, climate-resilient futures, while for the first time encouraging voluntary contributions by other Parties. Provision of resources should also aim to achieve a balance between adaptation and mitigation. In addition to reporting on finance already provided, developed country Parties commit to submit indicative information on future support every two years, including projected levels of public finance. The agreement also provides that the Financial Mechanism of the Convention, including the Green Climate Fund (GCF), shall serve the Agreement. International cooperation on climate-safe technology development and transfer and building capacity in the developing world are also strengthened: a technology framework is established under the Agreement and capacity-building activities will be strengthened through, inter alia, enhanced support for capacity building actions in developing country Parties and appropriate institutional arrangements. Climate change education, training as well as public awareness, participation and access to information (Art 12) is also to be enhanced under the Agreement.
- **Climate change education, training, public awareness, public participation and public access to information** (Art 12) is also to be enhanced under the Agreement.
- **Transparency** (Art. 13), implementation and compliance (Art. 15) – The Paris Agreement relies on a robust transparency and accounting system to provide clarity on action and support by Parties, with flexibility for their differing capabilities of Parties. In addition to reporting information on mitigation, adaptation and support, the Agreement requires that the information submitted by each Party undergoes international technical expert review. The Agreement also includes a mechanism that will facilitate implementation and promote compliance in a non-adversarial and non-punitive manner, and will report annually to the CMA.
- **Global Stocktake** (Art. 14) – A "global stocktake", to take place in 2023 and every 5 years thereafter, will assess collective progress toward achieving the purpose of the Agreement in a comprehensive and facilitative manner. It will be based on the best available science and its long-term global goal. Its outcome will inform Parties in updating and enhancing their actions and support and enhancing international cooperation on climate action.

- **Decision 1/CP.21** also sets out a number of measures to enhance action prior to 2020, including strengthening the technical examination process, enhancement of provision of urgent finance, technology and support and measures to strengthen high-level engagement. For 2018 a facilitative dialogue is envisaged to take stock of collective progress towards the long-term emission reduction goal of Art 4. The decision also welcomes the efforts of all non-Party stakeholders to address and respond to climate change, including those of civil society, the private sector, financial institutions, cities and other subnational authorities. These stakeholders are invited to scale up their efforts and showcase them via the Non-State Actor Zone for Climate Action platform (*www.climateaction.unfccc.int*). Parties also recognized the need to strengthen the knowledge, technologies, practices and efforts of local communities and indigenous peoples, as well as the important role of providing incentives through tools such as domestic policies and carbon pricing.

World Meteorological Organization

The World Meteorological Organization (WMO) is the successor of the International Meteorological Organization (IMO) which was created in 1873. Its fundamental mission is to support the countries of the world in providing meteorological and hydrological services to protect life and property from natural disasters related to weather, climate, and water, to safeguard the environment, and to contribute to sustainable development. This cannot happen without the necessary observations, research and operations that develop the understanding and knowledge of weather and climate.

The structure of the WMO which has headquarters in Geneva involves the Congress, the Executive Council, and eight Technical Commissions. The World Meteorological Congress, the supreme body of the Organization, assembles delegates of Members (countries) once every four years to determine general policies for the fulfilment of the purposes of the Organization; to consider membership of the Organization; to determine the general, technical, financial and staff regulations; to establish and coordinate the activities of constituent bodies of the Organization; to approve long-term plans and budget for the following financial period; to elect the President and Vice Presidents of the Organization and members of the Executive Council; and to appoint the Secretary-General.

The Executive Council is the executive body of the Organization, which meets annually, implements decisions of Congress, coordinates the programmes, examines the utilization of budgetary resources, considers and takes action on recommendations of regional associations and technical commissions and guides their work programme, provides technical information, counsel and assistance in the fields of activity of the Organization and studies and takes action on matters affecting international meteorology and related activities.

The Council is composed of 37 directors of National Meteorological or Hydrometeorological Services, serving in an individual capacity as representatives of the Organization and not as representatives of particular Members thereof. They include the President and three Vice-Presidents who are elected by Congress, and the presidents of the six regional associations. The remaining 27 members are elected by Congress.

There are also eight Technical Commissions which are composed of experts designated by Members and are responsible for studying meteorological, climatological, and hydrological operational systems, applications and research. They establish methodology and procedures and make recommendations to the Executive Council and the Congress. The Technical Commissions usually meet once every four years, when they elect a President and Vice-President. From 1989 to 1996, I was President of one of Technical Commissions, namely the "Commission for Climatology". In addition, three other New Zealanders have been Presidents of WMO Technical Commissions; Dr Jim Salinger (Commission for Agricultural Meteorology), Dr Neil Gordon (Commission for Aeronautical Meteorology), and Dr John Gabites (Commission for Atmospheric Sciences).

The WMO Commission for Climatology (CCl) of which I was privileged to be President from 1989 to 1996, and earlier Vice President from 1981-1989, was established in 1929. The WMO website in commenting on the CCl says that climate is one of our greatest natural resources. With its seasonal patterns and the potential for extreme variations, climate affects the daily lives of everyone on the planet, influencing the type of clothing we wear, the kind of housing we need, the modes of transport we use, the range of sports and recreational activities we engage in, what we eat, and how we work.

Early civilizations had a vital interest in the Sun, the stars, the planets and the atmospheric environment. Indeed, thousands of years ago, in some Asian and African societies, the keeping of weather records was common – a practice that gave the leaders of these societies some ability to forecast natural hazards and other weather-related events.

The Greeks were the first ancient civilization to take scientific climate observations and attempt to develop meteorological theory based on these observations. Later, in the 17th century, the invention and development of basic instruments to measure various climate parameters marked the beginning of modern quantitative climatology. Awareness of the enormous practical advantages created by having access to data and information on local and national weather and climate meant that governments were keen to obtain such information.

By the early 19th century, networks of weather observing stations were beginning to extend throughout a number of countries. The invention of the electric telegraph in the mid-19th century facilitated the rapid transmission of weather observation data among nations. Known as "weather telegraphy", this early form of operational meteorology developed rapidly, and soon national services began expanding climate observing station networks further afield.

In 1873, the International Meteorological Organization (IMO) was founded. During the organization's early years, the need to create a special commission to deal with climatology was never seriously considered. At the 1929 Conference of Directors in Copenhagen, however, where the conference agenda was dominated by climatological issues, it was unanimously recommended that a Commission for Climatology be created.

Accordingly, the Commission for Climatology (CCl) was established in 1929 under the auspices of IMO. After the Second World War, the United Nations was formed and the World Meteorological Organization (WMO) was incorporated on 23 March 1950 as a Specialized Agency of the United Nations, and the successor to IMO. Shortly after WMO was incorporated, the WMO Commission for Climatology (CCl) was established and the Commission's first session was held in Washington, DC, in March 1953.

A brochure *Commission for Climatology: Eighty Years of Service* published by WMO in 2011 (WMO No 1079) covers historical information relating to the period following the establishment of WMO. This brochure incorporates much of the information in another brochure written by former CCl President Morley Thomas and myself prepared specifically for the CCl Session held in Havana, Cuba, in February 1993.

Since 1953 CCl has continued to organize sessions for Members every four years. It has contributed significantly to the scientific community and it has developed cooperation with other bodies and institutions whose work is focused on climate-sensitive sectors.

Today, CCl is a major channel for organized collaboration among climatologists throughout the world. Its aim is to advance all aspects of climatology, ranging from the collection and management of high-quality weather observations to turning data, climate forecasts and projections into useful information. As one of the WMO 8 technical commissions, the role of CCl is to promote and facilitate action related to climate and its relationship with human activities and sustainable development.

I was involved during 20 years of the Commissions activities and the following are summaries of the five four-yearly CCl Sessions in which I was either President or Vice-President.

EIGHTH SESSION (CCl-VIII), WASHINGTON, DC, APRIL 1982

In April 1982, the United States hosted the eighth session of the Commission, which by this time had been renamed the Commission for Climatology and Applications of Meteorology (CCAM); the session was held in Washington, DC.

Three years earlier, in February 1979, the First World Climate Conference took place in Geneva. Later the same year, the World Meteorological Congress gave formal approval for the establishment of the World Climate Programme (WCP).

With the WCP opening up opportunities for the use of climate information throughout the world, delegates attending the eighth session of the Commission insisted that there was a significant need for increased training activities in climatology. Accordingly, a rapporteur was appointed to study problems in relation to education, training and the transfer of information. The establishment of the WCP meant that the Commission focused more attention on climatological operations at its eighth session than it had done at previous sessions.

It was agreed to prepare up-to-date climate normals, preferably using a standard thirty-year period and beginning with a year whose last digit is "1", such as 1991. In relation to the World Climate Applications Programme (WCAP), the session participants indicated that significant contributions could be made to the proposed high-priority areas of food, water and energy. At the end of the session, James L. Rasmussen (United States) was elected President, and W. John Maunder (New Zealand) was elected Vice-President.

NINTH SESSION (CCl-IX), GENEVA, 1985

The ninth session of the Commisison for Climatology was held in Geneva in 1985, at a time when there was a marked resurgence of interest worldwide in the issue of climate change. A number of significant achievements took place during the period following the eighth session. Many of these achievements were the result of specific Commission initiatives. They included the implementation of the Climate System Monitoring Programme, data rescue, improvements in climate data management and the development of several components of the Climate Applications Referral System (CARS).

The period 1982 to 1985 was also characterized by considerable activity in the field of climate change. I briefed the Commission on the main findings and recommendations presented at the joint United

Official viewpoints 359

Nations Environment Programme/World Meteorological Organization/ International Council for Science (UNEP/WMO/ICSU) international assessment conference held in Villach, Austria, in October 1985. The conference focused on the role played by carbon dioxide and other greenhouse gases in climate variations and its associated impacts, which affect the well-being, property and lives of people around the world.

At the ninth session, the Commission discussed the structure of the WCP and it reviewed the various activities and plans under the Programme's four components: the World Climate Data Programme (WCDP), the World Climate Applications Programme (WCAP), the World Climate Impacts Studies Programme (WCISP), and the World Climate Research Programme (WCRP).

Following a review of research findings suggesting that an increase in global temperatures is due to an increased concentration of greenhouse gases in the Earth's atmosphere, it was decided to establish more comprehensive climate databases to support climate monitoring, climate applications, research and impact studies. To ensure that reliable reference climate data were available, the Commission reviewed a proposal made by the Working Group on Climate Data Management, and it adopted a recommendation that work should begin on the creation of a global network of Reference Climatological Stations (RCS).

The Commission also recommended the inclusion of non-instrumental records, measurements and other information, such as proxy climatological data from tree rings, ice cores and archeological records, in the overall process of climate data management.

During 1982 and 1983, a severe El Niño event occurred, with catastrophic effects in the tropics. In order to carry out climatic studies on a coupled ocean–atmosphere system such as El Niño, oceanographic and air–sea interaction data are required. As a result of the severe El Niño event, the WCDP and the relevant national oceanographic centres agreed to work in close collaboration to support the Tropical Ocean and Global Atmosphere (TOGA) programme.

At the end of the session, J.L. Rasmussen (United States) and W.J. Maunder (New Zealand) were unanimously re-elected for a further term as President and Vice-President of the Commission, respectively.

TENTH SESSION (CCl-X), LISBON, APRIL 1989
A major highlight of the tenth session, which was held in Lisbon, was the proposal that WMO initiate the Climate Change Detection Project (CCDP) in collaboration with other agencies, and with the Commission

acting as the lead institution within WMO. In its discussions on the CCDP, the Commission stated that it viewed the project as an international effort, primarily by Meteorological Services, to collect additional climate data along with well-documented station information (metadata), and to process these data using uniform procedures; ultimately, the objective was to prepare more reliable analyses of climate trends and climate variability.

The session expressed great interest in the establishment of the WMO/UNEP Intergovernmental Panel on Climate Change (IPCC). This initiative had been agreed by the WMO Executive Council at its fortieth session (in 1988) and had subsequently been endorsed by the UNEP Governing Council. The announcement that the IPCC had arranged to produce its first assessment report by October 1990 was widely welcomed at the session.

By April 1989, significant progress had been made in the area of climate data management, including the production of manuals and the creation of the DAta REscue (DARE) and CLICOM (CLImate COMputing) projects. To support the DARE project, an International Data Rescue Coordination Centre (IDCC) was established in Brussels, with financial assistance provided by Belgium and UNEP.

For the first time, the Commission also recommended that CCI focal persons be identified in each WMO Region to assist the Commission president in communicating with Members in the Regions. In its discussions on the National Climate Programmes (NCPs), the Commission reaffirmed its belief that setting up the NCPs represented a major step in the development of all aspects of climatology. Indeed, such programmes and the WCP were in fact complementary, the Commission noted.

The session also initiated the completion of climate normal based on thirty years of climate data (1961 to 1990). In the election of officers, W.J. Maunder (New Zealand), who had been Vice-President for the previous eight years, was unanimously elected President, and Y. Boodhoo (Mauritius) was unanimously elected Vice-President.

ELEVENTH SESSION (CCl-XI), HAVANA, FEBRUARY 1993
The eleventh session was held at a time when a number of crucial developments were taking place in the area of climate and climate change. The IPCC published its first assessment report in 1990, and the Second World Climate Conference also took place that same year. Other major developments occurring around this time included the establishment of a negotiating process for the United Nations Framework Convention on

Climate Change (UNFCCC) and the inclusion of climate-related matters in Agenda 21, the action plan adopted at the Earth Summit held in Rio de Janeiro in 1992.

The World Meteorological Congress had renamed both the data component and the applications component of the WCP. These now became known as the World Climate Data and Monitoring Programme (WCDMP) and the World Climate Applications and Services Programme (WCASP), respectively. The objective of renaming the two components was to emphasize the climate monitoring and services aspects of the WCP. Detailed discussions about the WCDMP and the WCASP took place at the eleventh session.

The Commission also held in-depth discussions about the outcome of the United Nations Conference on Environment and Development (UNCED). In particular, discussions focused on the UNCED Agenda 21 and its comprehensive, long-term programme of specific objectives and actions aimed at creating a new global partnership for sustainable development.

By the time the eleventh session took place in February 1993, the second edition of the Guide to Climatological Practices (WMO-No 100) had been published in English, French, Russian and Spanish. At the session, the Commission considered a recommendation made by one of its expert groups in relation to the preparation of the third edition of the Guide.

Significant progress was made on the installation of CLICOM software in National Meteorological and Hydrological Services (NMHSs). By February 1993, 104 Members had implemented CLICOM; this compared with just 54 Members around the time of the previous session in 1989. The successful implementation of the system was mainly due to the efforts of donor countries, which helped to fund the acquisition of CLICOM software and the training of NMHS staff in its use.

The Commission emphasized the fundamental importance of climate research being carried out under the WCRP; this was particularly relevant in the context of increased worldwide interest in, and activities relating to, the impacts of potential global climate change and practical measures for preventing or mitigating the anticipated harmful effects of such impacts.

The Commission felt that many of its activities – especially those being carried out under the WCDMP and the climate change detection project – constituted essential support for the study of climate variations and climate change. With regard to the issue of the Climate System

Monitoring Bulletin, the Commission emphasized the significance of its timely publication and it discussed a mechanism to accelerate its distribution.

At the end of the session, W.J. Maunder (New Zealand) and Y. Boodhoo (Mauritius) were unanimously re-elected President and Vice-President of the Commission, respectively.

TWELFTH SESSION (CCl-XII), GENEVA, AUGUST 1997
The main topics discussed at this session were: climate system monitoring, including climate change detection; climate data management, including DARE; Climate Information and Prediction Services (CLIPS), which was formed in 1995; and the development of climate application methodologies for various socio-economic sectors.

In addition, the Commission discussed one of the key challenges facing it during the four-year period 1997 to 2001 – the need to focus on issues related to providing climate services for sustainable development. These issues included the provision of support through the Climate Agenda for the IPCC process of assessing climate change, as well as support for the implementation of the United Nations Framework Convention on Climate Change.

Recognizing the need for continued guidance on how the Commission should prioritize its activities in order to meet the objectives of the WCP, the Commission decided to re-establish its Advisory Working Group. The role of this group was to assist the President in guiding and coordinating the activities of the Commission and its various working groups and rapporteurs. The Working Group on Climate Data was also re-established.

In view of the enormous interest in, and concern about, the variability of climate and the early detection of climate change, and also due to the requirement for ongoing evaluation of climate on both global and regional scales, the Commission decided to set up a Joint Working Group on Climate Change Detection in conjunction with the WCRP/CLIVAR (Climate Variability and Predictability) project.

It also set up a working group to assist the CLIPS programme, and in particular to help CLIPS review and keep abreast of developments in national climate services and also to provide scientific and technical guidance on the optimal use of climate services. In addition, rapporteurs were appointed for international exchange of climate data and products; urban and building climatology; climate and health; tourism and recreation; energy, including solar energy; and capacity-building. At the end of the session, Y. Boodhoo (Mauritius) was unanimously elected President, and J.M. Nicholls (United Kingdom) was unanimously elected Vice-President.

World Climate Conferences
Through its long history WMO has organised many conferences on meteorology, climatology and related subjects. Of significance WMO organised three World Climate Conferences. The First World Climate Conference was held on 12-23 February 1979 in Geneva and sponsored by the WMO. It was one of the first major international meetings on climate change. Essentially a scientific conference, it was attended by scientists from a wide range of disciplines. I was one was of those who was invited and I Co-chaired several of the sessions. In addition to the main plenary sessions, the conference organized four working groups to look into climate data, the identification of climate topics, integrated impact studies, and research on climate variability and change. The Conference led to the establishment of the World Climate Programme (WCP) and the World Climate Research Programme. It also led to the creation of the Intergovernmental Panel on Climate Change (IPCC) by WMO and UNEP in 1988.

The Second Climate Conference was held on 29 October to 7 November 1990, again in Geneva. It was an important step towards a global climate treaty and somewhat more political than the first conference. The main task of the conference, of which I was on the secretariat, was to review the WCP set up by the first conference. The IPCC first assessment report had been completed in time for this conference. The scientists and technology experts at the conference issued a strong statement highlighting the risk of climate change. The conference issued a Ministerial Declaration only after hard bargaining over a number of difficult issues; the declaration disappointed many of the participating scientists as well as some observers because it did not offer a high level of commitment. Eventually, however, developments at the conference led to the establishment of the United Nations Framework Convention on Climate Change (UNFCCC), of which the Kyoto Protocol is a part, and to the establishment of the Global Climate Observing System (GCOS), a global observing system for climate and climate-related observations.

World Climate Conference-3 (WCC-3) was held in Geneva, Switzerland, 31 August - 4 September 2009. Its focus was on climate predictions and information for decision-making at the seasonal to multi-decadal timescales. The goal was to create a global framework that will link scientific advances in these climate predictions and the needs of their users for decision-making to better cope with changing conditions. Key users of climate predictions include food producers, water managers, energy developers and managers, public health workers, national planners, tourism managers and others, as well as society at large. Participants in WCC-3 included these users, as well as climate service providers and high-level policy-makers. The Conference also aimed to increase commitment to, and advancements in, climate observations and monitoring to better provide climate information and services worldwide that will improve public safety and well-being.

WCC-3 outcomes also intended to contribute to the achievement of the United Nations Millennium Development Goals and broader UN climate goals, including the Hyogo Framework for Action on Disaster Risk Reduction. The Conference theme complemented global work under way to help societies adapt to climate change in line with Bali Action Plan, especially the Nairobi Work Programme. The outcomes formed part of WMO input to the 2009 UNFCC COP-15 meeting for climate mitigation in Copenhagen.

World Meteorological Day
Since 1961, World Meteorological Day has commemorated the coming into force on 23 March 1950 of the Convention establishing the World Meteorological Organization (WMO) and the essential contribution that National Meteorological and Hydrological Services make to the safety and well-being of society. Each year, the celebrations focus on a theme of topical interest. The theme for the 2015 World Meteorological Day, "Climate knowledge for climate action," provided an opportunity to take stock of the climate knowledge built during the last decades, as an essential base to support the path towards more ambitious action to address climate change and climate variability.

"Understanding Clouds" the theme of World Meteorological Day 2017, was to highlight the enormous importance of clouds for weather, climate and water. It also marked the launch of the new edition of the International Cloud Atlas, the single authoritative and most comprehensive reference for identifying clouds and a treasure trove of hundreds of images of clouds, including a few newly-classified cloud types.

The theme of World Meteorological Day 2018 was "Weather-ready, climate-smart", which looked at the growing hazards – such as tropical cyclones, storm surges, heavy rains, heat waves, and droughts – that are threatening global populations. It is one of WMO's top priorities to protect lives, livelihoods, and property from the risks related to weather, climate and water events.

World Meteorological Day in 2019 looked at "The Sun, the Earth and the Weather". The Sun delivers the energy that powers all life on Earth. It drives the weather, ocean currents and daily activities. It is the inspiration for music, photography and art.

In 2020, World Meteorological Day and World Water Day shared the theme, "Climate and Water". The focus is on managing climate and water in a more coordinated and sustainable manner because they are inextricably linked. Both lie at the heart of the global goals on sustainable development, climate change and disaster risk reduction.

During 2020, WMO wants its Members (that is countries) to focus their attention on the theme of water conservation with the central idea being "Count Every Drop, Every Drop Counts". Through World Meteorological Day 2020, the organization aims to bring to light water crisis, floods and droughts, and lack of access to clean water for the people of the world.

UN Climate Conference 2014

The purpose of the 2014 Climate Summit was to raise political momentum for a meaningful, universal climate agreement in Paris in 2015 and to galvanize transformative action in all countries to reduce emissions and build resilience to the adverse impacts of climate change. An unprecedented number of world leaders attended the Summit, including 100 Heads of State and Government. They were joined by more than 800 leaders from business, finance and civil society. This summary details their most significant announcements. A comprehensive global vision on climate change emerged from the statements of leaders at the Summit including the following:

Leaders acknowledged that climate action should be undertaken within the context of efforts to eradicate extreme poverty and promote sustainable development.

Leaders committed to limit global temperature rise to less than 2°C from pre-industrial levels.

Many leaders called for all countries to take national actions consistent with a less than 2°C pathway and a number of countries committed to doing so.

Leaders committed to finalise a meaningful, universal new agreement under the United Nations Framework Convention on Climate Change (UNFCCC) in Paris in 2015, and to arrive at the first draft of such an agreement at a meeting in Lima, in December 2014.

Leaders concurred that the new agreement should be effective, durable and comprehensive and that it should balance support for mitigation and adaptation. Many underlined the importance of addressing loss and damage.

Many leaders, from all regions and all levels of economic development advocated for a peak in greenhouse gas emissions before 2020, dramatically reduced emissions thereafter, and climate neutrality in the second-half of the century.

Leaders from more than 40 countries, 30 cities and dozens of corporations launched a large-scale commitment to double the rate of global energy efficiency by 2030 through vehicle fuel efficiency, lighting, appliances, buildings and district energy.

Seventy-three national Governments, 11 regional governments and more than 1,000 businesses and investors signalled their support for pricing carbon. Together these leaders represent 52% of global GDP,

5% of global greenhouse gas emissions and almost half of the world's population.

Some leaders agreed to join a new Carbon Pricing Leadership Coalition to drive action aimed at strengthening carbon pricing policies and redirecting investment

Of course, not withstanding the importance of the event, not all of the world's media were focused on the Climate Summit. Indeed, Christopher Booker, writing in the UK's *Daily Telegraph*, stated: "Apart from the Middle East, there can have been few more depressing places to be in the world last Tuesday than the UN General Assembly in New York, where an endless queue of world leaders, including Barack Obama and David Cameron, treated an increasingly soporific audience to leaden little appeals for humanity to take urgent action to halt global warming."

14

Political aspects

"WE DECLARE that the average global temperatures should not be allowed to exceed more than 2°C".

From the UN Climate Conference, 2014.

Does "Nature" no longer have any say?

Politics and science

In January 2010, I was interviewed by Andrew Campbell of the Tauranga *Weekend Sun* about the politicisation of the climate change issue and how it is ruining the debate on it. I mentioned that in 1985 there were about 100 people at a World Meteorological Organization meeting in Villach, Austria, which I believe was the beginning of the manmade climate change debate.

This is what I said....

"I was the only one from New Zealand at that meeting. Our job was to express climate issues in words the politicians can understand. In many ways I regret some of the words I wrote. I think the politicians have taken it lock, stock and barrel.

The polarisation and politicising of climate change from a debate into a belief system has seen many scientists muzzled. It takes a bold person to be questioning the IPCC (Intergovernmental Panel on Climate Change) movement because if they are not in favour, they don't get much funding.

These days there are two camps in this whole climate area. In simple terms, most of the people who are supporting manmade climate change - the IPCC's argument - work for governments round the world.

Most governments are following what the official climate agencies are saying. The people who have concern about this are mostly retired, like myself. We have no axe to grind, and we are not being paid by anyone.

We think of things differently mainly because we have seen things in the past. There's nothing new under the sun in terms of climate. Mark Twain said 'climate is what we expect, weather is what we get.'

I blame it on the weather dice. The weather dice appeared on the cover of my 1986 book, *The Uncertainty Business: Risks and opportunities in weather and climate*.

The weather's always changing, the climate's always changing. The weather dice decide. Something happens to make the weather dice come down in a certain way and we have very little control over the weather dice. Any committee that sets out to state how global climate is to be controlled, or that an average temperature be kept within 2°C, is behaving similarly to the early English King Canute who set an example for his bragging courtiers by decreeing the tide stop, to '*let all men know how empty and worthless is the power of kings*'. "

Climate change: three sides of the story

Dr Ross McKitrick, an environmental economist, and Associate Professor and Director of Graduate Studies, at the University of Guelph in Canada, and co-author of the Donner Prize-winning *Taken By Storm: The Troubled Science, Policy and Politics of Global Warming*, and an IPCC Reviewer, wrote the following in February 2020. It was originally published on the website *WattsUpWithThat.com* and was reproduced on the Cornwall Alliance website (*CornwallAlliance.org*).

Last year was the year the climate issue took a sharp turn towards extremism. Let's hope 2020 is the year sanity makes a comeback. There have long been three groups occupying the climate issue. To avoid pejoratives, I will call them A, B and C.

The A group are the doubters; they don't believe greenhouse gases (GHGs) do much harm and they don't support expensive climate policy interventions. If we must choose between climate policy and the continued use of inexpensive fossil energy, they readily choose the latter.

The C group think the opposite; they fear a climate catastrophe, they foresee a crisis and they want urgent action, regardless of cost, to stop it.

The B group are in the middle. They believe, or say they believe, that GHG emissions are a problem and must be reduced. They are vague on the question of how much and when, but in general they try to balance environmental goals with the provision of inexpensive energy and robust economic growth.

The leaders in business, government and the bureaucracy tend to be in this group. They have spent the last 20 years verbally acknowledging the concerns of group C and even borrowing their slogans, while quietly letting the A agenda mostly win out, which the underlying economics pretty much necessitates. This uneasy compromise fell apart last year.

Despite A being a more natural ally for B, the B group long ago marginalized the A crowd and instead tried to ingratiate themselves with the Cs. They funded them, welcomed the more congenial elements into their circles and adopted their rhetoric about sustainability, the low-carbon transition and the imperative for climate leadership. To the B crowd, these were just nice-sounding sentiments – a bit of green window-dressing to help sell the growth agenda. But their new friends in the C crowd meant every word.

Thanks to 20 years of patronage and endorsement from the B crowd, group C is now in control and has dropped any pretence of commonality with B. They raised a generation convinced the apocalypse is nigh and they proved over the past year they can dictate terms of surrender to politicians everywhere.

To take one example, the decision by the European Investment Bank to phase out all investments in fossil fuel projects – even natural gas – by 2022 and redirect a trillion euros into "climate action and environmental sustainability" is a clear signal that the Cs are not only at the table, they run the show. Likewise, the worldwide declarations of a "climate emergency" and the embrace of net-zero targets means the B group is officially sidelined, at least in the West.

The exception among developed countries is the United States, where the Bs long ago recognized the true aspirations of the Cs and aligned themselves with the A crowd. They realized in the process that it's a surprisingly large and energetic constituency, thus creating a coalition capable of keeping the U.S. energy sector alive and the economy growing. Other exceptions include the developing powerhouses of China, Russia (who both must relish the prospect of their democratic Western rivals abandoning world economic and energy leadership for climate's sake) and India.

To those in the B group who are bewildered by the turn of events, I say this: you must win this fight and right now you are losing badly. At stake are the livelihoods of millions of ordinary people whose jobs and living standards will be destroyed if C prevails, not to mention the hopes of billions of people who want to rise out of poverty.

The old compromise is dead. Stop using C jargon in your speeches. Start learning the deep details of the science and economics instead of letting the C crowd dictate what you're allowed to think or say. Figure out a new way of talking about the climate issue based on what you actually believe.

You, and by extension everyone who depends on your leadership, face an existential threat. It was 20 years in the making, so dig in for a 20-year battle to turn it around. Stop demonizing potential allies in the A camp; you need all the help you can get.

Climate and energy policy has fallen into the hands of a worldwide movement that openly declares its extremism. The would-be moderates on this issue have pretended for 20 years they could keep the status quo without having to fight for it. Those days are over.

The Kyoto Protocol

The Kyoto Protocol was adopted on 11 December 1997. Owing to a complex ratification process, it entered into force on 16 February 2005. Currently, there are 192 Parties to the Kyoto Protocol. The Kyoto Protocol operationalizes the United Nations Framework Convention on Climate Change by committing industrialized countries to limit and reduce greenhouse gases (GHG) emissions in accordance with agreed individual targets. The Convention itself only asks those countries to adopt policies and measures on mitigation and to report periodically.

The Kyoto Protocol is based on the principles and provisions of the Convention and follows its annex-based structure. It only binds developed countries, and places a heavier burden on them under the principle of "common but differentiated responsibility and respective capabilities", because it recognizes that they are largely responsible for the current high levels of GHG emissions in the atmosphere. In its Annex B, the Kyoto Protocol set binding emission reduction targets for 36 industrialized countries and the European Union. Overall, these targets add up to an average 5% emission reduction compared to 1990 levels over the first five year period 2008–2012.

In Doha, Qatar, on 8 December 2012, the Doha Amendment to the Kyoto Protocol was adopted for a second commitment period, starting in 2013 and lasting until 2020. However, the Doha Amendment has not as yet (in 2020) entered into force; a total of 144 instruments of acceptance are required for entry into force of the amendment.

The amendment includes: New commitments for Annex I Parties to the Kyoto Protocol who agreed to take on commitments in a second commitment period from 1 January 2013 to 31 December 2020; a revised list of GHG to be reported on by Parties in the second commitment period; and Amendments to several articles of the Kyoto Protocol which specifically referenced issues pertaining to the first commitment period and which needed to be updated for the second commitment period. On 21 December 2012, the amendment was circulated by the Secretary-General of the United Nations, acting in his capacity as Depositary, to all Parties to the Kyoto Protocol in accordance with Articles 20 and 21 of the Protocol.

During the first commitment period, 37 industrialized countries and the European Community committed to reduce GHG emissions to an average of 5% against 1990 levels. During the second commitment period, Parties committed to reduce GHG emissions by at least 18% below 1990 levels in the eight-year period from 2013 to 2020; however, the composition of Parties in the second commitment period is different from the first.

One important element of the Kyoto Protocol was the establishment of flexible market mechanisms, which are based on the trade of emissions permits. Under the Protocol, countries must meet their targets primarily through national measures. However, the Protocol also offers them an additional means to meet their targets by way of three market-based mechanisms: International Emissions Trading, Clean Development Mechanism (CDM), and Joint Implementation (JI).

These mechanisms ideally encourage GHG abatement to start where it is most cost-effective, for example, in the developing world. It does not matter where emissions are reduced, as long as they are removed from the atmosphere. This has the parallel benefits of stimulating green investment in developing countries and including the private sector in this endeavour to cut and hold steady GHG emissions at a safe level. It also makes leap-frogging–that is, the possibility of skipping the use of older, dirtier technology for newer, cleaner infrastructure and systems, with obvious longer-term benefits–more economical.

Monitoring emission targets

The Kyoto Protocol also established a rigorous monitoring, review and verification system, as well as a compliance system to ensure transparency and hold Parties to account. Under the Protocol, countries' actual emissions have to be monitored and precise records have to be kept of the trades carried out. Registry systems track and record transactions by Parties under the mechanisms. The UN Climate Change Secretariat, based in Bonn, Germany, keeps an international transaction log to verify that transactions are consistent with the rules of the Protocol. Reporting is by Parties submitting annual emission inventories and national reports under the Protocol at regular intervals. A compliance system ensures that Parties are meeting their commitments and helps them to meet their commitments if they have problems doing so.

Adaptation

The Kyoto Protocol, like the Convention, is also designed to assist countries in adapting to the adverse effects of climate change. It facilitates the development and deployment of technologies that can help increase resilience to the impacts of climate change.

The Adaptation Fund was established to finance adaptation projects and programmes in developing countries that are Parties to the Kyoto Protocol. In the first commitment period, the Fund was financed mainly with a share of proceeds from CDM project activities. In Doha, in 2012, it was decided that for the second commitment period, international emissions trading and joint implementation would also provide the Adaptation Fund with a 2% share of proceeds.

Ozone and the 1987 Montreal Protocol

The US National Aeronautics and Space Administration (NASA) states that ozone (O_3) is a naturally occurring gas found in the stratosphere, 20-25 kilometres above Earth, in what is known as the ozone layer. The ozone "hole" is an area of reduced ozone (below 220 Dobson units (DU)) that forms over Antarctica. In winter, low temperatures over Antarctica form polar stratospheric clouds. Ozone-depleting substances react with these clouds, producing reservoirs of chlorine and bromine. Sunlight transforms these chemicals into forms that are destructive to ozone, so the ozone hole grows when the sun rises over Antarctica at the end of winter.

Mean ozone refers to total column ozone, measured in DU. One DU represents the amount of ozone molecules needed to produce a 0.01mm layer of pure ozone. Minimum daily ozone (DU) is taken from annual measurements over the period 21 September to 16 October. The mean ozone hole area (million km^2) is measured over the period 7 September to 13 October. In the 1970s, NASA began using satellite measurements to infer the depth and extent of the ozone hole. These estimates are validated against point observations, such as those from the Dobson spectrophotometer.

Ozone-depleting substances are emitted through human activities, such as refrigerant and aerosol production. These substances can last up to several centuries, making their way up to the stratosphere and damaging the ozone layer. While the ozone hole does not directly affect ozone concentrations over Southern Hemisphere countries such as New Zealand, when it breaks up in spring it can send 'plumes' of ozone-depleted air towards us. This briefly decreases column ozone levels by around 5%, about the same amount as normal daily variation (Ajtić et al., 2004). The ozone hole also affects atmospheric circulation and has led to an increase in the occurrence of positive phases of the Southern Annular Mode climate oscillation (Thompson et al., 2011).

In 2016, the mean maximum size of the ozone hole was 20.9 million km^2, a 21% decrease from its largest mean maximum size in 2006 (26.6 million km^2). The mean minimum ozone concentration was 124.3 Dobson units (DU), a 35% increase from the lowest mean minimum in 1994 (92.3 DU). According to NOAA smaller ozone hole areas in 1988 and 2002 were a result of warmer than normal temperatures, caused by disturbed stratospheric weather conditions (NOAA, 2002).

Maximum ozone hole size in 2016, 28 September

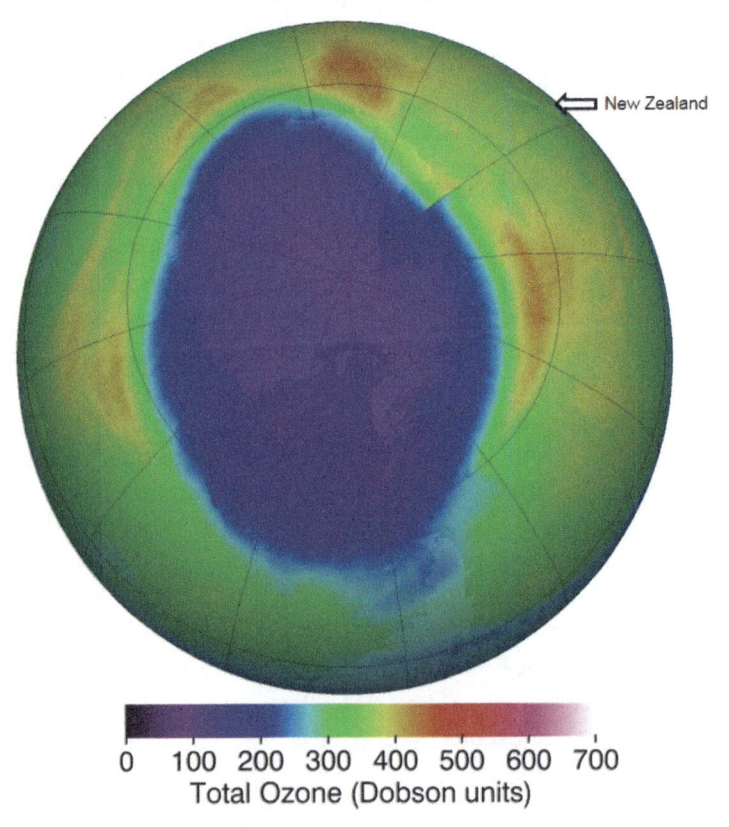

← New Zealand

Total Ozone (Dobson units)
0　100　200　300　400　500　600　700

Source: National Aeronautics and Space Administration

Mean minimum ozone concentrations and mean maximum ozone hole sizes
1979–2016

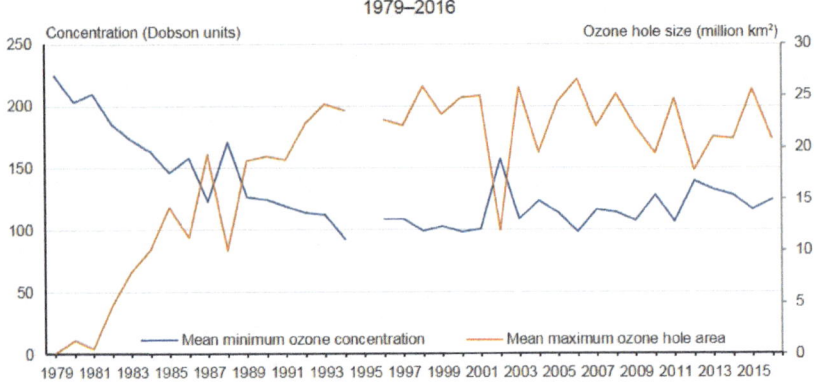

Source: National Aeronautics and Space Administration

378　*Climate Change : Nature is in Control*

Montreal Protocol

The *Montreal Protocol on Substances that Deplete the Ozone Layer* (a protocol to the Vienna Convention for the Protection of the Ozone Layer) is an international treaty designed to protect the ozone layer by phasing out the production of numerous substances that are responsible for ozone depletion. It was agreed on 26 August 1987, and entered into force on 26 August 1989, following a first meeting in Helsinki, May 1989. Since then, it has undergone nine revisions, 1990 (London), 1991 (Nairobi), 1992 (Copenhagen), 1993 (Bangkok), 1995 (Vienna), 1997 (Montreal), 1998 (Australia), 1999 (Beijing) and 2016 (Kigali). As a result of the international agreement, the ozone hole in Antarctica is slowly recovering. Climate projections indicate that the ozone layer will return to 1980 levels between 2050 and 2070. Due to its widespread adoption and implementation it has been hailed as an example of exceptional international co-operation, with UN Secretary General Kofi Annan quoted as saying that "perhaps the single most successful international agreement to date has been the Montreal Protocol". The effective burden sharing and solution proposals mitigating regional conflicts of interest have been among the success factors for the ozone depletion challenge, where global regulation based on the climate related Kyoto Protocol has failed to do so. In the case of the ozone depletion challenge, there was global regulation already being installed before a scientific consensus was established. Also, overall public opinion was convinced of the possible imminent risks

The ozone treaties have been ratified by 197 parties (196 states and the European Union), making them the first universally ratified treaties in United Nations history. These truly universal treaties have also been remarkable in the expedience of the policy-making process at the global scale, where only 14 years lapsed between a basic scientific research discovery of the adverse effects of ozone depletion in 1973, and the international agreement signed in 1985 and 1987).

Ozone and Health

The word 'ozone' is derived from the Greek word όζειν which means "to smell". Its strong smell allows scientists to detect it in low amounts. The ozone layer covers the entire planet and protects life on earth by absorbing harmful ultraviolet-B (UV-B) radiation from the sun. Prolonged exposure to UV-B radiation is linked to skin cancer, cataracts, genetic damage and immune system suppression in living organisms, and reduced productivity in agricultural crops and the food chain.

Atmospheric data demonstrates that ozone depleting substances are destroying ozone in the stratosphere and thinning the earth's ozone layer. Ozone depleting substances are chemicals that include chlorofluorocarbons (CFCs), halons, carbon tetrachloride (CCl$_4$), methyl chloroform (CH$_3$CCl$_3$), hydrobromofluorocarbons (HBFCs), hydrochlorofluorocarbons (HCFCs), methyl bromide (CH$_3$Br) and bromochloromethane (CH$_2$BrCl). They deplete the ozone layer by releasing chlorine and bromine atoms into the stratosphere, which destroy ozone molecules. These and other ozone depleting substances also contribute, to varying extents, to global warming.

In 1974, chemists Mario Molina and Frank Sherwood Rowland discovered a link between CFCs and the breakdown of ozone in the stratosphere. In 1985, geophysicist Joe Farman, along with meteorologists Brian G Gardiner and Jon Shanklin published findings of abnormally low ozone concentrations above the Antarctic, which galvanized worldwide action. In 1995, Mario Molina, Frank Sherwood Rowland and Paul Crutzen, also an atmospheric chemist, were jointly awarded the Nobel Prize in Chemistry "for their work in atmospheric chemistry, particularly concerning the formation and decomposition of ozone".

The ozone layer is depleted in two ways. Firstly, the ozone layer in the mid-latitude (e.g. over Australia and New Zealand) is thinned, leading to more UV radiation reaching the earth. Data collected in the upper atmosphere have shown that there has been a general thinning of the ozone layer over most of the globe. This includes 5 - 9% depletion over Australia since the 1960s, which has increased the risk that Australians already face from over-exposure to UV radiation resulting from their outdoor lifestyle.

Every four years, the World Meteorological Organization (WMO) and the United Nations Environment Programme (UNEP) review the state of the ozone layer. These reviews show that the abundance of ozone depleting chemicals in the atmosphere is now declining and the ozone layer is expected to recover to pre-1980 levels over the mid-latitudes by 2050 and over the Antarctic by 2065.

Right and left of climate policies

Why are climate sceptics often right-wing conservatives is a question asked by a report in the Australian based *Conservation.com* website. The report notes that human activities appear, according to the majority of the media and many climate scientists, to be causing global warming. Given the same evidence, *Conservation.com* asks why do some people become concerned about human-caused climate change while others deny it? In particular, why are people who remain sceptical about climate change often identified as right-wing conservatives. According to a recent poll conducted in Canada, 81% of Liberal and 85% of New Democrat voters believe that climate change is a fact and is mostly caused by emissions from vehicles and industrial facilities. In contrast, only 35% of Conservative voters believe the same thing.

Within the United States, a poll in 2006 showed that 79% of Democrats versus 59% of Republicans said there was solid evidence that the average temperature on Earth has been getting warmer. This divide has not only endured, but widened over time to 92% of Democrats and 52% of Republicans by 2017. Such a growing divide has significant implications for setting policy agendas that aim to fight climate change. For example, 77% of Democrats versus 36% of Republicans in 2017 said that stricter environmental laws and regulations are worth the cost.

A related question is which came first: the climate change "bias" between human induced causes, or the "political bias" between the Left and the Right. I would suggest that from my observations of the climate scene since the 1950's, my climate colleagues are from all political shades, but they are either "pro sun and pro ocean" or "pro greenhouse gases". I am not sure why, except many of the "pro sun and pro ocean" people have had a longer history in the old subject of "climatology" rather than the current subject of "climate change". Many have seen it all before and are not surprised with what happens to the climate, noting of course the flip of the butterfly wings.

Past studies, according to *Conservation.com* provide several accounts to explain public scepticism on climate change, such as a lack of knowledge or understanding of the causes of climate change, a lack of sense of urgency or insufficient awareness about the issue. However, these accounts do not completely explain the partisan polarization over the years when an increasing volume of information and evidence on climate change has been presented to the public. Recent efforts to explain partisan polarization suggest that people seek and interpret information that is consistent with their political ideology and party identification, and selectively expose themselves to news media that is consistent with their existing motivations and beliefs. Conservatives may seek evidence that challenges the scientific knowledge regarding climate change, which aligns with their existing knowledge acquired from political leaders whom they trust. Extending beyond these studies, we suggested a new explanation of how motivations and ideologies lead to this polarized view on climate change.

Previous work by *Conservation.com* demonstrates that liberals who are concerned about climate change pay more attention to climate-related words, such as carbon, over neutral words, such as coffee. Conservatives who are not concerned about climate change do not show a difference in the amount of attention they pay to climate-related words and neutral words, suggesting that political orientations are associated with the amount of attention paid to climate-related information.

Based on these findings, the *Conservation.com* study found that people's political motivations shape their visual attention to climate change evidence, which influences their perception of the evidence and subsequent actions to mitigate climate change. These altered perceptions and actions can reinforce their initial motivations, further entrenching the divide. To put simply, what you believe influences what you see, and guides your future actions. The study presented a graph showing the global temperature change from 1880 to 2013 to participants. It found that the more liberal people were, the more attention they paid to the rising phase of the temperature curve (1990 to 2013) relative to the flat phase of the curve (1940 to 1980). This shows that liberals and conservatives naturally pay more attention to the part of the graph that is consistent with their beliefs.

In another experiment, the study manipulated attention by colouring different parts of the temperature curve to deliberately bias attention to stronger change (the rising phase) or smaller change (the flat phase) in temperature. It tested whether biasing people's attention to different climate evidence influenced their actions to mitigate climate change. Would they, for example, sign a climate change petition or donate to an environmental organization? The study found that liberals were more likely to sign the petition or donate when the rising phase was highlighted than when the flat phase was highlighted. In other words, when attention was drawn to climate evidence that aligns with their prior beliefs, people were more likely to act. In contrast, conservatives were less likely to sign the petition or donate when the rising phase was highlighted than when the flat phase was highlighted. This shows that when attention was drawn to motivational evidence that was inconsistent with their beliefs, people were less likely to act.

It may seem paradoxical, but the *Conservation.com* research shows that an action can be encouraged by drawing people's attention to the evidence that matches their prior motivations. Overall, the study suggested that people's motivations prevent them from attending to and perceiving climate change evidence accurately, which influences their subsequent actions. Specifically, conservatives may focus selectively on climate data that confirm their beliefs, leading to inaction on mitigating climate change. The findings, along with traditional accounts, offer a few ideas to aid our understanding on why conservatives are more sceptical about climate change. *Conservation.com* notes that to encourage accurate interpretation of climate data and actions among conservatives, we can frame climate change consistently with their values, such as framing mitigation efforts as promoting economic or technological development. Or, we can provide information on peer group norms to shift attention, since people may have incorrect beliefs of how their peers view a controversial issue.

Empiricism and Dogma: Why Left and Right Can't Agree on Climate Change
Patrick T. Brown writing in the Australian journal *Quillette* on July 30, 2019 commented that. "As a climate scientist, I often hear puzzled complaints about the political polarization of the public discussion about anthropogenic global warming. If it is an empirical and scientific matter, such people ask, then why is opinion so firmly divided along political lines? Since it tends to be the political Right that opposes policies designed to address and mitigate global warming, responsibility for this partisanship is often placed solely on the ideological stubbornness of conservatives." He further comments:

This is a theme common to research on political attitudes to scientific questions. Division is often studied from the perspective of researchers on the Left who, rather self-servingly, frame the research question as something like: "Our side is logical and correct, so what exactly makes the people who disagree with us so biased and ideologically motivated?" I would put books like Chris Mooney's *The Republican Brain: The Science* of *Why They Deny Science—and Reality* in this category. Works like *The Republican Brain* correctly point out that those most dismissive of global warming tend to be on the Right, but they incorrectly assume that the Left's position is therefore informed by dispassionate logic. If the Left was motivated by pure reason then it would not be the case that liberals are just as likely as conservatives to deny science on the safety of vaccines and genetically modified foods. Additionally, as Mooney has argued elsewhere, the Left is more eager than the Right to deny mainstream science when it doesn't support a blank-slate view of human nature. This suggests that fidelity to science and logic are not what motivates the Left's concern about global warming.

The political divide on global warming
Rather than thinking about the political divide on global warming as the result of dogma versus logic, a better explanation is that people tend to embrace conclusions–scientific or otherwise–that support themes, ideologies, and narratives that are pre-existing components of their worldview. It just so happens that the themes, ideologies, and narratives associated with human-caused global warming and its proposed solutions align well with the political predispositions of the Left and create tension with those of the Right. The definitional distinction between the political Right and the political Left originated during the French Revolution, and relates most fundamentally to the desirability and perceived validity of social hierarchies. Those on the Right see hierarchies as natural, meritocratic, and justified, while those on the Left see hierarchies primarily as a product of chance and exploitation.

A secondary distinction, at least contemporarily in the West, is that those on the Right tend to emphasize individualism at the expense of collectivism and those on the Left prefer the reverse. There are several aspects of the contemporary global warming narrative that align well with an anti-hierarchy, collectivist worldview. This makes the issue gratifying to the sensibilities of the Left and offensive to the sensibilities of the Right. The most fundamental of these themes is the degree to which humanity itself can be placed at the top of the hierarchy of life on the planet. Those on the Right are more likely to privilege the interests of humanity over the interests of other species or the "interests" of the planet as a whole (to the degree that there is such a thing). On the other hand, those on the Left are more likely to emphasize a kind of pan-species egalitarianism and care for our shared environment, even if that means implementing policies that run counter to humans' short-term interests.

Within humanity, there are at least two additional ways in which narratives about hierarchies influence thinking on global warming. One of these concerns attitudes towards developed versus developing countries. Firstly, the blame for global warming falls disproportionately on developed countries (in terms of historical greenhouse gas emissions) and proposed solutions therefore often call on developed countries to bear the brunt of the cost of reducing emissions going forward. (Additionally, it is argued that developed countries have the luxury of being able to afford increases in the cost of energy.) Overall, the solutions proposed for global warming imply that wealthy countries owe a debt to the rest of humanity that should be paid due at once. Those on the Right are more likely to see the wealth of developed countries as rightfully earned by their own industriousness, while those on the Left are more likely to view the disproportionate wealth as fundamentally unjust and likely caused by exploitation. The idea that wealthy countries must therefore be penalized and made to subsidize poor countries is one that aligns well with the Left's views about rebalancing unfairness. An accentuating factor is the Right's tendency to favour national autonomy and therefore to oppose global governance and especially international redistribution.

Hierarchy narratives also help to determine political positions on the wealth of corporations and individuals. On the Right, oil and gas companies (as well as electric utilities that utilize fossil fuels) are held to be a product of innovation and a source of wealth creation; the smartest and most deserving people and organizations found the most efficient ways to transform idle fossil fuel resources into the power that runs society and, consequently, have greatly enhanced human wellbeing. For conservatives, it is therefore fundamentally unjust to blame those corporations and individuals that have done so much for human progress. The counter-narrative from the Left is that greedy corporations and individuals exploited natural resources for their own gain at the expense of the planet and the general public. They therefore support policies that blame and punish the fossil fuel industry in the name of cosmic justice and atonement.

Green movements around the world and their climate agenda

Green Parties around the world and related organisations such as *Greenpeace* have very strong views on climate change and almost without exception consider that "Global Warming" is caused by the release of greenhouse gases and that it is a major problem. Why the Greens have such an anathema to "global warming" but apparently have no problem about "global cooling" is to some extent a mystery but is related to the overriding concern of Green political parties to protect the natural environment.

Of significance, *Greenpeace* was originally founded with entirely different goals, and co-founder Patrick Moore sums it up nicely:

"The organization I co-founded has become a monster. When I was a member of its central committee in the early days, we campaigned – usually with success – on genuine environmental issues such as atmospheric nuclear tests, whaling and seal-clubbing. But when *Greenpeace* turned anti-science by campaigning against chlorine (imagine the sheer stupidity of campaigning against one of the elements in the periodic table), I decided that it had lost its purpose and that, having achieved its original objectives, had turned to extremism to try to justify its continued existence.

Now *Greenpeace* has knowingly made itself the sworn enemy of all life on Earth. By opposing capitalism, it stands against the one system of economics that has been most successful in regulating and restoring the environment. By opposing the use of DDT inside the homes of children exposed to the anopheles mosquito that carries malaria, *Greenpeace* contributed to the deaths of 40 million people and counting, most of them children. It now pretends it did not oppose DDT, but the record shows otherwise. On this, as on so many issues, it got the science wrong. It has the deaths of those children on (what passes for) its conscience. Also, by opposing fossil-fuelled power, it not only contributes to the deaths of many tens of millions every year because they are among the 1.2 billion to whom its campaigns deny affordable, reliable, clean, continuous, low-tech, base-load, fossil-fuelled electrical power: it also denies to all trees and plants on Earth the food they need.

Paradoxically, an organization that calls itself "Green" is against the harmless, beneficial, natural trace gas that nourishes and sustains all green things. *Greenpeace* is against greenery. Bizarrely, it is opposed to returning to the atmosphere a tiny fraction of the CO_2 that was once present there."

At the Second World Climate Conference held in Geneva in October/November 1990, I was a member of the organising Secretariat. After one of the lunch breaks I returned to the Conference Centre to be confronted with a large banner over the entrance to the International Conference Centre with the words "Climate Criminals" and many of the *Greenpeace* people had chained themselves to the entrance of the building. The banner had been erected by *Greenpeace* and as I knew several of the *Greenpeace* people, many from their headquarters in Amsterdam, I asked whether they had obtained the necessary photos for the media and then asked them to kindly remove the banner so the conference could continue. The "Climate Criminals" mentioned were of course the then UK Prime Minister Margaret Thatcher, and the then US President George Bush. Thirty years later similar banners and related billboards are to the forefront of climate marches.

Government decisions on climate change in New Zealand by the Minister for Climate Change

Major decisions made by the New Zealand Government are now being considered under a climate change lens, Minister for Climate Change, James Shaw announced on December 4, 2019. (James Shaw is co-leader of the Green Party, which along with the Labour and New Zealand First political parties is in a coalition government currently governing New Zealand.) "Cabinet routinely considers the effects of its decisions on human rights, the Treaty of Waitangi, rural communities, the disability community, and gender – now climate change will be a standard part of Cabinet's decision-making too," James Shaw said.

"A 'climate impacts assessment' will be mandatory for policy and legislative proposals that are designed to reduce emissions, or which are likely to have consequential impacts on greenhouse emissions greater than 250,000 tonnes a year. Passing the Zero Carbon Act earlier this year set New Zealand on a path to a zero carbon future – and this is about working together to get there. Ensuring Ministers are aware of the implications a decision may have for New Zealand's future greenhouse gas emissions will be vital to ensure we are all playing our part in meeting the commitments we've made. The Ministry for the Environment has developed a tool that can be used to estimate emissions impacts and its effectiveness will be reviewed in mid-2020."

"Decisions we take now and in the future about everything from the places we live, to how we get around, to public health, to how we relate to one another will be impacted one way or another by climate change. It's crucial therefore that when we're making big decisions climate change is at the forefront of our minds. I'm delighted that we've developed a tool for the whole government to easily assess whether policies we're considering at Cabinet will increase or reduce the emissions that impact on New Zealanders' quality of life in decades to come," James Shaw said.

The new guidance fulfils an important commitment in the Confidence and Supply Agreement between the Labour and Green Parties, and builds on a Green Party member's bill which would have required climate change impact statements in all legislation.

By 2020, this government will, according to the Act, have done more to help solve climate change than the last 30 years of government combined, including:

- Passing the Zero Carbon Act
- Ending new offshore oil and gas exploration permits
- Funding a new energy research centre in Taranaki
- Committing to plant 1 billion trees by 2028
- Agreeing a world-first partnership with farmers to reduce emissions
- Making cleaner cars more affordable
- Legislation to reform the Emissions Trading Scheme
- A Green Investment Fund

The Australian Greens

According to their Policy dated November 2018, the Australian Greens consider that human-induced climate change poses the greatest threat to our world, civilisation and way of life. Climate change touches all aspects of modern life, contributing to disruption of human societies through sea level rise, extreme weather events, desertification and changing weather patterns, and threatening food security, water, the economy, social cohesion and the well-being of humans and other living things. These impacts will escalate in the future. Urgent and sustained local, national and global action is required to avoid catastrophe and ensure a safe climate. A safe climate will require a return to an atmospheric concentration of 350 parts per million or lower of greenhouse gases (and CO_2 equivalents).

Australia's climate policy should be consistent with its commitment under the Paris Agreement to pursue efforts to limit the temperature increase to 1.5°C above pre-industrial levels, recognising that this is essential to reduce the risks and impacts of climate change. Australia's primary responsibility is to reduce its contribution to emissions; it cannot rely on as-yet undeveloped and undemonstrated draw down mechanisms. Climate change is resulting in the displacement of people, having a disproportionate impact on people in less developed countries, creating environmental refugees and intensifying the threat of regional and global conflict. Australia has a responsibility to assist in resettling and rehousing displaced populations. Australia needs to plan for a future that does not rely on fossil fuels for export or domestic use.

Australia is a wealthy nation with extensive renewable energy resources that should be used to benefit all Australians, and it should become a world leader in addressing climate change. Australia needs to urgently and substantially reduce greenhouse gas emissions, actively support international mitigation measures to reduce global emissions, and plan to adapt to climate change impacts which are now inevitable.

Many of the harshest impacts of climate change, according to the Australian Greens, is that climate change disproportionately affects those already experiencing disadvantage. Addressing climate change and building a just society go hand in hand. Climate action needs to include and respond to the differentiated needs, experiences, priorities and capacities of Aboriginal and Torres Strait Islander peoples and other communities. Equity must be at the core of climate change negotiations and measures, and the transition to an economy that supports a safe climate. Climate change necessitates a transition away from an economy reliant on unsustainable consumption and production of greenhouse gases. The cost of creating an economy that adapts to climate change and supports a safe climate must be distributed fairly, both domestically and internationally. In moving to a low-carbon economy, it is essential to minimise the adverse impacts of that transition on communities that are most at risk and most disadvantaged. Failing to transition to a low carbon future will have adverse impacts on the economy and society throughout: the increased cost of adaptation; increased risk of extreme weather events and bushfires; and risks to water resources, agriculture and food security.

Economic opportunities may be lost or diminished by failing to encourage a rapid transition to a more sustainable economy.

Australia has the capacity to ensure that its electricity needs can be provided by renewable energy. Australia must develop the capacity to drastically reduce emissions from all sectors, draw down greenhouse gases, and be greenhouse gas neutral or negative within a generation. Early action to reduce greenhouse gas emissions will ultimately be fairer and more cost effective than delaying action. A systematic response by all levels of government is required to achieve significant reductions in greenhouse gas emissions across all sectors.

Australia's international commitment to address climate change
The Australian Greens point out that the extraction of fossil fuels for domestic and international consumption, is not consistent with Australia's international commitment to address climate change. Significant reductions in greenhouse gas emissions may be achieved by reducing the demand for material goods. Australia must use its scientific, diplomatic and economic influence to promote the development and deployment of non-polluting alternatives to fossil fuel based energy. Energy prices should reflect the environmental, social, health and other external costs of its production and use. Subsidies to the fossil fuel sector, including funding for research and development, should be removed, while investment in the renewable energy, energy efficiency, sustainable public transport, energy efficient social housing, agriculture and other relevant sectors should be increased. The major refurbishment of existing coal fired power stations, except for transitions to renewable energy, undermines the effort to increase end-use energy efficiency, demand management and renewable energy.

A just transition for communities and workers affected by closure of fossil fuel based mining and electricity generation industries is essential.

Climate change will have a greater impact on our neighbours in the Pacific and Asia. Australia has a responsibility to assist other nations, particularly in our region, to create safe climate economies, and adapt to climate change through appropriate technology transfer and other forms of assistance. As an essential utility, regulation of all energy infrastructure must be government controlled, and the ownership of electricity retail, generation and networks should be in public or community hands.

The Australian Greens also want net zero or net negative Australian greenhouse gas emissions by no later than 2040. A leading role for Australia is negotiation of a multilateral emission abatement treaty which shares the burden equitably, recognising the proportionately greater historical and current contribution of wealthy industrialised nations to climate change. Removal of all subsidies to the fossil fuel industry.

An orderly phase out of fossil fuel mining, fossil fuel based electricity generation and consumption of fossil fuels consistent with the emissions reduction plan. A just transition to a net zero carbon economy through a range of mechanisms including a plan to replace fossil fuels with renewable energy through strong regulatory intervention and a strong effective price on carbon.

Binding national emission limits for each year through to 2050 supported by a well-funded, comprehensive, integrated and research-based emissions reduction plan with appropriate targets and reporting for all sectors with significant greenhouse emissions. A legislative framework to ensure that: addressing climate change is acknowledged as a federal government responsibility; all relevant legislation and regulations require that climate change is to be considered; long-term and interim targets to achieve reductions in emissions of greenhouse gases, and reductions in atmospheric greenhouse gas levels, are set, adhered to and achieved; climate is considered in all National Energy Market (NEM) decisions and relevant interim and long-term targets and goals are met; climate is considered in all decision and approval processes involving the federal government and/or involving matters of national environmental significance as currently set out under the Environment Protection and Biodiversity Conservation Act 1999 (EPBC Act).

Annex

"The important thing is not to stop questioning. Curiosity has its own reason for existing. One cannot help but be in awe when he contemplates the mysteries of eternity, of life, of the marvellous structure of reality. It is enough if one tries merely to comprehend a little of this mystery every day."

-Albert Einstein

The *climate4you.com* website

Climate4you.com is a website developed by Professor Ole Humlum who is a Danish Professor Emeritus of Physical Geography at the University of Oslo, and Adjunct Professor of Physical Geography at the University Centre in Svalbard. His academic focus includes glacial and periglacial geomorphology and climatology. He earned a Ph.D degree in glacial geomorphology in 1980.

After having held post-doc positions 1980-1983, Professor Humlum became scientific director at the University of Copenhagen Arctic Station near Qeqertarsuaq where he lived for three years. He subsequently worked as Assistant Professor at the University of Copenhagen from 1986-1999. He became Professor at the University Centre in Svalbard in 1999. In 2003, he became full Professor at the University of Oslo, Department of Geosciences. He became a member of the Norwegian Scientific Academy for Polar Research in 2008.

The website climate4you.com which he edits endeavours to provide an ongoing climate data website which is updated monthly. It uses data of significant national and global sites such as NASA, WMO, NOAA, UEA, NCDC, IPCC, BoM, SIDA, UAH, NIWA.

The objective of the website is to provide information on meteorological and climatological issues of general and specific interest.

The purpose is to assist reflective people to form a personal opinion on meteorological and climate matters. The purpose is not to provide a forum for discussions, as there are many fine websites providing excellent possibilities for this.

It is definitely not the purpose to encourage a passive personal approach by providing a list of 'correct' answers to a list of 'key' questions, but rather to stimulate active, personal thought and analysis. The motto of the *Royal Society, nullius in verba* - take nobody's word for it, is still highly relevant.

The main emphasis of the present website is to provide the interested reader with data and other information on meteorology and climate. Climate change information needs to be both accurate and undistorted, and analysis unemotional. Respecting the notion that information always should be the starting point for personal thought, analysis and interpretation, links to information sources (digital and written) are provided throughout the website.

The least objective part of the present website is the section on 'Climate Reflections', which is constructed around some of the webmaster's personal interpretations of certain data series.

Some debates, books and other initiatives relating to global climatic changes, appear to be somewhat frustrated by an apparent lack of basic knowledge on updated meteorological conditions and their variations across time and space. Also when it comes to the likely effects of climate change, the lessons of history often appear to be unknown or forgotten. In Europe it is only little more than 200 years since the recognition that Earth is a dynamic planet began to transpire as a result of basic geological research. Previously, in Europe it was widely believed that Earth essentially was unchanging, and only about 6000 years old according to a study of the *Bible* by James Ussher (1581-1656), the Anglican Archbishop of Armagh, Ireland. Today it is equally easy to forget that it is only about 160 years since about one million people in Europe died of starvation and epidemic diseases because of climate-induced harvest failures.

The recent focus on climate change has resulted in an increased awareness that climate is not as constant as it may have appeared previously. In this context, even the most extreme and divergent forecasts of future climate may have done some good. This is, however, a situation that should not continue much longer, as it confuses and disillusionates political decision-makers and the general public about the value of so-called 'climate experts'. In addition, the initial humble scientific attempts of modelling the future climate have unfortunately developed into a large-scale example of groupthink with its own dynamics, making informed political judgment difficult.

Air temperature remains a central theme in discussions on global climate change, and admirable attempts to estimate the global temperature have been published by different research teams or institutions. However, a number of issues relating to obtaining representative measurements of surface air temperature still remains, especially in or near areas affected by urban development. Even in Arctic regions it might be difficult to obtain representative air temperature measurements, despite all professional efforts. Also the varying degree of temporal stability displayed by the various global temperature records deserves attention.

The difficulty of identifying a new climatic trend deviating from a background of natural variations is therefore real and constitutes an important difficulty for both scientists and policy-makers. As an example: Is it possible to conclude that the late 20th century global temperature increase is unique in relation to previous temperature increases? Or could it just as well represent part of the natural temperature increase following the end of the Little Ice Age? Another important issue is the relationship between atmospheric CO_2 and global temperature in recent times?

The immediate need for climate scientists appears to be improving empirical knowledge on climate change, past and present, and to understand the limitations of the different types of approach to forecasting climate. For the decision-makers the lesson presumably is to allow wider margins for future climatic change; cooler as well as warmer, wetter as well as drier, windier as well as less windy, etc. Preparing for warming only may not be entirely prudent. After all, modern climate change may just be a continuation of everlasting natural rhythms of climate change.

Climate science remains a highly complex issue where simplification tends to lead to confusion, and where understanding requires knowledge, openness to new hypotheses, thought and effort.

The present website is under continuous development, and updates and new material are added whenever possible.

Typical "List of Contents" on the website:
- July 2019 global surface air temperature overview
- Comments to the July 2019 global surface air temperature overview
- Temperature quality Class 1: Lower troposphere temperature from satellites
- Temperature quality Class 2: HadCRUT global surface air temperature
- Temperature quality Class 3: GISS and NCDC global surface air temperature
- Comparing global surface air temperature and satellite-based temperatures
- Global air temperature linear trends
- Global temperatures: All in one... Quality Class 1, 2 and 3
- Global sea surface temperature
- Ocean temperature in uppermost 100 m
- North Atlantic heat content uppermost 700 m
- North Atlantic temperatures 0-800 m depth along 59N, 30-0W
- Global ocean temperature 0-2000 m depth summary
- Troposphere and stratosphere temperatures from satellites
- Zonal lower troposphere temperatures from satellites
- Arctic and Antarctic lower troposphere temperatures from satellites
- Arctic and Antarctic surface air temperatures
- Arctic and Antarctic sea ice
- Sea level in general
- Global sea level from satellite altimetry

- Global sea level from tide gauges
- Northern Hemisphere weekly snow cover
- Atmospheric specific humidity
- Atmospheric CO_2
- The phase relation between atmospheric CO_2 and global temperature
- Global surface air temperature and atmospheric CO_2
- Latest 20-year QC1 global monthly air temperature change
- Sunspot activity and QC1 average satellite global air temperature
- Climate and history (this changes each month): 1916: Lord Kitchener drowns near Scapa Flow

Two typical charts from *climate4you.com*:

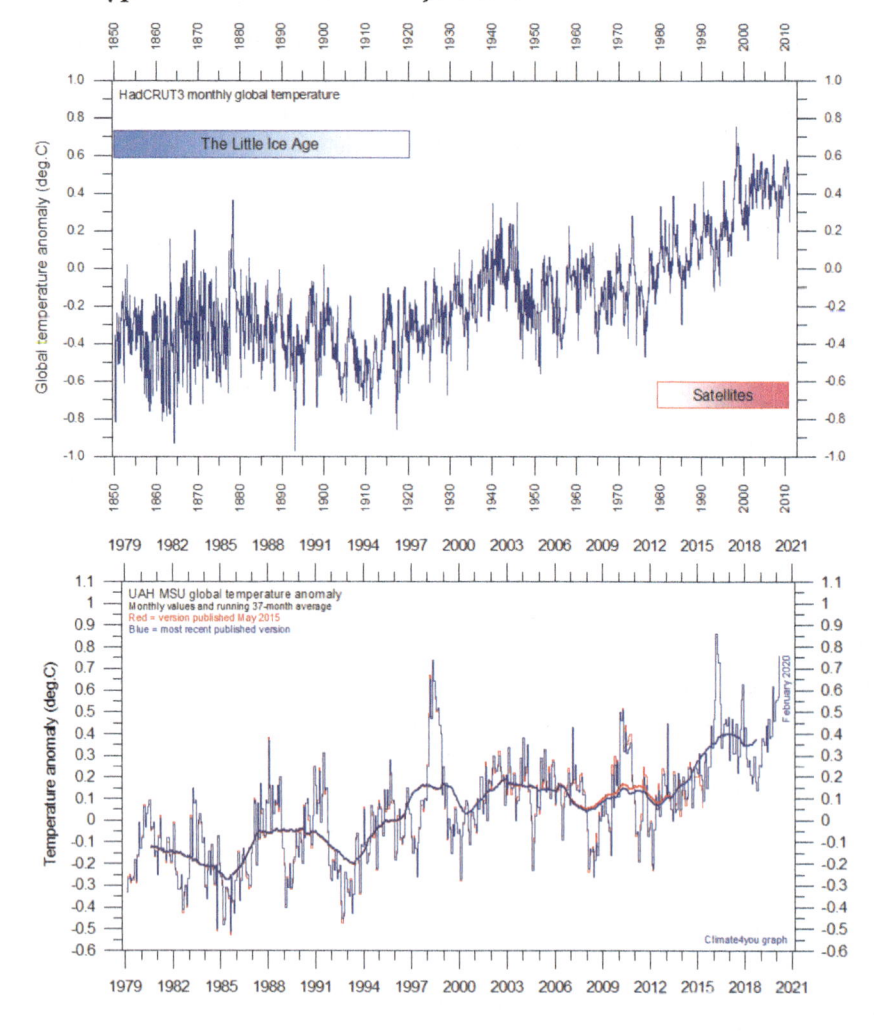

Bibliography

Alexandersson A., 1986: A homogeneity test applied to precipitation data. J. Climatol., 6, pp. 661-675.

Alexandersson H. and Moberg A., 1997: Homogenization of Swedish temperature data. 1. Homogeneity test for linear trends. Int. J. Climatol., 17, pp. 25-34.

Bakker R.J., et al. 2012: Impact of wind turbine sound on annoyance, self-reported sleep disturbance and psychological distress. Author links open overlay panel https://doi.org/10.1016/j.scitotenv.2012.03.005

Bogdan T., 2000: On the Disposition of Maunders' Original Butterfly Diagram. AAS 196th Meeting, June 2000

Bastings L. and Simmons P., 1950: Climatic Zones and Domestic Heating in New Zealand. N.Z. Jour. Sci. and Tech., Sec. B, 32, p. 50

Brazol D., 1954: Bosquejo Bioclimàtico de la Repùblica Argentina. Meteoros, 4, pp. 381-394.

Brunt D., 1945: Climate and human comfort. Proc. Royal Institution of Great Britain 33. No 151

Campuzano S. A., et al. 2018: "New perspectives in the study of the Earth's magnetic field and climate connection: The use of transfer entropy." PLoS ONE 13(11):e0207270

Caussinus H. and Mestre O., 2004: Detection and correction of artificial shifts in climate series. Appl. Statist., 53, Part 3, pp. 405-425.

Conrad V., 1925: Homogenitätsbestimmung meteorologischer Beobachtungsreihen. Meteorologische Zeitschrift, pp.482–485.

Domonkos P., Venema V. and Mestre O., 2013: Efficiencies of homogenization methods: our present knowledge and its limitation. Proceedings of the Seventh seminar for homogenization and quality control in climatological databases, Budapest, Hungary, 24 – 28 October 2011, WMO report, Climate data and monitoring, WCDMP-No. 78, pp. 11-24.

Flannery T., 2002:The Future Eaters: An Ecological History of the Australasian Lands and People Paperback – October 16, 2002 Amazon.

Flohn H., 1950: Neue Anschauubgen uber die allgemeine Zirkulation der Atmosphare und ihre Klimatische Bedeutung Erdkunde 4 pp.141-162.

French P.W., 2001: Coastal defences: Processes, Problems and Solutions. London: Routledge

Garnier B.J., 1950: The climate of New Zealand: According to Thornthwaite's classification, in New Zealand Weather and Climate BJ Garnier Whitcombe and Tombs, Christchurch, pp. 84-101.

Garnier B. J., 1951: Thornthwaite's New System of Climate Classification in its application to New Zealand. Tran. Roy. Soc. NZ 79, pp. 87-103.

Gemenne F., 2009: Environmental Migration: Normative Frameworks and Policy Prescriptions, Doctoral Thesis, Sciences-Po, Paris

Gentilli J., 1958: A Geography of Climate. University of Western Australia Press, Perth. pp. 120-166.

Gorczynski W., 1941: Decimal scheme of World Climates. Scripps Inst. Oceanog.

Heidke P., 1923: Quantitative Begriffsbestimmung homogener Temperatur- und Niederschlagsreihen. Meteorologische Zeitschrift, pp. 114-115.

Kidson E., 1932: Climatology of New Zealand, being Vol. 4, Part 5 of Handbuch der Klimatotogie, W. Köppen and R. Geiger, Editors. Gebrüder Borntraeger, Berlin.

Kidson E., 1937: The Climate of New Zealand. Quart. J. R. Met. Soc., 62, pp. 83-92.

Kininmonth William, 2004: Climate Change: A Natural Hazard Multi-Science Publishing Co.Ltd, Essex, UK

Koppen W., 1931: Grundviss dev Klimakunde. Walter de Gruyter Company, Berlin.

Koppen W., 1936 : Das Geographische System der Klimate, being Vol. 1, Part C of Handbuch Zer Klimatologie, W. Köppen and R. Geiger, Editors. Gebrüder Borntraeger, Berlin

Linham M.W. and Nicholls R. J., 2010: Technologies for Climate Change Adaptation – Coastal Erosion and Flooding Editor: Xianli Zhu and others published Technologies for Climate Change Adaptation... Book · January 2010   Isbn: 978-87-550-3855-4 Publisher: UNEP Risoe Centre on Energy, Climate and Sustainable Development

Loehle C., 1998: Corrections to the Mann et. al. (1998) Proxy Data Base and Northern Hemispheric Average Temperature Series First Published November 1, 2003 Research Article https://doi.org/10.1260/095830503322793632

Loehle C., 2007: A 2000-Year Global Temperature Reconstruction Based on Non-Treering Proxies First Published December 1, 2007 Research Article. https://doi.org/10.1260/095830507782616797

Lorenz E.N., March 1963: Deterministic Nonperiodic Flow. Journal of the Atmospheric Sciences. 20 (2): 130–141.

Manley G., 1974: Central England temperatures: monthly means 1659 to 1973., Quarterly Journal of the Royal Meteorological Society, vol. 100, pp. 389–405 (1974).

Mann M.E., Bradley R. S. and Hughes, M. K., 1998: Global scale temperature patterns and climate forcing over the past six centuries, Nature, 392, pp.779-787, 1998

Maunder W.J., 1956: A Study of the Diurnal Variation of Rainfall in New Zealand, Unpublished M.Sc. Thesis, University of New Zealand, pp. 207-216

Maunder W.J., 1965: The effect of climate variations on some aspects of agricultural production in New Zealand. and an assessment of their significance in the National agricultural income. A thesis presented to the University of Otago for the Degree of Doctor of Philosophy.

Maunder W.J., 1970: The Value of the Weather, Methuen. (Also reprinted/published in 2020 by Routledge)

Maunder W.J., 1986: The Uncertainty Business, Methuen. (Also reprinted/published in 2020 by Routledge)

Maunder W.J., 1989: The Human Impact of Climate Uncertainty, Methuen. (Also reprinted/published in 2020 by Routledge)

Maunder W.J., 1992: Dictionary of Global Climate Change, UCL Press.

Maunder W.J., 2020: Climate Change: Fifteen Shades of Climate, Amazon

Maunder W.J., 2023: Climate Change: A Realistic Perspective, Amazon

Mestre O., 1999: Step-by-step procedures for choosing a model with change-points. In Proceedings of the second seminar for homogenization of surface climatological data, Budapest, Hungary, WCDMP-No.41, WMO-TD No.962, pp.15-26.

Monnin E., et al. 2004: Evidence for substantial accumulation rate variability in Antarctica during the Holocene, through synchronization of CO_2 in the Taylor Dome, Dome C and DML ice cores Earth and Planetary Science Letters 224(1-2):pp.45-54.

Myers N., 1997: Environmental Refugees. Population and Environment 19, pp.167–182https://doi.org/10.1023/A:1024623431 9

Myrup L.O., 1969: A numerical model of the urban heat island. J. Appl. Meteorol., 8 (1969), pp. 908-918.

Robertson N. G., 1957: Climatic districts in New Zealand. Proc. N.Z. Ecological Soc.,No.4,pp.21-23.

Seager R. & Battisti D. S., 2007: Challenges to our understanding of the general circulation: Abrupt climate change, in The Global Circulation of the Atmosphere: Phenomena, Theory, Challenges, eds. Schneider T. & Sobel A.S., (Princeton, NJ: Princeton University Press, 2007) pp.331-371.

Sewell W.R.D., Kates R.W. and Phillips L., 1968: Human Response to Weather and Climate: Geographical Contributions, The Geographical Review, Vol. LVIII.

Sicre M.A.,et al. 2008: Decadal variability of sea surface temperatures off North Iceland over the last 2000 years. Earth and Planetary Science Letters, Elsevier,2008,268,pp.137-142.

Sweney H.M., 1946: The Climates of New Zealand according to the Thornthwaite System, Unpublished M.A. Thesis, University of New Zealand

Szentimrey T., 1999: Multiple Analysis of Series for Homogenization (MASH). Proceedings of the second seminar for homogenization of surface climatological data, Budapest, Hungary; WMO, WCDMP-No. 41, pp.27-46.

Thornthwaite C.W., 1931: The climates of North America according to a new classification. Geog. Review, 21, pp. 633-655.

Thornthwaite C.W., 1948: An approach toward a Rational Classification of Climate, Geog. Review, 38, pp. 55-94.

Trewartha G.T 1954: An Introduction to Climate. Mc Graw Hill, New York, pp.234.237.

Ungar S., 2003: Global warming versus ozone depletion: failure and success in North America CR 23:263-274 (2003)

Venema V.O., et al. 2012: Benchmarking homogenization algorithms for monthly data. Climate of the Past, 8, pp. 89-115, doi: 10.5194/cp-8-89-2012, 2012.

Made in the USA
Las Vegas, NV
04 November 2024